JOKES AND TARGETS

JOKES AND TARGETS

CHRISTIE DAVIES

INDIANA UNIVERSITY PRESS

Bloomington & Indianapolis

This book is a publication of

Indiana University Press
601 North Morton Street
Bloomington, Indiana 47404-3797 USA

iupress.indiana.edu

Telephone orders	*800-842-6796*
Fax orders	*812-855-7931*
Orders by e-mail	*iuporder@indiana.edu*

⊖ The paper used in this publication meets
the minimum requirements of the American
National Standard for Information
Sciences—Permanence of Paper for
Printed Library Materials, ANSI
Z39.48-1992.

Manufactured in the United States of
America

Library of Congress Cataloging-in-
Publication Data

Davies, Christie.
  Jokes and targets / Christie Davies.
    p. cm.
  Includes bibliographical references and
index.
  ISBN 978-0-253-35619-2 (cloth : alk. paper) — ISBN 978-0-253-22302-9 (pbk. : alk.
paper) 1. Wit and humor—Social aspects.
2. Wit and humor—Psychological aspects.
3. Wit and humor—Political aspects. I.
Title.
  PN6149.S62D36 2012
  152.4'3—dc22

2010039258
1 2 3 4 5 16 15 14 13 12 11

For Janetta,
and in memory of my father,
Christy Davies

CONTENTS

ACKNOWLEDGMENTS

The writing of this book was made possible by a research fellowship from the Leverhulme Trust in 2008–2009 that enabled me to make two extended visits to the Folklore Archive at the University of California, Berkeley and the Schmulowitz collection at the San Francisco public library and also to work in the Cummings Library of Humour at University College Cork in Ireland. I must thank the Leverhulme Trust and also all the exceptionally helpful and friendly archivists and librarians in these institutions, notably Jean Bascom, Joy Tang, and Ted Biggs in the Berkeley archive, Andrea Grimes and her colleagues in the Schmulowitz collection, and John Fitzgerald and his colleagues at the Boole library in Cork. I should also remember here the late Alan Dundes, who created the Berkeley archive and who first encouraged me to make use of it. My final debt is to the staff of the library of the University of Reading in England and particularly the interlibrary loan department, who as always proved adept at finding the unfindable.

I also acknowledge the financial assistance of the British Academy and the Estonian Academy of Sciences, who funded my visit to the University of Tartu and the Estonian Literary Museum, and I thank Piret Press for helping to arrange my visit there. It enabled me to consult the leading Estonian humor researchers Arvo Krikmann, whose work was being celebrated, and Liisi Laineste.

There are two institutions to which all humor scholars are grateful, namely, the well-established International Society for Humor Studies and its executive secretary, Martin Lampert, and Willibald Ruch's celebrated

International Summer School and Symposium on Humour and Laughter. At the annual meetings of these institutions, scholars give papers and lectures, meet and discuss humor, and later consult and exchange information by e-mail. During the writing of this book, I have received a great deal of advice and assistance from the members of these fellowships of humor scholars, and in particular I would like to thank Salvatore Attardo, Janet Bing, Dorota Brzozowska, Hugo Carretero Dios, Delia Chiaro, Władysław Chłopicki, Marc Galanter, Giselinde Kuipers, Paul Lewis, Anna Litovkina, Jessica Milner-Davis, Ofra Nevo, and Victor Raskin.

In as broad a work as this, it is also vital to consult experts in many diverse fields that impinge on humor, and Robert Barnidge, Clémentine Bry, Roger Evans, Richard Gee, Sandy Ghandhi, Seth Graham, Heinrich Härke, Dana Heller, Andy Knapp, Peter Kruschwitz, Peter Noble, Sean O'Leary, Robert Olley, Walter Redfern, Ian Roe, Beatrice Santorini, Desmond Tobin, Chris Wagstaff, Brian Whitaker, and Roy Wolfe were especially helpful in answering my questions.

I owe a particular debt to Elliott Oring and to Rabbi Barry Schechter not only for patiently answering so many e-mails but for decades of communication about humor.

All of the above provided vital information, suggestions, comments, and disagreements, but I alone am responsible for any errors in the text.

My colleague Dawn Clarke has as usual provided invaluable help in preparing the manuscript. Without Rebecca Tolen, my editor, with whom I first discussed the writing of *Jokes and Targets,* this book would never have existed; I am grateful to her for her continued help and encouragement throughout its preparation. I must also thank Brian Herrmann and Peter Froehlich at Indiana University Press who ably steered the author and this work through the complexities of modern publishing.

My wife, Janetta, has as always provided the consistent support that enabled me to complete this work, and it is dedicated to her and to the memory of my father, Christy Davies, who first encouraged me to study humor.

JOKES AND TARGETS

Introduction

The purpose of this book is to explain how certain large joke cycles come about and why particular groups rather than others become the targets of these jokes. The explanations will be social and historical and will be based on comparing large aggregates of the jokes in one country with those in another and also seeing how individual sets of jokes change or persist over time. Why do joke tellers in many North American and European countries tell jokes about blondes being stupid and about the French taking too great an interest in sex? The jokes could have been pinned on the "stupidity" of those with red hair or the "oversexed Germans," but they were not. Why are the members and inhabitants of some occupations, social classes, nations, and cities the butt of jokes about their supposed preference for male same-sex activities rather than others? Why are there jokes in this respect about Greeks and not Canadians, about the citizens of Qazvin in Iran rather than Tehran, about gold prospectors and ladies' hairdressers and not about physicians or carpenters, about aristocrats but not bankers? Why were political jokes so overwhelmingly dominant in the former Soviet Union and its satrapies but not in democracies or indeed under other kinds of dictatorship? Why did the great wave of American jokes about greedy, unscrupulous lawyers not spread to Britain, Europe, or Australia, given that many other great American joke cycles from Polish jokes to blonde jokes to disaster jokes had earlier been taken up and rapidly adapted elsewhere? Why do Jews produce and circulate so many unique jokes about the sex roles of their own people, types of jokes that it would

1

never have occurred to gentiles of any kind to invent, either about Jews or about their own men and women? None of these orderly patterns are planned by anyone; they are an instance of spontaneous order, an order resulting from the independent behavior of a large number of individuals, rather in the way that large numbers of competing producers, searching consumers, and eager entrepreneurs create a market order or individual experimenters and theorists a scientific order or judges using the common law and precedents a coherent legal order. The orderliness to be seen in patterns of jokes is perhaps the most spontaneous of all because it is not shaped or regulated by institutions. Where jokes are concerned, there are no tariffs, no cartels, no monopolies, no political appointees on the bench given to distorting the law, no funding bodies with agendas—it is the freest of all forms of spontaneous order and worth studying for this reason alone.

These questions are difficult, and one of the reasons for trying to answer them is that so many amateurs in the field of studying humor have assumed that it is an easy task to explain jokes and have barged in and applied odd notions of their own to particular sets of jokes. They force the jokes willy-nilly to fit into an arbitrary and unsophisticated "common sense" explanation because it feels right, even though it does not work. Even worse are those who draw on a dubious "theoretical perspective," often with a strong ideological underpinning, but never ask themselves the questions "Why should the unbiased intelligent reader believe me?" "How can my thesis be tested?" and "Would my thesis work for a different set of jokes and if not why not?"

It is important to study jokes, not because they have any significant social consequences or express profound moral or existential truths, which in general they do not, but because they are such a widespread and popular social phenomenon and one from which so many people derive so much pleasure. Those whose tastes run to ultra-elevated highbrow humor and biting wit are unable to understand how very important canned jokes are to the mass of the people, who spend a large part of their leisure enjoying the sheer sociability of an exchange of jokes. A dislike of canned jokes is usually an affectation and a sign of social and cultural snobbery. A liking for such jokes is entirely compatible with a love of the humor of Cervantes, Hašek, Proust, or H. G. Wells.

THE NATURE OF JOKES

In writing about "jokes" and "targets," it is necessary first to explain how these terms will be used. Jokes are narratives or riddles whose main, though not exclusive, humorous force lies in the punch line, the line at the end of the joke, when there is a sudden and unexpected shift in meaning. The joke has appeared to be a straightforward if incongruous narrative or question with a single script, but then suddenly a second hidden and unexpected script of a very different kind is revealed (Raskin 1985, 99). The pleasure we take in such humor lies in this combination of appropriate incongruity and suddenness. The joker has broken the rules of serious bona fide communication in a pleasurable way, for example by using false logic or exploiting the double meanings of words, and we have entered another domain, that of humor, where different rules apply. Jokes cannot be reduced to serious statements. They are complex, elusive, ambiguous, and playful. There is often a further humorous bonus to a joke (Riesman 1954, 331), for the second script revealed in the punch line may evade the conventional rules of a particular society or group about what may or may not be said. Jokes may make reference to sexuality or blasphemy or some other taboo subject, play with the idea of aggression against or great superiority over an individual or a group, mock the powerful or those powerless ones under the protection of the powerful, or speak in an apparently callous way about death or disaster. Jokes play with the forbidden. The fabric of the unmentionables is briefly revealed. Sometimes the jokers accept and believe in the rules regarding permitted forms of speech that are being defied, sometimes they go along with these rules as a social convention, and sometimes they see them as arbitrary restrictions imposed by the powerful. Whichever it is, it is fun to break them. Jokes are a brief time off from the everyday inhibitions and restrictions that bind the ways we speak. Jokes mean we can indulge in ambiguity, blatant and obvious departures from reality or logic, absurdity, impropriety, and the utterly shocking. Societies and groups differ a great deal in the kinds of speech they forbid, which is one of the reasons why one society or group may produce different kinds of jokes from another, a central interest of this study.

Quite deliberately this book sets out to analyze jokes, rather than other forms of humor, though it will also often refer to their closest relatives, anecdotes, witticisms, humorous slang, anonymous funny songs and chants, and urban legends, and will refer in places to cartoons and to longer humorous pieces written by particular authors. Jokes have the great advantage of being short, numerous, and anonymous. They have no authors and travel mainly by word of mouth, though increasingly also via the internet. They emerge from the interactions of ordinary individuals but unlike witticisms are free of any particular context. Jokes are truly the humor of the people. Jokes are an oral and a social phenomenon. Jokes exist to be told, indeed performed, in company, and a further source of pleasure to be derived from them is that they promote sociability, give the tellers a chance to demonstrate their skill as narrators and actors, and offer the listeners a form of entertainment that is more immediate and intimate than that provided by professional comics.

In some societies, the jokes that are told most often cannot be published or broadcast because of direct censorship or due to the self-censorship of editors, journalists, and broadcasters who fear controversy or the protests of those who are offended. This does not seriously impede the invention and circulation of forbidden jokes, even in totalitarian societies such as the former Soviet Union or in places obsessed with political correctness such as Toronto or The Hague. It is precisely because jokes in circulation are unfiltered that we can use them as a true indication of what a people laugh at. The jokes told on radio or television tell us mainly what particular writers, performers, producers, broadcasting officials, sponsors, and buyers of programs have decided; jokes in oral circulation reflect the tastes and perceptions of ordinary individuals. The types of jokes discussed in this work have been chosen because they exist in very large numbers, sometimes as part of a long-lasting tradition of joke telling, sometimes arriving as joke cycles, great new waves of jokes that in some cases hardly existed before and which after a time will give way to another cycle of jokes. It is difficult and dangerous to deduce much from the analysis of a single joke, but one is on far, far surer ground when considerable numbers of jokes exist with a common theme. Such a cycle or large aggregate of jokes constitutes what the sociologist Emile Durkheim termed a "social fact," a facet of a particular social world that has to be explained in social terms. Jokes are preeminently a social phenomenon. We are not concerned here with individuals or even with the interactions of individuals in small groups, even though the study of these by academic psychologists is of great importance and enormous value, but with the aggregate consequences of their behavior which, as sociologists, economists, and political scientists have long realized, have to be understood on their own terms and studied by looking at their relations at a different level of analysis. The key question to ask is why this particular set of jokes is in circulation at this particular time in this particular society rather than some other possible set. It is always necessary to consider the kind of jokes that could have multiplied and circulated but did not. The jokes that could exist but do not exist help us to understand those that do.

JOKES AND THEIR CONTEXTS

Jokes do not have fixed texts, for they change from one telling to another. Just as important, jokes vary in tone, which is one reason why it is almost impossible to try to infer the intentions of a putative joke teller or the feelings of his or her listeners just from the text of a joke. Likewise, it is dangerous to generalize about these from observing a particular telling of a joke. Tone and context are highly variable, and it is the tone that makes the music. Which tone a teller adopts will be influenced by where and to whom the joke is being told. You can tell a joke straight-faced or straight out, exuberantly or with understatement, directly or ironically, as yourself or by attributing it to someone else. Every joke is a little production and can be produced in many ways. Every telling is a "presentation of self," usually in an affiliative way because the teller wants the listeners to laugh and the sociability of the occasion to be enhanced. In some cases the teller may indeed have a serious purpose and add a gloss to the joke (Oring 2003, 95), a serious comment that conveys how the joke is being used. That it should be necessary to do so is an indication of how unserious and ambiguous jokes are; the gloss is used to move the joke into a framework of bona fide communication, a place where it does not naturally belong. Anyone who has ever deployed a joke in a speech or a lecture knows how easy it is to change a joke's implications. In a debate a joke may be fitted into a provocative speech in such a way as further to enrage the opposition while drawing laughter from one's supporters. The laughter of amusement that usually follows a joke has been amplified by a laughter of triumph, yet it is easy enough to produce a laughter of mere and sheer triumph by means of other kinds of rhetorical tricks that are not intrinsically funny or intended to be (Davies 1992). The relationship between laughter and humor is complicated and beyond the scope of this work.

It is for these reasons that arguments between individuals about the "real" meaning of a joke are often utterly futile, for there is no way of resolving them. The rationalizations provided by the sometimes emotional combatants are often merely a way of expressing different "residues," the contrasting idiosyncratic bundles of habits and feelings possessed by those disagreeably disagreeing (Pareto 1968). This is why it is important to try to avoid questions of the motives and feelings of individuals who tell jokes and not to engage in arguments with those who foolishly try to use their own speculations about motive and feeling to explain why a particular set of jokes exists. They employ a circular argument. They infer from a particular set of jokes that the jokers feel anxious or angry or frustrated and then use these feelings, for whose existence they provide no independent evidence, to explain the jokes. It is not worth taking such arguments seriously, and any such approaches and assumptions are easily refuted.

THE NATURE OF TARGETS

Targets are groups of people who are the butt of jokes upon whom a conventional comic script pins some undesirable quality. Most jokes are about the undesirable, for people joke not about good things or virtuous people but about failure and wickedness and about matters that they might well find disturbing outside the context of the joke (Brottman 2004, 44). Many jokes depict politicians as venal, psychoanalysts as crazy, Newfoundlanders as dirty, Scotsmen as tightfisted, Finns as drunks, Roman Catholic priests as child molesters, Muslims as suicide bombers, mothers-in-law as disagreeable, economists as out of touch with reality, Scousers (Liverpudlians, people from Liverpool) as thieving and work-shy, plumbers as forgetful, or actresses as vain because that is what jokes do. It is difficult to envisage jokes that depict particular groups as the sane, the clean, the generous, the sober, the moral, the peaceable, the practical, the honest, the reliable, the equitable, the efficient, and the modest. In order to do so, it would be necessary to manipulate the situation in the joke in such a way that these qualities became a problem. It is difficult to make a joke out of a virtue except when it is cultivated to an absurd and inappropriate extent, by which time most observers will have ceased to regard it as a virtue. Sometimes jokes can be arranged in pairs to fit around Aristotle's golden mean (Book 2 1104a32 and 1107a28 to 1108b9) as with, say, jokes about cowardly Italian soldiers versus overly disciplined or ruthless German ones, both of which are viewed from some kind of "reasonable" middle position. Both loyalty to things military and self-preservation have their value, but an excess of either may be perceived as ludicrous foolishness that is a fitting subject for jokes (Davies 1990).

Among the targets that will be discussed in this book are occupations and professions, such as lawyers, bankers, orthopedic surgeons, or Marines, social classes such as aristocrats or laborers, national groups such as the French and the Greeks, the inhabitants of a region or city, such as the Alentejos in Portugal or the citizens of Qazvin in Iran, and people who constitute a recognizable category but not a social group, such as blonde women or men who have sex with men. The last of these categories embraces gay men, who do constitute a social group with an identity, but most of the men having sex with men in the jokes that will be discussed are not gay. I am primarily interested in why certain occupations, classes, cities, and nations are the subject of jokes about their supposed sexual preferences. In the case of political jokes from the former Soviet Union and its colonial empire, the target has turned out to be an entire social and political order, for the individual targets of these jokes proved to be so strongly interrelated that it made no sense to separate them out.

SOCIAL FACTS

In each case the targets have to be studied on the basis of evidence that is independent of the jokes and their tellers. The existence of a large set of jokes with a common theme is a social fact, and it needs to be explained in terms of other social facts (Durkheim 1982). It makes no sense to study jokes about the Soviet Union or the French without considering the history of these societies and their distinctive social, political and cultural qualities. To explain Jewish jokes, it helps to look at them in relation to the contradictions between traditional Jewish ways and values and the preservation of a distinctive identity and the pressures of the wider society to conform to very different patterns of behavior and outlook; this in turn requires a knowledge both of Jewish mores and of the ways of the gentiles and to see both on their own terms. Likewise, in order to understand why blondes are the butt of jokes about their stupidity and promiscuity, it is necessary to establish that blondeness is for men a sexually desired quality and for women who are not natural blondes something worth striving to attain. However, this can involve social contradictions in a modern society where most organizations depend on women efficiently and disinterestedly performing difficult tasks and exercising authority. The lawyer joke cycle that flourished in America in the latter decades of the twentieth century, and which still has some life in it, did not spread to Britain, Ireland, or Europe because lawyers and the law are less important to the way these societies operate and because individual success is more important to Americans. Yet this creates stronger contradictions in America than in Europe between the law as a calling and the law as a profit-maximizing business, between a profession as a protection for the public and a profession as a conspiracy against the public, between the law as the sacred foundation of a nationally defining constitution and the mundane and sometimes dubious and unfair use of the law to settle disputes. When Europeans tell modern American lawyer jokes, they retain the original American settings of the jokes and do not move them to their own societies or adapt them to fit their own institutions. Although they find the jokes funny, they could not have originated the jokes themselves, nor do they invent new ones, because they do not experience the American contradictions in their own countries. The British, the Irish, the Europeans, the Canadians, and the Australians know a good deal about America because it is a powerful and influential country whose institutions are familiar from the news media, which is why they can understand and appreciate American jokes but Americans neither know, nor in their eyes need to know, very much about the rest of the world. It is notable that jokes and television comedy programs alike are exported abroad from America, but very little is imported.

This brief preview should give the reader an insight into the kind of explanations I provide by linking the origins of aggregates of jokes to social contradictions which in most cases it is reasonable to assume are visible to the joke tellers and important to them. For the reasons I have already given, I shall not speculate as to how those among whom the jokes originate or those individuals who circulate them feel about their social situation either in general or at the time when they are joking about it. I am certain of only one thing, and that is that individuals in any particular common situation will differ a great deal but will be able to take part in the joking.

SCRIPTS AND STEREOTYPES

The scripts that make a joke work, such as dumb blonde, greedy lawyer, or the oversexed French, are convenient fictions (Raskin 1985, 180), but in some cases there may well also exist a corresponding stereotype, by which I mean that many people believe the script to be true to the point where it could influence how they behave (Bry, Follenfant, and Meyer 2008). Some stereotypes have been very strongly held, such as that of the "fiendish and treacherous Japanese" of World War II, which led to the utterly unjust and unconstitutional deportation of people of Japanese ancestry living in California (Tateishi 1999), but did not give rise to any jokes at all, and there are the Canadian jokes about dirty Newfoundlanders which have no corresponding stereotype. If in explaining why the script of a particular joke exists, I have also accounted for a seriously held stereotypical belief, whether in the form of a reasoned generalization that can be tested or an irrational and unshakeable prejudice, that is merely a useful bonus. The joke cannot cause the stereotype, but it is likely that both have a common social origin. However, that is for someone else to follow up. The concerns of this book lie purely with the jokes.

JOKES AND THEIR RELATIONS

Jokes have many close relatives, such as witticisms, anecdotes, urban legends, riddles, humorous songs, chants, and slang that are also short, numerous, and funny. In some cases they are so very close to being jokes that they can be treated as jokes. The categories are not difficult to define, but the boundaries between them can be uncertain and permeable. When an item is clearly not a joke but has the same theme as a set of jokes, it can be invaluable in helping us to get a hold on a broader pattern of humor of which the jokes are part. Here, though, it is necessary to emphasize how each category differs from jokes. Witticisms are made by a particular person in a particular context and often with an intention that goes beyond a wish to say something humorous. Yet they have often been handed down to us freed from their original context and remain funny in the way that jokes are. For instance, some of the wisecracks and witty sayings of Mark Twain about subjects as diverse as financiers in America or adultery in France can be treated as jokes because today they are still remembered and cited and can stand alone, exactly as jokes do, even though in this particular case we know or think we know who the inventor was. They are not funny merely because Mark Twain said them, and they would remain funny even if the author were unknown. If witticisms can be detached from their original context, reshaped, and possibly ascribed to other individuals including fictitious ones, they become as jokes because they are now adaptable and transportable. Indeed they may well have the full structure of a joke with a discernible punch line. Many jokes may well have begun life as a spontaneous witty comment that was remembered, used away from its original context, repeatedly polished, and in being transmitted given the formal characteristics of a joke. In the process, what began as wit loses altogether the qualities of authorship and fixed context, which are what distinguish a witticism from a joke. It has become a "canned" joke, which can be moved around at will and has no fixed wording or tone. It is partly for this reason that it is impossible to trace the originators of jokes and futile to try to do so (Kuipers 2006, 23). A joke's origins are collective and social. This is equally true in the case where a joke has been adapted or switched from a similar joke that is known to have existed much earlier. Likewise a generic joke can be told in such a way that the punch line is placed in the mouth of a person known to be witty, even though he or she never said it. Jokes and witticisms are overlapping sets, and movement between them is often easy. Yet some witty remarks cannot be transformed in this way, for they are not funny out of context and not only lack but cannot be given anything close to the formal structure of a joke with two overlapping scripts joined by a punch line. The humor of such witticisms lay mainly in the particular interaction that generated them and the speed and cleverness of the original speaker, which may be difficult to recall or re-create. Many clever witticisms are no longer funny. They are admired because we also know about the speed and cleverness with which they were uttered; this is why they are often fathered or mothered on a person known for these skills. They cannot float alone like a joke. Even when first uttered, they may not have been perceived as particularly funny, and the laughter they elicited was one of appreciation or triumph at a smart, sharp piece of rhetoric rather than a laugh of amusement; laughter without mirth but still enjoyable. That is why there are so many books with the title "The Wit and Wisdom of X." Often they contain neither of these, and X, who may be anyone from Michel Foucault to President McKinley, may never have said them anyway, and the compilers are not trying to sell joke books. Aphorisms are quite unlike jokes, which have to or at least have to be intended to amuse someone. If jokes never do so, then they have failed, whereas an aphorism remains an aphorism even if it is banal or so obscure that it is considered profound by those who have no idea what it means. Jokes are by definition a form of humor and not of serious discourse. Witticisms by contrast are sometimes humorous, sometimes intended to convey a truth succinctly, sometimes a form of deliberate deception through a clever use of language. Sometimes they are very like jokes and sometimes merely cousins to a joke.

Similar points can be made about the anecdotes and urban legends that will be used alongside the jokes, though these tend to be discursive narratives, unlike the quick and succinct witticism. Some anecdotes are meant to be humorous and indeed are or can easily be reshaped into narrative jokes, but many are entirely serious stories and may even be trying to make a moral point. In many early joke books it is difficult to say whether a particular item should be called a joke or an anecdote. However, what is strange to the modern reader is that the editor will often choose to add a solemn postscript to a merry tale that purports to draw out a serious moral from it. Jokes are too ambiguous and frivolous to be moral statements, and the postscripts are often linked to the joke in a very arbitrary way. Likewise, whereas jokes are known to be fictions, even when told with a straight face, it is often claimed that anecdotes are true accounts of actual events; that many anecdotes are funny, though in a more discursive and less surprising and sudden way than jokes, simply shows that human beings like to be amused. In another mood people may prefer anecdotes that are parables or exhortatory tales or simply skillfully constructed little stories. Perhaps the oddest kind of anecdote is the "shaggy dog story," which is a long, repetitive story that deliberately mimics the narrative buildup of a joke but which ends not in a surprise punch line but in a letdown. The humor intended is at the expense of the listener who has waited intently for an amusing ending but who has then been foiled. As is the case with witticisms, jokes and anecdotes are overlapping sets.

Modern urban legends, anonymous "foaf tales" (tales ascribed to a "friend of a friend"), such as the tale of the woman whose cat exploded when she tried to dry her cold, wet pet in the microwave (Brunvand 1981; P. Smith 1983, 1986) can be very close to humorous anecdotes; they are sometimes structured rather like jokes and indeed can sometimes be converted into disaster jokes. Yet the thrust of most of them is to suggest that they are true stories that have a real and shocking ending. When we are amused, as we very often are, it is a bonus, and those who laugh may well be laughing because they are shocked or because others are shocked, rather than because they find the story funny in the sense that a joke is. A variant on the urban legend, though usually with a hidden author, that will be discussed in relation to American lawyer jokes, is the fake tort case in which a frivolous or vexatious litigant is unjustly awarded enormous damages in compensation for a trivial or self-inflicted injury. These hoaxes are uncomfortably close to reality, and it takes skilled researchers to prove that these particular cases never happened, even though others just as grotesque did. Urban legends are also relatives of jokes but rather more distant ones; if witticisms and anecdotes are first cousins, urban legends are second cousins as are many riddles. Often modern jokes take a question-and-answer form, just like a riddle, but they still conform to the standard punch line structure we find in narrative jokes. Indeed a simple question-and-answer joke can often be used as a do-it-yourself kit from which a more elaborate joke could be constructed. Yet many riddles are not jokes, merely exercises in pseudo-logic for its own sake; like witticisms, anecdotes, and urban legends, riddles possess some but not all of the characteristics of a joke.

IDENTIFYING JOKES BY TOPIC

Most of the jokes discussed in this book come from four of the largest sets of jokes that exist, namely, jokes about stupidity and its opposed counterpart, craftiness, as well as Jewish jokes, sex jokes, and Soviet political jokes. Particular attention has been paid to two of the major joke cycles that came out of the United States in the late twentieth century: blonde jokes and lawyer jokes. Thus this work can make some claim to comprehensiveness. Where a major topic has been left out, it is often because there is nothing new to add to the analyses and conclusions in my 1990 book, *Ethnic Humor around the World: A Comparative Analysis.* That is why there is so little here about thriftiness, dirt, food and drink, or Italians, fascinating and important though these themes are. In some cases a topic has been omitted because it posed problems that could not be solved without several more years of work. It would have been interesting and worthwhile to have written more about religious jokes, jokes about families, husbands, wives, and extended kin, and jokes about gays and lesbians treated as coherent groups with a distinct social identity, but further new comparative material, either in the form of jokes or of studies of the social settings of these jokes, would have been needed to do so properly. Research is the art of the possible.

SOURCES OF THE JOKES

Ideally, I collected the jokes myself or found them in a folklore archive. In such cases it is known who told the joke and when and something at least of how the teller perceived the joke. This information has not been used directly, but it does amply confirm that individual joke tellers vary greatly in these respects. Archive work provides clues as to the authenticity of a set of jokes and a very rough idea of how many jokes might be in the set such as "very few," "quite a lot," or "a very large number." These quantities are crude but important. To specify actual numbers would be merely to provide a misleading pretence to a greater precision and better sampling than is possible. Other securely embedded jokes have come from reading works on other subjects for other purposes, particularly social history and biographies, in which jokes are cited. Many of the jokes used have come from joke books and particularly from the internet; the chief trouble with these as sources is that, in order artificially to boost the numbers of jokes, editors and website compilers are always tempted to take and adapt jokes from other sources in a way that produces jokes that bear no relationship at all to their new setting. Those who send the sites jokes by letter or e-mail can be equally guilty of distortion. The internet is an increasingly vital source of material that has been used a great deal in this study, but it has to be supplemented, checked, and confirmed by other independent sources; studies of humor that rely on the internet alone are often badly flawed. Victor Raskin (1985, 205–209) long ago drew attention to the large numbers of pseudo-ethnic jokes in existence whose only ethnic aspects are the names of the characters and an unnecessary and artificial use of the vernacular. Many jokes are the genuine descendants of similar jokes told in another country or about another group and remain appropriate. The key question is whether the joke fits snugly into its current context and is phrased in an appropriate way. It is essential to have heard or read literally thousands of jokes and ideally to have spent many years studying and comparing jokes from many different places and sources to decide this. Experience helps.

The complementary experience of specialists on particular types of jokes also helps a great deal, and I am grateful to those who have, for their own scholarly purposes, collected and sifted for authenticity hundreds of jokes on a particular theme, notably the thorough and pioneering work in this respect of Victor Raskin, of Bruce Adams on Soviet jokes, Marc Galanter on lawyer jokes, Gershon Legman on sex jokes, and Rabbi Joseph Telushkin on Jewish jokes. They were not the inventors of these jokes, for jokes are a collective product and belong to the people. But these respected experts have brought to their work a degree of thoughtful scholarship that makes their books reliable sources. I have not always agreed with their interpretations and have sometimes substituted my own, but their works truly provide a series of very important reference points; any future student of humor should have them on his or her bookshelf.

Wherever possible, the source of each joke is given, but in some cases this could not be done. Jokes are oral communication and have no fixed texts. We do not memorize them but instead remember very roughly the punch line and the gist of the story, and when it comes to telling them, we spontaneously reconstruct them. Often I find in my notebooks just this brief reminder and a note of place and teller, possibly made a little later to avoid disturbing a session of joke telling. For those I heard a very long time ago, the information on source may be missing. It is perfectly valid to use these jokes because that is how jokes travel, but I have avoided relying on these sources alone; they are a way of supplementing the other jokes with further examples that I at least know to be genuine. If by accident I have used someone else's precise wording because I no longer have a record of a particular written or internet source, my apologies. No one owns jokes, for they have no authors, but as a courtesy I have tried to acknowledge individual collectors, including the many folklore students without whom folklore archives would not be possible.

It is to be hoped that the reader will find this a work rich in jokes, for it would make no sense at all not to show extensively the raw material that is being studied. Some of the jokes that follow are very funny, others only mildly so, some are such that the morally primmest and most ideologically bigoted of readers will find them heartwarming, others will offend someone or other, some are highly sophisticated, and others are very simple though effective. These factors were not important in choosing them, for the overwhelming considerations were relevance and representativeness. They may not be representative of the jokes told today in any one particular reader's social circle, but this is a comparative study taking in the jokes of many nations that have differing social structures, differing patterns of power, and differing clusters of values; these are the jokes of many disparate social classes and ethnic and religious groups. If a particular joke appears strange, unfamiliar, incomprehensible, disgraceful, or outrageous, that is because we live in a highly plural world. For this reason, an explanation has been added to some of the jokes, giving supplementary facts or events or providing synonyms of uncommon or foreign words in order to help the reader appreciate the understandings the jokers brought to their telling.

ANALYZING JOKES

Where there exists a great diversity of targets with a common theme, as with the jokes about stupidity and the jokes about men who have sex with men, my aim is to try to discover a few key variables that will explain the existence of what at first appear to be a great mass of disparate jokes. By chance there have also emerged from these comparative analyses some useful new approaches to the understanding of Jewish jokes about Jewish women and men that can now be seen in a new light.

In the case of the newer American jokes about lawyers and the old Soviet political jokes, what is most significant is that the jokes do not exist outside these societies. The Soviet jokes were not told in democratic countries with freedom of speech except in relation to the Soviet Union or its dependencies. Most of them did not circulate in other kinds of authoritarian societies, dictatorships, or oligarchies outside the Soviet orbit. After the collapse of the Soviet empire, they ceased to be invented in the newly free republics of Eastern and Central Europe. The modern lawyer jokes are well known in other countries as American jokes, but they have no imitators. In each of these cases there exist or existed distinctive local patterns of power and ideology that give or gave the jokes a special relevance to the peoples of the countries where they were invented but which did not exist elsewhere. It is here that the origins and significance of these jokes must be sought.

The other important but tricky factor is timing. Why did the blonde joke cycle and the lawyer joke cycle emerge in America when they did? Were there any particular circumstances that might have triggered their emergence, not necessarily events or crises, but more likely a slow intensification of a particular set of social contradictions that finally set off a new cycle? In the case of the jokes about sex and the French or about the Soviet Union that existed over a long period of time, what is of interest and will be studied at length is the way the jokes grew and changed, such that they have come to incorporate particular aspects of the history of those societies. In the case of the sex jokes about the French, the social circumstances that gave rise to these jokes have largely disappeared, but the jokes still persist. In the Soviet case it would almost be possible to write a history of the entire social, economic, and political order in terms of its jokes, something closely approached in Bruce Adams's admirable 2005 study, *Tiny Revolutions in Russia*. It would not be possible to use jokes to provide anything like as full and thorough a history of any other country or empire (see Ginger 1974), which is why the jokes about the Soviet system are unique and have been given an entire chapter of their own. The jokes about the French and sex are largely of British and American origin, though with some good German contributions and a strong input from the French themselves. Their setting is not just the history of France but the history of the experience of France by those who tell the jokes.

OUTSIDE EVIDENCE

In building a picture of the social settings from which the jokes have emerged, many sources and kinds of information from statistics to paintings have been drawn on. I have not tried to do anything difficult or complicated with the statistics, and they have been used sparingly and with a full understanding of their limitations, but such quantitative data is vital; a book-length study of jokes in which the only numbers were the page numbers would be of limited value. More important still is to remember that everything that exists exists to some extent, even if there is no possibility of measuring that extent properly.

Most of the information has come from social, economic, and historical studies, including in some cases my own, that were carried out for some independent purpose but that are here brought to bear on the study of humor. The alternative would be to rely, as many others have done, on processing texts through a mess of speculative assumptions rooted in an untestable cultural theory, to disguise the fact by recourse to obscurity decked out as profundity and to justify it by citing the equally unsupported observations of those with common sympathies. One way of spotting those who have gone down this dubious route is to check whether those sources cited in support are described with highly favorable if unrealistic adjectives often magnified by gushing adverbs. They refer to a supporting source as "a landmark study," "remarkably insightful," "in all senses groundbreaking," "wonderfully illuminating," or "truly revolutionary." But are these opinions true and testable, or are they merely arbitrary marks on the land, breaks in the ground, and spins of the wheel? It is necessary to stress the importance of always seeking and deploying well-founded empirical knowledge of the real world. The details of a social situation cannot be assumed to be the case just because they feel right to a coterie. The facts have to be checked out by reference to those who have measured them. It is necessary to check, as best one can, the number of lawyers and the costs of torts in America relative to other countries, the changing rate of intermarriage between Jews and gentiles, and the history of French brothel culture, Soviet famines, and the attractiveness of blondes.

Literary evidence has been used to provide extra examples of what is being laughed at in a particular set of jokes, as when I cite Sinclair Lewis's humor about realtors, Shakespeare's humor about honor, Nathanael West's humor about bankers, Oscar Wilde on blondes, the French and sex, and Philip Roth on Jews and sport. Literary humor differs radically from jokes, but it often draws on the same themes.

There are problems with using literary or artistic products as direct sources of social information, but in the case of the study of sex jokes about the French, extensive use has been made of them and of art in particular because they were and are such an important part of how France is perceived. For those who did not or indeed do not know the French language, the famous prints and paintings of France of necessity have shaped how they saw and see the French people, and questionable French cartoons have been one of the most exported aspects of French humor.

Occasionally literary references have been embedded in the text as mere hidden playfulness and sometimes as irony; this is the only aspect of this work that can be called postmodern. Postmodernism as a style is enriching. As a mode of thought, it is not.

BUT IS IT TRUE?

I do not claim to have discovered any definitive truths, for that would be impossible, but it is to be hoped that this study comes closer to the truth than previous accounts, and rational criteria have been provided for the reader to judge whether this is so. I have attempted to identify cases where a pattern of jokes exists in one society or for one group but not for another and to make sense of the evidence and to provide better explanations than were previously available. By "better explanations" I mean those that account for many phenomena in terms of a few variables. It may well be that some future scholar can improve on these and discover patterns that explain more but without having to add too many more complications. Too much complexity, too much richly obese description leads to that map with a scale of a mile to a mile mocked by Lewis Carroll in *Sylvie and Bruno Concluded,* a map that contains everything but is utterly useless. Likewise someone may derive a prediction from what I have said that turns out to be manifestly false, in which case that section of my argument will have to be reconsidered. The question of prediction and testing will be examined in greater detail in the conclusion, where the new models devised here will be compared with those employed in *Ethnic Humor around the World.*

ONE

‒♠‒

Mind over Matter

The jokes that target all manner of groups with the labels "stupid" and "canny" (clever, calculating, crafty) are more numerous than any other kind of jokes with targets. They are told about various groups and are told in many countries, indeed almost universally. It is thus appropriate to begin with them.

Apart from jokes about sex, there are probably more jokes about human stupidity than about any other theme. Such humor is not limited to jokes or even to words. It has long been with us in the form of circus clowns, royal fools (Amelunxen 1992; Southworth 1998), films featuring such buffoons as Stan Laurel and Oliver Hardy (McCabe 1961), television comedies such as *Father Ted,* with its wonderfully dim Father Dougal (Matthews and Linehan 1998); they all catered to the amusement people feel at watching someone being stupid. Those at whom we are laughing are behaving in ways that are incongruous and which break the social conventions that prohibit and exclude such foolishness in speech and behavior but in a context that we know is fictitious and harmless. Even in the real world the lesser stupidities of others are caught on candid camera or recorded, edited, and published as collections of humorous blunders and errors, slips of the tongue, or misprints. There exist particular collections of the asinine statements made by members of groups thought to be distinctively stupid, such as athletes doing sports commentaries (Fantoni 1982–2008) or quiz contestants who fail to answer easy questions. There is even a mocking Darwin award (Northcutt 2000) for those so stupid that their fatal blunders eliminate them from the gene pool through timely death.

Likewise a great deal of humor has long been about the sly and clever men and women who can use their wits to extract themselves from a difficult situation (Patel 1946). Here, though, we are concerned not with individuals but with groups who have been made the butt of jokes. In the case of the stupidity jokes these are very diverse indeed. Stupidity jokes are told about many occupations and indeed social classes, about rustics and aristocrats, about dictators and *apparatchiks*, about "military blimps and illiterate Samurai" (Speier 1998, 1376–77), carabinieri and militia, blondes and Essex girls, and, of course, about specific "stupid" local, ethnic, regional, and national groups that are dealt with in detail in my earlier comparative study, *Ethnic Humor around the World*. The challenge is to find an explanatory category that will embrace all these very different groups and the jokes that go with them and which will also cast light on jokes about groups made to appear canny.

The contrast that will be deployed is that between things mental and things physical, whether of the body or of the earth, that between mind and matter. Those whose occupations or very being are most strongly associated with material things are likely to become the butt of stupidity jokes. Yet, as we shall see when we come to discuss the canny jokes, the word *material* has many, sometimes conflicting, meanings. Those who are the butts of the jokes about their being shrewd and calculating are usually depicted as using these qualities in pursuit of "material," that is to say financial, gain. There is an interesting asymmetry between the two sets of jokes in that stupidity is always laughable but intelligence is funny only when it is linked to the morally dubious acquisition of rewards.

Let us first consider some particular occupations that have been made the butt of jokes about their being stupid or canny in order to see how the model works and to look at some of the difficulties.

JOKES ABOUT OCCUPATIONS

In looking at stupidity jokes told about those with a particular occupation, it is as well to begin with jokes about those that are well paid and of high standing, such as engineers or orthopedic surgeons. These examples undermine utterly the "power relations" view of stupidity jokes which assumes that the butts of such jokes are inevitably an easy target, picked on because they are powerless people at the bottom end of the social order. The very term power relations is incoherent and it is worthless for any kind of comparative analysis. The distribution of power is of necessity an important factor in shaping jokes, for it is a central aspect of all societies, but power takes many different forms, and power differentials vary greatly in degree and with context; jokes reflect this diversity.

The stupidity jokes told about engineers and about orthopedic surgeons are sometimes generic stupidity jokes but with a specific twist and sometimes specialized jokes that demand a greater degree of knowledge and understanding than is the case with, say, jokes about dumb blondes or Polish Americans (Davies and Chłopicki 2004), but they are all in essence the same kind of joke. Many of the jokes about engineers depict engineering as lacking in analytical precision and as crudely material and engineers as neither understanding nor needing to understand the science behind what they are doing in order to carry out their work.

> **Mathematician:** In Euclidean geometry you can always draw a straight line between any two points.
> **Engineer:** Any three, if it is thick enough. (Told to me by a Greek colleague)

> A mathematician, a physicist, and an engineer were all given a red rubber ball and told to find the volume.
> The mathematician carefully measured the diameter and evaluated a triple integral.
> The physicist filled a beaker with water and measured the total displacement.
> The engineer looked up the model and serial numbers in his red-rubber-ball table.
> (http://workjoke.com/projoke27.htm; accessed September 2009)

> An engineer, lawyer, and a businessman are all sentenced to death in an electric chair. They are told, "The law says that we only get one chance at killing you. We are not allowed to reset the device, so if the machine fails,

then you are free to go. Before we flip the machine, you can have a last request." The businessman sits down and is asked if he has any last requests. He says no. When they flip the switch, nothing happens, so he is free to go. The lawyer sits down and is asked if he has any last requests. He says no. They flip the switch, and nothing happens again. So he is happy and walks away. The engineer sits down and is asked if he has any last statements. He says, "See the wire up there? You need to short the ground."

(UCBFA Anglo American Blason Populaire File 02; collected by Angela Wong 1977)

There exist many more jokes like the one about the big red rubber ball, some of them demanding a good deal of specialist knowledge. The joke about the electric chair also exists as an ethnic as well as an engineer joke but refers to simpler modes of execution such as the guillotine. Here it is pinned on an engineer, who stupidly loses his life because he is so obsessed with pointing out a fault in the electrical system that he fails to realize the consequence of imparting this knowledge to his executioners. Here we can see a link to the huge cycle of Aggie jokes, long popular in Texas and in the American South, which refer to the "agricultural and mechanical" students of Texas A&M University, which is often contrasted in the jokes with the supposedly more intellectually demanding University of Texas with its emphasis on science and the humanities (*Best of 606 Aggie Jokes* 1976). The jokes about Virginia Tech are very similar.

> Q: Why do Va. Tech grads hang their diplomas on their rearview mirrors?
> A: They have to show some proof that they deserve to park in that handicap parking space. (http://users.erols.com/geary/humor/uvatech.htm)

The same principles underline the jokes about orthopedic surgeons, which are popular among physicians, other kinds of surgeon, and orthopedic surgeons themselves. The image of the orthopedic surgeon is of one who does not need to communicate with the patient. Working with bones is seen as requiring mere physical strength and manual skill rather than a subtle understanding of medical processes.

> An orthopedic surgeon is as strong as an ox and twice as intelligent.

> What is a double-blind study?
> Two orthopedic surgeons looking at an electrocardiogram.
> (Told to me by an Israeli physician in Hungary in 2007)

What is the difference between a carpenter and an orthopedic surgeon?
geon?
A carpenter knows more than one antibiotic!

How do you spot the orthopedic surgeon's car in the car park?
It's the Porsche with a comic on the back shelf!

The modern holistic approach to orthopedics.
You don't JUST treat the fracture . . . you treat the whole bone.
(The last three were collected by Professor Peter Richard Kay, FRCS, of the University of Manchester, and a consultant orthopedic surgeon at Wrightington Hospital.) (http://www.kayr.demon.co.uk/#joke; accessed October 2008)

Professional humorists have made similar wisecracks. After an operation on her hand, Laura Jimenez (2001, 85) wrote with what she calls "characteristic lesbian humor":

Orthopedic surgeons are the car body repairmen of the medical community. Their tools look remarkably like the stuff I buy at Home Depot. Things like glue guns, hammers, and, when they get really crazy, little saws and cordless drills.

Jimenez's humor is both about the crudely physical nature of orthopedic surgery and about lesbians' supposed love of "male" tools that cater to the conventional male obsession with hammering and drilling.

Bones are the most material part of the body, the very antithesis of mind, the bits left behind when the soul has departed and other tissues have decayed. The skeleton is the very symbol of mortality. To deal with bones is to be at the opposite end of the scale from brain surgery, the very image of work requiring knowledge and skill. For the jokers, brainy surgeons work on brains and the bone-headed on bones. Despite the remarkable advances in both knowledge and techniques in orthopedic surgery, bones remain bones, and an orthopedic surgeon can show a patient his or her own X-rays and explain what needs to be done or what has been done. The processes of the brain cannot be as easily explained to an outsider in this way.

Jokes told within and between professions have their counterparts in the jokes told by one set of skilled blue-collar workers about another; predictably those whose area of work is the more physical and material become the butt of stupidity jokes.

What do you get when you make an electrician a carpenter?
A bad carpenter.
What do you get when you make a carpenter an electrician?
A dead carpenter.
(UCBFA Blason Populaire American 02; collected by Brian Haughwont
1999)

Both craftsmen perform skilled manual tasks, but to be an electrician requires an understanding of the complex rules governing the transmission of electricity, which is invisible and for many people imponderable. According to the joke, a lack of such understanding is fatal, whereas a lack of manual dexterity merely makes for bad carpentry. For an electrician in the building trade, the carpenter is merely a cutter and fitter of a coarse building material, whereas he or she deals with the flows and fluctuations of electrons and the mysteries of electromagnetic fields.

Yet both kinds of skilled worker have to be able to think flexibly and provide different solutions to specific and possibly unfamiliar problems; it is this that sets the craftsman apart from the routine manual worker who is the butt of many stupidity jokes, including many ethnic ones.

Two men were digging a ditch on a very hot day. One said to the other, "Why are we down in this hole digging a ditch when our boss is standing up there in the shade of a tree?"

"I don't know," responded the other. "I'll ask him."

So he climbed out of the hole and went to his boss. "Why are we digging in the hot sun and you're standing in the shade?"

"Intelligence," the boss said.

"What do you mean, 'intelligence'?"

The boss said, "Well, I'll show you. I'll put my hand on this tree, and I want you to hit it with your fist as hard as you can." The ditch digger took a mighty swing and tried to hit the boss's hand. The boss removed his hand, and the ditch digger hit the tree. The boss said, "That's intelligence!"

The ditch digger went back to his hole. His friend asked, "What did he say?"

"He said we are down here because of intelligence."

"What's intelligence?" said the friend.

The ditch digger put his hand on his face and said, "Take your shovel and hit my hand."

(http://www.ang.pl/jokes_7418.html; accessed September 2009)

The symbol of having a crude relation to the material world is the hammer, a blunt instrument, the tool of the supposedly unthinking metal-bashers. In the British West Midlands, a center of the manufacturing industry, a hammer is known as a "Birmingham screwdriver," implying that the Brummies (citizens of Birmingham) use force where others apply knowledge. There is a similar Brazilian joke told by the Paulistas, the people of industrial São Paulo, about those who come there from the backward state of Bahia looking for work.

> What is a Baiano's scooter?
> His jackhammer.
> (UCBFA 1977)

It is no accident that the Soviet Union, whose ideology was crude and forceful and whose modes of production were fossilized, should have chosen as its symbol the hammer and sickle, the implements of two of the most frequent butts of stupidity jokes, the peasants and the unskilled metal-bashers. The Soviet Union was supposedly the "dictatorship of the proletariat," the class falsely asserted under the labor theory of value to be the creator of all wealth. The political leaders would select individual unskilled toilers and call them "heroes of labor," known as Stakhanovites after the coal-face miner Alexei Grigoryevich Stakhanov, who had allegedly beaten all production records. It was partly fakery and partly a trick to force the others to work faster, harder, and more intensively, so as to raise the rate of socialist exploitation and "extract more surplus" from the starveling workers. Stakhanovites were in consequence sometimes killed by other resentful workers who saw them as the ultimate in rate-busters. These "heroes of socialist labor" were feted in the press, which reported their stories and published their photographs in the company of political leaders. Later such "heroes" were awarded the gold hammer and sickle medal, though rather a high proportion of these seem to have gone to high-level party officials. The much publicized heroes and heroines of labor could well become the butt of stupidity jokes, as in the case of the Estonian super-milkmaid Leida Peips.

> The kolkhoz (collective farm) chairman says to Leida: "Tomorrow a reporter will come to interview you."

"What about?" Leida asks.

"I don't know either, but put on a clean slip, just in case!" (Krikmann 2006)

A sculptor comes to Leida and says: "Let's make a bust [of you] (understood as do it, i.e., sex) standing up ('püsti')."

Leida: "I have no time."

"We'll do the bust [do it standing up] quite quickly. It won't take long."

"I have never before done it standing up. Let's do it lying down instead."
(Krikmann 2006)

JOKES ABOUT AND WITHIN THE MILITARY

Within the armed forces, at least in the United States, though historically also in Britain, those in the Navy and Air Force tell stupidity jokes about the Marines. Here is another basis of the Texas Aggie jokes, for Texas A&M at College Station has strong links with the U.S. Marine Corps (Legman 1982). Both in Britain and in the United States, the Marines have a well-deserved reputation for toughness and bravery. Yet this very reputation for tough, masculine aggressiveness leads to jokes about their stupidity from those in charge of the sophisticated naval vessels and aircraft that get the Marines to the point where the fighting starts. This is the origin of the British phrase "Tell that to the Marines," said originally by sailors on being told an improbable story and implying that only a Marine would be gullible enough to believe it. In the Royal Navy, useless empty bottles were called "Marines" by the regular seamen, for the seamen alone knew how to work the ship (Brewer 1894, 808–809).

> Last week while I was at the Presidio, I heard over the loudspeaker, "It is now twelve o'clock for all you civilians, for the Navy personnel it is twelve hundred hours, and for you Marines, Mickey's little hand is pointing straight up and Mickey's big hand is also pointing straight up."
> (UCBFA Blason Populaire—anti-marine; collected by Ellen Chin 1970)

An Army Ranger was on vacation in Louisiana and wanted a pair of genuine alligator shoes. However, the local vendors were asking very high prices. So the Army Ranger decided to go into the swamps and get his own alligator and then have the shoes made at a more reasonable price. When he mentioned this to one of the shopkeepers, he was told that he might run into a couple of Marines who had decided to do the same thing. So the Ranger headed into the bayou and a few hours later he saw the two Marines. They were standing waist deep in the water. The Ranger then saw a huge 'gator swimming rapidly underwater toward one of the Marines. Just as the 'gator was about to attack, the Marine grabbed its neck with both hands and strangled it to death with very little effort. Then both Marines dragged it on shore and flipped it on its back. Laying nearby were several more of the creatures. The Ranger than heard one of the Marines shout, "Damn, this one doesn't have any shoes either."

(http://militaryjokes.informationresourcenetwork.com/index.php? entry=entry080303-220605; see also http://usmilitary.about.com/od/military humor/a/alligator.htm; accessed September 2009)

The U.S. Marines' riposte to these jokes is to tell jokes about sailors being passive homosexuals and thus, as we shall see in a later chapter, deficient in masculinity. The Marines refer to sailors as squids, after those soft formless creatures of the sea. That this kind of humorous banter should occur between rival branches of the armed services is unremarkable. The jokes told about the Marines' bravery refer to behavior that in terms of civilian values seems wild and irrational. The aircrew of bombers and the crews of submarines in World War II were just as brave, and a high proportion of them never came back, but their bravery was exercised in a less direct way and through the fine control of sophisticated machinery; it was not as visible as the close combat fighting of the U.S. Marines at Iwo Jima or the Royal Marines in the Falklands. The Marines and the commandos were the most physical of these elite forces. The jokes about the Marines being tough but stupid can be placed in contrast to the jokes told by Marines about military personnel involved in rather more knowledge-intensive forms of fighting, whom they depict as lacking in masculinity and physicality. Once again there is a contrast between mind and body, with the Marines winning battles through their willingness and ability to indulge in highly physical fighting under the roughest of circumstances, as distinct from the sophisticated thinking involved in the control of modern ships and aircraft. In a world of very varied threats and dangers, both kinds of fighter are necessary.

Are you fit to be a Marine?
Are you a muscle head?
Was your high school GPA put down as N/A?
Do you have explosive rage and curse excessively?

Do you have a strange desire to kill everything in sight?

Have you found yourself in solitary confinement on occasion?

If you've answered yes to any of these questions, the United States Marine Corps may be right for you.

Call 1-800-MARINES. The few, the proud, the downright fucking crazy. The Marines.

(http://www.dirtyjokesinc.com/joke-marine_jokes-14 287.htm; accessed September 2009)

Why do Marines like to be surrounded by the enemy?

Because it enables them to shoot in any direction and kill them.

A reality TV manager was interviewing one person from each of the armed forces for a spot on the new TV show. A soldier came in first, and the manager handed him a berretta and said, "Go into the other room there and shoot whoever it is in there." The soldier goes in and came back out and said, "I can't do it." He didn't get the spot.

Next a sailor came in, and the manager said the same thing to him. The sailor went into the room, came out, and said, "I can't do that." He didn't get the spot.

Then an Air Force pilot came in and was handed the same berretta and was told to do the same thing. Before he even went in, he turned the manager down.

Finally a Marine came in and stood in front of the manager at parade rest. The manager handed him the berretta and told him to kill whoever it was in the other room. The Marine walked in and from behind the door came a loud BANG!! Then what sounded like braking [sic] wood and screaming. The Marine walked out, covered in blood. The manager yelled, "What the hell happened?" The Marine replied, "Some dumbass put blanks in the gun, so I had to brake [sic] off a table leg and beat her to death, sir."

(http://www.dirtyjokesinc.com/joke-marine_jokes-14047.htm; accessed October 2009)

And, of course, the Aggies of Texas A&M, a university with a strong connection with the Marines, cannot be kept out of the jokes:

A guy walks into a bar and says to the bartender, "Hey, bartender, I know a great Aggie joke. You want to hear it?"

The bartender says, "Well, before you tell it, I should probably tell you that I went to A&M. And you see those two big guys sitting next to you—they were linebackers for the A&M football team. And those two guys on your other side—they're Marines, and they used to be in the Corps of Cadets at A&M. Now, are you sure you really want to tell that Aggie joke?"

The guy thinks for a second. "I guess not," he said. "I wouldn't want to have to explain it five times."

(http://signesays.com/blog/aggie-jokes-for-my-dad/; accessed October 2009)

The word *mad* is often used positively of soldiers who choose to take high risks. Field Marshall Montgomery said of David Stirling, O.B.E., and D.S.O. founder of the elite British Special Air Services in North Africa in World War II: "The boy Stirling is quite mad, quite, quite mad. However, in a war there is often a place for mad people." (www.undiscoredscotland .co.uk/usbiography/stu/davidstirling.html; accessed October 2009)

Outside of a war there is no place for mad people; the civilian world is one of caution and prudence, and it is out of this contrast that the jokes emerge.

Shakespeare's Falstaff would have seen Stirling's bravery as mad as well as "mad," much as he did the exhortations as well as the battling of Prince Hal, Henry of Monmouth, in *Henry IV,* Part 1. The comic rogue Falstaff provides a reasoned mockery of the very irrationality of honor itself:

> Falstaff: . . . Well, 'tis no matter, honour pricks me on. Yea, but how if honour prick me off when I come on, how then? Can honour set to a leg? No. Or an arm? No. Or take away the grief of a wound? No. Honour hath no skill in surgery, then? No. What is honour? A word. What is in that word honour? What is that honour? Air. A trim reckoning! Who hath it? He that died a' Wednesday. Doth he feel it? No. Doth he hear it? No. 'Tis insensible, then? Yea, to the dead. But will it not live with the living? No. Why? Detraction will not suffer it. Therefore I'll none of it. Honour is a mere scutcheon—and so ends my catechism. (Shakespeare *Henry IV,* Part 1, act 5, scene 1, lines 127–38)

DIM BLIMPS

Military intelligence: an oxymoron

We can see the opposition between and the mental and the material in George Orwell's (1982, 61) two "symbolic opposites—the half-pay colonel with his bull neck and diminutive brain like a dinosaur, the highbrow with his domed forehead and stalk-like neck." Orwell had in mind the comic and very British Colonel Blimp, invented in the 1930s by the Anglo–New Zealand cartoonist David Low (1956, 265–75) as a symbol of the stupidity of the traditional military mind. The Blimp cartoons ran for many years, and the words *blimp* and *blimpish* entered British English to describe those like him and their qualities. Low (1956, 265) claimed that his character, Colonel Blimp, a military airhead built like a dirigible, was based on direct observation of "chaps of a military bearing" talking in a Turkish bath. Low was further inspired when he read a letter in the press by "some colonel or other . . . to protest against the mechanization of cavalry and insisting that even if horses had to go, the uniform and trappings must remain inviolate and troops must continue to wear their spurs in their tanks." The British had been the first to develop the tank and in 1916 to use it in battle, but according to Low, the Blimps disliked sophisticated machinery that required brains and wanted the physicality of a good old-fashioned cavalry charge with much use of knightly spurs. The horse is a common symbol of faithful stupidity, as are those who ride it. For Low, the Blimps, together with their civilian adherents, stood for an entire British class, one trapped in military tradition and enthusiasts for the use of instant force to resolve all disputes of any kind. Here again it is a case of the powerful being mocked as stupid. It is the nature of the power being exercised or of the power that could be exercised that determines jokes about a target, not the mere possession of power as such. If that power is based on force or physicality, then it leads to stupidity jokes.

We can see this again in the jokes about dim military men that were told by Soviet students doing compulsory military courses at the university about their instructors, men brought in from the regular army:

> Instructor: "Suppose we have a unit of M tanks . . . no, M is not enough. Suppose we have a unit of N tanks!"

> Instructor: "Cadets, write down: the temperature of boiling water is 90°." One of the privates replies, "Comrade *praporshchik* (warrant officer), you're mistaken—it's 100°!" The officer checks in the book, and then replies, "Right, 100°. It is the right angle that boils at 90°."

> A missile silo officer falls asleep during his watch, with his face on the control board and the "red button." As the colonel comes in, the officer snaps up and proudly reports: "Nothing to report during my watch, comrade Colonel."
> "Nothing to report, you say? Nothing to report?! *Then where the hell is Belgium?!!*"
> (http://en.wikipedia.org/wiki/Russian_jokes; accessed January 2010)

STUPID ARISTOCRATS

It may be surmised that Colonel Blimp's love of force and horse and his sheer bone-headedness have their ancestry in an unthinking regard many have had for a long-dead, indeed to a large extent imaginary, feudal past of knights on horseback, honor and chivalry and colorful tradition, a time when commerce and technology did not dominate the world as they did in Blimp's time. Their imagined world was, to use Herbert Spencer's (1969, 499–533 and see 534–71) term, a "militant society," in which goodness was equated with bravery and strength as opposed to the values of the industrial and commercial society in which they lived. The feudal era had been a time when the use of force within a hierarchical social order to hold land determined who was powerful; it was the kind of power that today gives rise to jokes and parody. Nonetheless, in nineteenth-century Britain, the world's first industrial country, vestiges of these premodern traditions survived and to them was added a new mythical version of this world with deeds of derring-do by knights who defended swooning maidens and protected grateful, deferential, square-deal serfs. The combination took hold in the minds of many who did not like the newly modern utilitarian, calculative, ever-changing world, the world of the canny. It has been argued with reason that such fantasies led in England to the "decline of the industrial spirit," much to the detriment of the economy (Wiener 2004, 12–14, 97).

An extreme and somewhat comical example of this may be seen in the case of Julius Drew, an English businessman who made a very large fortune out of trading in tea. In his thirties he retired and hired a dubious genealogist, who persuaded him that he was a descendant of the ancient Drewe family of Honiton in rural Devon and even of Drogo de Teign, a Norman baron who had arrived with William the Conqueror. The good tea-wallah then changed his name to Drewe and in the early years of the twentieth century employed the leading architect Sir Edward Lutyens to build him a rugged medieval castle near Honiton to live in. He took as his family's and the castle's motto *Drogo Nomen et Virtus Arma Dedit,* "Drogo is my name and valour gave me arms," which he saw as having more dignity than the more truthful alternative, "Julius is my name and tea-pots poured me money." Like Don Quixote, he was tilting at dark satanic mills.

It was a view of the world that became the basis of ethnic, as well as class-based, jokes about English aristocrats that bring out the foolishness of such pride in a distant martial ancestry.

> An English sportsman in the Highlands, not getting all the respect he expected from his ghillie, said, "Look here, my man! You are evidently unaware that my family has been entitled to bear arms since the time of William the Conqueror."
> "Well, well, and you are fery welcome," was the mild reply. "My family was entitled to bare legs since the time of Noah." (Bell 1929, 27)

The identity of the Scottish Highlander is emphasized by an accompanying cartoon in which he wears a tartan kilt and by his pronunciation of the word *very* as "fery," a characteristic of Gaelic speakers. The phrase "entitled to bear arms," as used here, refers to the puce-faced, plus-foured Englishman's possession of a "coat of arms," of armorial bearings as a heraldic device, a badge of standing and ancestry. But coats of arms do relate to armor, and his ancestors would have displayed their coat of arms on a shield (escutcheon) and on a surcoat worn over their armor. It was the mark of the superiority of the noble warrior and thus of his descendant gone to Scotland to shoot deer and employing a local man to attend him, the ghillie.

Aristocrats were and are not particularly stupid, but the high social position that they had inherited and the power and influence that went with it meant that those who had risen by ability would have seen them as stupid and as hide-bound. What had they ever achieved as individuals to gain their high position? A valiant ancestor is no guarantee of an able scion. Tradition and instrumental rationality tend to conflict, and this is likely to be perceived as the powerful but stupid obstructing the intelligent. Aristocrats were often the butt of Gilbert and Sullivan's humor, as in their comic opera *Iolanthe* (1882), where the House of Lords (Peers) are told that their members are to be selected by competitive examination:

> Lord Tolloller: Well, but think what it all means. I don't so much mind for myself, but with a House of Peers with no grandfathers worth mentioning, the country must go to the dogs!
> Leila: I suppose it must!
> Lord Mountararat: I don't want to say a word against brains—I've a great respect for brains—I often wish I had some myself. (*Iolanthe*, act 2)

In the United States, a country whose republican Constitution (Article 1, Sections 9 and 10) sought from the inception to prevent the formation of a landed aristocracy, by banning the creation of titles and of permanently entailed estates, English class-based jokes about "upper-class twits" and "chinless wonders" become ethnic jokes about the English, jokes about tongue-tied old buffers who cannot even understand the simplest of jokes (Davies 1990, 254–56; Dundes 1980).

There are many European equivalents of such jokes, such as the *hrabia* (count) jokes in Poland, in Austria and South Germany jokes about the dim-witted Graf Bobby (Count Bobby) and his sidekick, Baron Rudi or Baron Mucki (*Die besten Graf Bobby Witze* 1982; Scholten 1971, 23–24; Stalzer 1982), and in Hungary about the two aristocrats Arisztid and Taszil
ó.

> Taszilió decides to visit Austria and tells his friend Arisztid. Arisztid says, "I'd like to go with you, and Taszilió says, "All right, I'll put you in my bag, and at customs I'll say I'm carrying porcelain."
>
> At customs the official asks Taszilió what he has in the bag, and Taszilió says, "Porcelain." Then the official kicked the bag and Arisztid made a noise like "csohrump, csohrump, csohrump" (crunch, crunch, crunch).
>
> (UCBFA Blason Populaire Hungarian; collected by Joanne Howard 1971)
>
> When Bobby was still better off financially, he had a manservant. One day he sent his manservant down to the Drogerie to get some insect repellant to fight the bedbugs. As his man is about to leave on the errand, Bobby calls him back and says, "No, wait a minute, Johann. You can't just get bedbug powder. They know us at the Drogerie, and they'll think we have bedbugs. We have to do this in a different way. You know what? Ask them to gift wrap it." (Lopez 2003)
>
> A count (hrabia) is asked, "Does speaking English cause you any difficulty?"
>
> "To me, no, but to the English, yes."
>
> Butler: "That beggar is at the door again. He claims to be a relative of yours."
>
> Hrabia: "He must be some kind of idiot!"
>
> Butler: "I agree, my lord, but that hardly disproves his claim."
>
> (Both *hrabia* jokes were sent to me by a Polish humor scholar by e-mail in January 2010).

Humor about a clever servant and his stupid aristocrat employer has a long and rich tradition in Europe, as in the Estonian jokes about the German Baltic barons, who were once a dominant class in that country (Vesilind 2009). P. G. Wodehouse's humor depends on the interaction between a dim aristocrat, the Hon. Bertie Wooster, and his shrewd valet, Jeeves. In the novel *Thank you, Jeeves,* Jeeves threatens to resign his post if Bertie continues playing the banjolele. Bertie, feeling that he is being manipulated by Jeeves, thinks to himself:

> . . . . what is Jeeves after all? A valet. A salaried attendant. And a fellow simply can't go on truckling—do I mean truckling? I know it begins with a "t"—to his valet for ever. There comes a moment when he must remember that his ancestors did dashed well at the Battle of Crecy and put the old foot down. (Wodehouse 1986, 15).

Kirby Olson (1996, 74) comments on this passage:

> As Bertie is well aware, he earned the right to be the master when his ancestors won at the Battle of Crecy. . . . Wodehouse's Bertie extends this notion [of mastery] to indicate that one's *ancestors'* fight earns *him* the privilege of continuing mastery, and he is furious to have to fight it out again and again with Jeeves, when to him the matter should be settled.

Similarly, there are old Indian humorous tales about canny advisors at court running rings around autocratic rulers (Patel 1946), which leads us to jokes about dictators.

STUPID DICTATORS

All states are ultimately based on force and claim a monopoly of legitimate force within their territory, but they differ greatly in their capacity, willingness, and need to use it internally to maintain a particular social order or simply to keep the rulers in power. Democracy was possible in Britain, the United States, and Switzerland historically because of the restricted amount of force the central state could deploy relative to its citizens. At the opposite extreme are dictators whose rule is primarily built on force, who may well have come to power in a civil war or military coup and may be toppled in the same way. Samuel Finer (1978) called his book on the role of the military in politics *The Man on Horseback,* a title which hints at some of their limitations when they have to try to rule a complex society. Military rulers are apt to become the butt of stupidity jokes, and so are the heads of one-party states, who stay in power only or mainly because they have the means forcibly and easily to suppress internal discontent. They and their entourage are very often the butt of stupidity jokes (García 1977; Pi-Sunyer 1977; Umeasiegbu 1986).

> Muzenda (vice president of Zimbabwe). "When the phone rings, green, green, green, I pink it up and say yellow!
> (Collected by a student from Sierra Leone from Zimbabweans studying in Britain 2001).

> Brezhnev travels to Central Asia. He is met by local party dignitaries who greet him. "Salaam Aleikum!" (Peace be upon you).
> Brezhnev has been trained to respond politely in the local fashion. "Aleikum Salaam!" (Upon you be peace), he replies immediately.
> "Salaam Aleikum!" they repeat.
> "Aleikum Salaam!" Brezhnev responds.
> A dissident, who has sneaked in, shouts, "Gulag Archipelago."
> "Archipelago Gulag!" replies Brezhnev.

> What is the average IQ of Poland? Fifty Ochab.
> (UCBFA Polish file; collected by Juliana Roth 1969)

Edward Ochab was a prominent Polish communist politician until 1968, when he was forced out by anti-Semites because his wife was Jewish.

STUPID MILITIAS

Those who controlled the direct use of force locally to keep a dictator in power were also the butt of stupidity jokes, notably the militia in communist Poland and Czechoslovakia. Those militiamen who policed the urban areas were recruited from failed peasants, men willing to take on a job everyone despised in order to get residence and work permits to live in one of the big cities. In these cities, living conditions and facilities were far better than elsewhere, since the party bosses lived there. Under socialism the state controlled where one was allowed to live and work through a system of permits, and this was an important tool for exercising social and political control. Those who got on the wrong side of the authorities could lose their permits to remain in a desirable city, but those who agreed to be the state's instruments instantly obtained them.

Why do militiamen go round in threes?

One can read, one can write, and one is there to keep an eye on the two intellectuals.

Jokes of this kind can also exist in a democratic society like Italy, where they are told about Italy's armed gendarmerie, the once carbine-toting carabinieri, a military force with police duties. They were created in case of a violent disturbance in a country where few have had much confidence in or loyalty to the central government. Unlike the ordinary police, the carabinieri live apart from the people in military barracks and have, when required, fought with distinction on the battlefield. They are recruited from the rustics of southern Italy or from Italy's "deep North" and are in consequence seen as less sophisticated than the people they control. They are sometimes mounted and provide a mounted guard of honor for the president, dressed in splendid uniforms. Once again horse = force = stupid.

> Carabiniere al maneggio: Carabiniere at the stable
> -Buongiorno, vorrei un cavallo. Good morning, I want a horse.
> -Da montare? To ride or to be assembled from a building kit?
> -No, no, già pronto . . . No, no, ready to go.

> Two carabinieri on horseback are patrolling through the Villa Borghese and telling stories about carabinieri heroes of the past. The first one begins: "One day Salvo D'Aquisto was riding a horse—oh, between 1930 and 1940." The other replies: "Good God! The horse must have been tired." (Both jokes from http://www.flickr.com/photos/firenzesca /2137529059/)

> In order to save the lives of Italian hostages held by the German army in 1943, the carabiniere, Sgt. Salvo D'Aquisto, confessed to having set off deliberately what had in fact been a purely accidental explosion in which German troops were killed. He was executed. He was a true Christian hero and is being considered for beatification. (For more jokes about carabinieri and some background, see Aquisti 1988; Necchi 2006.)

JOKES ABOUT THE STUPIDITY OF WARRIOR PEOPLES

It is not necessary for those who are the butts of stupidity jokes about their use of crude force to be in a position of authority as agents of the state. The members of any ethnic group who take pride in their physical strength or martial traditions can be the subject of stupidity jokes. In

India the jokes are often told about the Sikhs, a warrior religion (Uberoi 1967) that emerged at a time when it was necessary to defend the Punjab from invasion and conquest by the Muslims. An observant male Sikh carries his *kirpan,* his sword or dagger, with him at all times. The Sikhs have served with great bravery and distinction in the British army and today are overrepresented in the Indian army by a factor of ten. In the jokes they are called Sardars or Sardarjis. The suffix *-ji* is simply an honorific. The Nihangs are a traditional Sikh military order.

> Brain food
>
> A Sardar and a Bengali were travelling in the same railway compartment. It was very hot and the Bengali was having trouble undoing the steel strap of his wristwatch. The Sardar went across and with one mighty jerk undid the buckle. "You Bengalis should eat gehoon (wheat). It makes you strong."
>
> The Bengali did not appreciate the advice. A few minutes later he grasped the alarm chain and pretended to be unable to pull it. Once again the Sardar leapt to his assistance and pulled the chain with a triumphant yell: "There! You Bengalis should eat——"
>
> The train came to a halt. The conductor, accompanied by a couple of policemen, asked the Sardar to explain why he had pulled the chain and, on his failure to do so, fined him Rs. 50.
>
> After they had left, the Bengali gently advised the Sardar, "You Punjabis should eat rice. It is better for the brain."
>
> (http://www.indianjokes.in/Bengali_Jokes_jokes/joke-839.asp; accessed August 29, 2009)

The largely rural Punjabis grow and eat wheat and tend to be bigger and stronger than the Bengalis, who eat rice and are often city-dwellers, merchants, lawyers, or white-collar workers.

> The merciful Nihang
>
> A Nihang decided to stop an express train at a non-stop station. He stood in the middle of the rail track brandishing his kirpan and spear and yelling defiance at the oncoming train. A crowd watched the confrontation with bated breath.
>
> When the engine driver noticed the Nihang on the track and realised he would not be able to stop the train in time; he blew his whistle as frantically as he could. Just as the engine was almost upon him, the Nihang jumped aside and let the train pass.
>
> "What happened, Nihangji?" asked the onlookers. "Did you take fright?"

"Never!" replied the Nihang with bravado. "You see how I made it scream! (Cheekaan kaddh dittiyan!) A Nihang never kills anyone who cries for mercy."

(http://jokes.maxabout.com/punjabi-jokes/the-merciful-nihang/21047; posted May 29, 2008; accessed August 29, 2009)

STUPID ATHLETES

The central theme of many of the jokes cited above is that a person with merely physical skills is stupid. Sometimes there is a military or political dimension to such jokes involving power based on force, but this is not necessary, for there are also many jokes about stupid athletes or sportspersons, as in the jokes below that were told about David Beckham, known as Becks, a soccer celebrity in England, Spain, Italy, and the United States. Blake Morrison (2009) has written about Beckham, "Intelligence? His shortness up top is legendary and nothing to do with close-cropped hair," but it does not really matter whether he is stupid or not. The stupidity jokes are not really about him but about all football players and indeed athletes in general. Some sports stars are intelligent, but what matters is that they do not need be. They merely need to have certain highly specific physical aptitudes that can make them very rich but that have no real use outside that sport.

The Real Madrid players are in the dressing room on Saturday, just before the game, when Zidane walks in. "Boss," he says, "there's a problem. I'm not playing unless I get a cortisone injection."

"Hey," says Becks. "If he's having a new car, so am I."

(http://www.wanguoqunxing.com/cms4/modules.php?name=Nuke Jokes&func=JokeView&jokeid=31; accessed 20 January 20, 2010; see also Enodreven 2005)

David Beckham goes shopping and sees something interesting in the kitchen department of a large department store.

"What's that?" he asks.

"A Thermos flask," replies the assistant.

"What does it do?" asks Becks.

The assistant tells him it keeps hot things hot and cold things cold.

Really impressed, Beckham buys one and takes it along to his next training session. "Here, boys, look at this," Beckham says proudly. "It's a Thermos flask."

The lads are impressed. "What does it do?" they ask.

"It keeps hot things hot and cold things cold," says David.

"And what have you got in it?" ask the lads.

"Two cups of coffee and a Choc ice," replies David. (Enodreven 2005)

Posh (Beckham's wife) takes her car into a garage to have some dents removed.

The mechanic, knowing she isn't the brightest Spice Girl in the world, decides to play a joke on her.

"You don't need me to take those dents out," he says. "Just blow up the exhaust pipe, and the metal will pop back into place."

So she takes the car home and tries it. David spots her from the house and shouts, "You silly cow! You have to wind the windows up first!" (Enodreven 2005)

Beckham's statements in real life may have something in common with the fictitious ones in the jokes, and the comments of dim athletes generally have been collected and published by Barry Fantoni (1982–2008)

As with the jokes about the Marines, jokes about athletes can take in the Texas Aggies.

The star football player for the Aggies was failing his math class at the semester and had to pass his exam in order to play in the game that weekend at Kyle Field. The professor and the school board get together and decide to ask him one question at halftime of the game. If the Aggie answers the question correctly, he passes and can play. However, if he answers incorrectly, he fails the course and is ineligible. Well, the game finally rolls around, and everyone is anxious about the question. At halftime the player and his professor go to the center of the field and over the loudspeaker the professor asks the question: "What is two plus two?" The Aggie thinks and thinks. Finally he asks the professor if he can use a calculator. The professor says, "No, your time is up." In desperation the Aggie shouts into the microphone "Four!"

With that, Kyle Field erupts into the chant of "Give him another chance. Give him another chance!"

(http://home.earthlink.net/~mike_scott/aggjoke.htm; accessed February 16, 2010) (For a very similar joke told about the students of a college in Tafili in the southern part of Jordan, see Al-Khatib 1999, 268.)

A BLONDE MOMENT

Jokes about blondes and sex have long existed, but most of those in the recent blonde joke cycle were about the blonde's stupidity. Over a half of Elliott Oring's (2003, 62) sample of blonde jokes from the internet were about stupidity, compared with under a third about promiscuity. Nonetheless, her promiscuity is the key to her stupidity. The blonde's mindless sexual body corresponds to the mindless tough body of the warrior or athlete. Her unthinking use of it in bed or in the back of a car is categorized in humor along with the unthinking risks men take with their bodies when fighting, and both are the bases of jokes about comic stupidity. Both of them lack calculativeness. Both adhere unthinkingly to stereotypical sex roles, to tough masculinity, and to the uses of feminine allure. The blonde joke fits the opposition between body and mind, between mental and material that characterizes all the other stupidity jokes. It will be shown in the next chapter that blondes are sexually attractive and that this leads to jokes about their being sexually available. The jokes about blonde stupidity evolved out of the earlier sex jokes. Jokes about blondes and sex were common long before the huge cycle of blonde jokes of the late twentieth century. The blondes in these earlier jokes are not usually depicted as particularly stupid. The potential for stupidity jokes was already there, based on the contrast between sex as an unthinking urge, an expression of the instinctual, on the one hand, and the possession and use of a thoughtful and calculative intelligence, on the other, but the great wave of jokes about stupid blondes really only got going at the beginning of the 1990s (Oring 2003, 59).

> Which third-grader has the best body: the blonde, brunette, or redhead?
> The blonde; she is eighteen.

> What do you call it when a blonde dies her hair black?
> Artificial intelligence. (Oring 2003, 60)

The jokes began in America, but they rapidly spread to Croatia, France, Germany, Hungary, Poland, and even Brazil, where the dumb blondes of the jokes are known as *louras burras* (blonde she-mules). These jokes are not merely imported. They include new local inventions that depend on local knowledge and on forms of wordplay only possible in the local language.

> A blonde is trying to pass history at school.
> "Can you tell us what the first capital of Poland was?"
> After thinking long and receiving many hints from the examiners, she finally comes up with Gniezno and receives a C.

When she leaves, the other girls keep pestering her: "What do the examiners ask about?"

The blonde tells them the question, and the other blonde writes the answer down on a piece of paper and puts it into her shoe.

Her turn comes, and after a long time of sweating before the examiners, she is asked to name the first capital of Poland.

Happy, she reaches for her shoe, takes out the paper, and reads out with confidence: Radom Shoe Factory. (Sent to me by a humor scholar from Kraków, Poland, 2008)

A brunette meets a blonde and asks her, "Have you heard of this rail disaster at Skierniewice?"

"No, what happened?"

"A train was derailed, and 100 people are injured."

"One hundred? One hundred? . . . That's a million before redenomination."

(Sent to me by a humor scholar from Kraków, Poland, 2008)

Due to cumulative hidden inflation followed by hyperinflation, the Polish złoty was denominated in millions. The currency had to undergo redenomination, and on January 1, 1995, 10,000 old Polish złotych became one new Polish złoty.

A blonde buys herself a new car. She gets in and says, "The mirrors must be wrongly adjusted. I cannot see myself, just some cars."

(Sent to me by a humor scholar from Kraków, Poland, 2008)

A friend is taking a blonde to the cinema. Above the entrance there is an illuminated advertisement that proclaims: "Two hours of excitement! Two hours of thrill! Two hours of relaxation! Two hours of real entertainment!"

The blonde says, "Are you crazy? Why have you brought me here? Do you think that I am going to sit eight hours in the cinema?" (Sent to me by a humor scholar from Hungary 2008)

Elliott Oring (2003, 69) has explained the timing of the blonde joke cycle in terms of the cumulative expansion of the numbers of women occupying responsible positions in the workplace that required the steady exercise of intelligence. The flaunting of sexual attractiveness or the seeking of easy sexual relations with male colleagues does not fit with this. Blondes may "have more fun," but there is an antithesis between fun and work, particularly when it is the kind of fun conventionally associated with blondes. Oring backs up his argument by reference to earlier university-based stupidity jokes that mocked female students seen as having gone to college not to work or to prepare for work but to find sexual partners. The blonde of the jokes is just a "placeholder" in jokes that employ a playful manipulation of moral values in response to a contemporary situation. The blonde is a symbol of the inept, the sexual, the easy, and the easy route to approbation (Oring 2003, 65). The previous tradition of jokes about sexy blondes set her up for this.

Oring is right to stress the workplace as the key factor, for this is the area where intelligence is most valued and stupidity is most deplored and seen as ludicrous. This is why so many stupidity jokes are attached to particular professions, occupations, and social classes. Historically these stupidity jokes were nearly all about men. The few jokes about stupid women were given a family or domestic setting, and the only occupation about which female stupidity jokes were told was that of the domestic servant, who was also often shown as in search of a man or as having sex with the men of the house. Ethnic jokes about stupid, though loyal and amiable, male Irish domestic servants had already begun to appear in Britain by the reign of Charles II in the late seventeenth century, and ethnic jokes about "Bridget," the simple Irish maid servant, were common in nineteenth-century America as well as in Britain. There were many American ethnic jokes about other immigrant maid servants from a peasant background such as Swedes and Finns, all quite unused to the sophisticated American household.

A much earlier case of jokes about the confusion and conjunction of work and sex occurs in the "boss and secretary" jokes, which were made possible by the influx of women into routine white-collar jobs in the late nineteenth century, when the female typist replaced the unexciting and often comically dim and dull male clerks like Mr. Pooter in *The Diary of a Nobody* (Grossmith and Grossmith 1889). The boss in the jokes has a "blonde" stenographer (H. Norden 1937, 182–83; Loos 1928, 99, 118), with blonde being shorthand for sexually available. She appears in cartoons and in comic postcards sitting on the boss's lap or bending over in a short skirt to rummage in the bottom drawers of the filing cabinet. A pun on "drawers" predictably follows.

Confucius say: Secretary not permanent till screwed on the table.
(UCBFA File Joke IC 65; collected by Helene Blaustein 1983)

The businessman's wife, who had called at his office, regarded the pretty young stenographer with a baleful eye.
"You told me that your typewriter was an old maid," she accused.
The husband, at a loss, faltered in his reply, but at last contrived:
"Yes, but she's sick to-day, and sent her grandchild in her place."
(Jokes from the Late Nineteenth Century 2008)

Malborn sat in his attorney's office. "Do you want the bad news first or the terrible news?" the lawyer said.
"Give me the bad news first."
"Your wife found a picture worth a half-million dollars."
"That's the bad news?" asked Malborn, incredulously. "I can't wait to hear the terrible news."
"The terrible news is that it's of you and your secretary." (Fuqua 2000)

However, the focus in these earlier jokes is always on the breaking of sexual rules, not work rules. The essence of the joke is the deception of the boss's wife rather than the disruption of the routines of the office. The jokes are domestic jokes displaced to an office setting. Nonetheless, by the 1920s there were many more women working in responsible jobs outside the home that required the exercise of independence and intelligence, and it is at this time that their comic antithesis, the dumb blonde, first emerged. Far from being a joke about the stupidity of women in general, it is an acknowledgment that the new world of work requires intelligent rather than merely decorative women. The dumb blonde is a comic misfit and anachronism, who can only succeed by using her physical attractiveness and that alone to manipulate men.

The classic dumb blonde was Lorelei Lee, invented by Anita Loos (1925) for her humorous novel *Gentlemen Prefer Blondes* (1925). Lorelei is attractive enough to have been acquitted of a murder, of which she was guilty, by an all-male jury in Little Rock, Arkansas. She is seriously deficient in understanding. She tells the reader that an Englishman has sent a friend of hers books "by a gentleman called Mr. Conrad. They all seem to be about ocean travel" (20). She asks her rather more literate black maid to read *Lord Jim* for her, but manages to give her *The Nigger of the Narcissus* by mistake (28–29). Lorelei's errors are not just chance ignorance; she is a siren as thick as the rock after which she is named.

That her schemes pay off says much about the sheer irrational force of sexual attraction; she is not only stupid but a generator of utterly stupid behavior in her entranced followers.

Anita Loos records in her memoirs that she had the idea for the book on a long train journey from New York to Hollywood, when all the men who were with her drooled over a "Broadway cutie" who was "a quite unnatural blonde. Concerning our mental acumen, there was nothing to discuss; I was the smarter. But there was some mystifying difference between us. Why did she so far outdistance me in feminine allure? Could her power like that of Samson have something to do with her hair?" (1977, 73–74). Loos continues: "As the train sped on its way I began to harbor a resentment of blondes that cut quite deeply and presently I singled out another stupid creature who had bedazzled one of America's foremost intellectuals, H. L. Mencken. . . . I sometimes caused Menck to laugh but in the matter of sentiment he preferred the witless blonde" (Loos 1977, 74). Mencken could see the humor in the situation, for he much enjoyed her story and encouraged Loos to publish it (Bode 1969, 161). Her book became a best-seller and gave rise to several films and a musical. The humor Loos created out of her experience of a modern cultural conflict is an ancestor of the later joke cycle about dumb blondes.

It has been suggested that the image of the dim blonde is taken seriously and could affect how people behave in the real world (Bry et al. 2008). In Hungary in November 2004, blonde women held an angry protest outside the Parliament building in Budapest, claiming they were being discriminated against in the workplace and the job market. "Blondes—real and bleached—waved banners outside the ministry with slogans saying, "We're blonde, not stupid" and "Love us for our minds" ("Blonde Discrimination Is No Joke" 2004). The demonstrators from Hungary's "Blonde Women's Movement" also attacked a bar called Blondy with eggs and cakes and urged the blonde barmaids working there to go on strike. Al-Nasser, a subscriber to the Muslim discussion forum Ummah, which also reported the incident in 2004, commented, "Now this protest is the ultimate proof . . . how stupid! and will be the subject of the new wave of blond jokes." Another subscriber responded:

Blond gets caught speeding; the cop is also a blond. Cop: "Let me see your driver's license." Driver: "What's that?" Cop: "A square thing with your picture on it." Blond fumbles thru her purse, finds a mirror, sees herself in it, and hands it to the cop. Cop looks at it, then hands it back. "I'm gonna let you go without a ticket. I didn't know you were a cop." (Hungary to Ban Blonde Jokes? 2004)

What is curious is that for most blondes, including many of the protesters, blondeness is chosen. If blondeness truly were to carry with it the heavy social penalty of being thought stupid and treated accordingly, why is it chosen to the point where artificial blondes outnumber real ones by ten to one. It is easy to see why, in societies obsessed with youth, so many should wish to avoid discrimination against the gray-haired. But why choose blonde when many other youthful but "intelligent" hair colors are on offer? Even the woman who is naturally blonde can easily and cheaply dissolve her follicles of gold in henna or coat them with pitch and no one will ever know. The subjective payoff to those who choose to "have more fun," or be thought by others to have more fun, is presumably greater than the negative experience of being considered dim blondes. These choices and dilemmas reinforce the thesis expounded here, namely, that there is a tension and an ambiguity in the social order as traditional sex roles fail to mesh with the impersonal and instrumental rationality required by modern occupations, which is what gives rise to the blonde jokes.

There is a curious parallel between hair dilemmas and those faced by those who wear spectacles. For a variety of reasons, boys and girls who are short-sighted and have to correct this by wearing eyeglasses are far more successful in the educational system and far more likely to be upwardly mobile into a higher social class than those with normal eyesight (Douglas et al. 1971, 166, 239–40). However, myopia is also a stigmatized physical defect, and those who can afford it spend large sums of money on laser surgery to correct the shape of the natural lenses within their eyes. Likewise, those who wear spectacles are seen as ugly and unattractive and are the subject of jokes and banter and nicknames such as "four-eyes," "specs," or "gig lamps." Thick glasses are described as "pebble-lensed," and they stretch their wearers' eyes round their heads like a Picasso. Actors with eyeglasses such as Woody Allen, Phil Silvers, the Two Ronnies, or Eric Morecambe tend to end up in comedy and to use their eyeglasses as a prop. There is a scarcity of short-sighted men in the acting profession playing serious parts, and so when a role calls for a man to wear eyeglasses, they have to wear frames with plain glass, not lenses, which looks wrong on screen.

Dorothy Parker once wrote, "Men seldom make passes at girls who wear glasses." Yet the girls who wear glasses have better career prospects (Douglas et al. 1971, 166, 239–40). Also, they will appear more serious, efficient, and intelligent in the workplace—the female boss or P.A. as opposed to the image of the "dolly-bird secretary," the airhead who only knows how to manipulate the senior male staff. The woman who has to exercise authority in the workplace and be taken seriously or the efficient and experienced secretary, the one who holds the office together, may well choose to wear spectacles at work but contact lenses in her leisure hours.

Spectacles for long sight are often a sign of aging as the eye muscles lose their elasticity, and many men avoid wearing them for this reason. In the days before contact lenses, men would have their prescriptions built into mild sunglasses, and military men carried monocles for reading maps on which hills and targets are identified by tiny numbers. Hitler had his long ranting speeches printed in extra-large type so that he did not have to wear spectacles in public. Spectacles detract from an image of virile power and forcefulness. Eyeglasses, like baldness or blondeness, may seem to be superficial in all senses of the word, but they are not. We need only consider how much people spend on expensive frames and how much advertisers compete for their money. Appearance sells, and so they sell appearance.

There is once again in our imagery and in social reality a contrast between body and mind, between things material and things intelligent. Images of the physical, of the military, of force and strength, and of sexual attractiveness are opposed to brainpower and the images that go with it. In men it is brawn versus brain, the monocled, mustached warrior and the heavy dragoon versus the bespectacled intellectual and the bald-headed boffin, the backroom scientist. In the case of women it is, rather predictably, about sexual attraction, the unfair tyranny of appearance. Many jokes and much humor grow out of these dichotomies.

CANNY LAWYERS AND BANKERS

It might be expected that if those whose occupations are physical and material are the butt of stupidity jokes, then there should be jokes about the intelligence of those whose occupations are mentally demanding. This is not necessarily so. In and of itself, intelligence is a valuable quality, but jokes about targets must have a negative aspect such as the unduly self-interested behavior of the canny and crafty. To be the butt of jokes about being canny, it is necessary to master and to be the master of that most abstract and most material of things—money. Money is credit, and property is legal entitlement, both of which are abstract. Lawyers and bankers determine who owns what and how much of the material world others can claim and when they can claim it. They are the gatekeepers of power in a society based on large corporations, most of whose shares are owned by other corporations such as pension funds, insurance companies, or unit trusts, all of which are modern legal creations. Lawyers have long been the butt of "canny" jokes about their applying their intelligence in unscrupulous ways to take advantage of those who cannot understand what they are doing or why they are being paid so much. Essentially similar jokes are told about bankers, whose dealings are equally abstract and mysterious. This is the reason why members of these great and honorable professions are made the subject of so many jokes about their being clever swindlers. Such jokes became especially popular in America in the late twentieth century, but they are built upon a much older tradition.

LAWYER AND BANKER JOKES

In a society where most of the inhabitants work in agriculture or in the production of basic material items, there are often jokes about lawyers, for the lawyers' activities seem to produce nothing and to be based on nothing. In the jokes the lawyers are portrayed as "fomenters of strife" (Galanter 2005, 67–141), without whom the many conflicts over boundaries, over inheritance, and over reputation would not exist and as "economic predators" whose work does not add to but subtracts from the resources of the community. This view was particularly strongly held in early modern England, a very litigious place in the sixteenth and seventeenth centuries, which may account for Shakespeare's many jibes about lawyers, and in the early years of the newly independent United States (Galanter 2005, 3–5). The image of the evil lawyer, who toils not but only spins, reinforces the sustaining myth that the joke tellers are part of a united productive community of hard-working, self-sufficient people, a community in which there is no spite, envy, greed, or spontaneous conflict; the richly ambiguous jokes about lawyers may well also give the lie to that myth.

> A small town that cannot support one lawyer can always support two. (http://www.vakilno1.com/lawoneliner.htm; accessed March 2, 2010)

The DECEASED AND HIS HEIRS
A Man died leaving a large estate and many sorrowful relations who claimed it. After some years, when all but one had had judgment given against them, that one was awarded the estate which he asked his Attorney to have appraised.
"There is nothing to appraise," said the Attorney, pocketing his last fee.
"Then," said the Successful Claimant, "what good has all this litigation done me?"
"You have been a good client to me," the Attorney replied, gathering up his books and papers, "but I must say you betray a surprising ignorance of the purpose of litigation" (Myers 1984, 345).

> Lawyer to French client: "Take him to Court . . . that would be a good trick to play on your neighbor . . . he would have to eat into his savings to the extent of at least 300 francs."
> Client: "Yes, but I would have to eat into my savings too and I have no appetite for that."
> Added text beneath a Daumier engraving. Author's translation (Daumier 1970 [c. 1851], 29)

THE WISE PEASANT
A wealthy Peasant, who felt that his hours were numbered, called his sons around his bedside and began: "James, you are the eldest and I bequeath you my blessing."
The second son came forward, with bowed head, and the father said: "John Henry, you have been a good boy, and I bequeath you my good name."
The third son showed up, and the old man kindly remarked: "Andrew Jackson, you are my youngest, and I bequeath you the care of my grave. Goodbye, my dear sons. Each of you press my hand for the last time and then skip back to the field, for this is glorious weather for corn."

"But, dad, you are worth $90,000!" they protested in chorus.

"That is true, boys, but I have tried to make an equal division. I have let fall the honor to you and all the money to the lawyers. They would have got the sugar, anyhow, and in the getting would have left you nothing and proved your mother a fool and your father a lunatic; besides I die happy and full of peace. Bury me just to the left of the old cow-shed, and pay for my tombstone on the monthly installment system."

MORAL: The Lawyers were of course dissatisfied with the will and carried the case into court.

(C. B. Lewis 1884, 142–43).

At a revival meeting a young lawyer was called upon to deliver a prayer. Totally unprepared he got to his feet and these words tumbled out: "Oh, Lord, stir up much strife amongst thy people, lest Thy humble servant perish." (Shafer and Papadakis 1988, cited in Galanter 2005, 118)

The alternative to blaming the lawyers would be to accept what is true but inadmissible, namely, that there are always irreconcilable conflicts, even among equals, and that by definition there is never enough justice to go round. All communities are flawed, and all have devices for avoiding knowing that the flaws are there. It is an uneasy contradiction in which jokes flourish. When the lawyers win, no one knows how, for their knowledge and procedures are mysterious to outsiders, and their observed actions, such as talking to clients, do not seem to justify what they charge.

When Lloyd George was a young country solicitor in Wales, he was riding home in his dogcart one day and came upon a little Welsh girl trudging along so wearily that he offered her a ride. She accepted silently and all the way along, although the future statesman tried to engage her in conversation, he could not get her to say anything more than "Yes" or "No."

Some days afterwards the little girl's mother happened to meet Mr. Lloyd George and said to him smilingly, "Do you remember my little girl riding with you the other day? Well, when she got home, she said, "Mamma, I rode from school with Mr. Lloyd George, the lawyer, and he kept talking to me and I didn't know whatever to do, for you know Mr. Lloyd George, the lawyer, charges you to talk to him and I hadn't any money.'" (Galanter 2005, 83)

There is no doubt that my lawyer is honest. For example, when he filed his income tax return last year, he declared half of his salary as "unearned income." (Fuqua 2000)

There are relatively few jokes known to the public about the special knowledge and expertise that lawyers or indeed bankers or brokers have, even though it is this which enables them both to occupy a high place in society and to be the subject of jokes about their lack of moral probity. They are at the center of a huge corpus of canny jokes because they possess forms of extreme cleverness which set them apart from the "stupid" material world and yet which enable them to control that world. Yet precisely because their knowledge is arcane, there are few jokes about it, only a few hints that the intrinsic difficulty of the law is made even more difficult than it need be by lawyers clinging to obscure and even antiquated terminology and procedures that are unnecessarily opaque.

> Have you heard about the new word processor for lawyers?
> Whatever font you select, everything comes out in small print.

> ·Judge: Your client is, I take it, Mr. Smith, aware of the principle of
> *vigilantes et non dormientes inveniunt legem*?
> F. E. Smith: I do assure you, m'lud, in Barnsley they talk of little else.
> (Cited in Collins 1998, 1)

There are many versions of this humorous anecdote, some English and some Irish. Many sharp retorts to judges in English jokes are ascribed to the famously acerbic lawyer and politician F. E. Smith. Barnsley is an English mining town in South Yorkshire where Latin would be all Greek to the locals and the law a foreign language. Very roughly the Latin means "It is the alert, not the sleeping, who find out what the law is."

Jokes rarely refer to the content of the law, which the layman rarely knows, but concentrate on the final point where lawyer and client meet— the bill.

> What can a duck do that a lawyer should do?
> Stick his bill up his ass.

In addition to the intricacies of the system, individual cases differ so much that the client is not in a position to know how much time and expertise were required to settle his or her case and may well suspect that too much of these were expended or even pretended and the bill inflated.

Litigant—"You take nine-tenths of the judgment? Outrageous!"
Lawyer—"I furnish all the skill and eloquence and legal learning for your cause."
Litigant—"But I furnish the cause."
Lawyer—"Oh, anybody could do that." (Galanter 2005, 78)

As Galanter observes, the above joke from 1895 was still going strong a century later. The central idea remains the same, but the differences in style and language reflect how much society has changed:

> The man looked at the check he received after winning his suit against the city.
> "Wait a minute!" he said to his attorney. "This is only a third of the full amount!"
> "That's right," said the attorney. "I took the rest."
> "You!" screamed the man. "I was the one who was hurt!"
> "You forget. I provided the intelligence required to build the case, the expertise to find precedents, and the oratory to convince the jury. Any asshole could fall down a manhole."
> (Galanter 2005, 78)

What the lawyer is saying may well be entirely true, and his services may well be worth that in the marketplace, but all this is undercut by the cynical punch line. Sometimes in the joke the suspicion is that the victim has paid over the odds for a seemingly trivial consultation. Here again the lawyer may be in the right either because it quickly revealed that the client's case was hopeless or because the conversation had an "opportunity cost," that is, it took up time that the lawyer could have devoted to work that paid well or indeed better. However, the jokes are always told from the point of view of the doubting client.

Additional variations on this theme have to do with the practice of lawyers charging by the hour rather than having a set fee for a particular task. In many respects this is fairer than averaging the fee across simple and lengthy cases alike, but again the client has no way of telling how many hours were put in or whether they were necessary or whether the hourly rate will be higher for his case than for tasks requiring less mental expertise and ingenuity.

> Have you heard about the new microwave lawyer?
> You spend ten minutes in his office and get billed as if you had been there ten days.

Q: What's the difference between a lawyer and a boxing referee?
A: A boxing referee doesn't get paid more for a longer fight.
(http://www.turkhukuksitesi.com/turkishlaw/lawjokes.shtml; accessed
March 2, 2010)

Galanter cites a joke about billing told by a Judge Wilkie in a dissenting opinion in a case before the U.S. Court of Appeals in 1980:

An immediately deceased lawyer arrived at the Pearly Gates to seek admittance from St. Peter. The Keeper of the Keys was surprisingly warm in his welcome: "We are so glad to see you, Mr. (X). We are particularly happy to have you here, not only because we get so few lawyers up here but because you lived to the wonderful age of 165." Mr. (X) was a bit doubtful and hesitant. "Now, St. Peter, if there's one place I didn't want to get into under false pretenses, it's Heaven. I really died at age seventy-eight." St. Peter looked perplexed, frowned, and consulted the scroll in his hand, "Ah, I see where we made our mistake as to your age. We just added up your time sheets!" (Galanter 2005, 79)

Crucial to our understanding of the jokes about both lawyers and bankers is the idea of "information asymmetry," of asymmetrical knowledge, a characteristic of a trade in which the client or buyer knows far less about what is being purchased than the provider. *Caveat emptor*—let the buyer beware. In our agrarian and pre-automobile past, jokes and other humor had as their target dubious horse dealers (*Hebrew Jokes* 1902), who knew more about the age and condition of the horse than a would-be buyer and were in a position to swindle the purchaser. Likewise, there was humor about swindling millers, as in Geoffrey Chaucer's (1926 [1387], 3993–4011, 4243–47, 4091–97) lewd "Reeve's Tale," for the miller alone knew the true amount of flour derived from the grain that the peasant had brought to be ground. A grind for a grind. In modern times, the targets have been the used car salesman, trying to pass on and pass off a lemon, or the realtor (real estate agent) dealing in houses, who knows more about market values than his or her client. Galanter (2005, 159) wryly reports that in one opinion poll in the United States in response to the question "Which profession do you trust the least ?" 23 percent spontaneously replied lawyers, 13 percent car salesmen, and 11 percent politicians. They are all selling the unknown.

Levitt and Dubner (2006, 63–69) have shown convincingly how real estate agents exploit their advantage in the possession of greater information and how a lessening of this asymmetry due to trading on the internet has led to a squeezing of their profit margins. When novelist Sinclair Lewis wanted to satirize a "not too unreasonably honest" provincial businessman, he created an estate agent, George Follansbee Babbitt of the Babbitt-Thompson Realty Co. When Babbitt, a pillar of the Chatham Road Presbyterian Church, wanted a loan to do something particularly dubious, he sought out his co-religionist, the dignified, "old-money" William Washington Eathorne, president of the First State Bank of Zenith (Lewis 1950, 182). *Babbitt* is a satire not of financial manipulators on Wall Street, nor of mega real-estate speculators, but of very ordinary realtors and bankers in a medium-sized city. Lewis chose well, for he chose two professions who know more than their clients and are thus in a position to exploit them. In Nathanael West's (1961 [1934], 78–81) savagely comic tale *A Cool Million; or, The Dismantling of Lemuel Pitkin,* there is another portrayal of a grasping small-town banker, Nathan "Shagpoke" Whipple, president of the Rat River National Bank in Ottsville, Vermont, in the 1930s, who defrauds the widow and the orphan. Not surprisingly, the swindling small-town banker turns up in jokes.

> Two Saarlast (men from Saaremaa), Ats and Priit, were walking by a bank. Ats asked, "Why do the bank windows have bars on them?"
> Priit thought for a moment and then suggested, "Perhaps they are there so that the bank managers will get used to them." (Vesilind 2009, 9, Joke 15)

> A banker and his cashier were discussing a certain contingency.
> The cashier: "If this gets out, our depositors will be down on us in force tomorrow."
> The President: "Well, we'll give them a run for their money." (*Wit and Humor of Business* 1908, 236–37)

Significantly the dubious sellers of used cars and houses are linked in jokes to the legal profession, the cost and quality of whose services and product are equally difficult to judge and far more intangible. The customer may find out about and can understand the dry rot and the subsidence, the clapped out engine and the sticking gears after the purchase, but *caveat emptor* (let the buyer beware) says the lawyer. What? Why? If you are tricked by a used car salesman or a real estate agent, at least you have a rough idea how they did it, but the workings of the legal and financial systems are a mystery to all except initiates and even then often only to specialists in particular areas.

> Why did God invent lawyers?
> So that realtors would have someone to look down on. (Field 2003).

> What are lawyers good for?
> They make used car salesmen feel good. (Field 2003).

The realtors together with their colleagues, the mortgage brokers and lawyers, are probably seen by the public as having done well out of the sub-prime mortgage fiasco and the illusory boom in house prices, which like all bubbles burst. Bubbles always do because the buyers see an apparently ever-improving asset, obtain credit to get it and drive the price up and this pulls in more buyers. Then there comes a point where the doubts start or the credit turns sour and everybody loses except those who had, for a substantial fee, been urging the lemmings up the slope on the other side of the cliff. The greatest skepticism is expressed in jokes about the financiers, whose activities are seen by the jokers as at best a form of mere gambling and at worst of fraud.

> It is told how a great modern "financier," head of a trust company, remarked jovially that he had "tried" both poker and banking and he liked banking best. (*Wit and Humor of Business* 1908, 187)

> OCTOBER: This is one of the peculiarly dangerous months to speculate in stocks in. The other are July, January, September, April, November, May, March, June, December, August, and February. (Mark Twain 1894)

> There are two times in a man's life when he should not speculate: when he can't afford it and when he can. (Mark Twain 1897)

> How many stockbrokers does it take to change a light bulb?
> 1. My God! It burned out. Sell all my G.E. (General Electric) stock NOW!!
> 2. Two—one to take out the bulb and drop it and the other to try and sell it before it crashes, knowing that it's already burned out.
> http://www.workjoke.com/stockbrokers-jokes.html; accessed August 24, 2009

> A stock analyst and a Wall Street broker went to the races. The broker suggested he bet $10,000 on a horse. The analyst was skeptical, saying that he wanted first to understand the rules, to look on horses, etc. The broker whispered that he knew a secret algorithm for the success, but he could not convince the analyst.

"You are too theoretical," he said and bet on a horse. Surely that horse came first, bringing him a lot of money. Triumphantly, he exclaimed: "I told you I knew the secret!"

"What is your secret?" the analyst asked.

"It is rather easy. I have two kids, three and five year old. I sum up their ages, and I bet on number nine."

"But three and five is eight," the analyst protested.

"I told you, you are too theoretical!" the broker replied "Haven't I just shown experimentally that my calculation is correct?!"

(http://www.workjoke.com/stockbrokers-jokes.html; accessed August 24, 2009)

It is worth noting that a joke about stock market speculation has to be turned into one about horse racing in order to go into circulation.

Once upon a time in a village swarming with monkeys, a strange man arrived and told the people that he would buy all their monkeys for $10 each. The villagers, knowing that the forest was full of monkeys, went out and caught them. The man bought thousands of monkeys at $10 a time. Soon there was a scarcity of monkeys and they were difficult to catch, so the villagers stopped looking for them

The stranger next said that he would pay $20 for each one. This gave the villagers an incentive to start hunting them again. But the supply had diminished and the monkeys were even harder to catch, so people went back to work on their farms and gave up monkey catching. The stranger increased the price to $30, and soon monkeys became so scarce it was almost impossible to find one, let alone catch it. The stranger now offered to pay $100 but said he had to go away to the city on business, so his assistant would buy monkeys as his agent. As soon as he had left, the agent told the villagers, "He still has the monkeys you brought him in these cages. I will sell them back to you for $50, and when he comes back next month you can sell them to him at $100 each." The villagers got together all the money they had saved over the years and bought all the monkeys from him. They never saw the man or his assistant again, and the village is swarming with monkeys.

Well, now you have a good idea of how the stock market works!

A long time ago, a visitor from out of town came to a tour in Manhattan. At the end of the tour they took him to the financial district. When they arrived to Battery Park, the guide showed him some nice yachts anchoring there and said, "Here are the yachts of our bankers and stockbrokers."

"And where are the yachts of the investors?" asked the naive visitor.

(http://www.workjoke.com/stockbrokers-jokes.html; accessed August 24, 2009)

Not surprisingly, these jokes became very popular during the great crash of 2008–10, which also led to much satire and derision at the expense of the financiers. A characteristic humorous comment on the crisis was provided in his cartoon strip *Pearls before Swine* by Stephen Pastis, an artist who very skillfully captures something of the primitive quality of children's drawings in the form of a story told by little animals:

Rat's Fairy Tale o' Fairness and Justice
Rat: "Once upon a time there was a bank C.E.O.
Who decided to make loans to people he knew could not pay them back.
As a result Mr. Bank C.E.O made $50,000,000 in bonuses and stock options.
But then the loans went bad.
And as a result all the bank's employees lost their jobs.
And the bank's shareholders lost their money.
And the homeowners lost their homes.
And taxpayers with no connection with the bank had to pay off all the money to fix it.
And Mr. Bank C.E.O got to keep all of his $50,000,000 and to live happily ever after in his Connecticut mansion."
(Pastin's cartoon animals respond to Rat's story)
Goat: "Where's the Fairness and Justice in THAT?!"
Rat: "Whoa, perhaps I should retitle this."
Piglet: "Oh, I just love happy endings." (Pastis, April 19, 2009)

But how are the lawyers involved in these dubious transactions? Well, someone drew up the contracts that enabled bankers to walk away rich when everyone else was ruined and to create bonus without hazard contracts, whereby the holders are rewarded when the bank does well for the time being, but escape all penalty when, due to their gross incompetence, it collapses. As Judge Louis D. Brandeis told Ferdinand Pecora when he conducted a Senate investigation of the banking industry in the 1930s after the crash of 1929, "You should be kind to the bankers. Bankers are not men of ingenuity. It's always the lawyers who develop the chicanery" (Hay 1989, 21–22). The ruinous bankers and lawyers of the twenty-first century may not have broken the law, but their actions hardly correspond to the common notions of morality held by the joke tellers who see these events as kleptocracy and schnorrocracy in action—

the rule of thieves who then become impudent beggars. For the joke tellers, utterances like "I've done nothing illegal" or "my contract means I'm entitled to" emphasize the great gap between what the law says and what is generally regarded as ethical, which is also one of the main bases of the jokes about lawyers.

> A bank president was giving some fatherly advice to his son, who was about to go to another part of the country to engage in some business for himself.
>
> "Son," said the father, "what I want to impress upon you at the beginning of your business career is this—Honesty is always and forever the best policy."
>
> "Yes, father," agreed the youth.
>
> "And, by the way," added the old man, "I would advise you to read up a little on corporation law. It will amaze you how many things you can do in a business way and still be honest." (Galanter 2005, 242)
>
> A man who never graduated from school might steal from a freight car. But a man who attends college and graduates as a lawyer might steal the whole railroad. (Ascribed to Theodore Roosevelt)
>
> Between grand theft and a legal fee,
> There only stands a law degree.
> (http://www.vakilno1.com/lawoneliner.htm; accessed 2 March 2010)

A similar humor prevailed in Britain at the expense of the bankers after the crash, when many of those most responsible had prospered mightily. An example of this was *Silly Money,* a set of comedy documentaries by Rory Bremner, John Bird, and John Fortune shown on Britain's Channel 4 in four one-hour episodes in November 2008 (*Silly Money* 2009). Bremner did impersonations of President Bill Clinton and the British chancellor of the exchequer and later prime minister and first lord of the treasury, Gordon Brown, while Bird and Fortune played a variety of dubious financiers who had done very well out of others' ruin. It was a rare example of a comedy documentary succeeding both as comedy and as a vehicle for serious reflection. Clinton was there because the roots of the subprime mortgage crisis lay in the Community Reinvestment Act of 1995, which forced banks to grant mortgages on easy terms to people with no assets and low and uncertain incomes and provided a very good income indeed for lawyers doing the forcing. It is a good example of how using lawyers and legal measures to manage a problem that ought to be dealt with directly and transparently by the government leads to disaster. One mendacity led to another, as the bankers in their turn tried to hide and pass on the poisonous mortgages in a securities sandwich. In *Silly Money* Bremner has Clinton saying, "You know, I knew there was a fanny in there somewhere." It was a measure of Fannie Mae's dubious reputation worldwide that a foreign audience got the joke. Clintonomics and its consequences are summed up by an old Jewish joke about the stupid people of Chelm.

> Hockman, the Hebrew teacher, was having tea with Luchinsky, the rabbi of Chelm, and discussing the town's economy. "There is a great injustice heaped on the poor," sighed Hockman. "The rich, who have more money than they need, can buy on credit. But the poor, who haven't two coins to rub together, have to pay cash for everything. Is that fair?"
>
> "Of course," answered the Rabbi.
>
> "But it should be the other way around," insisted Hockman. "The rich, who have money, should pay cash, and the poor should be able to buy on credit."
>
> "I admire your ideals," said the rabbi. "But a merchant who extends credit to the poor instead of the rich will soon become a poor man himself."
>
> "So," retorted the Hebrew teacher, "then he'd be able to buy on credit, too!"
>
> (http://freespace.virgin.net/dick.worth/Jokes.htm; accessed March 2, 2010)

Gordon Brown, an Edinburgh alumnus, a son of the manse, and Thane of Fife, became the subject of many British jokes, as in the one below circulating by e-mail in 2009:

> Gordon Brown, the Chancellor of the Exchequer in charge of the British economy and then Prime Minister when it collapsed, finally decided to resign.
>
> His cabinet colleagues decided it would be a worthy gesture to name a historic railway locomotive after him. So a senior civil servant, "Sir Humphrey," went from Whitehall to the National Railway Museum in York in his chauffeur-driven car to investigate the possibilities.
>
> "We have a number of locomotives here without names," the Museum under-under-manager told him, "but most of them are just freight locomotives."
>
> "Oh dear, that's not very fitting for an ex-prime minister," said Sir Humphrey. "How about that big green one over there?" he said, pointing to locomotive 4472.

"That's the old-London Edinburgh express, the fastest train in the world in its day. But it's already got a name," said the manager. "It's called the 'Flying Scotsman.'"

"Oh. Couldn't it be renamed?" asked Sir Humphrey. "After all, this is a national museum paid for by the taxpayer."

"I suppose it might be considered," said the manager. "After all, the entire old owner London North-Eastern Railways renamed a number of their locomotives after directors of the company, and even renamed one of them 'Dwight D. Eisenhower.'"

"That's excellent," said Sir Humphrey. "So that's settled then. Let's look at renaming 4472. But how much will it cost? We can't spend too much, given the last expenses scandal!"

"Don't worry," said the manager. "We will simply paint out the 'F.'"

The joke could just as well have been told about one of the many crooked Scottish bankers who pocketed large sums of money when the Scottish banks collapsed in ruin. But, despite the long tradition of ethnic jokes about canny Scotsmen, there were no new ethnic jokes, nor did the comedy programs emphasize the seemingly disproportionate role of the Scottish banks in the crisis. After the crash there were many jokes in Britain about formerly wealthy City of London bankers who had suddenly come down in the world, and of course there were jokes about the banks in Iceland where only the glaciers had failed to melt down.

Q: What's the definition of optimism?
A: An investment banker who irons five shirts on a Sunday evening. (Mika, Shields, and Boulding 2008)

An investment banker said he was going to concentrate on the big issues from now on. He sold me one in the street yesterday. (The *Big Issue* is the name of a newspaper sold in the streets of British cities by the unemployed.) (Mika et al. 2008)

Q: What is the difference between an investment banker and a pigeon?
A: A pigeon can still make a deposit on a BMW. (Mika et al. 2008)

Q: What is the capital of Iceland?
A: About $3.50. [Iceland, a very small country with an over-large financial services sector, saw all its banks collapse suddenly in 2008, dragging the entire country's economy down in a way reminiscent of Scotland's Darien crisis. As a consequence, Iceland may be forced into the European Union and lose its independence and its fish] (Mika et al. 2008)

The *Toronto Star* repeated a joke said to be popular in the City of London following the Icelandic collapse. What's the difference between Iceland and Ireland? One letter and about six weeks. (Hearne 2009)

Meanwhile, in San Francisco, a man neatly dressed in a suit and tie sat in the gutter in Larkin Street holding up a sign saying, "Will litigate for food."

Some of those who tell jokes about bankers and lawyers being crooks may well believe that they are crooks, as we can see from the populist resistance to President George W. Bush's decision to use government funding to bail the bankers out when the crash hit in 2008. The voters' indignant phone calls, e-mails, and letters delayed approval of his urgent rescue measures by Congress. Similar sentiments were expressed in Britain and in Europe. It was as if they believed one of the possible meanings of the late J. Edgar Hoover's ambiguous statement that "Banks are an almost irresistible attraction for that element of our society which seeks unearned money" (Crime: Easy Money 1955). But what do people mean when they say that "bankers are crooks" or "lawyers are crooks"? Contrary to what is sometimes argued in relation to stereotypes, it is very unlikely that many of them are saying "all bankers are crooks" or "all lawyers are crooks," since their observable behavior does not support such an interpretation. They do not keep all their cash under the mattress or decline to sign documents drawn up by someone else's lawyer. Rather they are saying, albeit sloppily, that "a far greater proportion of bankers are crooks" or "a far greater proportion of lawyers are crooks" than is true for other professionals. Now this may be true or it may be false, but it is not in itself a bigoted or unreasonable view to hold, though it could be if used unfairly against any particular individual. Also, people came to such a view not because they had listened to the jokes but because they had seen some members of these professions getting very rich in ways that they could not understand and felt were unfair.

The point is not whether they are right to feel that way but rather that they are apt to do so and in consequence to tell canny jokes about those groups alone. Such jokes are told only about those whose occupations lack any visible, tangible basis and where financial rewards go directly to particular high-earning individuals. It is necessary to consider the jokes that are not invented. Why are there no jokes about dishonest farmers or fishermen, even though there are many of them and the consequences of their cheating are horrendous? It is very likely that EU fishermen will destroy the entire fishing grounds around Europe and parts of Africa both by preventing the imposition of proper limits on the size of their catch and by blatantly ignoring such limits as exist. The captains of commercial fishing vessels are often crooks, but there are no jokes about their canny, crooked activities. Likewise, the huge and unjustifiable protection and subsidies given to EU farmers in general, and to the growers of sugar beets and tobacco in particular, are the product of a dubious and self-interested misuse of political power and are administered so dishonestly that the European Union's books never get passed by the auditors (Buitenen 2000). The auditors have made it clear that crooked things are going on. The growers of sugar cane in poor countries cannot gain entry into the European market, and their governments are not even allowed to raise the issue in trade negotiations. Yet the inefficient production of sugar from beets unjustly enriches EU farmers. Diabetes could be much cheaper than it is. But there are no jokes at all about crooked, canny farmers. If you are of the earth, you are immune from such jokes. You may be called a wurzel, a swede, or a turnip-head and be mocked as stupid, but jokes about the canny are reserved for bankers, lawyers, merchants, and dealers because the value they add to the economy seems "immaterial" and their very real economic contribution is difficult to understand, even though it may greatly exceed that of the agricultural sector.

COUNTRY MATTERS

Peasants, farmers and farmhands, herdsmen and mountain men, and country people generally are very much the subject of jokes about their simple minds. In English to call someone a peasant or in French a *paysan* implies that he or she is stupid and uncouth. The Hebrew term for an ignoramus, *am ha-aretz* (Dershowitz 1991, 12), once meant a person of the soil, but it now has several connotations. *Bur ha-aretz* are dimwits whereas *melach ha-aretz* are the salt of the earth. Land, soil, peasant also convey images of sturdy, straightforward, uncomplicated continuity, the quality of a homeland, of belonging. The very lack of dynamism, simplicity and closeness to the earth that lead to country people being the subject of stupidity jokes may also constitute a virtue for the romantic nationalist. In the jokes rustics are known to the jokers as *catetos* in Andalucía (uncouth rustic, from the word for right angles or the sides of a square), as Loong Chay in Thailand (Uncle Hayseed), as Pak Pandir in Malaysia, as *suaku* (mountain tortoises) in Singapore, as *teuchters* in Scotland, and in many English-speaking countries as rustics, hicks, boobies, boors, bumpkins, bog trotters, briar hoppers, hillbillies, rednecks, rubes, yokels, clods, clodhoppers, clodpates, clowns, churls, chawbacons, hayseeds, swedes, wurzels, and turmots. In the jokes they live in places with names like Hicktown, Dogpatch, Pumpkin Creek, Podunk Hollow, Hayseed Corner, Gophersville, or Cwmtwp. Contrasted with them is the canny city slicker. Jokes of this kind began in the distant past, for as soon as there were towns and cities, merchants and scribes, there were jokes about the stupidity of those who lived in the rural areas and continued to work in agriculture. City jokes about rustics date back at least to the time when the Athenians laughed at their rural Boeotian neighbors (Fuller 1811, 2:206). Even today the word Boeotian is used to describe someone who is dopey and sluggish. They were earthy and illiterate and unable to grasp the "abstract" written word of the scribe or administrator or the calculations and recordkeeping of traders. In eighteenth- and nineteenth-century England, rustics often appeared in caricatures and cartoons. In jokes they are made to speak in an old-fashioned way. In England when jokes are told about them, the teller will put on a broad rustic accent such as Berkshire, Wiltshire, Devon, or Norfolk and make frequent use of the sound "Aaar!" The joke teller may even distort his facial expressions and gestures to mimic a simple yokel. The sound "Ooarr" is used in chants at soccer games in England when the opposing team comes from a rural area.

> We can't read
> and we can't write
> But that don't really matterrr
> We all come from Cheltenhamshire and we can droive a tractor
> ooarrr ooarrr ooarroooarrroooarrr
> Cheltenhamshire la la la
> (http://board.dogbomb.co.uk/archive/index.php/t-20595.html; accessed January 2009)

Jokes occur worldwide about ignorant peasants and pastoralists, backward hill and mountain herdsmen, desert dwelling camel-keeping Bedouin, and simple fishermen.

> A peasant is riding on his donkey when suddenly a Ferrari goes past at great speed. Later the farmer sees it standing at the side of the road and asks the driver, "How come your car can go so fast?"
>
> The driver tells the ignorant peasant, "It is because it is painted blue and green."
>
> The next day the farmer goes into town and buys two cans of paint, one blue and one green, and throws the whole of the blue can over the animal. The animal hates the feel of the paint so much that it bolts away up the road.
>
> The peasant looks on in amazement as the animal disappears and says, "And that's even before I added the green color."
>
> (http://www.chistes.com/Clasificacion.asp?ID=40&Pagina=2; accessed August 29, 2009; Joke 2404, Author's translation from the Spanish)

> A rustic came into town and asked a dentist how much he would charge to extract one of his teeth. "Just five pounds," said the dentist, "and I guarantee that you will feel no pain."
>
> "How long will it take?" asked the yokel.
>
> "About five minutes at most."
>
> "What!" cried the irate bumpkin. "Five pounds for only five minutes' work? Last time I needed a tooth out, I went to the village blacksmith and it took him nearly an hour pulling and tugging until it came out . . . and he only charged me a pound." (English origin, judging from the prices it is very old)

> One day a bania (merchant caste) boy quarreled with his jat (peasant caste) friend and called him *bewakoof jat*—stupid peasant.
>
> The jat rewarded him with a light slap across the face. The boy went and complained to his father.
>
> "You deserved what you got," reprimanded the father. "When you called him a *jat*, you did not have to add *bewakoof* to it."
>
> (http://jokes.maxabout.com/jatt-jokes/stupid-peasant/21691; accessed August 29, 2009)

This kind of stupid peasant, herdsman, or fisherman joke is often what underlies jokes about those living on the national or cultural periphery of a country (Davies 1990), for it is often also an economic periphery, where the people are peasants or fishermen, in contrast to the cities at the center and in particular the capital. The peasants and fishermen are, of course, those whose produce comes directly from the earth and the waters. They are the sons of the soil and those who go down to the sea. When peasants migrate to the towns, they are often employed as unskilled construction workers, the men of pick and shovel and wheelbarrow, the hod carriers and ditch diggers, as is the case of the Newfies in Ontario, the Laz in Turkey, and at one time the Irish throughout the English-speaking world. Peasant toil and construction labor alike involve squelching through mud and muck, wearing clogs, sabots, klompen, pattens, cha-kiaks, or other wooden shoes, heelless brogues or wellies, wellington boots. These are the symbols of their constant contact with the earth, and the local version often appears in ethnic jokes about stupidity, as do the thigh-high "long rubbers" worn by fishermen in Newfoundland when out at sea, which are referred to in Canadian jokes (Davies 2002). Even the Essex girl, the British version of the blonde joke, encounters, such men, for she too is from that social class.

> An Essex girl and an Irishman were in a pub. She noticed that he had *L* and *R* marked on his wellies. "'ere," she said. "Why 'ave yer got *L* and *R* written on yer wellies like that?"
>
> "Well, yer see," he replied, "being Irish, I'm a bit on the t'ick side, so I need to be reminded which welly is for my left foot and which is for my roight foot."
>
> "Ow!" said the Essex girl, "that must be why it says *C* and *A* in my knickers."

Wellies are cheap rubber boots that stop just below the knee. In Britain, the "Essex girl" is the butt of "blonde jokes" about stupidity and promiscuity, and here she is cast alongside an Irishman, the male butt of stupidity jokes. When the wave of American blonde jokes came to England, it was given a new social class dimension, and the jokers see the Essex girl as coming from that part of Essex on the flat, muddy coast between London and "Sarfend," up the creek and close to Barking and speaking mud-in-yer-mouf Estuary English. Many former slum-dwellers from the East End of London and their descendants live there and are employed in a variety of unskilled jobs. C and A was a chain store that sold cheap clothing (Coats and 'ats), including Essex-girl knickers, at the time when the jokes were being invented in the 1990s. In cartoons the Essex girl is shown as wearing very short skirts, very high heels, and earrings as big as quoits.

THE PEASANTS, HERDSMEN, AND
FISHERMEN OF THE PERIPHERY

Ethnic jokes about stupidity that draw on the supposed nature of rustics and herdsmen include among their targets the Afrikaners (the van der Merwe of South African jokes), the Arequipeños of Arequipa in Peruvian jokes, the Baianos (from Bahia) in Brazil about whom jokes are told in São Paulo, Berbers in jokes told in Tangiers, Bosnians in jokes from the former Yugoslavia, Burgenlanders and Carinthians in Austrian jokes, the people of Choong Chung Do in Korean jokes, Gallegos (Galicians) and Leperos (from Lepe) in Spanish jokes, the Gochos in Venezuelan jokes, the Alentejos in Portuguese jokes, the Hausas in Nigerian jokes, the Irish in British jokes, the Kerrymen in Irish jokes, the Kurds in Iraqi jokes, the Meridionali (southerners) in Italian jokes, the people of Oltenia in Romanian jokes, the Portuguese in the jokes told in Hawaii and California, the Sardarjis (Sikhs) in Indian and Pakistani jokes, the Šopi in Bulgarian jokes, the Tassies (Tasmanians) in Australian jokes, the Turks in Persian jokes, the Ukrainians in western Canadian jokes, and the Yucatecos (from Yucatan) in Mexican jokes.

We may reasonably include here the jokes told in Brazil, Hawaii, and California (San Leandro) about poor peasant immigrants from Portugal and in Mexico and Argentina about Gallegos, poor peasants emigrating there from Galicia in Spain. The Poles and Italians who figure in American stupidity jokes are the descendants of poor peasants from southern (rarely northern) Italy and from eastern Poland who took on unskilled blue-collar work and lived a kind of village life in distinctive ethnic neighborhoods.

Among the fishermen in stupidity jokes are the Newfoundlanders (Newfies) in Canadian jokes told both in English and in French, the islanders from Saaremaa and Hiiumaa and fishermen from the West Coast in traditional Estonian jokes, the inhabitants of the fishing port of Klaksvík in Faroese jokes, the Laz and their anchovies in Turkish jokes, the Molboer of Mols in Jutland with their *Molbohistorier* (now represented by jokes about nearby Aarhus), and the marsh men of Ostfriesland in German jokes.

MIND OVER MATTER

The mind-over-matter model of stupidity jokes is broader in scope than my earlier center-versus-periphery model, for it covers jokes about occupations, social classes, athletes, the use of force, and sexy blondes as well as the ethnic jokes. The connections between the two will be further discussed in the concluding chapter. There is nothing mysterious or esoteric about the central contrast between mind and matter that has been employed, which should be one familiar to all. It is a commonplace of how people think about the world, how they experience it, and how they evaluate social life, but it is also limited in its scope. It is broad enough to contain all the varied cases of stupidity jokes, but it is also bounded, which is what renders it meaningful, for to use a catchall dichotomy such as good versus bad, which embraced everything, would be untestable and pointless, whereas it is possible to imagine targets of stupidity jokes that would fall outside the mind-and-matter framework. The details differ from one set of circumstances to another and indeed from one kind of society to another, but this single thread links together neatly all the groups who are the butts of stupidity jokes. Jokes whose theme is stupidity differ markedly from all other jokes with targets, including the jokes about the canny. In order to understand these other jokes, such as the jokes about the French and sex or about American lawyers or Jewish marriages or jokes about the Italian army (Davies 1990, 2002), it is necessary to know in detail the highly particular historical circumstances in which the jokes were generated. But all that is needed in the case of the stupidity jokes is to recognize a linked set of social locations.

The pairing of the jokes with a stupidity theme with the jokes about the canny is merely a convenient way of arranging the material. The relationship between them is an asymmetrical one. Jokes about the canny have a lot in common with the jokes about other targets and require specific explanations. It is only jokes about the stupid that fit into reasonably simple formulae. This is not entirely a surprise. All stupid people are stupid in the same way, whereas clever people are clever in many ways. Stupidity is a lack of something, a zero. Some stupidity jokes refer to a lack of specialized skills and knowledge and are told within groups that possess that knowledge and those understandings, but most of them refer to an inability to comprehend everyday processes. They are stupidity as seen by the average person, not the most intelligent ones, and everyone can laugh at them; no one gets left out uncomprehending, which is important, given that jokes are part of a common sociability. The stupid are defined by not having to use their brains overmuch, and this is associated with occupations and roles that have about them a coarse physicality. It is here that we can speak of mind over matter. The canny use their brains, but in regard to something universally understood—trickery with money. Jokes about lawyers and bankers are not so much about the law or banks but about the trickeries of the traditional trader in a bazaar taken to a higher level. Nonetheless, they have a context and a history in a way that the stupidity jokes do not, and this will become clear in the later discussion of the new American lawyer jokes. By contrast, the sex jokes about blondes and the French that follow, though simple in content, call for detailed historical explanations. What needs to be explained is not the sex but why the jokes are pinned on these particular groups rather than on others.

TWO

♠

Blondes, Sex, and the French

Of the jokes told about the over vigorous sex lives of targeted groups, the ones with the most interesting histories are those relating to blondes and to the French. The blonde has already been met in the late twentieth-century jokes about stupidity, but the jokes about sexy blondes long predate them. The jokes about the supposed sex life of the French differ in that they can be about men as well as women, whereas the blonde is always female. The accounts of the two sets of jokes are very different. The key to jokes about blondes is their physical attractiveness, but this has no explanatory value in the case of the French. The explanation of the jokes about the French is of necessity longer and more intricate, and so we will begin with the blondes.

THE DESIRABLE BLONDE

When it comes to sex jokes, where are the blondes rooted? The answer lies in the long and widely held perception of blondes as remarkably attractive and in the frequent attempts by women with other hair colors to imitate their glory by going blonde through the use of wigs, bleaches, dyes, and tints. This is in itself comical because of the deception involved (Redgrove and Foan 1939, 15), which leads others to suspect that things are not quite what they seem. There is less in blonde hair than meets the eye.

Sex jokes about blondes have been part of the repertoire of the stand-up comedian since the days of vaudeville and the music hall. They flourished long before the big blonde joke cycle of the late twentieth century. In America, Britain, and France, they have been routinely built into sex jokes in which hair color was irrelevant, except as a message that the joke was going to be about sex. Phrases such as "luscious blonde," "gorgeous blonde," "big blonde," "well-endowed blonde," "*une magnifique blonde*," or "blonde bombshell" indicate exactly why we are being told the heroine's hair color. Such jokes are to be found scattered throughout the repertoire of the famously risqué British comedian and revue artist Max Miller (1894–1963), the "Cheeky Chappie," a comedy star from the 1930s to the 1950s. The jokes are still available on CDs and in *The Max Miller Blue Book* (Took 1975).

> Now when I started in this business many years ago, I started in a circus. I started in Billy Smart's circus—Billy Smart—not the Billy Smart who is today—his father—'cos I'm much older than Billy. And I remember his father said to me one day, he said, "Maxie, would you like to be a lion tamer?" I said, "I've no desire." He said, "There's money in it." I said, "What do I have to do?" He said, "All you've got to do is walk in the lion's cage and put your head in its mouth." I said, "I should think so." He said, "Are you scared?" I said, "I'm not scared—I'm just careful." He said, "I shouldn't be scared of that lion," he said. "That lion's as tame as a kitten. He was brought up on milk." I said, "SO WAS I, BUT I EAT MEAT!"
>
> So he advertised for a lion tamer and a beautiful blonde came along, like they are today—you've seen 'em, well out in front—a lovely roll top desk—and that's a lot of madam an' all—that's the ironing board stuck up there. So he said to this blonde, "Will you go into the cage?" She said, "I'll go in, 'cos I'm a lion tamer." And she walked into the cage, and as she walked into the cage the lion made a dash for her, and she thought quick, undid her zip, and all her clothes fell off her, and she stood there as naked as the day she was born, and the lion, he stopped—then he started to walk towards her, and when he got near enough, he started to kiss her. And he kissed her all over, and the governor said, "Would you do that?" I said, "Yes—get the lion out!"
>
> (Max Miller in Took 1975)

There was no need for the attractive women in Miller's blue jokes to be blonde. The lion wouldn't care. Yet Miller clearly thought that blonde meant beauty and blonde meant sex. He was not alone in this, for we find exactly the same equation in the United States in Henny Youngman's routine:

> A stunningly stacked blonde walked into a dress shop and asked the manager:
> "I wonder if I might try on that blue dress in the window?"
> "Go right ahead," he said. "It might help business." (Youngman 1974, 44)

These jokes were lasting and widespread, and it is significant how often the blonde is also given very large breasts, shown off to advantage, another important symbol of attractiveness and potential availability:

> What is the difference between a well-stacked blonde in the daytime and the same dame at night?
> In the daytime she's fair and buxom . . . (Hart 1971, 27)

In her collection of essays *The Hussy's Handbook* the witty American writer Helen Brown Norden (1942, 191–93) commented on such humor:

> [The blonde's] constant recurrence as the synonym for sin in vaudeville and burlesque jokes . . . he ran off with some blonde from the chorus, etc. That is sin—the gay doll, the bright lights, the whoop-de-doodle. If you even think the words "chorus girl," your accompanying mental image is of something glamorous, blonde and desirable, I am sure. In divorce cases the erring husband is always depicted as caught with "an unidentified blonde." The jokes about the boss concern his blonde stenographer, his blonde nurse, or simply "a blonde." "I saw you out with a brunette last night" doesn't carry the same connotation as does "I saw you out with a blonde last night!"

The ubiquitous image that equates blonde and sex, which has also been noted by Mikita Brottman (2004, xvi.), can be seen in the ingenious way Françoise Vreck (1999, 32) has tried to translate into French the English joke below, which is based on a pun. The original joke has nothing to do with blondes or sex, but in the French translation, both have been inserted:

> A man bought a bath and was just leaving the shop with his purchase when the shop assistant called, "Do you want a plug?"
> "Why?" asked the man. "Is it electric?"

The translation reads:

Un homme achète une beignoire et au moment qu' il quitte le magasin avec son achet, le vendeur l' interpelle: (as above)
Vous avez besoin d'une bonde? (Do you need a plug?)
Une blonde dans le beignoire? Porquoi pas? (A blonde in the bath? Why not?)

The original pun about plugs doesn't work in French, so the translator uses instead a pun on *bonde* (plug) and the similar sounding *blonde.* The pun works in French and permits a switch from a mundane script about plugs to a sexual script (Raskin 1985, 32), since that is what a naked blonde in a bath signifies, just as much in French as in English.

Did you hear about the new blonde paint?
It's not bright, but it's cheap and it spreads easy. (Lederer 2003, 118)

There is no evidence that blondes are cheaper or easier to spread than women with other hair colors, but it is clear that blondes have long been perceived in many parts of the world as far more sexually attractive than women whose hair is darker. As Richard Lederer (2003, 17) has quipped, "Genitals prefer blondes." This has long been the perception of men in the Mediterranean and the Middle East, where blondes are not very common and the dominant people are dark-haired. The ancient Romans would cut off the blonde hair of German slave girls captured in war to make false hair for their own womenfolk (Ovid 16 BC, book 1, elegy 14, lines 45–50; Pitman 2003, 26; Redgrove and Foan 1939, 14), some of whom had ruined their own hair with fierce bleaching. Later Arab and Turkish slave traders were keen to acquire blonde female slaves from Poland or the Baltic states (Pitman 2003, 61), and today pimps in wealthy Arab countries import and exploit blonde hookers from the Ukraine. Norden (1942, 175–79) described blondes as attention-getters the world over and "like cat-nip to a Latin." Blondes then are almost universally desirable and so presumably get more offers, and even if their acceptance rate is no different, they "have more fun" in consequence.

The key proof of the attractiveness of blonde hair, as far as modern Europe and America are concerned, is the sheer extent to which women who are not naturally blonde bleach or dye their hair blonde and pretend that this is its real color. The Irish maiden seeks to be the Colleen Bawn (*cailín bán*) with the entrancing flaxen tresses. Others imitate Goldilocks, who found a comfortable bed and was pursued. The old tales and legends are dyeing in.

By contrast it is unlikely that many blonde women dye their hair red or black, even though, should people take seriously the notion that blondes are stupid (Bry, Follenfant, and Meyer 2008), acquiring darker hair might be an easy way to look more capable in the workplace. Yet to do so might mean appearing less attractive, and this is a risk few apparently wish to take. These women are trapped in a very unfair trade-off.

> What is the difference between a brunette and the trash?
> The trash gets taken out once a week!

In Britain perhaps one in three women ages 18 to 50 seem to have light hair, but for very few is the color natural, even though they may have been truly blonde as children (Desmond J. Tobin personal communication 2008; see also Leake 2003). In Europe and North America, generally only about 5 percent of women have naturally fair hair as adults, yet there are blondes everywhere (Pitman 2003, 4–5). Blondeness signals youth, much as gray hair is the mark of age. Societies are not kind to those who look old. It is easy to see why so many seek to banish the gray and return to or achieve blondeness with the aid of a cornucopia of modern, gentle, artificial chemicals that have replaced the reeking pigeon dung or inauspicious horse urine used in times long past (Pitman 2003, 4–5), or indeed such harsh bleaching oxidants as the hydrogen peroxide once used by the fierce "peri-blonde." Coloring one's hair blonde is the poor woman's plastic surgery (Roppatte and Cohen 1985), a painless operation on the one part of the body that is already dead. The clinching evidence is that American women looking for male partners or dates through personal advertisements on the internet frequently misrepresent themselves as being blonde, for the same reason that they will claim to be thinner than they probably are. Blondeness and slenderness are linked in our minds to the sexual attractiveness of youth, and indeed women tend to get darker as well as fatter as they age. Becoming blonde has the same function as getting rid of gray hair. Men seem to agree, for the women who are or claim to be blonde get more email responses to their advertisements than others, and those with "salt and pepper" hair get the least (Levitt and Dubner 2006, 75–76).

However, the women who become blonde are often the target of jokes and witticisms about their duplicity and absurdity.

> **Confucius say:** Woman who have blonde hair on head have dark hair by cracky.
> (UCBFA, Confucius jokes file; collected in 1970 by Constance Chew from a Chinese-American informant)

The link between youth, blondeness, visible breasts, and female attractiveness, together with the deceptions of hair color and as a bonus the equation of sex and the French, was given a witty literary form by Oscar Wilde in *The Picture of Dorian Gray*.

> "How you men can fall in love with that woman!" exclaimed the old lady. "I really cannot understand it."
> "It is simply because she remembers you when you were a little girl, Lady Narborough," said Lord Henry. "She is the one link between us and your short frocks."
> "She does not remember my short frocks at all, Lord Henry. But I remember her very well at Vienna thirty years ago, and how *décolletée* she was then."
> "She is still *décolletée*," he answered, taking an olive in his long fingers; "and when she is in a very smart gown she looks like an *édition de luxe* of a bad French novel. She is really wonderful, and full of surprises. Her capacity for family affection is extraordinary. When her third husband died, her hair turned quite gold from grief." (Wilde 1981, 177–78)

In the late Victorian period, of which Wilde was writing, young girls of high station wore short frocks, but when they matured into sexual beings, they were expected to wear garments that reached much lower and entirely hid their nether limbs, though this could be compensated for at the other end by a lowering of the neckline. Wilde's use of the ambiguous term "bad French novel" implies that the work has a strongly sexual content and an *édition de luxe* of such a book would contain suggestive illustrations. French means sex, as we can also see from his use of the French sounding word *décolletée*, here meaning a woman wearing a dress that exposes a great deal of cleavage. Elsewhere Wilde describes Lady Narborough's pleasures as "French fiction, French cookery, and French *esprit* when she could get it" (175).

Wilde has gaily put in these amusing "jab lines" (Attardo 2001, 82–83) on his way to the punch line where a woman is spoken of as dyeing her hair gold in order to appear a young as well as a merry widow. This is an appropriate witticism in a Wilde tale full of artifice, in which the title character has sold his soul so that his face may stay young and handsome, and only his portrait reveals the ravages of age and debauchery.

Female readers may quite reasonably see all this as part of a tyranny of appearance under which they alone suffer, for men who go gray can sometimes still be described as looking handsome and distinguished. Equally to the point, when men do dye their hair or beards, they usually don't choose to go blonde. Gerald Ford said of Ronald Reagan that he had turned "prematurely orange" (Gardner 1994, 168). Most go for being "tall, dark, and handsome." They seek to retain the appearance of a dominant youthful maturity: "Look at me. I'm not too old to be powerful." They are playing quite a different game to the woman forced by social pressure to imitate a blonde bimbo. In fairness, men who go bald are also at a considerable disadvantage, and there exists much humor including jokes directed at luckless, lockless men, who suffer the cavities as well as the canities of age. Women often regard baldness in men as an ugly mark of aging, as is shown by their unwillingness to respond on dating sites to men who describe themselves as bald with a fringe, though men who shave their heads do better (Levitt and Dubner 2006, 76). Those who shave their heads are trying to make it look as if they have chosen this almost skinhead style, rather than having been haplessly overtaken by age and hair loss, which constitutes a kind of minor stigma.

> When Mr. Baldy went to the zoo, the ostrich chased him. She thought her egg was trying to run away.
>
> Are you really that bald. . . . or is your neck blowing a bubble?
>
> There is a new treatment for baldness. It doesn't cure the baldness, but it shrinks your head to fit the hair you've got.
>
> A bald man with a peg leg gets invited to a costume party. Being shy and self-conscious about his appearance, he goes to the best costume shop in town. When he gets there, he tells the shop owner his situation and that he would rather cover his head and leg with a costume instead of exploiting his apparent problems. So the shop owner comes back with a lifeguard costume. The man says, "No, no. That will show off my peg leg. I can't hide it with that. Try again." So the shop owner leaves and comes back with a monk costume. And again the man says, "No, no. I can't wear that. It will make people notice my head." Obviously pissed off, the shop owner

leaves and comes back with a five-pound bag of caramels, gives it to the man, and says, "Here. Just take this." Confused, the man says, "What am I supposed to do with a bag of caramels?" Smiling, the shop owner says, "Take home this bag of caramels, melt them, pour it all over your body, stick that peg leg up your ass, and tell everyone you're a caramel apple."
(http://hair-and-bald-jokes.allthejokes.com/hair_and_bald_jokes_2 .html; accessed March 6, 2010)

Only clowns and comedians can say, "Baldness be my friend." Clowns wear bald wigs and thus reverse the normal social order. Many leading American and British comedians and comedy actors both today and in the past have lost much or all of their hair. Baldness is a great advantage in constructing an image of such undesirable qualities as silliness or pomposity.

The hair of the sexy blonde is a part then of a more general humor about hair or its lack, and hair is of course an important part of the symbols of appearance that reveal a social identity. In the case of women, many cultures demand that in public places a woman must hide her hair because it is her glory (1 Corinthians 11:15), her beauty, and an indication of sexuality. Muslims, ultra-orthodox Jews, and the stricter Amish and Mennonites insist that women must cover their hair to show that they are controlled by their male relatives or their community and lack independence, particularly in relation to sexuality. Nuns "take the veil" when embarking on their life of chastity as a bride of Christ, and female Salvation Army officers, who until recently could only marry other officers, wore bonnets. For women, hair signifies sex, and blonde hair, the most glorious and desired of all, very much means sex. But it is time to leave beauty altogether and turn to the French.

THE FRENCH CONNECTION

Jokes about the French—and especially French women—being oversexed and ignoring all the conventional rules of fidelity, propriety, and decency are common throughout Europe, North America, and even farther afield (Khanaka 1990, 12). In the world's jokes, French men are seducers, rascals, and experts in sexual technique, particularly in the jokes the French tell about themselves (Quercy and Korsak 1993, 249). Until recently, jokes about the French were about little else than sex, and to label a sex joke "French" was a way of giving it an imagined reality. Often a joke or a cartoon that has nothing to do with the French will be spiced up by giving it an irrelevant French context.

A French lawyer at a convention in America denies the allegation that all French law cases are always about sex. "Why, take the case I'm handling right now," he says. "It has no sex element in it at all. My client was in love with a girl, but she was afraid of losing her virginity and made him promise to put in just the head of his penis and to stop when he got to her maidenhead. He did exactly as he promised, but just at that moment the girl's mother burst into the bedroom, saw what was going on, became furiously angry, and gave my client a tremendous kick up the ass that drove him right through the girl's maidenhead, all the way in. He came; the girl got pregnant; and my client claims that the girl's mother is the father of her child! (Legman 1982, 1:467; joke collected in New York 1952, earlier version 1907)

Often in Britain or America, a risqué joke or a cartoon that has nothing to do with the French at all will be provided with irrelevant French attributes. Sex jokes are told in a stage-French accent full of women who roll their r's. *Th* is always pronounced as "zee" or "ss," and *i* comes out as "ee." All aspirates are omitted, as in an imagined Paris street-vendor's approach to a tourist: "Pleeze 'ave some feelsee postcarrds, M'sieur." Joke tellers will also take care to put the stress in the wrong place in word and sentence alike to represent a French person speaking "Eengleesh." These stage pronunciations may even be indicated in a written text. Anglophone phrases of saucy French or mock French such as "Ooh la la," "Pièce de la Résistance," "Vive la Différence," and "Cherchez la femme" are often scattered randomly, irrelevantly, and inaccurately in collections of jokes and cartoons about the French. There are even menus of crudities that begin "Rabelais says" (Elgart 1973, 8) for readers whose sole perception of that author is that he is Rabelaisian. They are in the tradition of the one-liners that begin, "Confucius say," and they are about as French as the latter are Chinese. If it had been technically possible, the publishers of these "French" books would have made the pages smell of garlic.

The jokes about the French cover all manner of sexual encounters and indiscretions, but two in particular are portrayed in the jokes and in other humor as particularly characteristic of that nation. One of the main themes of the jokes is adultery, particularly the wife cuckolding the husband, who is often *le mari trompé*, deceived but unknowing and thus ridiculous, but in other jokes he is clearly complicit in his wife's affairs. Indeed his wife's lover, he, and his wife may even share the same household, possibly the very same bed, in a *ménage á trois*, a household of three; there is no equivalent term for this institutionalized gleesome threesome in English or in German, and so the language of its country of origin is normally used. The phrase in French itself dates from 1891. In Mina and André Guillois's 1980 French collection of sex jokes, there is an entire section called *ménages á trois . . . et á plus* containing ninety-one jokes (123–46). Whether in this household of three persons the mistress proceeds from her lover or from both her lover and her husband is still a contentious question.

Perhaps the most famous artistic expression of the *ménage á trois* were the murals painted by Max Ernst in 1923 in the bedroom of the house of Paul Éluard in the Parisian suburb of Eaubonne (Wood 2007, 45–48), which Ernst shared with Éluard and his wife, Gala. Ernst's own wife, Luise, was excluded. In France three's company, four's a crowd. Their Frankish relationship was quite frankly displayed, indeed celebrated, in the design of the room with its three doors, two real and one false. Everything is highly colored with a bright blue sky shining above ochre walls filled with mad plants, animals, and insects and particularly enticing red fruit. Above the bed a highly sexualized, long-fingered woman's hand sneaks through a false window to catch one of these round objects between her fingers. Only in France can such murals be found.

Curiously, the taking of lovers by married women in France was suggested by Jean Baptiste Moheau in 1778 (cited in Van de Walle and Muhsam 1995, 264) as responsible for the beginning of the fall in the French birthrate in the late eighteenth century, far earlier than elsewhere in Europe, even though French economic development was slow. Moheau rightly predicted that the French birthrate would continue to decline. The theory was that in certain classes marriages were arranged for reasons of money, landed property, or social status, without there being any affection between the parties. This happens in much of Asia anyway, but in the French case it was complicated by western sentiments regarding emotional fulfillment, and so no one was surprised when, after she had provided her husband with an heir and a back-up heir, the wife would take a lover. The lover did not want a child, and neither did the husband, because the paternity of the child would be uncertain. The wife did not want a child, because her infidelity did not stretch to possibly foisting on her husband a child that was not his. So both men threshed inside and winnowed without, and the birthrate declined. It is unlikely that Moheau's explanation is correct, but it is significant that a Frenchman should have even thought of, let alone express in writing, an account of an important social phenomenon in terms of an adultery that was not only connived at but expected. It is the stuff of which jokes, though not children, are made.

Jokes about those who deceive and triumph over a hapless, horned cuckold are, of course, common in countries other than France (Norden 1942, 69). There are many such jokes in Muslim countries (Khanaka 1990; Seifikar 2003), where women are often seen as property and the basis of their family's honor. This sexual property is jealously guarded, and when stolen, it is savagely avenged, but in stories this is seen to incite others daringly and secretly to obtain it, as much for the illicit thrill as for the sex. But only in and in regard to France are there jokes about the husband willingly colluding in his own situation:

> Mme Arouet had died. At the funeral her husband and her lover, Alphonse Moe de Cambronne, stood together at the graveside. Her lover was inconsolable and wept and wept. To comfort him, the husband put an arm round his shoulders and said, "Alphonse, don't cry so. I will marry again."

> Overheard in a French café: "The cuckolds are in a majority—*Voilà*." (Gramont 1969, 298)

> Two Frenchmen are standing on the platform of the train that is pulling out of Paris. One of them waves to a friend at the station and calls: "Thanks loads; had a marvelous time; your wife was a wonderful lay!" Then he turns to the man standing next to him and says, "It's not true. She's no good at all. I just wanted the husband to feel good." (*What Rugby Jokes Did Next* 1970, 62)

> *Ein Franzose ist ein Vagabund.* (One Frenchy is a tramp.)
> *Zwei Franzosen ist Liebe.* (Two Frenchies is a love affair.)
> *Drei Franzosen ist eine Ehe.* (Three Frenchies is a marriage.) (Scholten 1971, 34)

The image of the French *ménage* of three persons has even been introduced, somewhat arbitrarily, into the political jokes of Eastern Europe.

> In Bulgaria they tell of an ocean liner that sinks near a tropical island with two men and one woman surviving. If the survivors had been Italian, goes the story, one man would kill the other and live happily ever after with the woman. If the survivors had been French, all three would live together happily ever after in a peaceful *ménage á trois*. If the survivors had been German, the two men would make war on each other and end up killing themselves and the woman, too. But if the survivors had been Bulgarians, they would wire Moscow for instructions. (See B. Adams 2005, 66, joke 237; Lo Bello 1968, 241)
>
> For a similar joke in German about the French ending " . . . *in aller Seelenruhe á trois*" (calmly living as a threesome; note that the French word *trois,* not the German *drei,* is used to indicate three), see Scholten (1971, 32).

Other jokes deal with the married Frenchman's supposedly avid pursuit of mistresses.

> "Pierre, you have a mistress!"
> "But no, my darling, I have no mistress."
> "Don't lie to me, Pierre. This is the third time this week you washed your feet."
> (Legman 1982, 1:703. Told in fractured-French dialect. Collected in Paris 1959.)

The second distinctive theme in jokes about the French is the alleged French preference, indeed avidity, for oral sex, for the going down of the son or daughter of France. In English-speaking countries, when a prostitute advertises "French" or "French lessons," it implies that she will provide "Frenching," "French tricks," code words for oral sex. When a man and a woman perform oral sex on each other simultaneously, it is commonly described in other countries by a term from the French, *soixante-neuf* (sixty-nine), a reference to the position of the heads and tails in 69. Perhaps the use of this word in English is a genuflection to its French origins. Both *cunnilingus* and *fellatio* are Latinate words used to hide the meaning of what is being done in the decent obscurity of a classical tongue. These are, or were, referred to in demotic English as "to gamahuche" or at an earlier time "gamahuch" or "gamahouche" (Norton 2006, 174). All of these sound suitably and excitingly French, less blusterous than the Anglo-Saxon, less coldly clinical and legal than the Latin; they all derive from the French verb *gamahoucher,* to go down on.

The French are queer [strange] folk. There was a girl of this village who married a French sailor, and when she came home after a year or two her mother asked how it was that she was not in the family way and she said that she really thought it was her Man's [German Mann: husband] fault, for she always swallowed it all right. (Legman 1982, 1:553, taken from a book published in German in Leipzig, 1910)

What's a French abortion?
"Ptooey!" (spitting) (see Legman 1982, 1:553)

The Frenchman and the Italian were in the woods hunting together when suddenly a voluptuous blonde girl ran across their path totally nude.
"Would I love to eat that? *Oui, oui!*" the Frenchman said, smacking his lips.
So the Italian shot her. (Mr. J. 1984, 53)

The Perfect Lover
A Frenchman with a nine-inch tongue who can breathe through his ears. (*What Rugby Jokes Did Next* 1970, 37; also Legman 1982, 1:563)

A Frenchman is a man who kisses other men on cheeks and girls on all fours. (Coote 1998, 154)

"Take your glasses off, Pierre," Fifi demanded. "They are tearing my stockings."
Pierre did as he was commanded,
"You'd better put them back on again," she said a few minutes later. "You're licking the carpet." (Pease 1998, 243)

[An American girl, on her first trip to Paris and] on her first date with a Frenchman, asked him precisely what he intended to do with her.
"First," he replied, "I would remove ze dress. Zen I weel carry you to ze bed. And zen," he said triumphantly, "I weel kiss ze navel!"
"So what else is new?!" yawned the woman. "I've had my navel kissed a thousand times."
"Of course," said the Frenchman, "but from ze eenside?" (Jones 1987, 247)

A French family owned a cat. It died suddenly, and their fifteen-year-old daughter was so upset that she became very ill. The parents took her to see a psychiatrist, who said that they should have an autopsy done on the cat, which would reassure the daughter that her dear cat's death had been from natural causes. Later, the girl went to the pathologist's office and was told, "Many other little cats have died in the same way. When the cat licks itself, it can happen that it swallows some of its own fur. We found a solid ball of short curly hairs had matted together in its stomach and prevented it from digesting its food." The young girl looked sad and replied, "Ah, now I know what killed my dear Uncle Alphonse!"

There are many jokes involving a Frenchman using his mouth on the female genitalia like a sly Irish airline or an antitussive for rabbits. Legman (1982, 1:563) wrote, "The Frenchman is the traditional cunnilinctor." Indeed it has even been humorously suggested that this is the reason that the French invented the bidet and subtle perfume. By contrast, in British and American jokes on this topic where one of their own countrymen is involved, the man who goes down in this way is often portrayed as a loser, perhaps compelled by a gambling debt owed the woman, or as very drunk (Legman 1982, 1:568). The inference is that the man in the joke would not truly voluntarily have performed such an act involving "submission to the woman's dominance" (Legman 1982, 1:567).

> An expert pinochle-player is matched against a rich woman. He is to get $10,000 if he wins but must "go down on" her . . . if he loses. When he appears in his usual haunts he is asked, "Well, could she play pinochle?" "Ptooey!" he says, spitting. "Could that woman play pinochle!" (*Anecdota Americana* 1933, 441; Legman 1982, 1:567)

There is no reason to suppose that any of this American, British, or German humor describes the actual sexual behavior of the French population at the time when the jokes were being invented. The broad masses of France, particularly in the provinces, sought neither a lively night life nor sinful adventures (Gramont 1969, 38). Many expressed a sense of *l'atrophie de désir*, boredom with it all (Winokur 2005, 57). French women were conservative and restrained. Surveys indicated that few, even of the younger women, had had premarital sex (termed *faire des bêtises*, literally, to do something bad) (Gramont 1969, 413–14). It has been suggested that the French, whose birthrate fell earlier than anywhere else in Europe and long before the widespread availability of modern contraceptive methods, whether barrier or chemical, used oral sex as a way of avoiding pregnancy, but standards of hygiene in the countryside and among all but a small elite in the towns were too low to make this at all likely.

Have you heard about the new method of birth control used by French Catholics?

It's called *soixante-neuf du Pape* (pun on Châteauneuf du Pape, a wine from the Châteauneuf vineyard near Avignon sponsored by popes, a wine of the pope, *le Pape*.)

If the stork brings babies, and larks bring illegitimate babies, what kind of birds don't bring any babies at all? Swallows. (Legman 1982, 1:553; collected in the United States in 1941 and 1942)

Such evidence as we have implies that the main method of preventing conception employed was *coitus interruptus,* the "French sin" known in France as "jumping off while the train is still running," "fireworks on the lawn," or "to know how to blow one's nose" (Gramont 1969, 406; Van de Walle and Muhsam 1995). Moralists spoke of such matters as *funestes secrets,* the deadly secrets of the French peasantry and French Roman Catholic priests spoke of "conjugal onanism," a phrase that also included forms of mutual manual labor known as *les plaisirs de la petite oie,* the pleasures of the little goose. Such practices were used as a way of controlling marital fertility in other countries, but the French were the pioneers.

Yet oral sex in France does not seem to have aroused the kind of strong disgust that it once did in Britain (Abse 2000, xi–xii; Norton 2006, 174–75) and the United States (Brottman 2004, 6). In Alabama, Arizona, Florida, Idaho, Kansas, Louisiana, Massachusetts, Minnesota, Mississippi, Georgia, North Carolina, Oklahoma, Oregon, Rhode Island, South Carolina, Utah, Virginia, and Washington, D.C., oral sex was illegal until 2003, and in some states a married couple could have served a long jail sentence for a private infringement. An attempt to repeal the laws of Virginia that criminalized consensual oral sex between married couples in private failed in the early 1990s (Orleans 1992, 42) and again in 2001. It was only in 2003 that the U.S. Supreme Court decided in *Lawrence v Texas* that such laws were an unconstitutional invasion of privacy. The obduracy of the lawmakers and the sentiments lying behind that obduracy may help to explain why there were and are so many American jokes about the French and oral sex, acts not merely repugnant but illegal, and also why another kind of humor exists about the absurdity of the law concerning itself with trifles. There are few things more ridiculous than a public fit of moral indignation about sex. J. Edgar Hoover, the first director of the FBI, once robustly declared, "I regret to say that we of the FBI are powerless to act in the case of oral-genital intimacy, unless it has in some way obstructed interstate commerce," but his stirring statement ended up on a comic postcard published by Gathered Images of Brighton, Sussex, England. His very words were placed verbatim on the card in big letters beneath a picture of the pug-faced, pugnacious Hoover, a confirmed bachelor, squinting down the long (well, moderately long) phallic barrel of a gun, as if he were about to shoot at some offending organ. Humor can go either way, sometimes to mock the vicious preference for oral sex ascribed to the perverted French, and on other occasions to laugh at the absurdity of someone wishing to squander the power and resources of the federal government on obstructing commerce between consenting adults. When it became known in France that Monica Lewinsky had quite willingly and without any qualms blown President Bill Clinton's bugle, there were not only numerous jokes, as in America, about Clinton's sexual peccadilloes, but also humor at the expense of what the French saw as a puritanical America characterized by an obsessive legalism that had led to a trivial matter being dealt with in a ludicrously clumsy and hypocritical way (Abse 2000, 1–3).

> Clinton got a stain on a dress and Mitterand an *agrégation*. (Told to me by an English professor of modern French history)

President Mitterand, of Rainbow Warrior fame, had an illegitimate daughter, Mazarine Marie Pingeot, who took the degree of *agrégation de philosophie* at a distinguished French institution. When he died, Mitterand left three families (Lemonier and Dupouy 2003, 153), and at least one of his many mistresses was there up front with his wife at his funeral. This would not have been possible at the funeral of JFK, for America would have been far too shocked, and besides, there would not have been enough room in the church to fit them all in.

These jokes about the French are part of a much more expansive body of sexual humor, notably expressed in cartoons. Many of the collections of cartoons published in America or Britain in the 1940s and 1950s are genuinely of French origin, though selected for their "naughtiness," rather than as a representative sample of the best France had to offer, and the French language sometimes pops up through a badly, or deliberately badly, translated text. These cartoons are often just an excuse for showing a naked or half-clad pretty Frenchwoman in a compromising situation; her nationality could be changed without damage to the visual joke (Bellus 1957; Cole and McKee 1960 and 1962; House and Bennett 1956). The cover of *Love from France* (House and Bennett 1956) declares that the work is "hilarious proof that in France lovemanship is still a national art" and "like bubbling champagne." It is perhaps unfortunate, or perhaps deliberate, that the latter phrase is or was American slang for oral sex.

The collection *French Cartoons of the Twentieth Century* (Wallis 1945), which was rather lewd by American standards of that time, has an irrelevant introduction by the French scholar Claude Roger Marx, who speaks learnedly of Honoré Daumier and Gustave Doré and the rich tradition of French caricature and quotes the philosopher Bergson on laughter. The contents do not live up to this high-flown preface. In one of them a bald and bearded man in bed with his wife leans out and looks under the bed, where he sees his wife's equally bald and bearded lover in hiding. The husband says, "Thank God, it's you, Henri. I thought it was a robber" (Wallis 1945, 17). On the wall is a picture of Eve and an insinuating serpent. Crude and amusing, yes, but Daumier it ain't. The word *French* on the covers of cartoon collections translated into English is simply a signpost indicating naughtiness and vulgarity within. French equals sex. The many truly excellent French cartoons on other topics are rarely published for the Anglophone market.

These comic images in Anglo-American jokes and cartoons are paralleled by the way in which many of the consciously introduced French words in the English language are about the cuisine of either food or sex, much as the German words in English refer to war, philosophy, or rocks and the Italian ones to music. The French strongly resist taking in English words, but when they do, these are mere terms for mundane things they lack, as in *le parking, le weekend, le fairplay*. The peoples of the Anglophone world, by contrast, frequently use as ordinary English words French (or French-seeming) words pronounced, if badly, in a French way. These are spelled in the French way, indeed often with accents, and yet printed without italics, such as amour, négligée, peignoir, boudoir, décolleté, risqué, femme fatale, roué, cocotte, demi-monde, paramour, or lingerie, so as to imply or stress sexual connections or connotations. This is quite the opposite of rendering obscure the sexual meaning of the unmentionable by employing a Latin or a latinate term as in *coitus a tergo, membrum virile, pudenda,* or *pedicate,* or as when an oblique biblical reference is employed as in "the Cities of the Plain," "the sin of Onan," or "the sins of Egypt." Rather, it is a way of adding a frisson of "French naughtiness" to the way English is spoken or written. French culture is perceived as characterized by that very quality, a quality that also permeates many of the jokes about France. Hence, too, the French kiss and the French tickler.

HISTORICAL ORIGINS OF THE JOKES ABOUT THE FRENCH

Where then do the sex jokes about the French come from? What is the origin of the "nudge nudge, wink wink, know what I mean" leerings when France is mentioned? For most it is just a joke, but some believe in the myth of the easiness of French women, a belief that has led to misunderstandings and worse, with German (Scholten 1971, 30–31; Vinen 2006, 25), English and American men visiting France being disappointed at their lack of success in seduction and sometimes receiving an indignant rebuttal of their unwanted approaches by the offended local women. My sole task is to explain the jokes, but the explanation may also help to account for the existence of the myth.

The answers will be sought in French history, a history that has regularly brought to the attention of her neighbors the sexual excesses and promiscuity of small but highly visible groups within French society. In the eighteenth century it was the licentious French royal court and its patronage of both artistic erotica and pornography which led to a profitable French export trade to other countries, one that continued well into the twentieth century. It was also a time when in France the great and the gross kept mistresses in addition to their wives, much more openly than was possible in Britain or America. This gap in overtness of behavior and concern for propriety widened in Victorian times; indeed, as we have seen with Clinton and Mitterand, the gap is still there where politicians are concerned.

In the nineteenth century the lavish brothel culture of Paris attracted large numbers of sex tourists (Bauer and McKercher 2003), who returned with stories of their experiences. Others spoke of their great enjoyment or in some cases shocked repudiation of the other lewd entertainments on offer in that city, and this continued right up until World War II. In that war, as in World War I, the presence of very large allied and enemy armies in much of France led, as it often does, to the local women providing sex for the soldiers. A key theme throughout will be the asymmetries of travel and trade in relation to sex between France and those historically most middle-class and censorious of societies, Britain and the United States. In each and every case, the key questions are "how much?" "how openly?" and "in which direction?"

ASYMMETRIES

One marked feature of the eighteenth, nineteenth, and early twentieth centuries was the export of indecent books and prints from France to its neighbors and to the United States. In the receiving countries there was a significant home-based industry, but it may well have been limited in size or constrained by the authorities or just plain unimaginative, and so substantial illicit imports came from France. At that time there would not have been any sizeable trade in the opposite direction with American, British and German erotica being brought into France. Likewise, there were few French sex tourists going to these other countries, and no special facilities were laid on for them. The balance of the sex trade was in France's favor. British, American, and German politicians and notables often led irregular sex lives, but the force of public opinion, particularly Protestant and female middle-class opinion, meant that they had to be far more circumspect than their French counterparts. The British, German, and American armies have spent years occupying or squatting on French territory in modern times, but the reverse has not happened in England since the time of William the Conqueror. Thus we find one main direction of military occupation and of trade in the indecent, one major visible Parisian center of sexual activity, and one direction of travel by sex tourists and in consequence one set of jokes about one country with a single preponderant theme. This visible asymmetry provides in and of itself a sufficient explanation. There is no need for us to indulge in deep corvine chat about "the self" and "the other" or to speculate about the diffuse but inaccessible and unobservable emotions or so-called "anxieties" of the joke tellers. It would tell us nothing more of any interest or importance. There has been a slow but extensive accumulation of jokes about the debauched sex life of France, many related to particular events or times, and some of these jokes have persisted into the very different world of today.

LAUGHING THROUGH AND AT FRENCH EROTICA

It is arguable as to when the image of French licentiousness first became established in Europe. Some have suggested it can be traced back to the sixteenth century, and reference is sometimes made to the court of the French monarchs with its tradition of *paillardise,* lewdness (Gramont 1969, 398). For convenience we may begin with the orgies, courtesans and seductions of the court of Louis XV, the French age of rococo (1715–75), first during the regency of the Duc d'Orléans (Alexandrian 2007, 35) and then under Louis himself. The French monarchy was an absolutist one. The nobles did not normally live on their estates but were compelled to reside at court where they could not rebel against the king. In this way warriors were tamed into courtiers, remaining a privileged caste, yet one utterly dependent on the king and forever acting out elaborate codes of precedence and indulging in the cultivation of refined artistic tastes, elegant dress, exquisite haute cuisine, and sophisticated manners (Elias 1982, 5–6, 197, 259, 302; Goody 1982, 154). It was a way of life imitated by the other absolutist courts in Europe, even to the extent of speaking French rather than using the vernacular language of their own people. In the French court it was the age of "gallantry," of the erotic as entertainment and of intrigues as mere adventures without consequences, and all this came to be justified by a libertine philosophy (Ozerkov 2006a, 11, 15). Such a court generated a demand for erotic engravings, prints, and novels, some openly displayed, some hidden away, and also for rococo paintings to be hung in the salon showing the pleasures and pleasurings of courtiers and their coy indecencies and seductions, sometimes indicated through innuendo. Debauchery generated art, and art taught debauchery (Alexandrian 2006, 36–43). It was truly a land fit for Eros to live in. These explicit French materials were plentifully exported abroad, and they created and reinforced the image of French sexual sophistication and decadence. Rousseau referred to much French literature as "one-handed novels" (Ozerkov, Padiyar, and Alexandrian 2006, 80–81), and his point is illustrated in François Hubert's (after Jacques-Philippe

Caresme) 1775 print *Honi Soit qui Mal y Pense* (Shame on the one who has evil thoughts). The print shows a pensive French honey sitting with a curiously absorbed facial expression, a French translation of Ovid's *Ars Amatoria* (the art of love) in one hand, while her other hand is tucked strategically beneath her skirts. Other rousing prints of the time show voyeurs on the spy or discovered lovers tumbling out of cupboards.

The finest French artists of the day, Boucher, Fragonard, Jean-Baptiste Greuze, Watteau, and that great depicter of religious scenes, Subleyras, all provided suggestive paintings verging on the indecent that were known to cultured foreigners. Some of them are very amusing, notably Jean Honoré Fragonard's painting *The Swing* (1767). Swings on which women fly in ecstasy and men push and pull are a common theme in French erotic art. Metaphor and symbol were easily and fully discerned by the contemporary viewer. In Fragonard's famous painting, an earnest, innocent, toiling curate, standing in the darkness of the wood, works the swing with a rope, so that a fashionably dressed woman flies, accompanied by a colorful passing bird, high into the bright sunlight that comes through a gap in the trees. Reaching this high point she opens her legs to her lover who is hiding in the bushes, sprawled back against an antique statue of Cupid, pointing upwards with raised arm at her inviting bijou residence high above him. Equally amusing is Pierre Subleyras's *La Jument de compère Pierre* (The Mare of Peasant Pierre) from the 1740s, based on a scurrilous and obscene 1668 fable by Jean de la Fontaine in which Father Jean, the village priest, promises the peasant that through caresses he will transform Pierre's beautiful wife into a powerful mare for plowing but that the magic will only work if she is undressed and there is total silence. In the picture the wife bends over a couch and raises her shift to reveal her inviting thighs and sassy bottom. She turns her head to look directly back out of the picture at the viewer with a knowing expression. The lecherous priest leans toward her, one hand stroking where the mare's tail will grow and the other thrust through his pockets. The peasant protests, the spell is broken, and there is no more mare for him to ride. There is another version by Fragonard from the 1760s. It is the exact ancestor of our modern jokes and cartoons about the French, complete with wanton wife, cuckolded husband, and deceitful would-be lover. A real green mare's nest. It was not outsiders who invented these images of the French; they did it by and for themselves.

It may well be objected that only the cultivated élite in England, those who spoke French, knew French art, and appreciated the symbols and literary references, would know and fully understand these works. Never underestimate the power of the uneducated to work things out and pick ideas up, as they did with the Greeks and homosexuality, or the democratizing influence of the printing press and the translator. It is important to make this point to refute the nonsense talked about the dissolute French being invented as "the other" by the British. The French invented themselves, and the British merely reacted to what they saw. The English attitude to these French enticements and indeed to French luxury goods of all kinds was ambivalent. It is not a simple case of the English defining themselves as a direct straight-forward people characterized by industry, benevolence, and integrity in opposition to French frivolity. Rather, we are talking about two quite different actual social orders. Britain was a constitutional monarchy where there was a distrust of an over-mighty state like absolutist France and where the executive was kept in check by Parliament and by an independent judiciary. It was a very unequal society, but "British Liberty" was a reality, the prototype for American liberty and the antithesis of Continental absolutism. It was this liberty which made possible the outrageous caricatures of eighteenth-century England, notably those of Cruickshank and Gillray, who relentlessly ridiculed and lampooned monarchs, princes, aristocrats, and politicians alike, often in libelous and scurrilous ways (Donald 1996, 1–2; Hibbert 1998, 90; Gatrell 2006). They grew out of a uniquely British social order and were even then seen as distinctively British because Britain was rare in being a stable, wealthy, and effective society that lacked a powerful central government with a large standing army. An offended English member of the royal family or a politician was prevented by public opinion from using the power of the state to suppress or persecute those who drew, engraved, or published these mocking satirical prints. The best they could do was to hire the caricaturist themselves to mock their own opponents. This was not true of other European countries, such as France, Spain, or the various German states (Donald 1996, 2). They were a visible and enjoyable expression of "British Liberty." Only a limited circle of people could afford to buy the prints or could understand all the political nuances, and their production was based in London but the public was free to look at them in a

London shop window. Besides, the prints were extensively plagiarized and pirated, and cheaper versions and copies circulated extensively in the provinces. The very knowledge of their existence was also a matter of vicarious and even patriotic satisfaction to that much greater body of people who knew of their existence and of their symbolic importance as a denial of absolutism.

It was not possible to suppress them because no one had the power, nor would public opinion have permitted such an affront to liberty. One odd consequence was that there was an export trade in these satirical prints to absolutist countries where there was little interest in the details of British domestic politics but where they were prized as expressions of the possibility of liberty (Donald 1996, 20). The British exported images of political liberty to France, and the French repaid them with elegant pornography. During the eighteenth century, Britain became an increasingly commercial and eventually industrial society with classes whose wealth had been made in the market place exercising a degree of power and independence not possible in France. Many of the English aristocrats, such as Turnip Townsend, or their non-aristocratic younger sons were themselves entrepreneurs, bringing about the agricultural revolution by living on and improving their estates with crop rotation and animal breeding or by investing in drainage systems or transport canals. Even King George III, "Farmer George," took a keen interest in agriculture and in mechanical mechanisms (Ayling 1972, 206–207) and affected a degree of simplicity and frugality that was mocked in the prints, particularly by Gillray (Hibbert 1998, 272–73, 322). The perception that Britain and France were antithetical in ways that permitted France to be ridiculed was not a mere identity game but was rooted in the very different material circumstances and relations of the two peoples.

Unsurprisingly, these influential British commercial classes had a very different set of sensibilities and ideas about the proper relations between the sexes and priorities from the noble and courtier class that dominated French society. This is another source of a British humor that mocked the French as being decadent and licentious. It is to be seen in the work of William Hogarth, who saw France as a backward, unbusinesslike, militarist society run in the interests of two anachronistic estates, the nobility and the Roman clergy, as a place of luxurious excess, courtly intrigue, and effeminate display, that also represented corruption and temptation for his own country (Hallett 2000, 181; Jarrett 1976, 139). Hogarth's image of France as a place of pomp and poverty, of insolence and slavery, is well brought out in his comic 1748 masterpiece, *The Gate of Calais*. Hogarth's humorous caricatures are moral and didactic, portraying the contrast between the virtuous, steady and philanthropic merchants and gentry whose family lives are decorous and companionate and dissolute aristocrats who squander their fortunes on frivolous French luxuries. In the first picture of Hogarth's witty and satirical 1743 series *Marriage Á-la-Mode* (fashionable marriage, the title has a French feel), Lord Squanderfield, a foppish rake, is shown looking bored as his father bargains for him to marry the foolish daughter of a wealthy, social climbing alderman. The prospective groom is dressed in the very latest Paris fashions, complete with the red-heeled shoes, *les talons rouges*, of the higher French nobility who have been presented at court. Seated next to him, his prospective wife is reading an erotic French libertine novel, *Le Sopha* (The Sofa) (Hallett 2000, 181–82, see also 239) by Claude Prosper Jolyot de Crébillon. Predictably, the wife takes a lover, who then murders her husband. Both Hogarth's moralizing humor and the erotic frivolity coming out of France portrayed, albeit in opposed ways, the French ruling class as luxurious, salacious, and decadent.

The French export trade in pornography survived the French Revolution and became a huge industry during the nineteenth century, supplying the rest of Europe, not just England but as far afield as Russia (Ozerkov 2006b, 49). Ronald Pearsall (1969, 467) in his *The Worm in the Bud*, noted, "Throughout the century French pornography, either in the original or in translation, enjoyed a considerable vogue." Yet in England even the novels of Émile Zola were banned, and their translator was sent to jail. As important for the creation of an image of France were the distinctively French publications of saucy frivolity, such as *La Vie Parisienne* (Paris Life) founded in 1862. In the 1890s the cartoon *A Ticklish Moment* shows a female searcher at the customs groping under a fashionable woman's skirts close to the pubic area. In the 1900s we are shown a half-dressed woman telling us, "Illicit love, if nothing else, teaches one to dress at lightning speed." In the 1910s there is a drawing of a woman in corsets looking at a full-length mirror labeled "Reflections of a mirror on corsets: difficult to get into, yet when necessity calls, they can be left in a cab" (*The Girls from La Vie Parisienne* 1962). This cartoon is a reminder of one of Sigmund Freud's analyses of sex jokes:

> A wife is like an umbrella. Sooner or later one takes a cab.
> (Freud 1991, 119, from *The Book of Carnival*, a Viennese joke book)

For Freud, a cab is a protection from the rain and also a public vehicle, a metaphor for a public woman, a seller of sex, in contrast to an umbrella, which Freud sees as privately owned like a wife. However, an enclosed cab was also a protection from the possibility of others knowing about an illicit affair; the design of some of the old style French *fiacres* (hackney carriages) was such that it was possible even to have uncorseted pneumatic bliss there. It was a space fully enclosed from the gaze of those outside in which an illicit extramarital liaison could be conducted, while the couple were being driven around Paris (a city where Freud had once lived and worked). A different blissful space was enclosed by the then obligatory corset, which could only be entered if the corset were discarded.

SEX TOURISM AND FRANCE

In the nineteenth century and indeed until World War II, France was a great destination for sex tourists, particularly from England but also from Germany and America (Rugoff 1972, 247–49). France was a relatively poor country. The exchange rate favored foreigners, and for the English and the Germans it was close and easy to visit. Gramont (1969, 52) suggests that for "generations of Englishmen" a weekend in France meant "wenching in Paris." Americans went to Paris in the 1920s, when the dollar was strong against the franc, for the same reason. "Gay Paree" was seen as the brothel of Europe. There are jokes about German, American, and Czech sex tourists in Paris

> A German tells a friend that he has just been in the French capital for a week and has experienced Paris (*erlebt*, experienced, can also mean to have found a woman there).
> Friend: "*Du Schwein!*" (You pig!)
> "*Dann sagt er wieso Schwein?*" (Why do you call me a pig?)
> "*Ich war mit meiner Frau da.*" (When I went to Paris, I took my wife with me.)
> "*Du dummes Schwein!*" (You stupid pig!) (Scholten 1971, 30–31)

An American planning a trip to Paris for himself and his wife asked a travel agent what the total cost of the visit was likely to be.

"About ten thousand dollars," said the agent.

"That's a lot of money. How much would it cost if I went on my own?"

"Twenty thousand dollars."

Mr. Porsches is on a business trip to Paris. In that city of pleasure! He's already been there for two weeks when he receives an anxious telegram from his wife: "Samuel—stop—Don't forget—stop—that you're married."

The next day a messenger from the post office brings her the following telegram from Paris: "Received telegram—stop—unfortunately too late." (Karbusický 1998, 71)

In each case prostitution was widely available in these other countries (Chesney 1970, 307–65), but France offered openness with anonymity and an escape from customary social constraints, a place where the tourist could for a short time imagine that "everything is possible" and then return to home, family, and duty (McKercher and Bauer 2003, 3–17). The French were well aware of the profits to be made from English travelers. In his famous 1892 lithograph *L'Anglais au Moulin Rouge* (The Englishman at the Moulin Rouge), Toulouse-Lautrec has provided us with a wonderful caricature of just such an eager English customer, modeled by his friend and colleague, the English Lincolnshire artist William Warrener. The leering English visitor to the establishment is dressed in the height of fashion, gloves held in his hand, cylinder hat and cane, and is thrusting his mustache forward at two provocative, famously negotiable women, Rayon-d'Or and La Sauterelle. At the other end of the social scale, those who ran the Thomas Cook travel agency were uneasily aware that some of the working men, for whom even at that time they organized inexpensive visits to Paris to sample high culture, were more entranced by the great availability of sex and alcohol there. No doubt the doorkeepers of the more splendid and exclusive establishments were not very keen to admit them; too many Cook's spoil the brothel. They would have had to make do with the down-market whorehouses, *les maisons d'abattage*. They may have seen the wild, erotic *chahut* from the early days of the Moulin Rouge, again portrayed by Toulouse-Lautrec, which had begun as a literally all-revealing high-kicking display used by courtesans to attract custom. It was utterly different from the feeble, sanitized Hollywood can-can (Iverson 1963, 95) that so shocked Nikita Khrushchev on his visit to America. In order to make sure of the custom of even the humbler British visitors, those running the sex trade also set up bawdy houses, *maisons de passé, maisons de joie,* in Boulogne, Calais, Dieppe, and Le Havre, the main ports of arrival and departure for the boats to England. For the benefit of these customers passing through, most of whom knew little or no French, they would even lure and entrap Englishwomen to work there and trick them into signing legal agreements that made it difficult for them ever to escape (Chesney 1970, 343, 345; Mayhew 1950, 129–32).

It is possible that it was in these establishments that male British and American visitors in the late nineteenth and early twentieth centuries first experienced being blown and sucked, something that was taboo in their own countries, and so came to regard it as an intrinsically French activity. Labour MP Leo Abse, as a teenage chairman of the local branch of an extremely left-wing faction, the Young Socialists, went to Paris in 1934 for a Communist "people's conference" for "peace." He still remembered it at the age of 82: "As a callow provincial youth of seventeen, I was for the first time proffered a blow job. . . . I have no difficulty in recalling the exact address where the event occurred. I was . . . in an up-market bordello standing behind the Montparnasse Station in Paris at 31 Boulevard Edgar-Quinet—'Le Sphinx,' which with celebration had been formally opened by the Mayor of Paris. Today I would find the setting—a pot-pourri of Karnac and Pompeii, red plush and overblown chandeliers—burlesque." A "scantily dressed" young Frenchwoman then took him to a bedroom "with pink sheets and mirrored walls and ceiling" and "as part of her routine she sought to encourage me by moving on to fellatio, a name and practice unknown to me. . . . I recoiled with amazement and horror . . . and in the subsequent mêlée the girl fled the room" (Abse 2000, xi).

Abse (2000, xii) adds that in Britain at that time oral sex was unthinkable and that his entire generation was completely ignorant of the practice. Indeed, Britain was a rather restrained and conservative society sexually (Gorer 1955, 84–124; Gorer 1971, 30–31, 38–39). Abse also recalls a case, from his subsequent long practice as an attorney, where a man was charged with causing bodily harm to a woman, including forcing her to fellate him. It was claimed that the quite incredulous judge asked, "Didn't she have any teeth?" (Abse 2000, xii–xiv). Likewise, an American GI from a World War II survey cited by Roberts (2010, 121) said of his time in Paris in 1944, "Suassont-neuf (soixante-neuf) was a figure of speech and we knew that no normal person would practice it."

From the girl in the Paris brothel's point of view, giving Abse head made a good deal of sense. Whether it was provided as an hors d'oeuvre to stimulate the client or as a main course that did not require a full erection (L. Humphreys 1975, 69), it meant she could get through her work faster, perform a larger number of tricks in a day, and make more money both for herself and the house. For her, it was a commercial project, and she would have seen it in economic terms, in terms of "speeding up the line" and "opportunity cost" (spending longer with one customer takes up time that can be used for dealing with another). The problems she had with Abse would not have occurred with the French emperor, Napoleon III, who would have someone of her profession brought naked to his apartment; she would then be told by his equerry, "You may kiss his majesty on any part of his person with the exception of his face" (Rosner 1965, 115, citing *Goncourts Journal*, March 15, 1862). Fellation first seems to have entered female prostitutes' repertoire and to have become a common offering in the course of the nineteenth century, from which time there are photographs of them providing it (Norton 2006, 186). Fellation is much more commonly practiced in short-term as distinct from secure relationships, and the association with prostitution may possibly have reinforced the dislike of the practice among wives (Laumann et al. 1994, 101–104, 128–29, 157), which, as we shall see, is so strong a feature of Jewish jokes. In general, jokes about oral sex tend to be told in a context of commercial sex. In his encyclopedic collection of disgusting jokes, Geoff Tibballs (2005, 72–75, 360–74) includes fifteen jokes about blow jobs, and over half of them involve prostitutes.

> A Scotsman has a whore give him a blow job. He is about to come and shouts, "Swallow it and I'll give you an extra buck!"
> The whore says, "(gulp) What did you say?"
> The Scot answers, "Oh nothing." (Jones 1987, 327)

Not surprisingly, there have long been jokes about the visits of American or British provincials to Parisian establishments.

A gentleman from Idaho was in Paris and didn't want to make himself too conspicuous. So he asked a cabby to give him the address of a good whore-house. He went there by himself, quietly asked for a private room, and, after selecting his partner, ordered dinner with lots of wine. Afterwards the man entertained himself in various ways with his playmate, who taught him positions of which even Elephantis, Aretino, and Louisa Sigea were ignorant. Thoroughly drained, the gentleman from Idaho went downstairs, where he asked the madam what his bill was. "There is no charge," said the lady of the house. Astonished, but not disposed to argue the matter, her guest left. All next day he hugged his secret to himself. He could barely wait till dinner time before he again presented himself before the bands. Again he went through his performance, but this time, when he made a bluff at paying the piper, he was informed the charges were seven hundred francs. "What!" he shrieked. "Wasn't I here last evening, and didn't I go through every kind of screw, and you didn't charge me a sou?" "Mais oui, said the madam, "but last night was for the movies." (Schweinickle 1920)

Commercial sex was visible enough in nineteenth- and early twentieth-century London (Mayhew 1950), and before the 1959 Street Offences Act, female prostitutes could in many areas solicit custom from male passers-by in the street almost with impunity, but brothel keeping was illegal. Brothels were secluded, indeed to most people unknown or unmentionable, establishments. By contrast, France was famous for its *maison tolérée*, the legal, regulated, medically inspected brothel. Some of these were celebrated and sophisticated and "lavishly furnished with thick carpets, mirrors, statues and mythological motifs on ceilings and walls" (Rounding 2003, 10), such as Le Chabanais, at 12 rue Chabanais, conveniently close to the Louvre, where a notice in English in the main hall proclaimed, "House of All Nations." Others included Aux Belles Poules, le Sphinx, and le One Two Two (Lemonier and Dupouy 2003, 39). Today many of the brothel buildings with their fine, erotically decorated interiors are lovingly preserved by the French Ministry of Culture as an important statement about the history of the French way of life (Herbert 1998). There are available in the French language today vivid historical guidebooks to Paris, indicating the addresses and buildings where all manner of lewd and lascivious entertainment used to be provided—and in some cases still is (Lemonier and Dupouy 2003). The brothels' artifacts are displayed in privately owned museums in France open to the public, such as the Musée de l'Érotisme in Paris, which displays the *siège d'amour,* the love seat from Le Chabanais that enabled Bertie, Prince of Wales, later Edward VII, to enjoy sexual contact with two women at once. Being extremely corpulent, he required a system of hoists, pulleys, and stirrups to lift and lower him for this particular entente cordiale. The management of Le Chabanais housed him in a room decorated in the Hindu style, as befitted a king who was also emperor of India. They also provided him with a huge boat-shaped copper bathtub, with a half woman—half swan figurehead, in which he could cavort, or more likely loll, in water or champagne with the house whores. Edward's visits to Le Chabanais were the subject of caricatures in the French satirical press (Lemonier and Dupouy 2003, 39–40, 42, 198). Edward's love seat was described by Gramont (1969, 51) as being in the art nouveau style, though it seems to have been designed for conjunction rather than Secession and for the modes of the aged rather than Jugendstil (see also Pearl 1983, 25, 112; Lanoux 1983, 13–14). Le Chabanais itself has been parodied by Nathanael West (1957, 95–99) in his satire of American pieties and xenophobia, *A Cool Million.* In that satirical novel a virtuous New England girl, Betty Prail, is kidnapped and sold by villainous, Italian-speaking white-slave traders to the evil Chinese brothel keeper Wu Fong. Wu Fong runs a New York imitation of Le Chabanais' Hall of Nations where, dressed in period costume, Betty is shown ready to welcome an Armenian customer to her bed in a perfectly furnished, colonial style American room. Presumably many of West's 1930s readers understood the Parisian reference and concluded that what was perfectly normal and sophisticated in Paris would be profoundly shocking and sordid in New York.

The French political elite were so well aware of the appeal of elegant brothels to visiting politicians, monarchs, and diplomats that they would often insert into their official program of visit a little trip to one, discreetly described as a "visit to the president of the Senate" (Gramont 1969, 417; Lemonier and Dupouy 2003, 39). As far as foreigners in general were concerned, whether participants or not, it was all part of a single world of French sexuality, according to taste, exciting or abhorrently lewd. This world embraced not only regular sex workers, some of them girls from the provinces earning their *dot* (dowry) before returning home to marry and women who sold their services en bloc to a little syndicate of men on a time-share basis, but also the *demi-castors* (Lanoux 1983,

163), who occasionally did it on the side for a little money. *Demi-castors* means half-beavers; rather disappointingly the term refers to a hat made of mixed beaver and wool. Likewise, *hirondelle*, swallow, merely means a prostitute who displays herself in a window. Of equal fascination and remark to the foreign voyeur were the *lorettes* of Paris's Quartier Latin and the *grisettes*, girls of working-class origin, milliners, dressmakers, florists, who, when young and attracted by all things fashionable, shared their favors with the students and artists of Bohemia (Lanoux 1983, 13–14; Mayhew 1950, 106; Rounding 2003, 13–20). Visitors and Parisians alike talked about the celebrated mistresses and courtesans of the great, known as *les grandes horizontales* (on their backs), *les cocottes* (chicks), and *les abandonées* (abandoned women).These constituted *la haute gallanterie*, the highest practitioners of sexual "gallantry," who provided liaisons for the French elite and who were shown off in public and boasted about (Blyth 1972, 108–13; Rounding 2003, 18–20; Richardson 1971, 69); the group later become known as *la haute bicherie*, those who are very pleased with themselves. The top dozen or so courtesans were called "the lionesses," and during the Second Empire under the rule of Napoleon III (1852–70) they were known as *La Garde*, presumably a metaphorical comparison with the status of the *Garde Impériale*, the elite French guard units, who provided personal bodyguards to the emperor. There are many ways of surrounding the body of an emperor . . . or indeed a *président*.

Most tourists from Britain or America or Germany in these years did not go into the lavish brothels or other places of lewd entertainment, but they gawked at them from the outside and would have been well aware of what was for sale or on display. They were apt to buy erotically designed and decorated souvenirs, including household items, such as a mammary inkwell or a chamber pot with a large eye painted inside. Back home these would be goggled at and seen as being as characteristically French as an Eifel Tower paperweight.

THE COMIC TRAGEDY OF FELIX FAURE

Jokes were told in France about oral sex after the sudden death on February 16, 1899, of the president, Félix Faure, Félix *le bel* (the handsome), Félix *Oeil-Bleu* (blue eye), after he became over excited and collapsed while receiving a blow job from his mistress, Marguerite Steinheil, the wife of the painter Adolphe Steinheil (Lanoux 1983, 129; Lemonier and Dupouy 2003, 151). Faure was a "devotee of the *cinq à sept*" (5 PM to 7 PM), the customary time in France for "a late afternoon interlude for illicit sex," which he would spend with Madame Steinheil in the *salon bleu*, his private apartment in the Palais de l'Élysée. He had phoned her to come over that very afternoon. At quarter past five, the president's secretary, Blondel, heard some strange sounds coming from the room as orgasm led to seizure, and on peeking in, Blondel saw Faure lying on a couch clutching Mrs. Steinheil's curly head to his groin (Gramont 1969, 389). Rumors magnified this into the story that he had torn out strands of her hair during his final spasm and even that her hair had had to be cut free (somewhat unlikely) from his stiffening hands (Lanoux 1983, 157). The incident led to many jokes and cartoons.

> Before Faure died several hours later his wife, a doctor and a priest had been called in.
>
> Priest (or, in some versions, doctor): "*Le Président a-t-il encore sa connaissance?*" (Is he still conscious?)
>
> Policeman (or in some versions butler): "No, sir, she slipped away through the garden door." (Lemonier and Dupouy 2003, 152)
>
> (*Sa connaissance* can mean either "his consciousness," "his acquaintance," or "the woman he had just known.")

This is said to have been Charles de Gaulle's favorite joke (Gramont 1969, 391).

Faure's great political enemy, the tigerly Clémençeau, said in a parody of a funeral oration, "Faure! . . . he won't be missed" and cracked a still remembered joke:

> *Qui se croyait Caesar et qui mourut Pompée.* (Lemonier and Dupouy 2003, 151)
>
> (He who thought he was Caesar has died as Pompey/died being pumped.)

Or in an alternative version:

> "*Il voulait être César, il ne fut que Pompée.*"
> (He wished to be Caesar but could only be Pompey/pumped.)

Madame Steinheil was known thereafter as "*La Pompe Funèbre*" (funeral pomp/ funeral pump). Lemonier and Dupouy (2003, 151) claim that a theatrical company in Princeton subsequently performed a tableau, presumably a *tableau mourant,* of a scene they called "How oral sex saved Captain Dreyfus." President Faure had been unwilling to grant Dreyfus an appeal, but his successor, Émile Loubet, pardoned the innocent Dreyfus. The political opposition in France tried to create a scandal out of the way Faure died, but an amused public thought that it had been in all senses a felicitous death. It was one more stimulus for the French to tell jokes about oral sex and for outsiders to tell jokes about oral sex and the French.

FRANCE'S HIGH CULTURE AND HIGH SCANDALS

At the end of the nineteenth century, many were fascinated by tales about France's *demi-mondaines,* women who lived in a world that was not as respectable as it might have been, and loved stories about actresses, dancers, and models who posed nude for artists. It is not as utterly unfair a grouping together of the disparate as it might seem. Actresses, dancers, models, and prostitutes all provide a floating world of pretence and artifice in which there is a front stage and a backstage and all may be required to wear abbreviated or even no clothing and to act out parts and poses that other women would regard as indecent. This is one reason why artists who painted prostitutes, such as Degas, Walter Sickert, Picasso, and of course Toulouse-Lautrec, also chose to paint dancers and stage scenes. Édouard Manet's *The Bar at the Folies Bergère* (1882) depicts that part of the theater where prostitutes looked for customers. Where there's muck, there's Manet.

Many artists recruited their models from the ranks of the prostitutes, for they were willing and able to pose as they were placed without awkwardness, embarrassment, or presumably cramp. In France the nude models often had a very blurred relationship with the painter or sculptor. Auguste Rodin, who was already having sex with Rose Beuret (had his son) and Camile Claudel (had an abortion), even seduced the distinguished Welsh artist Gwen John of Dinbych-y-Pysgod, who posed naked for his statue *La Muse Nue, bras coupés* (1905–1906). She stands with one foot on the floor and the other held high and resting on a rock; Rodin has deliberately produced a statue with no arms, which draws our attention to country matters.

Not surprisingly, these matters get laughed at in French cartoons, which, as we have seen, get translated and republished in Britain and America.

> French artist at the start of a morning in the studio looking at a nude painting he had done the day before: I shall have to touch you up again.
> **Model:** But you said we had a lot of work to do today. (Wallis 1945)

In another much later cartoon, translated from the French, a bearded French artist with the obligatory black beret and beard slaps paint directly onto a nude model (Elgart 1973, 27). In a cartoon in the same collection, a high-kicking chorus girl complains to the next in line in a very odd mixture of French and American English speech: "That batard [bastard] with the bean shooter is here again" (Elgart 1973, 67. Circumflex accent on *bâtard* missing in original.)

Dancers and actresses often depended on the patronage of politicians in exchange for sexual favors to ensure their employment in state-run or subsidized establishments. Gramont (1969, 391), perhaps jokingly, perhaps seriously, suggests that it was seen as wrong for the minister of education *not* to have a mistress in the Comédie Française. When he was a young Prince of Wales, Edward VII asked his French hosts to arrange for him to have sex with a ballet girl at the Opéra whom he had seen onstage (Pearl 1983, 112). It was not regarded as an unusual request. He was one of the many lovers of the actress Sarah Bernhardt, who could be as profane as she was divine (Brandon 1992, 258, 359–60; Pearson 1975, 115, 120). The connections between the theater, irregular liaisons, and commercial sex in France were close and well recognized. Even in the mid-twentieth century, a president of the Assemblée Nationale, M. André le Troquer, recruited teenage girls, rather too young even by French standards, from the Ballet Rose for *partones* (orgies) in one of his official residences (Gramont 1969, 415). William Iverson (1963) commented that le Troquer had induced nymphets to perform "erotic pas de deux or *trois* or *quatre*."

The connection between high culture and high sex in regard to art and literature in France is important for several reasons. Notions of French licentiousness were often transmitted to other countries through a very prestigious French high culture, through much admired novels and paintings with a strong erotic aspect, as well as through commercial pornography. It is for this reason that it has been so important to discuss art in particular, which has not been necessary in relation to any other set of jokes. The French created their own sexual image. It was not a product of the imagination of others. The image was not that of a primitive, polymorphous promiscuity, the one that occurs in Russian jokes about Georgians or in jokes from the American Georgia about African Americans but of a sophisticated, aristocratic and Bohemian loucheness seen as distinctively French. In this mode it is a strong part of the jokes the French like to tell about themselves.

> What is a true Frenchman? A man who every morning arrives at his office coming from a different direction. (Quercy and Korsak 1993, 249; my translation)

> Where can one find the shortest book in the world?
> In the Bibliothèque Nationale in Paris.
> How long is it?
> Hardly three pages.
> Who is the author?
> A Frenchman.
> And what is it called?
> All the women that I have not had. (Quercy and Korsak 1993, 249; my translation)

Many countries have jokes about such studs, but they would not set the jokes in their country's most important scholarly library; only in France.

What the extensive evidence that has been discussed shows is that it was almost inevitable that jokes about the French and sex would proliferate. There is no need to invoke gobbledygook about the French being created by their neighbors as an exotic "other." All that was necessary was for foreigners to take seriously the way the dominant or most celebrated classes in France presented themselves or to observe the scale of sex tourism to that country. It is utterly pointless to ask whether the outsiders who laughed were hostile or Francophile, whether they felt superior to the French or admired them, or whether they saw France as enticing or decadent. In each case it would be quite easy to be both. The key factor is visibility, as was pointed out in my earlier accounts of jokes about the Italian army running away or about German militarism (Davies 1990, 171–219). French peasants, those who dwell in small and medium-sized towns, the highly respectable petit-bourgeoisie, the people of "deep France" (Chanfrault 1992) who made up the greater part of the French population were neither visible nor remarkable. It was the aristocratic, the fashionable, the artistic, and the sex workers in France who were visible and sometimes noisy, prominent, and distinctive, and they were the ones who gave France its sexy image on which the jokes are based. Given France's importance, it was almost inevitable that these jokes should be invented. Conflicts do not come into it, or at least not yet.

WAR AND THE SELLING OF SEX IN FRANCE

Conflicts do come into it but in a rather odd way. Wars led the Germans, British, Australians, Canadians and Americans alike to experience directly the apparently easy availability of sex with French women, as a consequence of France's nineteenth and twentieth century habit of losing wars or coming to disaster in them and having much of its territory occupied by invading armies or squatted on by the armies of its allies. This in itself has been the subject of many jokes

Why are the roads in France lined with trees?
So that the German infantry can march in the shade.

How do you get a French waiter's attention?
Order in German.

What did the "mayor" of Paris say to the German Army as they marched into the city in 1940?
"Table for 100,000, m'sieur?"

A very elderly British gentleman arrived in Paris by plane.
At the French immigration desk, the man took a few minutes to locate his passport in his carry-on bag.
"You have been to France before, Monsieur?" the immigration officer asked, sarcastically.
The elderly gentleman admitted he had been to France previously.
"Then you should know well enough to have your passport ready."
The British gentleman said, "The last time I was here, I didn't have to show it."
"Impossible. The British always have to show their passports on arrival in France!"
The elderly gentleman gave the French immigration officer a long, hard look.
Then he quietly explained;

"Well, the last time I was here, I came ashore on a beach on D-Day in June 1944, and I couldn't find any fucking Frenchman to show it to."
(See http://www.sickipedia.org/alljokes/1; accessed August 21, 2009)

In 1870, the overwhelming French defeat in the Franco-Prussian War led to much commerce between German soldiers and the local women, the basis of much subsequent humorous literature. In particular, Marcel Aymé's ribald farcical French novel *La Jument Verte* (The Green Mare) deals with the family feuds in a French village that lead Madame Haudouin to sleep with a young Prussian officer just when her son, Honoré, is hiding under the bed (Aymé 1933, 51). In Guy de Maupassant's (1880) grimly humorous tale of the perfidy of respectable but morally grimy France, a pleasingly zaftig little prostitute, Boule de Suif, butterball, is induced to lose her patriotic pride in the bed of a German officer, in order that her respectable traveling companions may be released from custody; when free, they sneer at her.

During World War I, several million British, Canadian, and other Commonwealth soldiers fought to defend France, and a substantial American army arrived in 1917. When facing the possibility of death tomorrow, soldiers tend to seek sex with the local women (Roberts 2010, 124–25) and in this case, the local women were French. Many of them were young widows or women who had lost their lovers or boyfriends in the slaughter of the French army, which had the highest casualties of any of the armies on the western front. In wartime, sexual restraints tend to break down; in France, the child of any unmarried woman who claimed that the father had died in the fighting was, by a decision of the French parliament, automatically legitimized (Grayzel 2002, 66). The British soldiers sang ribald comic songs about sex with the local women, such as *Mademoiselle from Armentières* and *Après la Guerre*, sung to the tune *Sous les Ponts de Paris* (Under the bridges of Paris).

> Après la guerre finie (When the war is over)
> Soldat anglais parti: (and the English soldier has left)
> Mam'selle Fransay boko pleuray (The French Miss will cry a good deal)
> Après la guerre finie.
> ***
> Après la guerre finie,
> Soldat anglais parti:
> Mademoiselle in the family way,
> Après le guerre finie. (Swineford 1989, 39; De Witt 1970, 9)

One of the verses of the Canadian-American-British song *Mademoiselle from Armentières* brings together the French reputation for oral sex and their distinctive foot boxing, *savate chausson, la boxe française*, giving a general picture of a funny people who do everything upside down.

> The French they are a funny race.
> They fight with their feet and fuck with their face.
> Hinky Dinky parlez vous.
> Oh Mademoiselle from Armenteers,
> Parlez vous.
> She'd readily agree to sixty nine
> With any rotten bastard from the line.

There are many slightly differing versions of the latter song (De Witt 1970, 60; Legman 1982, 1:703). The first two lines of these verses from World War I were still being collected by American folklorists in Michigan in 1964 and 2000, in California in 1986 (UCBFA Blason Populaire file F7), and in Arkansas in 1953 (http://www.mudcat.org/thread .cfm?threadid=2385; accessed July 28, 2009). The song must have a certain staying power, and it shows that the Anglophone soldiers acquired a little coarse French while over there.

The British returned to France in 1939 during World War II and sought similar liaisons, which allegedly were used in German propaganda but here form the basis of a joke.

> In 1939 another device was to drop leaflets on the soldiers in the Northern Provinces of France telling them that the British soldiers were raping their daughters. The French unit responded "We don't give a bugger, we're from the south." (Swineford 1989, 119)

When the British soldiers returned to France in 1944, along with the very substantial armies of their American and Canadian allies, it was business as usual, indeed more frantic than before. The Paris redlight district, Pigalle, became known as Pig Alley (Roberts 2010). One American joke links the troops' arrival in 1944 to the previous U.S. military presence in France in 1917–18, the experiences of which had already been transmitted to the new generation of fighting men. The sons reveled in anticipation in the sins of the fathers (Roberts 2010, 101–102).

The Flavor Lasted and Lasted.
(In 1944 a group of American soldiers were discussing how to obtain French women for sex.)
"I remember a movie I saw when I was a kid—this Yank so-jer had some gum—an' he teaches this French girl how to chew it! He did it all right."
"Well that might get us a look at Madame Lami's two daughters—everybody in the outfit's heard of 'em but nobody's seen 'em."
They go round to the house of a middle-aged French woman.
Soldier: "Bone swar, madame! . . . Je havez here beaucoup chewing gum. . . . mebbe so votre june fillies would like some of same. Tastez tray bone!"
"Chewing gom? Mais non, m'sieu!"
"Pour quah, Madame? Gee whiz. . . ."
"That's how I got the daughters soldat." (Caniff 1945)

In fairness to the French, there are many jokes about the attempted seduction of local women by American servicemen in Australia, Britain, and Germany ("Du schlafen mit me, baby, ich bringen du chocolate") as well as in France, and there were jokes about the "Piccadilly commandos" and "Piccadilly flak," London's finest hookers out cruising for good American business prior to D-Day in 1944 (Swineford 1989, 32, 49, 98). In Australia, cheap knickers were described as "one Yank and they're off."

During the last war, a large number of American soldiers were billeted in Brisbane and were very free spenders. One day a girl entered a furrier's and asked to see the best fur coat in the shop and paid five hundred pounds for it in ten pound notes. The shop assistant was aghast and said, "You must be sitting on a fortune." "I've been sitting on one all my life," came the reply, "but I didn't know it until the Yanks came." (Sent to me by a reader of the *Brisbane Courier-Mail*, Queensland, 1987; see also Cerf 1943, 101)

The fall of France in 1940 led to the occupation of most (and eventually all) of that country by the German army until 1944. An estimated 200,000 children were born to French mothers whose German fathers were either stationed in France or were briefly sent there from the eastern front for rest and recuperation. In some cases it was an affectionate relationship; in others it was a way of making money or obtaining gifts or favors by women whose economic situation was desperate and whose men were often POWs in Germany (Vinen 2006, 160, 172–75). In Paris many famous brothels including le Chabanais, le Sphinx, and le One

Two Two were requisitioned for use by German officers, with the very best houses reserved for the Gestapo (Lemonier and Dupouy 2003, 40–41; Roberts 2010, 104) and were organized with great efficiency to protect the fighting potential of the army. Other ranks picked up *les horizontales* (those who lie down for money) in the Place de la République in Paris, which became known as the *Marché de viande*, the meat market. After the German army left, during that vengeful and lawless period known as *L'épuration extrajudiciaire* (purge by vigilantes), many of the women who had fraternized with the occupiers were accused of horizontal collaboration. They had their heads shaved by latter-day patriots and were ostracized or run out of town (Vinen 2006, 175–76). Yet their behavior had not been political. *Femmes de guerre* are hors de combat. The point is well made in humorous anecdotes of the time.

> French collaborator to the postwar police who had arrested his daughter: "Why are you imprisoning my daughter for sleeping with the Germans? She would go to bed with the Americans." (Swineford 1989, 121)

> France, 1944. Two street-wise French "ladies of the evening" talking as two GIs approach: "It's disgusting the way the *Amis* [the Allies] ask, "*Voulez vous coucher avec moi?*" (Will you sleep with me?) *The Boche* "*Fraulein, du schlafen mit mir?*" [Miss, you sleep with me?] had a lilt to it the *Amis* never achieve." (Swineford 1989, 113)

The episode reinforced for the Germans the view of Parisian women as being easy that some of them, like some of the Americans, British, and Canadians, already held. As the French writer Gramont (1969, 53) wryly observed twenty-five years later, "The lip-smacking manner the Germans adopt when recalling the pleasures of Paris under the occupation is a form of tribute its citizens could do without."

> Thirty years after the war, a former German soldier went back to the little French village where his regiment had been stationed.
> He went into the cafe and said: "I vas in zis village during zer var. Vat a horrible var it vas."
> At a neighboring table were an old man and his son.
> **The old man, a little deaf, said to his son:** "What did he say?"
> **The son said:** "He was stationed here during the war."
> **The old man went on:** "Ask him if he knew Annie Dupont."
> The son asked the German this.

The German said: "Dit I know Annie Dumont? She vas the luff of mein life. I gave it to her all zer time. Her husbant vas not give her anyzing. Heh! Heh! Ho! Ho! Ja! Ja!"

The old man said to his son: "What did he say? I didn't understand a thing."

The son replied: "He says that you are not my father!" (Gaulet 2005, 240. My translation. In the French original the German speaks French with a very strong German accent, much as English speakers tell jokes about the French with a stage-French accent.)

LONG MEMORIES

Since 1945, France has not been occupied by a foreign army nor has one been stationed on its territory. The flamboyant major brothels were closed down in 1946 after Frenchwomen had been able to vote for the first time, although the system was already crumbling in 1945 (Roberts 2010, 125). As France became wealthy and French labor costs rose, sex tourism switched to other poorer countries in Southeast Asia, the Mediterranean, or the West Indies (Bauer and McKercher 2003), including egalitarian Cuba, where it caters to women as well as to men. The collapse of censorship in other countries, starting with Denmark (Kutchinsky 1978), has undermined the French pornography industry and the sexual revolution and a greater equality of the sexes means that France has come to look like any other modern country. But the jokes persist, like the jokes about the retreat of the Italian army or about efficient and obedient German brutality, which were still being invented sixty years later. Old jokes never die, they merely fade away, and they do so very slowly. In the French case there was a large stock in existence, and it went on being gradually added to, as often happens with settled historic comic traditions. The joke about the French and sex was part of such popular British television comedies as Jeremy Lloyd and David Croft's 'Allo!'Allo! (1982–92), set in a café in Nouvion, France, during World War II. The proprietor, René Artois, spends much of his time trying to cheat on his wife, Edith, with his three charming and underdressed waitresses—Yvette Récamier, Maria Carte-Blanche, and Mimi Labonq—all of whose names have double meanings. A récamier is a couch for reclining on or more, carte-blanche in this context means full discretion in indiscretion, and Labonq is a fake French spelling of *bonk,* meaning copulation. René Artois' diaries (Fairfax 1991) have been published in Dutch as well as in English.

Suddenly in 2003, when the French president refused to take part in and maliciously tried to frustrate the American-led invasion of Iraq, jokes of all kinds about the French, many quite elderly, were conscripted by irate Americans who felt that they had been betrayed by the very same people whom they had twice rescued from military disaster.

One American website of jokes began:

> We hope that this page is as deeply offensive to anti-American French people as their president's behavior has been to us. Please contribute new jokes. Don't forget to boycott French goods!
> (http://www.tinyvital.com/Misc/frenchjokes.htm; accessed March 6, 2010)

It is a good example of how to use preexisting jokes against a newly acquired enemy. The original jokes did not come into existence to be used in this way, but once jokes exist, they can be mobilized. The organizers of the websites made sure there could be no ambiguity by placing a stirring battle cry right at the beginning. The compilers made their motives and mood absolutely clear. All the jokes in the sites are about the French and only about the French, which is not how jokes are usually told, for there is a convention that targets are rotated (Kravitz 1977). The tone of the jokes is deliberately hostile and the glosses added to them make sure readers do not miss the point. The jokes are largely political, but the old sex themes have been woven in, as in the examples from another site, Cue Another Round of French Jokes (http://www.wbazone .com/forum/index.php?topic=2917.0).

> "President Bush has called for the end of the marriage tax, calling marriage a 'sacred institution recognized by God and man.' Wow, this guy can't stop slamming the French."—Craig Kilborn

> "You know why the French don't want to bomb Saddam Hussein? Because he hates America, he loves mistresses, and wears a beret. He *is* French, people."—Conan O'Brien

This collection contains slick political wisecracks that have probably come from late-night television shows; they have a hard-pressed scriptwriter feel about them. The good old "sex and the French" jokes tradition now became an extra resource for those who wanted to make a hostile political point against the French, much as Hogarth and the British caricaturists of the wars against Napoleon (Ashton 1888) had done.

It is a good example of the distinction between jokes as entities and the uses to which jokes can be put. The jokes about the beret-headed Frenchman and his mistress are not a product of America's dispute with France over the Iraq war but grew out of perceptions of France over a long period of time. They are not specifically American, and before the dispute over Iraq the French were seen as guilty of mere Gallic naughtiness. Had America come instead into conflict with England and Ireland, both of whose peoples are the subject of many American jokes, these jokes also would have been pressed into service. The American media and websites would have pullulated with jokes about drunken Irishmen and stuffy English gents. After a while the jokes about the French have returned to being what they had been and had remained in other countries, a specific set of sex jokes with strong and distinctive roots, whose numbers are still being added to and which are a gift to joke tellers.

THE DIFFERENCE BETWEEN BLONDES AND THE FRENCH

The sex jokes about the French differ greatly from those about blondes. The new blonde jokes are mainly part of a sudden joke cycle, whereas the French jokes evolved slowly, growing by accretion and often in response to particular events and institutions. The blonde in the jokes is a "placeholder" (Oring 2003, 65) who can easily be replaced with a member of some other category, as happened when the blonde jokes evolved into Britain's Essex girl jokes, much as the earlier wave of American Polack jokes had very little to do with real Poles (Davies and Chłopicki 2004). The blonde is the female successor to these earlier waves of stupidity jokes about ethnic groups, which were nearly all about men. The promiscuity is an integral part of the stupidity jokes because this aspect is about the usages of body as opposed to mind and the unthinking use of that body. The blonde's stupid male counterparts are often defined by their unthinking use of force. They are both grotesque caricatures of conventional sex roles; performing these crudely does not exactly require much thought or sophistication. Blonde jokes about sex have been around for a long time, but even in these older jokes, blondeness stands in for youth and beauty. Any other group of women having these latter characteristics could have been substituted. The great wave of blonde jokes in the late twentieth century was a response to a long cumulative process of social change, in which women came to occupy a more and more important part of that section of the workforce whose tasks involve serious thinking. Blonde jokes are not about blondes.

French jokes *are* about the French, and are about men as well as women. They are closely related to the humor of the French themselves and about themselves in farces and particularly in cartoons, which are primarily visual and whose captions are easy to translate. Blonde jokes can be told with any accent and are easily shifted to and between languages as diverse as Croatian, French, Polish, and Hungarian. French jokes are often told with the mock French accent and distinctive Frenchisms such as "'eet is 'ow you say?"—familiar to the joke tellers from the stage, films, and television, particularly in comedy. These jokes about the French travel between countries but do not get switched to local groups; they remain loyal to France. They are the product of historical circumstances peculiar to France, first the existence of the idle aristocracy of the *ancien régime,* given to pleasure, elegance, and seduction, to a "gallantry" poised between *fêtes galantes* and fetes worse than death, followed by a long period of being a venue for sex tourism and of providing camp followers for other nations' armies. French jokes refer to real people—not to the average French person, but to certain highly visible minorities and to particular explicit sexual images that were exported or known about. This is a common pattern in ethnic jokes in which a distinctive and visible and often quite atypical minority becomes the basis of jokes about a whole people, as in French jokes about stuffy English aristocrats, phlegmatic men in *chapeaux melons* (bowler hats) and laconic Empire builders (Isnard 1991, 227–28) and their ugly wives' big teeth, or humor about upper-class army officers (Daninos 1954; Maurois 1940). Things are always as they look but never how they seem.

THREE

❧

Jewish Women
and Jewish Men

The "opposite" of the jokes about the sex-obsessed French and over-sexed blondes of the last chapter is to be found in Jewish jokes about Jewish women who refuse and deny sex (Oring 2003, 61; Raskin 1985, 218). These jokes are entirely and exclusively Jewish. Gentiles would not have been able to invent them, for they would have had no interest in the matters raised by the jokes. Gentiles know them only because they have been told them by Jewish men, heard them from Jewish comedians, or read them on Jewish websites or in Jewish joke books. Once the gentiles know the theme and the scripts, they find them very funny, but when the great wave of these jokes first emerged in America, they must have been somewhat baffled by them. Many Jewish jokes play with comic images that relate in some way to negative views of the Jews held by anti-Semites (Oring 2001, 208: Saper 1991, 92), but not these; they are entirely homegrown. The jokes about the Jewish American Princess's greed for possessions may mesh with the perceptions of the anti-Semites, but I doubt that her antipathy to fellatio is part of their general and often ideological pattern of hostility. Likewise, the jokes about Jewish women are not part of a general humor of misogyny, for they have no real parallel elsewhere and they never get switched to women who are not Jewish.

Rather, the jokes emerge from social tensions and contradictions within the Jewish community about the rising tide of Jewish intermarriage (Krausz and Tulea 1998), a problem that gentiles probably do not know about, do not care about, and do not understand. Westerners are locked into a romantic myth of marriage based on the free choice of a partner within a framework of mutual attraction. In some cases the attraction has led to pregnancy, which then precipitates the marriage. In general, people marry within their own social class, religion, and ethnic group. If they do not, it may well cause embarrassment and family quarrels, but it does not threaten the very existence of the group to which they belong. A substantial proportion of Chinese American women marry men of European ancestry, but there are well over a billion Chinese in the world. There is a very strong Jewish tradition of marrying within the community, and it was long considered an utter disgrace if a son or daughter "married out." There is a contradiction between this tradition and the much more individualistic American way in which this kind of strong constraint is seen as an anachronistic restriction on "the pursuit of happiness." The jokes began when the contradiction became sharper as the rates of intermarriage rose sharply in the late twentieth century. Many of the children of these marriages are brought up in another religion, which in time will seriously diminish the size of the Jewish community (Sharot 1998, 96).

These jokes may be linked to two other sets of jokes. First, there are those about the alluring shiksa, the gentile woman who "tempts" Jewish men to depart from the marital paths of righteousness. She represents forbidden pleasures, in contrast to Jewish wives and girlfriends, who represent duty. Clashes between self and pleasure versus loyalty and duty are the bases of very many kinds of jokes of all types; what we have here is just one particular case, albeit a specifically Jewish one. There is a general clash between Jewish tradition and Americanism. Americanism is about individual choice including free choice of religion and of spouse, and this conflicts with the requirements of a religion based on ancestry and the maintenance of continuity.

However, the story cannot be completed without considering a second related set of jokes, Jewish jokes about Jewish men in regard to sport, another arena of contradiction between Jewish tradition and American mores, and also the marked absence of jokes about Jewish men getting drunk or into fights. This entire corpus of jokes will lead us back to the universal pattern of jokes about the stupid and the canny described in detail in chapter 1 and to Jewish humor about *goyishe kop* (gentile-head), the rumored stupidity of the gentiles.

JEWISH JOKES ABOUT JEWISH WOMEN

The opposite of the sexy, enticing, alluring blonde who is dependent on men is the JAP, the Jewish American Princess, who has an aversion to sex and particularly oral sex and is selfish and frigid. Whereas the blonde of the jokes is dumb, naïve, and giving, the JAP of the jokes dominates, manipulates, or refuses men (Oring 2003, 61). The sexy blonde joke, though, long precedes the Jewish jokes about sexless Jewish women.

> What does a JAP do when she has an orgasm? She drops her nail file. (See also Handwerker 2008.)
>
> What's a Jewish American Princess's idea of kinky sex? She moves.
>
> What is the difference between a Jewish American Princess and Russia? Russia sucks. (Raskin 1985, 218).
>
> What do you get when you cross a JAP with a computer? A computer that never goes down on you.
>
> What's the difference between a tidal wave and a JAP? A tidal wave swallows seamen.
>
> The only thing she [a JAP] will go down on is a store's elevator. (Prell 1999, 183)

When it was revealed in 1998 that Monica Lewinsky had freely and eagerly given Bill Clinton a blow job, indeed, that she had been down on her knees before the royal president within hours of meeting him (Abse 2000, 2–3), the Jewish comedian Jacky Mason was skeptical that a Jewish girl would be interested in oral sex. "In an oral *surgeon*, maybe" (Zinoman 2008).

The JAP jokes, though, are a subset of a much larger set of Jewish jokes about Jewish women, both as wives and as girlfriends, who are depicted as avoiding and disliking sex in general and especially oral sex; they constitute a large part of the "rich and complicated scripts used in Jewish humor [that] concerns the Jewish woman" (Raskin 1985, 217).

Medical research has revealed why Jewish women like Chinese food so much. It is because Won Ton spelled backwards is Not Now.

Why is a Jewish man like a ceramic tile? You lay it well the first time and then you walk all over it.

Mildred and I had doggy sex last night. I sat up and begged, and she rolled over and played dead. (Prell 1999, 183)

While Mr. and Mrs. Blumstein were gaping at the gorilla in the cage, the huge animal became sexually aroused, reached through the bars, pulled Mrs. Blumstein into the cage, and began ripping off her clothes. "What should I do?" she screamed hysterically to her husband. "Do what you do with me," replied Mr. Blumstein. "Tell him you got a headache." (Raskin 1985, 218)

There's a new one-hour Jewish porno movie just out.
There's 40 minutes of begging, 3 minutes of sex, and 17 minutes of guilt.
(Pease 1998, 82)

Mr. Cohn, Mr. Katz, and Mr. Rabinowitz are such avid golfers that their wives finally get fed up with being "golf widows" and insist on a two-week vacation in Miami Beach. On pain of divorce, each promises not to even mention golf to his wife. But by the third day all three are climbing the walls and, sure enough, where do they run into each other on the fourth day but the local golf course. "You wouldn't believe this, fellows," moans Cohn, "but this game is costing me $45,000 for a new Mercedes for my wife."
"You think that's bad," says Katz. "Listen to this: I've got to shell out $110,000 for a new condominium."
Rabinowitz smiles and says. "You poor schmucks. I'm here without it costing me a penny. At six AM I rolled over and said, 'Well, Becky, what's it going to be, golf course or intercourse?' She says, 'Take a sweater, so you don't catch cold'." (Knott 1985, 9–10).

These jokes are a peculiarly Jewish phenomenon that has no equivalent elsewhere. The gentiles have learned the jokes from Jewish joke tellers, have come to enjoy them and indeed to tell them, but they do not transfer the jokes to their own womenfolk. The jokes remain external to them. Even though the term and acronym JAP has been modified to include IAPs (Italian American Princesses), Happies (Hibernian American Princesses), and BAPs (Black American Princesses), there are no equivalent sex jokes about them. The jokes are jokes of the Jews, by the

Jews, and for the Jews. They are a Jewish cultural treasure, one of many in the world of jokes. They began as an internal joke and simply happened to be good enough to go public.

The no-sex jokes about Jewish women all date from the late twentieth century. They have no equivalent in the traditional Jewish jokes of Europe nor in earlier American Jewish jokes; indeed, in these earlier jokes Jewish women may well not only be willing but enthusiastic (*503 World's Worst* 1982 (1939), 136; Chambers 1958, 134, 145; Hall 1934, Joke 372, 153) and demanding from their spouses the sexual relations to which Jewish tradition says they are entitled (Exodus 21:10).

> A Jewish woman was dying and her saddened husband asked her if she had any last wishes. "Yes," she said, "I would like us to have sex one more time." They went at it vigorously and half an hour later she said to her husband, "I'm feeling a lot better. I think I'll get up." Soon she was bustling cheerfully round the house and behaving as if she had never been ill at all. Suddenly she realized that her husband was sitting in his chair looking almost depressed. "What's the matter, Abie?" she asked him. "Aren't you glad that I've recovered?"
>
> "Of course I am," said her husband. "It's just that if I'd known before that I had this power I could have saved Eleanor Roosevelt." (Roosevelt, who was revered by Jewish ultra-liberals, died in 1962, and this joke probably dates from that time.)

> "You're asking am I a good cook?" said the wife of a travelling man to a friend. "Why, my Abie is just crazy for the pot roast I make. In fact, when he comes home from the road, that's the second thing he asks for!" (Schweinickle 1920)

In contrast to Christianity, Hinduism, Jainism, and Buddhism, where traditionally celibacy and abstention were prized and monks and nuns given an honored status, mainstream Judaism has never been an ascetic religion in relation to sex. Marital sex for Jews was traditionally constrained by clear rules as to when it should take place, such as avoiding sex during and around menstruation for up to twelve days (Leviticus 18:19), and also on Yom Kippur, the Day of Atonement, when all must fast and refrain from sex, washing, and wearing leather shoes. But marriage and sex within marriage were a duty that must not be avoided. There is nothing in Jewish tradition or in the history of Jewish jokes that would have enabled an observer to predict in advance that the JAP joke cycle would have sprung into existence in the late 1970s and lasted so long or that Jewish wives would be joked about in this way. We need another kind of explanation.

QUESTIONS OF INTERMARRIAGE

For once, the explanation lies in the social circumstances of the joke tellers, Jewish men. In the past it was taken for granted that Jewish men would marry, indeed, marry early, and that they would marry Jewish women; there is no accepted Jewish bachelor culture of celibacy nor of carousing. In Eastern Europe this had been ensured by the employment of a matchmaker, the *schadchen,* about whom there were many jokes. These are also an early type of Jewish jokes about Jewish women, and perhaps for this reason new ones are being invented today, even though few have recourse to such an intermediary.

> A marriage-broker was trying to arrange a match between a business man and a beautiful young girl. But the business man was obdurate. "Before I buy goods from a mill I looked at snatches, and before I get married I must also have a sample," he said. "But, my God, you can't ask a virtuous, respectable girl for a thing like that," said the schadchen. "I'm a man from business," said the other, "and that's the way it will be done, or not at all." The broker went off in despair to talk with the girl. "I got for you a fine feller, with lots of money," he said. "He's a business man and his rating is O.K. But he's eppis a little meshuga [crazy]. He says he's a good business man, and wouldn't go into nothing blind. He must have a sample." "Listen," said the girl, "I'm so smart a business man as he is. Sample I wouldn't give him. References I'll give him!" (Schweinickle 1920)

> An old matchmaker had a student, a young matchmaker. Wherever the old one went, the young one would go with him, and that's how he learned how to negotiate a match.
>
> One day the old man said to him, "You understand, don't you, that a matchmaker has to constantly be exaggerating. For example, if the girl has, let's say, a thousand rubles, the matchmaker has to say that she's got three thousand. So keep that in mind, and when you accompany me, you should constantly exaggerate what I say, and I'll see if you are already good at this business."
>
> The young matchmaker understood all this. Once he went with the old one to a man to propose a match for the man's son. As usual, the old one

was the first one to talk, and he says, "You should be aware that the girl comes from a very good family."

So the young matchmaker goes, "What do you mean, a good family? She's of noble descent."

"And the girl's family is well-to-do?"

"What do you mean, well-to-do? They're millionaires."

"And the girl isn't bad-looking. In fact, she's quite good-looking."

"What do you mean, good-looking? She's a beauty!"

"However," said the old man, "she does have a small defect; she has a bit of a hunchback."

So the young man goes, "What do you mean, a bit of a hunchback? She's got a hunchback as big as a mountain!" (Olsvanger 1947, 11–12; Beatrice Santorini's translation)

These are as much jokes about Jewish women (Oring 2003, 41) as they are about the would-be crafty but in fact inept schadchen. In the jokes the potential bride has become almost a commodity, to be described, inspected, and traded as if she were a pack of goods to be haggled over. Elliott Oring (2003, 117–19; see also Riesman 1954, 349) has noted Freud's great liking for schadchen jokes and says that Freud saw the jokes as a criticism of arranged marriages, which gave too much weight to financial considerations and to the relative prestige of families as against the free choice of romantic partner. There is a tension here between the traditional Jewish world of Freud's ancestors, who, in common with hundreds of millions of others, Jew and gentile alike, saw arranged marriages as natural and the modern western individualistic view of marriage, where mutual choice based on affection is supposed to be the norm, a view that is probably particularly strongly held in America.

However, in America there remained for Jewish men an important constraint on that choice, the necessity to take a Jewish wife, since only the children of Jewish women are Jewish. Since Judaism, unlike Christianity, is not a proselytizing religion, the survival of Jewish identity depends on Jewish men marrying Jewish wives. Jewish men thus have two duties imposed on them by tradition. The first is that they must marry, for a Jewish man who does not marry was traditionally seen as imperfect, as deviant. There was no bachelor culture with its own way of life, no honored roles demanding or accepting celibacy, no pleasant clubby niches into which the Jewish man could retreat to escape the rigors of family duty. Jewish masculinity is domestic. The second duty is to choose a spouse from within the community; to marry out will lead to strong social disapproval. Among the Orthodox, if a son or daughter married out, it was the custom to sit *shiva*, to go through the weeklong period of grief and mourning that is customary when a close relative has died. It signified that those who married gentiles were socially dead, that they were no longer present in their family and community. There are jokes about this. "One story tells of a man who married a non-Jew, whereupon his brother sat seven days of *shiva*, mourning him as dead. On one of these days his intermarried brother paid him a condolence visit!" (Telushkin 1992, 138). Jokes (nearly always about the man marrying out) about intermarriage can reflect the horror with which it was regarded

> David came from an Orthodox family. One day he announced, "Mama, I'm going to marry an Irish girl named Maggie Coyle!"
> "That's nice, David," she said. "But don't tell your papa. You know he's got a weak heart. And I wouldn't tell your sister, Ida. Remember how strongly she feels about religious questions. And don't mention it to your brother, Louis; he might give you a bust in the mouth. Me, it's all right you told. I'm gonna commit suicide anyway." (Wilde 1978, 143; see also Telushkin 1992, 137–38)

> If you're visiting a mixed couple during the holidays, here are a couple of gift suggestions: for the Christian wife, a bayberry-scented candle or a fresh evergreen wreath; for the Jewish husband, a lovely framed portrait of his parents, rending their clothes and sobbing. (Rudnick 2009)

However, over time secularization and cultural assimilation reduced the force of these sanctions. At the same time social mobility into the upper-middle classes and the higher education this involved, together with the decline in social anti-Semitism in America, meant that intermarriage became more likely. It is at this point in the 1970s that jokes about JAPs appeared (Prell 1999, 178, 188–89) and jokes about Jewish wives began to proliferate. Both flourished in the late 1970s and 1980s (Dundes 1987, 62) and new ones are still being invented.

In the early 1960s only 10 percent of Jews intermarried and 20 percent of the gentile partners converted. Now over half intermarry. The figures on intermarriage speak for themselves (E. Norden 1991, 41; based on the 1990 National Jewish Population Survey).

Table 1. Jewish Intermarriage Rates

	% of Intermarriages in United States	% of Gentile Partners Converting to Judaism
Before 1965	10%	20%
1965–74	25%	18%
1974–84	42%	15%
Since 1985	over 50%	10%

Source: Norden 1991, 41; based on the 1990 National Jewish Population Survey.

A social change of this speed and size will have intensified the tension between duty and choice, between the traditional Jewish duty of marrying a Jewish wife and the American cultural emphasis on choosing a spouse on entirely personal and romantic grounds. The implication of the latter belief is comically to undervalue Jewish women because they represent duty as opposed to temptation and in most jokes duty loses. It is probably the case that individual Jewish men are far more likely to end up happily married if they marry Jewish women, who bring with them a familiar sense of community, tradition, and custom, but that in itself brings an extra set of known duties and obligations, since Jewish life is more rule-bound than that of most gentile groups. Thomas Szasz (1990, 229) has spoken of "the dull and distasteful sense of obligation engendered by the unremitting presence and availability of the partner, however beloved and sexually attractive." For men at least obligations of any kind are a source of jokes. Jokes about Jewish women are jokes told by Jewish men making fun of the women they ought to marry and increasingly ought to have married. Even the jokes about Jewish mothers are jokes about a set of duties and obligations to women, ones of which gentiles are perceived as relatively free. In America and Western Europe male gentiles tell jokes about mothers-in-law, not about mothers. There are no distinctively Jewish jokes about mothers-in-law.

Jewish women may well object that they are caught in the same dilemma in regard to intermarriage. Had they told jokes about it or about the deficiencies of Jewish lovers and husbands, I would have analyzed them in much the same way, but they do not. In addition, significantly more Jewish men marry out than Jewish women, leaving a residuum of Jewish spinsters (Telushkin 1992, 210n11), whose resentment is sometimes manifest but has not given rise to jokes. In the Orthodox community there has been an increase in the numbers of those who remain unmarried, but most of this glut is women. In Baltimore, it has led to a revival of the *shidduch*, matchmaking, and the schadchen, and even to the offering of cash incentives by the community to anyone who will arrange the marriage of a religious woman over twenty-two (B. Harris 2009).

Jewish men are more likely than Jewish women to marry out, partly because unmarried men spend a greater proportion of their days outside the constraints of family and community than women do and partly because women have a stronger internal sense of family duty and are less inclined to experiment, whereas men are more likely to see duty as an externally imposed constraint; it is also in consequence something to be joked about. For men, duty is joked about even when it is heeded and obeyed. Jokes are time off from duty.

AN INDIAN COMPARISON

In support of my argument, I would cite the curious recent appearance in America of jokes told by those of South Asian Indian ancestry about how unattractive their women are.

> Okay, so there were these three people walking down the street. One was a beautiful Indian girl. The second was a really ugly Indian girl, and the third was Santa Claus. So as they are walking, they suddenly come across a penny. Do you know who picks it up? The ugly Indian girl 'cause the other two don't exist. (UCBFA Blason Populaire file I.6; collected in 1998 by Tracy Hanna from a Jat Sikh, first generation in United States)

> Why do Indian women have that red dot on their forehead?
> Because their husbands are always asking them (take index finger and bang it against the other person's forehead), "Why are you so fucking ugly?"
> (UCBFA Blason Populaire file I.6; collected by Lynn D'Souza in 1995, from an American Anglo-Indian)

Outsiders tend to find South Asian Indian women handsome, and it would never have occurred to them to invent such jokes. Rather, such jokes are a product of the tension between the Indian expectation of a traditional arranged marriage within religion, community, and *jati* (caste), all of which are specified in Indian matrimonial advertisements, and the American emphasis on romantic choice. It is not the women who are ugly but the duty, a duty that in India would be taken for granted but in America can be a source of cultural conflict for the Hindus and Sikhs who have emigrated there. It is not possible to convert to Hinduism, nor to change one's caste, and each caste has its own distinctive duties and expectations, one of which is to marry within the caste into which you are born. Hence the jokes told by Indian men about the unattractiveness of the Indian women they will have to marry. It would not surprise me if one day South Asians in America were to do something no other group has done and adopt Jewish jokes about Jewish mothers to tell about their own mothers. Both South and East Asian women have a very bitter humor, though rarely jokes, about their mothers-in-law.

SHIKSA JOKES

Within Jewish humor the shiksa, the non-Jewish women whom Jewish men are supposed to avoid, is portrayed as beautiful, sexy, and utterly desirable, the humorous opposite of the Jewish women whom they are supposed to cherish. It is even said in Yiddish of a handsome Jewish woman that she is *shayn vee a shiksa,* as beautiful as a shiksa. She is often portrayed as a blonde, a (golden) shiksa, though red hair will do. A search in Google produces of the order of 500 hits for "blonde or golden (*goldene*) shiksa" (using different spellings in the roman alphabet) and about nine for red-haired ones but hardly any for those with darker hair. On October 23, 2009, there were at least 70,000 hits for just "shiksa," possibly far more, a large proportion of which refer to her sexual attractiveness or availability, to the shiksa goddess, the big Junoesque shiksa. These figures are very rough ones indeed, but the impression they give is accurate. Many of the entries play with a kind of humorous lasciviousness, as do the popular Jewish T-shirts inscribed "Shiksa goddess, every Jewish boy's secret fantasy" and "Shiksas are for practice."

(http://www.shalomshirts.com/Shiksas-are-for-Practice; accessed March 8, 2010; http://www.cafepress.com/shiksagoddessag; accessed March 8, 2010)

It is hardly surprising that there are so many Jewish jokes about shiksas and particularly blonde ones:

> A Jewish travelling salesman in a small town calls in the red-headed chambermaid, and without a word throws her on the bed and has intercourse with her. Afterwards she says, "You know, I'm not mad, but how is it you Jewish drummers never ask a girl the way the other fellows do? It's been the same way the last six Jewish drummers. They just throw me on the bed. What's the big idea?" He takes her by the hand into the bathroom and silently swings open the door of the medicine cabinet. Written in soap along the bottom in Yiddish is the legend: "*Die rōyte shicksa trennt* (the red-haired gentile screws)." (Legman 1982, 1:281; told to Legman in 1940 by the editor of *Anecdota Americana*)

> Jewish guy in a London hotel calls the operator and asks, in broken English with a heavy Lithuanian-Yiddish accent, for number 266419.
> A short time later there's a knock on the door, and when he opens the door, he sees two beautiful and sexy girls who ask him: "Are you the guy who ordered two shikses for one night?"
> (http://www.harryc.com/j-jokes905.htm#28; accessed March 8, 2010)

The shiksa jokes began earlier than the jokes about Jewish women at a time when intermarriage was unlikely but when, just occasionally, Jewish men might seek premarital adventures with gentile women, fearing that an approach to a Jewish woman might result in the rebuff "No chuppah, no stuppe" (no wedding canopy, no sex).

> Why does a Jew need legs?
> To school he must be forced, to marriage he must be led, to burial he is brought, to the synagogue he won't go, and after the Gentile girls he crawls.
> So why does he need legs? (Kumove 1986, 142)

> What are shiksas good for?
> Shiksas are good for practicing but not for marrying. (UCBFA American Jewish Blason Populaire miscellaneous jokes file; collected by Reginald P. Calaguas 1992)

It is a joke that often sneaks out. Philip Weiss (2008) recalls a debate at Yale on the relationship between the United States and Israel:

> There had been one funny speech. Matt Lee of the Progressive Party had chosen to mock the U.S. for being a Jewish mother to Israel, and Israel for being the princeling child—upsetting the mother by coming home with China.

When the questions came for Lee, someone stood up to ask if Israel could "marry a goyische country." Lee looked around, mystified. "I don't even know what that word means." Nicola stood up to clarify things. "Shiksa countries are for practice." It was a neat play on a dirty old line: Marry a Jew—shiksas are for practice. The neocon backbenchers roared.

The joke cropped up again when Eliot Spitzer, the Jewish governor of New York, whose wife was not Jewish, resigned in March 2008 after an intrusive investigation showed he had paid for sex with a twenty-two-year old Jewish woman through an escort agency. Here are some of the snider comments that ensued:

> Spitzer paid 5,000 bucks to cheat on his blonde Shiksa wife with a 22-year-old Jewish girl. Pretty funny for a guy with a genius IQ. . . .
> Pretty damn hilarious, isn't it. I can just hear Eliot's mom: "Eliot, Eliot . . . if you like Jewish girls so much then why didn't you marry one like I told you to do gazillion times! Oy Gevalt."
> (http://www.freerepublic.com/focus/f-news/1984893/posts; accessed March 8, 2010)

In the days before intermarriage became common, jokes about shiksas or blonde shiksas were simply the Jewish equivalent of the traditional gentile jokes about sex with blondes with which we began. An ethnic dimension had been added to a standard storyline. Jokes about the temptations of blonde shiksas are part of a long Jewish tradition of humor on the subject, as in the B. Kovner (Jacob Adler) story "Wanted a Man with Money."

> After having listened to my wife's recitation, I said to her:
> "Would you like to take in a maid?"
> "No, I would rather not. The maid would be more yours than mine. I remember well what happened a year ago this time when I engaged the German blonde with those long braids. The time she was here, you forgot completely that you had a wife. In the six months she was here you did not kiss me once."
> "What are you talking about? So whom did I kiss?"
> "Not me."
> "And I thought I was kissing you."
> "That shows how mixed up you were that you did not know whom you kissed."
> "What do you think! To support a family and keep up such an expensive home is enough to make any man lose his head."

"Only such a man as you would lose his head. When you see a blond young girl you get off your 'nut.' It is a lucky thing I sent her away in time."

(Kovner 1936, 34–35; for additional specifically Jewish jokes about blondes, see also Kramer 1980, 39, 171; Munn 1965)

For some, seeking a compliant blonde was just an ordinary part of growing up Jewish. In Myrna and Harvey Frommer's (1995, 230) oral history of Jews in America they note that "the ideal for a Jewish boy is a blue-eyed blonde shiksa or even a Jewish girl who looked like that." Among the interviews they recorded, there is one with an Ivy League astrophysicist from Brooklyn who reminisced fondly about his youth.

I had a blonde shiksa as a teenager. She lived in Bay Ridge. If you wanted sex you either joined the Young Communists or Socialists in Greenwich Village or you found a blonde shiksa. I did both. (Frommer and Frommer 1995, 230)

The humor about shiksas is sometimes associated with the Christian celebration of Christmas, so famously mocked by Philip Roth (1969, 143–44) in *Portnoy's Complaint*, when Portnoy complains of the tackiness of the compulsively smiling nativity gnomes and animals to be seen on the snowy lawns of the Christians of Irvington in the days leading up to that festival. The sloppy, sentimental song "I'm Dreaming of a White Christmas" has been parodied as "I'm Dreaming of a Blonde Shiksa." The humor embraces a parodic festival called Jewsmas.

On Jewsmas, we call to our houses all our *shiksa* friends and admire their beauty; we sing their praises and laugh at their jokes; we ply them with Manischevitz wine and wonder whether we will get in their pants. (http://www.jewsmas.org/traditions.html; accessed March 8, 2009)

It was all good clean Jewish fun, but then came accelerating intermarriage, and now and only now began the jokes about sexless Jewish women.

To a Jewish man, the shikse is:
Desirable because she is non-Jewish
Inferior because she is non-Jewish
Wonderful because she is non-Jewish
Forbidden because she is wonderful
Wonderful because she is forbidden

However, this comes from Richman and O'Donnell's (1978) humorous advice book, *The Shikse's Guide to Jewish Men*. For many Jewish women and for those concerned with the shrinking size of the Jewish population, the shiksa was no longer an amusing fantasy but a kind of threat. From the Jewish women's point of view she was a competitor for a scarce resource, suitable Jewish husbands. By the 1990s, only 28 percent of the children in mixed households were being brought up Jewish; 700,000 half-Jewish children were brought up in another religion, and 400,000 adults, the offspring of such marriages, practiced another religion; 210,000 Jews had converted out, usually as a result of intermarriage (E. Norden 1991, 41–42).

> What do you call the grandchildren of intermarried Jews?
> Christians. (Milton Himmelfarb, cited in E. Norden 1991, 42)

When Kristina Grish (2005), who describes herself as a "Love and Sex Coach," wrote her lighthearted *Boy Vey! The Shiksa's Guide to Dating Jewish Men*, many laughed, but others found it very threatening (Urquhart 2005). Grish's wisecrack "To find a Shiksa with a hilariously high-maintenance mixture of strength and prowess is an utter utopia for the libidinous Jew" is funny, though somewhat tasteless, but with intermarriage the shiksa has come to be seen by many Jewish women as predatory and not someone to be encouraged by a handbook, however farcical. There is great unease among Jewish women in particular when non-Jewish women advertise themselves on Jewish dating sites, thus poaching a scarce resource (see Raphael 2001). It is noteworthy that, despite Jewish women's many admirable qualities, no one has written a guidebook about them for gentile men. The humor is entirely asymmetrical. In the background is the suspicion that it may be a classic trade-off between female attractiveness and male social position (Chang 1997), as when English peers marry actresses (Bullock 1935). Blondes, who as we have seen are greatly desired by men in general, can use their attractiveness to marry prosperous professionals, a group in which Jewish men are highly represented. The Jewish mother's ambition for her sons has exposed them to a higher risk of intermarriage.

> A Jewish mother was pushing her two little sons down the street in a push-chair when they met an old friend who stopped to admire them.

"What lovely children! How old are they now?"

"The doctor is three, and the lawyer is nearly two." (see also Rosten 1970, 433)

Higher education tends to undermine commitment to ethnic and religious homogamy, and the social prestige of professionals means that they are more sought after as husbands than the old-time Jewish cutter, presser, packman, hand-cart peddler, drummer, or dealer in secondhand clothes would have been.

It all seems very unfair to Jewish women, but the unfairness lies in the world, not in the jokes. The jokes, like those about dumb blondes, are a product of a tension between two sets of values, in this case loyalty to a particular identity, tradition, and community on the one hand and American individualism on the other. For most Americans, "worship at the church of your choice" and "marry the spouse of your choice" are almost taken for granted, unthreatening, seemingly natural ideas. But for the Jews, they have come to create new sources of cultural contradiction and thus new forms of jokes.

The oldest tradition of jokes is that about the attractiveness of blondes, one embraced by Jews and gentiles alike. Both the joke cycle about stupid and promiscuous blondes and the Jewish jokes about blonde shiksas grew out of it independently. The Jewish jokes about Jewish women that have come to be appreciated, though not invented, by gentiles are the opposite of these, involving the construction of an unattractive, canny withholder of sex, everything the imagined blonde is not.

THE STRANGE CASE OF ORAL SEX

The one extra element in the Jewish jokes are the jokes about Jewish men specifically wanting oral sex and Jewish women denying it to them. Why does the question of oral sex come up in the jokes so often, far more often than might be expected? Why is its withholding far more common in jokes about Jewish women than its granting is in jokes about blondes? What is it about oral sex and the Jews?

Oral sex may have been placed off-limits by some Jewish authorities because it leads to the spilling of the seed in vain, thus paralleling the sin of Onan, or because it conjoins the pure upper body in whose products, such as tears or even spittle, no ritual pollution resides, and the impure, potentially polluting lower body, or because it involves the immodest thrusting into full and close visibility of the private parts, such that the couple see what is unseemly (and for some authorities that which must not be shown and seen at all). A jagged tooth could even lead to the consumption of a tiny spot of blood, the very life of the partner. It is, though, unlikely that such views would hold very much force in the increasingly liberal and secular late twentieth century, when the jokes about oral sex began to flourish. Even more speculatively, it may be related to the general emphasis placed in Jewish tradition on what goes into the mouth, the contrast between kosher and *treyf* (in this context the contrast between things that can be eaten and those which must not be) and the strict separating of meat and milk products. Nathan Abrams (2004) has written that "*treyf* signifies the whole world of forbidden sexuality, the sexuality of the *goyim*, and there all the delights are imagined to lie."

The dietary laws do find their way directly or indirectly into jokes about shiksas.

> A guy's mother dies; he feels bad because his father's left all alone. So he sends his father to Kutscher's in the Catskills where he'll be fed kosher food, he'll meet nice eligible older Jewish women, and he won't be lonely. So after his father's been there a week and he hasn't heard from him, he tries to get in touch with him, keeps calling and calling but his father's not there. So he gets in his car and drives up to Kutscher's and runs around looking for his father, but nobody's seen him. Finally someone says he's seen him go off with a blonde women to another hotel. So the guy goes off to the other hotel and he asks for the room of this woman. And so he goes up to the room, bursts open the door; there's his father embracing this beautiful blonde bombshell, 45 years his junior and clearly a shiksa. The guy cries out, "Father—what are you doing? What's going on here? I send you to Kutscher's where there are kosher meals and Jewish women, and here you are schtupping this shiksa!" His father turns around and says, "I don't eat here!" (UCBFA American Jewish Joke file; collected by Ruth Charloff 1986)

To *schtupp* or *shtup* means to have sex with. It is a bit like the British English verb "to tup," although in Britain it is more often used in connection with sheep.

Blonde lobsters are not okay to eat OR marry

Divers have discovered a new crustacean in the South Pacific that re-
sembles a lobster and is covered with what looks like silky, blond fur,
French researchers said Tuesday.

Scientists said the animal, which they named *Shiksa Treifus,* was so
distinct from other species that they created a new family and genus for
it. . . . In what Segonzac described as a "surprising characteristic," the
animal's pincers are covered with sinuous blonde hair-like strands, rang-
ing anywhere from $80–175 for monthly upkeep.

(http://www.jewlicious.com/2006/03/blonde-lobsters-are-not-okay-to-
eat-or-marry-2/ March 9, 2006)

A new species of crustacean fitting the above description really was
found by divers and has been named *Kiwa hirsute,* but a Jewish wit renamed it Shiksa because it was blonde and not okay to marry and Treifus
because it is forbidden to consume lobster, a sea creature that lacks fins
and scales (Leviticus 9:12); the phrase "not okay to eat" is somewhat
ambiguous.

However, it is more likely that the basis of the jokes about oral sex is
that the recipient of oral sex is seen as dominating the giver; this is not acceptable to Jewish women, and the Jewish men are portraying themselves
as not assertive enough in pushing them to do it; this fits the jokes into a
more general Jewish comic script about Jewish men and masculinity.

Of those Americans interviewed as part of a large sample of the population in the early 1990s, at the time when the jokes about oral sex were
very popular, most of the ones born after 1948 said that they had had some
experience of oral sex. However, oral sex was far more likely to occur in
short-term relationships than between married couples. Within marriage,
men were somewhat more likely to perform it on women (cunnilingus)
than to be the recipients of it (fellatio), but in short-term relationships
exactly the opposite was true, with more women performing it on the men
(Laumann et al. 1994, 101–104, 128–29). The strongest differences between
the sexes lay in their attitudes toward and enjoyment of oral sex rather
than in their actual behavior. Their tastes in this matter differ. Laumann
et al. (1994, 157, see also 152–53) comment on their survey results:

oral sex may be the most contested of the sexual practices that we consider. Its potential as a cause of conflict in sexual relationships . . . renders
the distribution of its appeal of particular interest.

> Compared with vaginal intercourse, the discrepancies between men and women with regard to the appeal of both giving and receiving oral sex were considerably larger. . . . While 45% of men found receiving oral sex (fellatio) very appealing, only 17% of women found giving oral sex very appealing. On the other hand, gender-based reports of the appeal of cunnilingus were markedly closer. . . . fellatio may be viewed as an obligation for women in a way that cunnilingus is not for men. (Laumann et al. 1994, 157)

What the authors of the sex survey report are saying is that performing oral sex is a sacrifice for women; they do it only to please their partners and are more likely to do it in short term relationships, where their situation is precarious and a partner has to be assuaged, than in marriage, where the woman's status is more secure (see also Wellings et al. 1994, 166, table 4.9).

Given that the central script in Jewish jokes about sex is the Jewish woman's and particularly the Jewish wife's refusal to comply with her partner's sexual requests, then the data from the surveys of the general population indicate why jokes about the woman's denial of oral sex to her man would be such an important part of the total set of Jewish jokes. While the general American survey is able to distinguish differences in behavior and attitudes to oral sex between different races and different kinds of Christians, the number of Jews in the sample is too small to be able to tell if they do or do not differ in this respect from the general population. It is further complicated by the fact that the Jews in the sample would in general have been older and better educated than the others and that by the end of the 1980s Jews had a later age of marriage than gentiles. For what it is worth, white men in America who are circumcised have had more experience of heterosexual oral sex, both active and passive, than uncircumcised men (Laumann, Masi, and Zuckerman 1997), but social class is again a confounding variable because the incidence of circumcision is strangely high among upper-middle-class American male gentiles.

The Jewish jokes about sex are part of a much larger and more general set of Jewish jokes whose theme is that Jewish women are more powerful in relation to their own men than gentile women are in relation to their men, the Jewish man's humorous lament that "I have measured out my life in apron-strings." There exists a complementary Jewish comic image of the gentile as an irresponsible, brawling, drunken wife-beater, like the heroine's husband in Woody Allen's 1985 film, *The Purple Rose of Cairo,* who is the antithesis of the uxorious Jewish husband, that saintly and virtuous man, who is also "good to his mother" all his life and indulges his daughters.

> Why does the groom smash a glass underfoot at a Jewish wedding? It's the last time he gets to put his foot down. (Sol the Answer Man 1990, 48)

(The breaking of the glass is a *momento mori* to remember the destruction of the Temple in Jerusalem and is also a reminder of something that is about to be broken.)

> Why do smart goyim [gentile men] seek to marry Jewish women? Because they know they will never again have to make a decision.

> A gentile man phones his mother and says, "Look, Mom, I know you're expecting me for dinner this evening, but something very important has come up and I just can't make it." His mother says, "OK, son. Maybe some other time."

The JAP jokes and the jokes about resentful Jewish husbands' and doting Jewish fathers' inability to curb the shopping extravaganzas of their wives and daughters are part of this same comic pattern of the Jewish man's supposed lifelong subordination.

> What's a JAP's favorite erotic position?
> Bending over the credit cards. (Goldman 1999)

> Mrs. Goldfarb takes her little boy to the beach, and as soon as she settles under an umbrella, the routine begins:
> "Alan, come here. Don't go into the water. You'll drown."
> "Alan, don't play in the sand. It'll get in your eyes."
> "Alan, come out of the sun. You'll get sunstroke!"
> "Oy vey, such a nervous child." (Novak and Waldoks 1990, 272)

JOKES ABOUT DRUNKEN BRAWLING GENTILES AND VIRTUOUS JEWISH MEN

In order fully to understand the Jewish jokes about Jewish women, it is necessary also to analyze carefully Jewish jokes about Jewish men and the ways in which they and their tradition of masculinity are depicted as differing from gentile men and their male mores. It has been shown that Jewish men, who are not violent and whose tradition is to drink only in moderation, very much appreciate (non-Jewish) jokes about drunken gentiles (Wolff et al. 1934). The gentiles who get drunk in these jokes and sometimes in reality have a style of "drunken comportment" that involves brawling in the street or in a bar and then going home drunk. If the gentile is married, he will have spent all his wages and will thump his wife if she objects or nags, or perhaps she will be hiding behind the door armed with a rolling pin (see Frommer and Frommer 1995, 7–8); this, too, is a subject of many jokes and cartoons. These jokes are not invented by Jews but are general jokes told by, for, and about gentiles, including jokes about drunks, ethnic jokes about the Australians or the Irish, social class jokes about tipsy Glaswegians, giving rise to the drunken comic song "I belong to Glasgow" or about belligerent Geordies, from the industrial northeast of England, who are the basis of the worldwide syndicated cartoon strip *Andy Capp* (Smythe 1963). In Hartlepool in the northeast of England, the work-shy, sport-mad, drunken, fist-fighting wife-beater Andy Capp is so revered that they have put up a statue of him. It is difficult to imagine a Jewish Andy Capp or a Jewish Tam o' Shanter (Burns 1868), and even if they did exist, they would not get statues. Rabby Burns is no Rabbi Burnstein.

> While we sit bousing at the nappy, (carousing on ale)
> An' getting fou and unco' happy (full and uncommonly happy),
> We think na on the lang Scots miles,
> The mosses, waters, slaps and stiles,
> That lie between us and our hame (home),
> Where sits our sulky, sullen dame,
> Gathering her brows like gathering storm,
> Nursing her wrath to keep it warm. (From Robert Burns, *Tam o' Shanter*)

These jokes are often invented and treasured by the groups about whom they are told, and the men see them as referring, through fictional exaggeration, to reckless rollicking good times, to the camaraderie of the inebriated, to a proudly macho, fun-loving world of sports, booze, and punch-ups, to the mateship of a culture from which women are excluded (Stivers 1976; Oxley 1978). Jewish men are not part of this world but from a culture emphasizing family and self-control and from which uncouth gentiles of this kind are regarded with a certain disdain. Jews greatly enjoy gentile jokes about gentile drunkenness (Wolff et al. 1934) but presumably from a very different perspective. Perhaps this is the basis of the traditional Yiddish comic song "*Shikker iz der goy*" (the gentile is a drunkard) in which gentiles get drunk and smash the Jews' windows while the Jewish men remain sober, so that they can remain attentive to their religious duties such as regular prayers.

> *Shikker iz der goy* (The gentile is a drunkard)
> *Shikker iz er* (A drunkard is he)
> *Trinken miz er* (He must drink)
> *Vayl er iz a goy.*" (Because he is a gentile)
> (Sung for me by a Jewish cantor in 2010; see also Bermant 1986, 71–72)

JEWISH JOKES ABOUT JEWISH MEN AND SPORT

We may set against the jokes about drunkenness and violence, jokes invented and told both by and about the gentiles, against an opposed set of jokes invented by Jews and about Jews, particularly (but not exclusively) in the United States about the distance that Jewish men place between themselves and the comic conventional masculine physicality of gentile America, with its emphasis on sports, outdoor pursuits, and hunting with guns.

> A marathon was being run in Chicago, and Llewelyn Jenkins was well in the lead. As he ran sweating and red-faced through an Irish neighborhood, a huge crowd gathered and shouted, "Hurrah! Hurrah!" Then he came to a Hispanic neighborhood, and the crowd all shouted, "Viva! Viva!" Still well in the lead but his face showing signs of pain and fatigue, he came to the Jewish suburb of Skokie. Passers-by looked at him in amazement and shouted, "Meshuggener!" (lunatic) (Told to me by a Jewish scholar from Skokie in 2009; name of Welsh runner has been added)

> Entering a bookstore, a man asks for a very short book. The salesman answers: "I have just what you're looking for: *Jewish Sports Figures*."

> In the film *Airplane!* a stewardess responds to a passenger's request for "light reading material" by handing over a microscopic pamphlet titled "Famous Jewish Sports Legends." (Boronson 2008)

> When I was a child, my father told me that sport was *Goyim Naches* (Yiddish from Hebrew, "pleasure of Gentiles"), and that the only Jewish

sport was to ponder the philosophies of Spinoza and Schopenhauer or, alternatively, the Talmud. Yeshayahu Leibovitch, an observant Orthodox Jew, described football teams as "eleven hooligans running after a ball." Another Jew suggested, for the sake of peace, "Why quarrel? Give each team their own ball." (Avnery 2006)

A Jewish rowing team challenged Oxford University to a rowing match on the Thames. Oxford won easily. Afterwards the Jews asked a spectator why he thought they had lost. "Well," he replied, "they had eight men rowing and one man shouting, and you had eight men shouting and one man rowing." (Told to me in 2009 by a Jewish Keynesian from King's College, Cambridge)

Ernst Stern, cognition theorist and wrestler, . . . turned an apparently inescapable defeat into a sensational victory and was asked afterwards by one of the journalists mobbing him what he had thought in those threatening seconds when he was almost pinned down to the mat with both shoulders. He answered, "That's when I thought: a Jew belongs in the coffeehouse." (Torberg 2008, 117)

Three bubbes were sitting around and bragging about their children. The first one says, "You know my son, he graduated first in his class from Stanford, he's now a doctor making $250,000 a year in Chicago."
The second woman says, "You know my son, he graduated first in his class from Harvard, he's now a lawyer making half a million dollars a year and he lives in Los Angeles." The last woman says, "You know, my son, he never did too well in school, he never went to any university, but he now makes 1 million dollars a year in New York working as a sports repairman."
The other two women ask "Vos is a sports repairman?" The bubbe replies, "He fixes hockey games, football games, baseball games . . ." (M. Weiss, September 3, 1996; see also Rockaway 1993, 5)

A sports contest took place between two Jewish schools, both of which claimed defeat. (Heddendorf 2009, 73)

The last joke is used in a theological discussion of humor by Russell Heddendorf, a devout Presbyterian and founder of the Association of Christians Teaching Sociology, who at the time of his death was professor emeritus at Covenant College, Lookout Mountain, Georgia, and based in Dayton, Tennessee. He was also a keen baseball fan. Dr. Heddendorf cited the joke as a piece of "characteristically self-deprecating" Jewish humor. To someone of his religious persuasion and living in the part of America where he did, that is the joke's main aspect. However, it is a far more complex and ambiguous joke than that. It is also a questioning of the value of sport in the first place and of the very sanity of those who think that the winning of a football match, a baseball game, or any other athletic contest by a school is a matter of some importance. There is a very good fictional illustration of this point in Philip Roth's celebrated piece of humorous Jewish fiction, *Portnoy's Complaint*.

> Which was more or less the prevailing attitude toward athletics in general and football in particular among the parents in the neighborhood; it was for the goyim. Let them knock their heads together for "glory," for victory in a ball game! As my Aunt Clara put it in that taut, violin-string voice of hers, "Heshie! Please! I do not need such *goyische naches!*" Didn't need, didn't want such ridiculous pleasures and satisfactions as made the gentiles happy. At football our Jewish high school was notoriously hopeless (though the band, may I say, was always winning prizes and commendations); our pathetic record was, of course, a disappointment to the young, no matter what the parents might feel, and yet even as a child one was able to understand that for us to lose at football was not exactly the ultimate catastrophe. . . . We were Jews—and not only were we not inferior to the goyim who beat us at football, but the chances were that because we could not commit our hearts to victory in such a thuggish game, we were superior! . . . the goyim pretended to be something special while *we* were actually *their* moral superiors. (Roth 1969, 55–56)

The jokes are part of a more general multilayered humor about a uniquely Jewish perception of the sheer joylessness and pointlessness of sports and athletics. At the "Jewish Olympics" below, the Jews are made to look absurd, but so by implication are the Olympics.

> The Jewish Olympics
>
> After reading through the list of this year's Olympic events, it was found that the Olympic Committee has made some significant changes. Some of the less-publicized events of particular interest to the world's Jewish communities, that you may have missed, may be:
>
> **Oyga Vault:** A sound-enhanced Pole Vault competition, the vaulter must clear the bar then yell "Oy" upon hitting the foam pad below. Any heights cleared without an "Oy" will be considered a fault. Points will be added for more enthusiastic exclamations of "Oy," such as "*Oy vay iz mir!*" (woe is me). "Oy, I've just landed on my *shana punim!*" (pretty face) or, the winner in the Olympic trials, "Oy, such *tsuris* (grief) this is causing me!" (M. Weiss, 1996)

What lies behind this humor at the expense of sport and sportsmen? Sport is once again a point of contradiction between Jewish tradition on the one hand and gentile, and in particular American, ways on the other. To most foreigners, American men's total obsession with sport seems very strange indeed. Sport and an interest in sport have become part of the American civic religion and so close to being compulsory as to be oppressive (Boyarin 1997, xiii, xxi; Goffman 1990, 153). It is not strange for children and youths to enjoy playing, but both the amount of time and interest that American parents invest in the sporting activities of their offspring (Gurock 2005, 172) and the centrality of sport and athletics to American educational institutions seem very odd to outsiders, as does the remarkable lack of skepticism in America as to the value of such activities. Does an enthusiasm for sport provide a pay-off in health and fitness, or are Americans steadily becoming more obese and short of breath? Does sport enhance military preparedness? Does a ruthless emphasis on winning provide moral benefits? What are the "opportunity costs" of sport? Could the time and resources that sports take up in schools and colleges be put to more productive educational uses? There was a similar lopsidedness in the curricula of the leading private boarding schools of nineteenth-century Britain (Honey 1977), which in the long run proved a disaster for that country, as it fell behind its economic and military competitors, due to the innumeracy and lack of scientific and technical expertise of its elites. The battle of the Somme was lost on the playing fields of Eton. By contrast, sport is largely neglected in Israel, the key military player in the Middle East and the only country in the region with a modern economy and educational system. Even if there were in fact a very strong and widespread Jewish dissent from the American obsession with sport, it would be a perfectly reasonable and rational position to adopt. Nonetheless, it is the uniqueness of such Jewish dissent as there is that calls for an explanation. By contrast, the American obsession does not call for an explanation. It is merely a bigger version of what happens in other countries, though these play international sports such as soccer and cricket, rather than the essentially local baseball and American football, which are peculiar to the United States and thus a mark of American identity.

JEWISH PIETY AND PAGAN ATHLETES

The Jewish repudiation of athletics began with the revolt of the Maccabees in the second century BC against their Seleucid Greek ruler from Syria, the wicked tyrant Antiochus IV Epiphanes, who wished to deprive the Jews of their distinctive identity. He was supported in this by those Jews who had assimilated to the ways of the Greeks, including the unspeakable Greek athletics and gymnasia, which were the very symbol of the profane and the heathen (2 Maccabees 4:7–20). Some Jews had previously become so Hellenized, indeed assimilated almost to apostasy, that they fully adopted the Greek cult of athletics, the gymnasium and *ephebion* (clubroom), and even had operations to reverse their circumcisions, so they could run around naked and not be laughed at by the Greeks. The Greek word *gymnos* means naked; our word gymnasium is derived from this. The more pious and nationalist Jews saw the Greeks' Olympic-style games as pagan and the nakedness of their male athletes as grossly indecent. At the core of the revolt was an objection to the alien Greek idealization, almost worship, of the body, which was quite contrary to the Jewish regard for things spiritual. Antiochus' armies were hammered by the Maccabees; their Hellenizing supporters among the Jews were suppressed, and for a brief time a true Jewish independence was restored under the Hasmonean dynasty (140–37 BC) and athletic contests were abolished. It is amusing to record that one muscular and devout Christian classicist, Harold Harris, knowing that the disciples of our Lord had all, without exception, been fully Jewish, as was Jesus himself, was upset to think that there could have been no athletes among them and sought to find a way around this. Well before the events of the New Testament, athletics and games had been reintroduced into Israel under Herod I, tetrarch of Galilee and then "king of the Jews," a title conferred on him by the Romans; he was a mere client-king of the Roman Empire. Herod I was an enthusiastic builder of gymnasiums and stadiums and so great a patron of the Greek Olympics that he was made life-president. On the strength of Jesus' disciples having come from Galilee where a great stadium had been built in the capital, Tiberias, Harris (1976, 95–106) concluded that the name Peter, *Kephas* in Aramaic, meaning the rock, given by Jesus to his faithful disciple Simon, might well have been based on an existing nickname, Rocky, conferred on him during his earlier days as a boxer. The rock on which the church is founded (Matthew 16:18) has been turned by Harris into a pugilist. However, John could run much faster than Peter and so was the first man to reach the empty tomb of our Lord (John 20:1–10), and Harris concluded that the disciple whom Jesus loved must have been a trained sprinter. I doubt if any of this should be taken seriously, except as an indication of how troubling some have found the Jewish rejection of that brutal, frivolous, and demeaning manifestation of paganism, Greek athletics. There is also an irony in the naming of modern Jewish sports clubs and competitions after the Maccabees, who had done their best to stamp out such abominations.

Closer to our own time is the distinctive position of the *yeshiva bochur*, the dedicated and, where possible, full-time studier of Jewish texts and commentaries, a man whom Jews in Eastern Europe held in high esteem and who was seen as an ideal of masculinity, elevated far above the warrior gentile or even the wealthy Jewish merchant. Such a man was admired for being gentle and studious, a man of *Edelkayt*, meaning part of a nobility of goodwill, intellectuality, and spirituality (Boyarin 1997, 2, 23). He was desired by women (Boyarin 1997, 68–69) and much sought after as a husband and as a son-in-law, even though he might well in many cases be unable either to protect or provide for his wife and numerous children. A wealthy man would see it as an honor for his daughter to marry such a man (Telushkin 1992, 42) and would willingly support him while he devoted himself to study. His wife might well accept that it was her duty to work outside and maintain him and the children, should that prove necessary. A wealthy Jewish peasant would defer to a poor scholar, and those ignorant men who worked without studying were seen within the community as "like women" (Boyarin 1997, 162). His was a masculine role by definition, rather like that of a priest, since women were not permitted such forms of study. Unlike the priest, he was expected to marry and have children, and indeed that marriage might be his means of support (Boyarin 1997, 146, 329). Like the Roman Catholic priest, he abjured weapons, but unlike the priest, he could be legitimately desired by a woman. The importance for the present argument is that this pale, slender, utterly sedentary man, his back bent by incessant study, stands in contrast to the manly warrior and sportsman and is an alternative masculine ideal to that of the rude gentiles (Boyarin 1997, 85). However, this very contrast, this very opposition, was bound to lead to jokes, once Jews were drawn out of their secluded communities into a wider world whose ways were different and tried both to adapt and yet to remain true to their own different, distinctive, and authentic tradition.

In modern America such a man may seem to be a rather unexciting marriage partner, and American fathers-in-law may not be so keen on supporting a husband who devotes himself entirely to the study of Torah.

> Mr. Shwartz goes to meet his new son-in-law to be, Sol. He says to Sol (who is very religious), "So nu, tell me Sol my boy what do you do?"
> "I study the Torah," he replies.
> "But Sol, you are going to marry my daughter, how are you going to feed and house her?"
> "No problem," says Sol. "I study Torah and it says G-d will provide."
> "But you will have children, how will you educate them?" asks Mr. Shwartz.
> "No problem," says Sol. "I study Torah and it says G-d will provide."
> Mr. Shwartz goes home, and Mrs. Shwartz, his wife, anxiously asks what Sol is like.
> "Well," says Mr. Shwartz, "he's a lovely boy. I only just met him and he already thinks I'm G-d."
> (http://www.hashkafah.com/index.php?/topic/804-son-in-law/30th July 2003; accessed February 16, 2010)

> Jewish Personal Ad
> Sincere rabbinical student, 27. Enjoys Yom Kippur, Tisha B'av, Taanis Esther, Tzom Gedaliah, Asarah B'Teves, Shiva Asar B'Tammuz. Seeks companion for living life in the "fast" lane. POB 90. (These are the names of the days on which Orthodox Jews are expected to refrain from eating.)
> (Seventeen Jewish Singles Ads 2005)

SPORT AS GOYISHE NACHES

In America, the Jews were initially able to retain a proper dislike of and distance from sporting activities and see them as *goyishe naches,* as part of the inferior pastimes and enthusiasms of the gentiles, but their children often gave in to the allure of the American sporting life and assimilated. Frommer and Frommer (1995) cite an amusing anecdote of the tension between a father's Jewish rejection of sports as pointless and tedious and a small boy's wish to watch the local baseball team, Brooklyn's artful Dodgers.

A little boy gets his father to take him to a baseball game. The Dodgers.
The father is sitting in the street afterwards. Someone asks, "Alex, how was your day?"
"Oysgematter farloiener tog." (An exhausting wasted day.)
(Frommer and Frommer, 1995, 86)

Some little American Jewish boys of all ages came to feel that it was not enough that their people were America's biggest winners of Nobel prizes. These included the prankster Richard Feynman, who made fun of frat boy masculinity and wrote, "I was never good in sports. I was always terrified if a tennis ball would come over the fence and land near me, because I could never get it across the fence—it usually went about a radian off where it was supposed to go" (Feynman 1986, 33). (A radian is the angle subtended at the center of a circle by an arc equal to the circle's radius. The humor lies in the tennis players' inability to understand what a radian is.) The builders of America's first nuclear weapons, who contributed rather more to the defense of America than tennis players, were largely Jewish, including J. Robert Oppenheimer, who loathed athletics (Bird and Sherwin 2006). You can't fight a war with tennis balls; even Henry V knew that. But all this was not enough for the Americanized youngsters. There had to be Jewish sports heroes, too. Accordingly, encyclopedias of Jewish sportsmen were produced that included anyone with a vaguely Jewish name, who had a Jewish great-grandparent, or who had been a sports manager or entrepreneur (Gurock 2005, 1–4). That such books of banal cheering should have been published at all shows how great the deformation of Jewish culture by the American cult of sports has been. Far more important than these mere lists is the detailed scholarly work done on Jews and sports in America that shows how contentious a question it was with Americanized rabbis who wanted to be regular guys who played baseball and called their more traditional colleagues "nerdy fellows"; the latter in their turn saw Jews who took part in sports as crass, vulgar betrayers of Jewish tradition with its veneration for things of the mind and sacred learning (Gurock 2005, 11–12, 58).

In central Europe in the late nineteenth and early twentieth centuries, the situation was far more unpleasant than mere spats between rabbis, and far more was at stake, since the political anti-Semites used the lack of Jewish sporting prowess as one more weapon in their vicious campaign of racial hatred. The Jews were called effeminate and degenerate (Weininger 1906, 304–19; see also Oring 1984, 110–12), and this accusation was used as a weapon by their political enemies. This hatred spurred both the formation of Jewish sports clubs like Hakoah (which also had an orchestra) in Vienna, in a vain attempt by the Jews to be better liked, and also the beginnings of Zionism, the wish to have a state of their own, far away from this threatening madness. Theodor Herzl and Max Nordau wanted a new breed of "muscle-Jews." The Jews of the Teutonic lands wanted to be accepted into the dueling corps from which they were excluded (Gurock 2005, 29–31; Oring 1984, 107) so that each might have a *Schmisse*, a scar on the face, like those inevitably given to German officers in British cartoons, and to have an equal right to be murdered in a duel (Frevert 1995).

TOUGH JEWS: THE JEWISH GANGSTER

There persists in American Jewish jokes an image of the Jews as not combative. This was also a part of how big-city Irish and later Polish hooligans saw the Jews. They thought they could go into Jewish neighborhoods with impunity and beat up Jewish immigrants and their children, sometimes for amusement, sometimes as an expression of Roman Catholic bigotry (Bayor 1978; R. Cohen 1998, 41; also see Frommer and Frommer 1995, 7, 33–34, 91) until the rise of the Jewish gangsters who drove the "Micks" out (R. Cohen 1998, 54; Rockaway 1993, 215–22). These Jews were violent mobsters and utterly ruthless murderers—not just the organizers and accountants of crime, but hit men and contract killers, though in fairness some Orthodox Jewish gangsters tried not to kill on the Sabbath (R. Cohen 1998, 65–66; Rockaway 1993, 148). There were more all-day gunfights in New York than there had ever been in Tombstone. The Jewish criminals were *schtarkers* (extreme toughs), who were employed to beat up and break the arms and legs of those who refused to fall in line with the gangsters' wishes, and *schlammers* (violent strike breakers), who would intervene forcibly in labor disputes. Much of the organized crime involving rackets, prostitution, alcohol, drugs, and gambling in America from the 1880s to the 1940s was in the hands of such tough Jews as Arthur "Dutch Schultz" Flegenheimer, Benjamin "Bugsy" Siegel, Arnold

Rothstein, Louis "Lepke" Buchalter, Abner "Langer" Zwillman, Morris "Moe" Dalitz, Hymie "Nigger Hymie" Altman, and Meyer "the little man" Lansky; they were easily the equals of the leaders of the Italian American Mafia. However, whereas for the Mafia crime was a way of life for entire families and they stayed in the business, the Jewish gangsters could see for themselves that violent crime was un-Jewish; they kept their work well away from their families and like other Jewish parents made sure their children went into legitimate professions (R. Cohen 1998, 150–53; Rockaway 1993, 188–203). After World War II, the Jewish gangsters faded away (R. Cohen 1998, 241; Rockaway 1993, 248), and many Jews now find their previous preeminence difficult to believe (R. Cohen 1998, 130). Before 1950, there were many films involving Jewish gangsters, but after that the films only had Jewish actors playing Italian gangsters (R. Cohen 1998, 154, 258).

The Jewish jokes about Jewish gangsters are very different from the general American ones (Bonfanti 1976) about their Italian counterparts.

> Sam "Killer" Kaplan, a hit man for Murder Inc., a notorious Jewish gang which operated in the Brownsville section of Brooklyn in the 1930s, was caught in a crossfire during a gang war. Severely wounded, he managed to escape and crawl the three blocks to his mother's house. Barely able to climb the stairs and bleeding profusely, he used all his strength to bang on the door. "Mama," he cried, "it's me, Sammy. I'm hurt bad!"
> "Sit down and eat," his mother said. "Later we'll talk."
> (Novak and Waldoks 1990, 71; see also Rockaway 1993, 1, 190, 203, 208).

> A rabbi had a brother who was a gangster, with whom he was not on speaking terms.
> One day they met in the street. "Why won't you talk to me?" said the gangster. "My brother is a rabbi. It's your brother who's a gangster." (Rockaway 1993, 212)

GOYISHE NACHES AND PEACEABLE JEWS

The memory of the Jewish gangsters has faded. The jokes based on the comic image of Jews not fighting have flourished:

> In this country Jews don't fight. I don't know if you noticed that. In this country they almost fight. Every Jew I know *almost* killed somebody. They'll all tell you that. "If he had said one more word . . . he would've

been dead today. That's right. I was ready. One more word.... What's the word? Nobody knows what the word is." (Mason 1989)

"I'm not the heroic type really. I was beaten up by the Quakers." (Woody Allen in *Sleeper*, 1973; cited by Telushkin 1992, 52)

"Swimming is not a sport. It's just not drowning." (Woody Allen quoted by Dershowitz 1991, 42)

Two Jews are walking through a rough part of town when they see two tough looking *schwartzers* (blacks) coming the other way.
"We'd better get out of here," says one to the other. "There are two of them, and we're alone." (Told to me by a Jewish Chicago economist in 2003. For another version, see Telushkin 1992, 77.)

In addition to the Jewish jokes about the Jewish abstention from sports and fighting, there is an extensive Jewish humor about the supposed Jewish distaste for and fear of adventure and the outdoor life, as seen in such compilations as *The Jewish Adventurers' Club* (Selitz et al. 1987) and *The Book of Jewish World Records* (Burns and Weinstein 1978). It is Jewish self-mockery, but it is also a mockery of central American myths such as the rugged frontiersmen, the cowboy, and the deer hunter. It is a humor contrasting the life of the "nice Jewish boy" in the city suburb with that of the ragged, uncivilized, and "bad" but also envied and iconic Huckleberry Finn on the Mississippi type of boy in a way that mocks both of them (Cooper 1996, 94; West 1961).

Our comedian Jules Farber recalls once going with his Uncle Shermie to the movies to see a Western:
I went one time to the movies with him—a western. With a scene—you know the scene? Morning, first thing in the morning. The gunslinger gets up. The gunslinger rubs his beard. The gunslinger takes out his razor. And he strops his razor, he gives himself a lovely shave, and again he rubs his beard. He rubs his beard, and he wipes his face, and he wipes his razor. He finishes wiping the razor, he takes his coffee pot, he goes to the stream, he fills the coffee pot with water from the stream, he collects twigs, with the twigs he makes fire, on the fire he makes coffee, he drinks a cup of coffee, he sloshes out the grinds, he finishes sloshing out the grinds, and he pours himself a second cup, he drinks the second cup—
And my Uncle Shermie yells out. "Nu und pisin darft m'nisht?"
(And he doesn't have to piss?)
(Markfield 1974, 128)

There's a term for the joy that a parent feels upon seeing their child sail off by themselves onto the open seas, knowing they won't see them again for more than a year—if ever. And that term is *goyishe naches* (gentile pride and satisfaction). Sure, it's not the same type of *goyishe naches* that comes from shooting a deer and tying it to the bonnet of your pickup truck, or having its head stuffed and mounted on the wall of your lounge-room. It's not even quite the same as the type of *goyishe naches* that comes from competing in motorsport, bungee jumping, setting a record for eating more hotdogs than anyone else, owning an extremely loud hi-fi, or drinking two dozen bottles of beer in less than an hour. No, this is more like the *goyishe naches* that comes from one's child endangering their life in order to climb to the top of Mt. Everest. Oy vey, don't get me started on that one. Real *naches* [joy] does not come from any of these meshugah [crazy] activities—it comes from seeing your child accepted into medical school. Now that's real Yiddishe naches! (Izzy 2009; a letter from Australia, another country with a myth of the outback and the sportsman)

It is clear that the American Jewish jokes about Jewish men, like the jokes about Jewish women, stem from the contradictions between "the American way" of sporting prowess, outdoor adventures, and unrestricted individual choice of marriage partner, which is taken for granted by most Americans, and a contrasting set of Jewish traditions. Most American Jews want both, but this not only fails to make the contradictions go away but leads to even more jokes. It is futile to speculate as to the feelings of those who tell and invent the jokes. There may well be among their number men and women who are anxious, angry, complacent, delighted, resigned, defensive, combative, optimistic, or depressed in the face of these contradictions, but we cannot know which, if any, predominates; there is always among jokers a great diversity of feeling, and these are not even constant or consistent for the individual. It is pointless to speculate, and it is quite wrong to use an intuition about how people feel as an explanation for why their jokes take the form they do. At the actual time of joking, the dominant feeling is one of amusement at an incongruity, the incongruity of living in two worlds that do not neatly fit together. How this relates to more serious reflection is impossible to say. Jewish jokes are an observable social fact, and so are the social contradictions. The humor scholar's task is to try to discern how these two are related, and that is all.

What is also now clear is how the Jewish jokes are related to the universal set of jokes about the stupid and the canny discussed earlier. Jewish jokes about Jews provide a very large proportion of all canny jokes, and many of the others show signs of Jewish origin (Davies 2002). Chelm apart, there are very few jokes about Jews being stupid. In Jewish humor, that quality is usually reserved for the gentile with his *goyishe kop,* his big gentile head, which is not overloaded with brains. It is contrasted with *Yiddishe kop,* the Jewish head (Patai 1977, 287), with its greater capacity for cerebration and for *saichel,* whether the latter is defined as deep insight or as prudent common sense.

> Professional Jewish athlete, winner of Davis Cup, America Cup, Stanley Cup. Seeking non-Jewish woman. Goyishe Cup. POB 58.
> (Jewish Personal Ads 1996)

The Jewish athlete who has won all the prizes is now looking for an appropriate woman to go with his gentile achievements, one who is not Jewish and will have a Goyishe Cup (*kop*), a gentile head, as stupid as his own

> Until I was 15, I didn't realize that "stupid" and "Goyim" (gentiles) were two different words. (UCBFA; collected by Bob Klass from a Jewish informant who first heard it in 1961)

It was postulated earlier that the qualities of those who figure in jokes about the canny would be the opposite of those we find in those who are the butt of stupidity jokes. The butt of stupidity jokes are athletes and those whose power is based on force, and these are the very roles which Jewish men, at least in Jewish jokes, strongly avoid. Likewise, the dumb blonde is nothing but a body and represents sex without thought; in Jewish jokes, Jewish women are constructed as the opposite of this, as thought without sex. Things physical, the things of the body, are the opposite of the things of the mind, which are so respected by Jews. We are back where we began. Likewise, jokes about the "stupid" often also show them as lacking in self-control or a proper sense of self-preservation. They lack not only brains but *saichel,* sense, insight. By contrast, Jewish jokes about Jewish women and Jewish men show them as, by gentile standards, too self-controlled, and not willing to take unnecessary physical risks; men who revel in physical danger that has no deeper purpose are depicted in Jewish humor as foolish and irrational. These points can be emphasized by returning to the earlier analysis of jokes about occupations, which showed that it is those whose tasks bind them to the world of earth and of things who are to be found in stupidity jokes.

JOKES ABOUT JEWISH OCCUPATIONAL PREFERENCES

The collection of jokes I compiled about my own people, *Welsh Jokes* (Davies 1978), included this joke:

> A Welshman was shipwrecked at sea and marooned on a desert island.
>
> When a passing vessel picked him up five years later, the crew were amazed to find his little island covered in fine buildings that he had built himself.
>
> With pride the Welsh Robinson Crusoe took the captain round the island and pointed out to him his house, workshop, electricity generator, and two chapels.
>
> "But what do you need the second chapel for?" asked the captain.
>
> "Oh, that's the one I don't go to," he replied. (Told to me by my father in 1976)

Later, I discovered that there existed a very similar Jewish joke (Spalding 1973, 255; see Dershowitz 1991, 269) and wrote a commentary pointing out that both individual Welsh Nonconformist chapels and synagogues were characterized by argumentative democracy and were in consequence at times quarrelsome and fissile in a way that would not be possible within the more hierarchical religious institutions that defined other nations (Davies 1986, 78). The joke and my comparison were then seized upon by that great expert on Jewish humor, Rabbi Joseph Telushkin (1992, 20), who commented on how the Welsh and the Jewish versions differed, writing:

> Although the joke's essence and punch line are virtually the same in the Welsh and Jewish versions, there is one important difference. In most Jewish versions when the man is rescued all he has built is a hut and two simple synagogues ("the one where I pray and the one I wouldn't set foot into"). On the dozens of occasions I have heard this joke told, the marooned Jew never puts up a workshop or constructs an electricity generator. Had such details been inserted the joke would no longer have sounded plausible, because in the Jewish self-image, Jews are lawyers, doctors, accountants and businessmen, not Robinson Crusoes or Mr. Wizards. And yet the Welshman's behavior corresponds exactly to what Jews expect of non-Jews.

Having spent much of my youth wandering alone in the wilder and rockier parts of Wales with a geological hammer and a chisel, hunting the elusive trilobite, I had always assumed that this was what people did on desert islands and that Jews would be much the same. Indeed, Hyman Rickover would have brought from the shipwreck a means for generating a strong magnetic field. But I can now see that, like my fellow-countrymen generally, I am a creature of the rocky wilderness with a weakness for its down-to-earth pleasures, the outdoor *goyishe naches* of the geologist. By contrast, the Jewish self-image excludes such employments and exalts the canny lawyers, accountants, and businessmen who use their minds and do not work with things. A predominantly bourgeois Jewish American population has invented jokes about an alleged Jewish aversion to and disdain for manual work, and this humor is central to the wonderful monologues of the comedian Jackie Mason:

> Let me tell you something; there's not a Jew in this world who can do anything with his hands. It's a well-known fact. And why? Because a Jew was raised never to use his hands to do anything but turn a page. To this day, a Jew can't fix a car. If a Jewish car breaks down, it's all over. He can't do anything. Watch a gentile car break down. In two seconds he's under the car, on top of the car, it becomes an airplane. A Jewish car breaks down, you hear the same thing:
>
> "It stopped."
>
> And the wife says, "It's your fault."
>
> The husband has an answer: "I know what it is. I know what it is. It's in the hood."
>
> The yenta says, "Where's the hood?"
>
> "I don't remember."
>
> Takes a Jew three hours to open a hood, and when he finally gets it open, he takes one look: "Boy is it busy under here!"
>
> But listen, why should a Jew know about cars? It's not his field. A Jewish kid has to be an intellectual. You find any Jewish family, and their son's a truck driver, it's already a tragedy. A Gentile family, they're proud if their son drives a truck. "Look at this, my son drives a truck." They take out pictures of the truck. "Look at this, my son drives this." But a Jew is ashamed. You ask him what his son does, he says, "He's in the trucking business."
>
> "In the trucking business? What does he do in the trucking business? Does he drive a truck?"
>
> "Drive a truck! My son!? Are you kidding? He doesn't exactly drive a truck. He controls a truck. How would it look, a truck moving by itself? He controls it. He's a controller in the trucking business!" (Mason 1989, 261–62)

THE FOUNDING OF ISRAEL: JOKES ABOUT
JEWISH PIONEERS AND SOLDIERS

The concentration of Jews in urban, commercial, and professional oc-cupations has been used against them in a hostile way by anti-Semites, from those who incited peasant pogroms in Eastern Europe, to those holding to the ideology of *Blut und Boden* (blood and soil), to Henry Ford, employer of metal bashers and sponsor of the *Dearborn Independent*. It was hostility of this kind that led the Zionist leader Theodor Herzl to want to build a Jewish state where Jews would be found in all oc-cupations. The early pioneering Jewish settlers in Palestine did the harsh physical work of clearing uncultivated land for their Jewish successors to farm; they were hewers of boulders and drainers of swamps (Oring 1981, 8). They were frontiersmen. From the very start there were repeated, unprovoked, and sometimes murderous Arab attacks on their farms and villages (Oring 1981, 11). The Jews were forced to defend themselves by forming the Palmach (platoons), an underground, commando-style militia (Oring 1981, 2) trained by Colonel Orde Wingate. They had be-come "farmer-soldiers," the old Roman ideal. There had been a complete culture change, driven by a Zionist ideology that wanted Jews no longer to be just merchants, lawyers, and intellectuals but laborers tied to the soil, farmers who worked their own land, watchmen-farmers able to defend it (Oring 1981, 9).

Out of this contrast came the distinctively Israeli *chizbat* humor that contrasted the new *sabra* (pioneer) and the old *galut* (exile, diaspora) Jewish styles, one more contradiction to joke about. The sabras and particularly the Palmach elite were seen as sturdy, bluff, simple, and straightforward men, robust and rough-edged, men of peasant mental-ity without the hang-ups of the Jewish urban intellectual. The diaspora qualities of softness, subtlety, familism, and verbosity were rejected (Or-ing 1981, 122). The Palmach were the highest form of sabra, and for many years the members of the Israeli elite were known as VASPs: *Vatik* (old-timer) Ashkenazi, *Smolani* (socialistic), *Palmachnik*.

The *chizbat* humor of the Palmach dwelt upon the incongruous contradictions of the two styles of culture and character, *galut* and *sabra* (Oring 1981, 123). An abbreviated version of Oring's figure 1 appears in table 2.

Table 2. Incongruity and Humor in Israel

SABRA	GALUT (diaspora)
Primitive	Civilized
Boorish	Cultured
Dirty	Clean
Slovenly	Disciplined
Self-assured	Sly
Terse	Rhetorical
Strong, violent	Weak, nonviolent
Unemotional	Emotional
Practical	Theoretical
Levantine	European

The Palmach was the nucleus of the Israeli army that against all odds defeated invading armies from several Arab countries in the war of independence in 1948. The Arab leaders had foolishly acted on their own false view of the Jews as the cowardly conquered ones, as mere traders who would be unable and unwilling to fight (ibn Khaldûn, 1950, 60–61, 68–69). There were further convincing Israeli victories over the Arabs in 1956, in the Six Days' War in 1967, and in the Yom Kippur war of 1973. After the Six Days' War there emerged jokes about the Jews of Israel as being invincible warriors. The Arab armies had not merely been defeated; they had been trounced and driven back, bootless and humiliated.

What is the Six Days' War? It's a weeklong festival of Jewish military art held in Arab countries. (Draitser 1994, 261)

What is the difference between the Israelis and the Italians?
The Israelis are the world's best soldiers and the world's worst waiters.

NO SPORT IN ISRAEL: THE MAINTENANCE
OF A JEWISH TRADITION

Yet all is not quite what it seems. The kibbutzim have long been in decline. They have switched back to traditional family structures, and some employ nonmembers hired for wages to do unskilled work; they are going bourgeois. Most immigrants prefer the fleshpots of Tel-Aviv to roughing it in agriculture. Sport is not important in and to Israel. Israeli soccer draws heavily on players from the Arab minority (Chabin 2005), and when the Israeli boxing champion Yuri Foreman, a *frum* (observant) rabbinical student, lived in Israel, he had to train in an Arab gymnasium with Arab sparring partners (Frosh 2009). The Israeli National Centre for Physical Education and Sport (Machon Wingate) was named after a member of the Plymouth Brethren, the British Major-General Orde Wingate D.S.O., a fervent Christian. The Machon Wingate proudly says that among its specialties and greatest achievements are sports medicine and the rehabilitation of the injured and handicapped. It provides employment for sons who have become doctors. Any decent person who gives a proper priority to the relief of human suffering and to restoring the injured to health can see that these Israeli achievements are morally superior to the frantic pursuit of Olympic medals, a drive which may well damage the body through the use of steroids, amphetamines, or hormones and even become an abuse of human rights, something that shamed the former DDR, East Germany.

> Ben Johnson (Canadian sprinter accused of taking steroids) swears it was just his birth control pills.
> (http://www.netfunny.com/rhf/jokes/88q4/bennie.html; accessed March 8, 2010)

In the 2008 Olympics, Israel came in 83rd and not that far from last, well behind countries as small as Iceland and Estonia. The great Jewish tradition of contempt for the physical and the athletic had been magnificently maintained. In Australia, such a disgraceful result would have led to an official day of national despair and the rending of tracksuits, but the Jews have more sense and the Israelis have more confidence. Hillel Halkin (2008) wrote in the *Jerusalem Post* and in the *New York Sun* about Israel's Olympic failure:

> It's all *goyishe naches*. These are two Yiddish/Hebrew words that are difficult to translate A short version of them might be: "The kind of things Jews should know better than to lose any sleep over." . . . I for one couldn't care less that my country came in 83rd.

Israelis know that what matters is having a mighty army to repel the enemy and that the antics of the "flannelled fools at the wicket or the muddied oafs at the goals" (Kipling, *The Islanders*) are a useless and foolish distraction from the demands of international conflict.

It is sometimes claimed that the "new men" of Israel have lost the old Jewish gift for self-mocking jokes, but it is not so. Israeli values and behavior are mocked with jokes about the gap between Zionist ideals and everyday reality—yet another contradiction.

> An Israeli boy went for a walk with his proud grandfather. As they passed an embankment, the grandfather pointed at it and said, "When I was young I helped to build that." A little later they came to a drainage channel. "When I was young I helped to dig that," said the grandfather. The boy looked at him in amazement and said: "Grandpa, did you used to be an Arab?" (Told to me in Israel in 1975. For a similar version see Telushkin 1992, 179; predictably his version is less "physical" than mine.)

This joke probably dates from the time after the 1967 war when Arabs from the West Bank came to work as unskilled laborers in Israel. In what sense can Israel now be called an agricultural country of pioneers? Diamonds and software are exported, and grain is bought in. Within Israel most manual tasks are carried out not by the descendants of the Ashkenazi Jews from Eastern and Central Europe, who formulated the Zionist ideology and were the early settlers, but by Israel's own Arab citizens (a fifth of the population) or by Oriental Jews, the Mizrahim, whose ancestors came to Israel in the 1950s from the Middle East and other Arab countries, often as refugees from persecution. Israel is a country where the Jewish population remains stratified by place of origin or of ancestors' origin, either directly or because the various Jewish ethnic groups are concentrated in different social classes. Israeli ethnic jokes are shaped by the existence of this hierarchy. The Ashkenazim earn on average over a third more than the Mizrahim and fill the universities and the professions. We are back to the United States, where a predominantly middle-class Jewish population jokes about construction workers.

THE STUPID AND THE CANNY

We are also now back where we started with the Jewish jokes about Jewish women as the opposite of those about dumb and recklessly promiscuous blondes and the Jewish jokes about Jewish men as the opposite of the jokes about dim athletes and stupidly 'mad' risk takers. The blonde and the athlete are merely unthinking bodies, but the distinctive and observable attributes of the Jews are intelligence, acumen, and a considered self-control, and self-preservation. It is mind over matter. The Jewish jokes about men and women are one more version of the Jewish jokes about clever, canny, unstupid Jews.

The bulk of the Jewish jokes about Jewish women and men have come out of the United States; like most Jewish jokes they are the jokes of a distinctive people, rightly proud of their distinctiveness, living among a majority population whose ways are different from their own traditions and which holds out the seductions of assimilation. No other group has lived so long with a foot in two social worlds and understood both of these worlds and the contradictions between them with such clarity and with so much explicit analysis and fierce arguments. In few other groups is the question 'what does it mean to be us?' asked so often and so intensively. A strong awareness of such contradictions has led to the celebrated Jewish tradition of inventing and telling self-mocking jokes.

Here American Jewish jokes about Jewish women have been analyzed in terms of the contradiction between the duty to marry within the community on the one hand and American individualism and the concomitant American myth of free romantic choice of partner on the other. For the Jewish jokes about Jewish men, it is the contradiction between the American obsession with sport and the outdoors, something required for full acceptance into America, and the traditional Jewish disdain for sport that is important, as is an allied contradiction rooted in the Jewish respect for things intellectual in a fiercely egalitarian and populist country where these are often not properly valued (Hofstadter 1964). Jews in America today are entirely American and live alongside other religious and ethnic groups in mutual and equal regard and respect, something that was lacking in the past (Gurock 2005, 189). This has made no difference to the flourishing of the jokes. The jokes of exclusion have become the jokes of inclusion, but inclusion brings with it new contradictions to laugh about.

-●

FOUR

Sex between Men

PLACES, OCCUPATIONS, AND CLASSES

The subject of the analysis that follows is not sex jokes as such, nor even gay men as a target of jokes, but the targets of jokes told about ethnic, occupational, and other social groups and classes portrayed as taking part in or having a preference for sex between men and particularly anal sex. These groups include Greeks, the citizens of Qazvin and Idlib, soldiers in remote outposts, sailors, prisoners, boys in single-sex boarding schools, aristocrats, monks, and priests. One very frequent common factor is that the butts of the jokes are men living in temporary but lengthy isolation from women.

Very similar kinds of ethnic and occupational jokes are told about lonely shepherds and sheep. By coincidence, this conjunction matches the linked condemnation of both sodomy and bestiality, "the detestable and abominable crime of buggery with man or beast." Both are seen as defying and breaking down the fundamental categories of human existence and of the story of the creation, namely, human and animal, male and female (Davies 1982, 1983). This is one of the main sources of the condemnation of homosexual behavior and in consequence of prejudice against gay men. It is reinforced by the biblical (Romans 1:26–27) and theological (it has no support from biology) view that sexual contact between two men or between two women is "unnatural," since it defies the "design" and "purpose" of the sexual organs, cannot possibly lead to

154

procreation, and frustrates the natural order that God created and His purposes. The other source of prejudice that is relevant to any explanation of the jokes is an obsession on the part of many men with masculine dominance, which leads them to despise a man who has sex with other men as a kind of traitor to the ruling sex. He could have enjoyed its special prestige and privileges, but he willfully chose to be "inferior," particularly if he is a "pathic," a "pogue," a catamite, who passively allows himself to be penetrated. Even in those cities in ancient Greece at times when homosexual relations were tolerated, it was not regarded as proper for an adult male citizen to play the passive role, for this was seen as a crime, not against heterosexuality but against masculinity (Halperin 2002).To be penetrated was to be dominated, a fundamental transgression, the mark of giving up the struggle to be masculine and lapsing into shamelessness. Only boys, slaves, or foreigners, those who lacked the status of full citizen, might allow themselves to be penetrated and become "as women." The jokes that follow can only be fully understood if these sources of disapproval of homosexual behavior are kept in mind. Here, though, our main concern will be to discover how and why jokes about sex between men got pinned upon a number of very disparate groups and to see what common qualities these groups have.

JOKES OF PLACE AND ETHNICITY

Many places and nations have been made the subject of jokes about their homosexual proclivities, such as the peoples of Central Asia in the former Soviet Union (Hellberg 1985, 95), the inhabitants of Fujian province in China during the later years of the Ming dynasty (much to the disgust of the Jesuit missionary Matteo Ricci), the citizens of Qazvin in Iranian jokes and those of Idlib in Syrian jokes (Whitaker 2006, 205).

> Why do birds fly over Qazvin using only one wing?
> Because they are using the other to protect their ass. (Told to me in 2000 by an Iranian when travelling past Qazvin in Iran on a bus)

> Why did they take pictures of the backside of the moon?
> On public request from Central Asia. (A Radio Yerevan joke from Soviet times; Hellberg 1985, 95)

In the western world such jokes are mainly told about Greeks. Indeed, the slang of many European languages uses "Greek" as a synonym for anal sex, sometimes euphemistically, sometimes insultingly, as in "doing it the Greek way" or "Greek love." In circumstances where the English will vigorously tell someone to go away by saying, "Bugger off," the French will say, *"Allez se faire foutre* (or *voir* or *mettre*) *chez les Grecs,"* go and fuck like the Greeks.

Prostitutes advertising anal sex, whether gay or heterosexual, often use the word *Greek* in their advertisements, and this in turn leads to humor.

Anglo-German G/M 29 seeks North African for Greek passive/French active. Translator provided. Eric 211-3344. (Curzon 2006, 80. G/M is gay male. For similar examples of putatively genuine gay and kinky sex advertisements used as humor, see Bracewall, Livingstone, and Debbault 2007; Forney 2008.)

The supposed preference of Greek men for anal sex with their girl-friends (virgins in front and martyrs behind) and wives is also a source of jokes.

The Greek bride was so confused she didn't know which way to turn. . . . Her husband was indifferent (Legman 1982, 2:78; told by a nightclub comedian in Florida in 1945)

Sex between men is no more common in Greece than in other countries, and indeed there is more disapproval of it in a country like Greece, where the Greek Orthodox Church enjoys something close to a religious and moral monopoly, than in more secular parts of Europe. Europe's other Greek Orthodox country, the Republic of Cyprus, was the last state in Europe to decriminalize sodomy, which was referred to in their criminal code as having "carnal knowledge against the order of nature." The Cypriots scrapped this law very reluctantly in 1998 because doing so was one of the conditions of their being granted membership of the European Union. Earlier the Greek Cypriots had been unwilling to drop their laws against sex between men, even when a gay activist, Alexandros Modinos, had won a case against his own government in the European Court of Human Rights in 1993. The ECHR judges declared almost unanimously that the very existence of such a law infringed Modinos's human rights. The only exception was Georghios Pikis, the Greek Cypriot judge in the ECHR, whose rambling, dissenting judgment runs to several pages of absurd legal hair-splitting (*Modinos v Cyprus,* judgment April 22, 1993).

Archbishop Chrysostomos, the head of the Greek Church, regularly denounced homosexuality as immoral and wanted it kept illegal. In Greece itself, levels of hostility toward and discrimination against gay men and lesbians are far higher than in most other EC countries; in this respect, the Greeks take a very backward position indeed.

Nonetheless, jokes about gay Greeks proliferate, and young Greek men complain about being propositioned by gay foreigners both abroad and in their own country. For the latter, Greek gayness is not just a joke but a stereotype to be acted on, despite being quite untrue of modern Greeks. Such jokes about Greeks are common in both North America and Europe.

> What do you call a Greek faggot?
> Andros, Miklos, Vassilis, Giorgos, Manos, or just plain "Hey, you!"
> (Wilde 1978, 53)

Larry Wilde's collection of jokes about "queer" Greeks is accompanied by a cartoon of two well-endowed Greek women in trousers whistling at a group of embarrassed modern Greek soldiers wearing a caricature version of the Evzone soldier-dancer skirts and petticoats and pompomed shoes (Legman 1982, 2:78).

> How do you define a Greek gentleman?
> A man who goes out with a girl for at least three months before propositioning her brother. (Quercy and Korsak 1993, 260; my translation from the French)

> What is a Greek tragedy?
> Hemorrhoids. (Quercy and Korsak 1993, 261; my translation from the French)

The comic image of the Greeks as great indulgers in sex with other men comes not from the observed behavior of modern Greeks but rather from a knowledge of the literature of the ancient Greeks, a key part of elite education in the past in both Europe and America. The contemporary Iranian jokes about Qazvin have a similar origin, for the town was the home of the fourteenth-century Persian poet Ubayd-i Zākāni, who wrote ribald homoerotic verse. Greek classical literature and its study were until the early twentieth century the main context in which homosexual behavior and relationships were fully described and discussed as something ordinary and sometimes even acceptable and praiseworthy, rather than wicked or pathological, although this view was often kept within the decent obscurity of the classical languages. Likewise, overt images of homosexual acts appeared on items of ancient Greek art in museums and private collections, though much of it was hidden away from the general public (Dover 1978, 118–19; Wallace, Kemp, and Bernstein 2007). For gay men or for those who indulged in same-sex practices at elite boarding schools for boys, ancient Greece provided one of the few available justifications for what they did. Greek authors offered an idealized version of male friendships, relationships, and behavior (Grosskurth 1964, 34; Symonds 1975, 11, 17–18, 64; see also Burke 2008, 117–28; Houlbrook 2005, 204) for those whose own sex lives were far from platonic. Hellenism was the only respected alternative to that of the Christian religion with its Hebraic antecedents, and offered a rare moral escape (Dowling 1994, 78; Rosario 1997, 103–104, 111) from the relentless condemnation by religion, law, and social prejudice of "sodomitical practices" of any kind, regardless of the nature of the relationship between the parties concerned or the context in which they occurred. Likewise, in a world that despised homosexuals as effeminate "pansies" and "nancy boys," the literature of the ancient Greeks provided alternative accounts of them as manly and athletic comrades (Dowling 1994, 78–9, 130; Grosskurth 1964, 267) and as masculine warriors, such as the sacred band of Thebes, supposedly made up of gay lovers (Symonds 1975, 29, 41). The ancient Greek city-states were in fact very varied, and their customs changed over time, so that accounts of them as gay-friendly can be disputed, but that is beside the point. What is important is that they were believed to be so by many of those who studied the literature and the art of the Classical period in Greece (Rosario 1997, 103–104, 111) and that this view was widely known.

SEX WITH MEN FOR MEN WITHOUT WOMEN

In order to understand jokes about same-sex activities, it is necessary to stress that the proportion of committed homosexuals among men is low, being only about 1–3 percent of the male population in Britain, the United States, France, and Norway. These are men who identify themselves as homosexual or who seek out other men for sex even when female partners are available. However, the proportion of men in both Britain and the United States who have at some time had sexual contact with another man is greater, perhaps 6–9 percent, which is three times as many (Laumann et al. 1994, 283–314; Wellings et al. 1994, 183–216). These are very uncertain and approximate figures, since homosexuality is not a simple attribute but has to be viewed in terms of complicated patterns of desire, behavior, and identity that cannot be easily reduced to a single number. In the United States, only 2.0 percent of the men in Laumann et al.'s 1994 sample referred to themselves as homosexual and 0.8 percent as bisexual. Only 2 percent said that they had had only other men as sex partners (and no female partners) in the last year, and a mere 0.6 percent said that since puberty they had only had sex with men and boys and never with women. By contrast 9 percent of the men in Laumann's 1994 sample reported some same sex activity since puberty. In the Wellings et al. 1994 British sample, just over 1 percent of the men reported having had any homosexual partners or genital contact with other men in the past five years, but 5–6 percent reported having had same-sex experience at some time.

One likely reason for the much higher figure for those who are not involved in same-sex activities but who have some experience of them is that these men had an extended period in their lives when they were separated from the company of women for geographical, institutional, or social reasons (Laumann et al. 1994, 291; Wellings et al. 1994, 204). They may well have been living in a single-sex total institution (Goffman 1968), which is the opposite of family life (Davies 2000), one where the same group of men or boys must spend twenty-four hours of the day together. It is a context where one might expect some of them to find a male sexual partner, until such time as they can return to women, what has been termed facultative or situational homosexuality (Richardson 1981, 17). It may happen in a geographically isolated military base, among those employed on a distant construction site or logging operation, on a ship at sea, or in a prison (Laumann et al. 1994, 291), monastery, or single-sex boarding school (Wellings et al. 1994, 204–206).

> Two sailors are talking aboard ship.
> "You know," says one, "the best tail I have ever had was right here on this ship."

"No shit?"

"Well, not really enough to matter." (Brottman 2004, 81)

An ex-sailor and his son entered a saloon.

Son: "Golly, look at the fanny on that blonde."

Father: "Cut that out. . . . Wow, look at the can on that bartender."
(Elgart 1973, 65)

The sailors' alleged habit of alternating between a girl in every port and a shipmate in every porthole has gives us the comic saying "Ashore it's wine, women, and song. Aboard it's rum, bum, and concertina" (Melly 1978, 5) and the comic greeting "Hello sailor!" a parody of a pickup line used by gay "sea queens" cruising the ports looking for "seafood," "fishy franny," sailors in tight bell-bottoms (Melly 1978, 65).

Bumper sticker: "Love the Navy. Eat a Sailor" (Mr. J. 1984, 169).

DOMINANCE AND SUBMISSION

A common assumption of the jokes about sex between men who are isolated from women is that these men want penetrative sex and seek to get it, but they are unwilling to be penetrated. The convention in such jokes is that the catamite, the passive "feminine" receiver, whether orally or anally, is either coerced or tricked into taking this position, sometimes as the price of having been, albeit unknowingly, the active one earlier. Only the victim is humiliated and reduced to being female.

Gold miner comes to Alaska. He's lookin' around a nice bar, says, "Hey, this is nice, good drinks, good food."

Bartender says, "Yes, why don't you go down about four hundred yards and go to the left. There's a little creek there. You can pan a little bit of gold there."

He says, "Oh, great." He goes over there. Sure as hell, he hits a bunch of nuggets. Comes over, says, "Hey, you people are fantastic. Here I get a whole bunch of gold."

He says, "Oh, that's not bad."

"But tell me one thing. What do you guys do for women around here?"

He says, "Women? Oh no, I'm sorry. We don't have any."

He says, "Well, okay. Are you sure there's nothing?"

"Well, we got the barrel over there with a knothole in it."

He says, "Whaddya do?"

He says, "Well you take the rag out of the knothole and put your thing in there till you're contented."

He says, "Alright." So he goes over there, pulls the thing out. Does it a bit. He's humpin' away. "Hey this is great. How often do I get to do this?"

"Every day except Thursday."

He says, "Why Thursday?"

"That's your night in the barrel."

(UCBFA File Jokes American V H6; collected by Bryan Arellanes, 1994. In the same file are many similar jokes with varied settings. It is recorded in 1971 as having been being told in 1947 in the Alameda Fire Department about a new convict in San Quentin and in 1985 about the army. See also Legman 1982, 2:165–66 for a version told in New York in 1938.)

After a week on board the new bosun asked, "What do you do for sex on this ship?"

He was told, "On Friday nights we fuck the Chinese cook for $23"

"Why does it cost so much?"

"Well the captain doesn't like it, so we slip him $10, the padre doesn't approve, so we slip him $5 and the cook doesn't like it, so we slip $2 each for four blokes to hold him down.

(Coote 1996, 27–28. For another version see Hall 1934, 90 joke 227 and Legman 1982, 2:158, where it is set in a western camp and the Chinese cook is a laundryman.)

Arse-hole rules the Navy.
Arse-hole rules the sea.
If you wants a bit o' bum,
You can fuck my chum,
But you'll get no arse from me.
Fly away, you bumble bee.
(*Rugby Songs* 1967, 141).

A king and his jester were stranded on a desert island. At the end of the first week, the king was desperate for sex. At the end of the second week, he was going crazy with frustration. At the end of the third week, he was at his wit's end.

(British, 1960s; another version in Legman 1982, 2:147; collected in Washington, D.C., in 1940)

After serving in the [Soviet] army a Chukchi comes home. His neighbors are kidding him.

"We bet you were the most stupid soldier."

"Well, no. There was one even more stupid: for two years he took me for a woman." (Draitser 1998, 85)

In these jokes there is a dominant party who penetrates and a loser who gets penetrated. Often the victim is the physically weaker party, a servant like the king's jester, the performer of traditionally female tasks such as a cook or laundryman, or belongs to a subordinate ethnic minority such as a Chinese, French Canadian, (Red) Indian, or Chukchi. Thus the direction of sexual domination in the jokes follows patterns of social domination.

The dichotomy of penetrator and penetrated is most stark in jokes set in prisons in which the use of force determines who will play the dominant role of the master and who will be humiliated by being effeminized.

> This joke is about . . . a tax lawyer that gets caught. . . . And he is thrown in jail down South . . . with this huge big guy. . . . A hardcore criminal. . . . And so he's in there and the little guy is in sitting in his bunk and the big guy comes up to him and he says:
>
> "Okay. Me and you gonna be in here a long time . . . you'd better figure something out. Are you the dude or are you the bitch?"
>
> And the little guy says, "uh . . . I'll be the guy . . . the dude."
>
> And the big guy says, "Good, get down on your knees and eat my pussy. (UCBFA 1994; collected by Toti Argue. The joke is from Hawaii. The gaps are in the original. For a French version, see Gaulet 2005, 97.)
>
> A Russian and a Chukchi are fighting on the street. A policeman approaches them:—"What is going on here?"—"We are arguing about who is the master of Chukotka (the remote peninsula, where the Chukchis come from)."—"You will continue the argument in jail," answers the police officer. Next morning the policeman asks them:—"Did you solve your issue?"—"Yes," answers the Chukchi.—"The Russian is the master, and I'm the mistress . . ." (Delfi, Dr. Huibolit, May 28, 2004; cited in Laineste 2008b and 2009, 47)

In practice, many sexual contacts in these all-male institutions will be voluntary, perhaps a mutual exchange of pleasure, perhaps affectionate, perhaps an item in a system of illicit informal trading and may not involve dominance or indeed penetration (Humphreys 1970, 150; Woog 2001, 20), but the jokes nearly all involve penetration by force or by trick. By contrast, in the many jokes about sex between Roman Catholic priests or Christian Brothers and altar boys, choir boys, and boys in church-run institutions, the jokes often describe compliance without coercion, even though the reality was often very brutal indeed. Father

Joseph James Hickey. a Newfoundland priest, organizer of the local altar boys' jamboree, was convicted in 1988 on a very large number of charges of sexually abusing these boys over decades. There was universal moral disgust with him, his fellow-abusers, and the hierarchy, and the public's anger grew as yet more priests and the cruel as well as lustful Christian Brothers of Ireland who ran the Mount Cashel orphanage were convicted of sex crimes. Yet there was a large wave of Father Hickey jokes in Newfoundland in which the boys were shown as cooperating for rewards. Within the frame of the jokes, the boys could be represented as willingly passive because they had no full male status to lose. Such jokes were already in general circulation in Boston well before the Archdiocese was overtaken by a wave of scandals involving priests and boys (P. Lewis 2006, 152–53).

> **Choirboy 1:** Hi! I have to go to confession today, and I'm a bit worried. You've known this priest a long time already. What would he give for committing sodomy?
> **Choirboy 2:** That's two chocolate bars. (P. Lewis 2006, 152)

When there is sexual violence in a jail, the perpetrators are rarely gay men but heterosexuals seeking to assert masculinity through dominance, much in the way that members of a victorious army might sodomize the prisoners of a defeated enemy. Indeed, a gay man may well become the victim of an attack and be forcibly penetrated as a way of punishing and stigmatizing him for his sexual preferences (Shilts 1993, 178–79). The driving force is the same one that led the members of the Soviet and French armies in World War II to rape the women of the countries through which they were advancing or the Pakistani soldiers to rape the women of East Bengal during the Bangladesh liberation war (Aydelott 1993). On August 21–22, 1973, Stephen Donaldson, a bisexual Quaker pacifist, was raped orally and anally sixty times in two days by forty to fifty black inmates in a prison in Washington, D.C. (Fletcher 1992, 39). Given the opportunity, these violators of men might well choose to rape women instead, since their main aim is to enjoy the exercise of brutal and arbitrary power that defines sex without consent, rather than for the sex itself.

The instances of same-sex acts given in the scriptures are of this kind as with the men of Sodom wanting to "know," i.e. forcibly to bugger, two handsome young male angels (Genesis 1:24–31, 19:1–29; Kreeft 2004, 78, 115–16, 126) or the members of the tribe of Benjamin from Gibeah wishing forcibly to sodomize a Levite (Judges 19:22–30). These are stories about dominance, as we can see from the attempt in either case to placate the men bent on sodomy by offering them desirable young women to be raped as an alternative. The attackers did not manage to rape the virgin daughters offered to them by Lot, but when the Levite's concubine was handed over to them, they abused her all night, and in the morning she died. The men's attempt at the sexual domination of other men is portrayed as the abomination of homosexuality, yet it is clear that they were indifferent as to the sex of the victim. What is shocking, but rarely remarked on, is that Lot and the Levite are quite willing to offer up their women to appease the mob. They are stories not about the protection of guests but about women being mere disposable possessions.

An imagery drawn from such assaults is employed in exchanges of quasi-humorous abuse between sailors as in "How would you like to be cornholed?" and "I'll deck ya and dick ya before you can throw me (meaning I will knock you down on the deck and stick my penis up your anus before you can wrestle me to the floor). It is a statement of the dominance of the winner of a fight over the loser, who then gets penetrated. (UCBFA; collected by Sandra Fini, 1968, from U.S. Navy World War II veteran; filed under "Retorts")

For most of those living in tough all-male institutions or indeed in the social classes from which their members tend to be recruited, to be gay is a departure from masculinity rather than heterosexuality. It has something in common with the view taken by those ancient Greeks who were tolerant of pederasts but who totally condemned the taking of a passive role by adult male citizens. Likewise, Arabs today often see only the passive role as demeaning, there being nothing shameful about those who are active (Whitaker 2006, 206). A piece of humorous Mexican folklore makes the same point.

A Mexican man's dream is to have seven wives and a faggot. (UCBFA Blason Populaire, Mexican, 1992; collected by Susan Schliesser)

Julius Caesar was widely believed to have been buggered by Nicomedes, king of Bithynia, when a young man, and there was much joking about him as the "Queen of Bithynia," and as "every woman's man and every man's woman." After Caesar's conquest of Gaul, his troops sang:

> All the Gauls did Caesar conquer. Nicomedes conquered him.
> Behold our Caesar rides in triumph, subjugator of the Gauls.
> Nicomedes had no triumph, though he triumphed over Caesar.
> (Suetonius, 121, XLIX; my translation from the Latin)

The humor at the expense of the catamite has been very widespread.

For lower-class lads, it is not same-sex contact as such that is utterly taboo but taking a passive role and being feminized or having any kind of emotional involvement with another man (Reiss 1963). They define only the passive penetrated one as homosexual and thus inferior; when they sell penetrative sex to gay men, the sellers are not in their own view acting in a homosexual way, whatever others might think. Sailors, guardsmen, and delinquents alike will sell sex to gay men who want "rough trade" with macho, straight hunks (Forth 2004, 45; Houlbrook 2005, 48, 89, 177), but only if it is impersonal and with very strict limits as to what they will do. These rules of the game are shared, learned, and handed down from older to younger "real" men and imposed on gays who wish to pick them up (Houlbrook 2005, 180; Reiss 1963, 251–72; Richardson 1981, 39). The world against which gay men are judged and condemned is not that of heterosexual family life but that of a lower-class bachelor culture of toughness, fighting, asserting dominance, hard drinking, gambling, and whoring. Jokes about gay men are rooted in these assumptions and perceptions and to that extent are the jokes of a particular social class. Sometimes the class aspect is made explicit.

> An effeminate little queer was walking to his office when he saw a brawny, muscular labourer with his shirt off, digging a hole in the road.
> He went up to him and said, "Do let's be friends."
> "Sod off," said the man in the trench.
> "Now, don't be nasty," said the little poof. "We could be such good friends, and I could teach you a thing or two."
> "If you don't clear off," said the labouring, shirtless one, "I'll come up there and stick your umbrella right up your arse."
> The little fairy was not deterred. "Oh, come on," he said, "we could have such a lovely time."
> The labourer leapt out of the trench, grabbed the umbrella out of his hand, and stuffed it up his arse as he had threatened.

"Ooooh, ooooh," cried the little nancy, "now open it slowly." (Told to me in Leeds, England, in 1970, complete with graphic gestures and a contrast of voices, one brutal and masculine, the other one piping and lisping, so that *slowly* became *thlowly*. See also Legman 1982, 2:86, 91.)

A Scouse guy is in a bar having a quiet drink alone when he's approached by a little gay camp guy who cuddles up alongside him at the bar and says, "Do you fancy a blow job?" at which point the Liverpudlian guy jumps up, takes him by the throat, knocks him to the floor, beats him unconscious, kicks him out the door, and leaves him for dead. He returns to his seat at the bar, and the barman says to him, "I don't know what he did to warrant that treatment. What did he actually say to you?" and the Scouser says, "He said something about a fucking job!" (Told in a joke booth set up in Blackpool, England, to collect jokes from the public in connection with a TV program in 2006. The main focus of the joke is the work-shy Scouser [man from Liverpool], but the image of the "little gay camp guy" looking for rough trade and coming off worst again highlights the social class dimension.)

The only group which the jokes do not tend to divide decisively into penetrators and penetrated is monks.

A visitor to a monastery was amazed to find the entire company lined up and buggering one another simultaneously. At the front of the line was Brother Anthony, who kept shouting, "Form a circle, form a circle." (British 1960s)[1]

Monks with their vow of celibacy have permanently left the world of sex with women. They have no conventional masculine status to defend, and they are expected to be peaceable. All sex breaks their rules of celibacy, and they are shown as playing both parts and even both at once in a group linked together in a daisy chain. Daisies of the world, unite; you have nothing to lose but your chains.

MEN WITHOUT WOMEN, JOKES ABOUT SHEEP

The jokes told about the same-sex sex of men working where there are no women are very similar to the extremely numerous occupational and ethnic jokes about men having carnal connection with sheep, told about the Welsh, the Scots, the New Zealanders, the Sardinians, or any other country or U.S. state (*101 Jokes about Sheep*, http://www.the-joke-shop. com/showjoke.asp?joke=1834), where sheep farming is important, or in

Greece (Orso 1979) about shepherds generally. One may even wonder who Corydon was really interested in.

An English tourist, watching an old Welsh farmer ploughing, noticed that he always left one corner of the field untouched.

He asked him why.

"Oh," said the farmer, "that's where I had my first sexual experience."

"How touching," said the Englishman. "You must have felt so proud."

"Not really," said the Welsh farmer. "It was all rather embarrassing. You see her mother was watching us the whole time."

"Good gracious!" said the Englishman, greatly shocked. "What did she say?"

"Baa-baa-baa!"

(Welsh 1990s. There are also New Zealand and Greek [Orso 1979] versions.)

The Welsh have just discovered two new uses for sheep. Meat and wool. (Welsh 1980s. There are also Vermont and Montana versions.)

How can you tell when you're at an Australian stag party?

A sheep jumps out of the cake.

How does a Welshman count his sheep?

"*Un, dau, tri,* hello, my pretty one, *pump, chwech . . .*"

(Welsh 1990s. The words in italics are the numbers in Welsh for 1, 2, 3 . . . 5, 6)

What's the difference between the Rolling Stones and an Aberdeen sheep farmer?

The Rolling Stones say, "Hey, you, get off of my cloud."

And an Aberdeen sheep farmer says: "Hey, McCloud, get off of my ewe."

(www.sickipedia.org/tag/Glasgow; accessed September 2008)

Why do Scotsmen wear kilts? So the sheep won't hear the zipper.

(http://www.scotster.com/forums/scottish-jokes-humour/Why-do-Scotsmen-wear-kilts.303.html; accessed February 16, 2010)

How do you know when a Kiwi has broken into your house?

Your Ugg boots are missing, and there's love bites on the lamb roast.

(www.kevinbloodyunloon.com/site/laughs; accessed September 3, 2008)

Ugg boots are high sheepskin boots worn by Australian and New Zealander farmers and especially sheep shearers. Many of the jokes involve the use of Ugg boots or wellies (wellington boots) to hold the sheep's back legs in place. Such boots are, as we have already seen, the occupational badge of the rustic in stupidity jokes. When discussing sex with sheep jokes, Masters (1962, 29) refers to "the American legend of the western sheep farmer in his knee boots."

Despite the jokes about sheep, most of the cases about bestiality that are reported and recorded and which have come before the Scottish and presumably Australian and New Zealand courts have involved animals other than sheep, often larger animals, and have occurred in less remote places where detection is more likely.

> "I hear Major Carruthers has been court-martialed for having sex with a horse."
> "Good Lord! A mare or a stallion?"
> "Oh, a mare, of course. Nothing queer about old Carruthers." (Told to me by a television presenter in London in the 1970s)

The ethnic jokes about sheep are again very much jokes about men in lonely and remote places where women are scarce. They are imaginative with regard to the shepherds' behavior, since their occupational isolation means that if such sex does happen, it is unlikely to be detected and reported to others.

> Why do the Welsh shag sheep on cliff edges?
> So the sheep push back harder. (Also told about New Zealand)
> (Jokes.Rellacool.co.uk; www.jokes-o-matic.com/jokes/Dont-Welsh-On-Me.html)

There is another likely reason why sheep rather than other animals feature in the jokes. A sheep is a weak and placid animal; it does not fight and struggle but goes meekly to the slaughter. Orwell uses them to represent unthinking, unresisting Communist Party members in *Animal Farm*. "Sheep-sex good, men-sex better baaaah!" "Sheep-shagging" in the jokes may well be a metaphor for sexual dominance, and the emphasis given to the way the sheep is trapped with its legs in the man's boots also suggests this. In support of this possibility, we may cite jokes in which a hunter gets buggered by a large and savage male animal, such as a moose or a bear, which have a similar narrative to some of the earlier jokes about homosexual acts. The victim is once again physically weak or a man from an ethnic minority working as a servant.

> A promising but distraught young business executive is advised to take a two-week vacation in the north woods. The company plane flies him to

Canada, where the travel agent has been alerted to prepare him the de luxe hunting trip. The agent explains to him that the key to the whole trip is the French-Canadian guide, Pierre, who paddles the canoe, baits the fish-hooks, builds the fire, cooks the food, and arranges the eiderdown sleeping bag for the executive. Then, when they reach the hunting grounds, the executive is to load his gun while Pierre makes the sound of the female moose in heat: "Be-ee-eep! Br-e-e-e-eep!" And from far away will come the reply of the male moose. "Bo-o-oop! Br-o-o-o-oooop!" coming closer and closer, until finally the bull-moose is right there, and all the executive must do is shoot him. "But what if I miss?" he asks nervously. "Oh, well," says the agent, "in that case Pierre gets fucked." (Legman 1982, 2:172; see also D'Arcangelo 1972, 73)

A guy from the city, fed up with being called a wimp, decides to go to bear hunting. He goes off into the woods, and there is the biggest bear imaginable. He puts his gun to his shoulder and shoots at point-blank range. There is a huge bang, but when the smoke clears, the bear is still there. The bear strolls over and indicates that he must kneel down and give the bear a blow job.

He is utterly humiliated and angrily goes back to the gun shop and buys a more powerful gun. Back in the woods he meets the same bear and shoots him at close range. There is a huge explosion that knocks the would-be hunter over, but when he looks up, the bear is still there. The bear signals that he must bend over, and then buggers him.

Even more angry and upset, he goes back to the gun shop and buys the biggest gun they've got. Once more he meets the same bear, takes aim, and fires. But afterwards, the bear is still there and unharmed. The bear strolls over to the terrified man and says genially: "You know, something tells me that you don't come here for the hunting." (Told to me by a Californian anthropologist in Aberdeen, Scotland, 2007; see also http://www.sodomy.org/jokes/bears.html)

It is also noticeable that in the 1980s cycle of jokes involving gay men having sex with animals, the man is the passive partner. The gerbilling or gerbil stuffing jokes that flourished briefly in America in the 1980s involved a gay man inserting a declawed gerbil into the rectum of another so that the latter could enjoy the little rodent's squirming and struggling inside him. In the background to the jokes was an absurd urban legend about gay men. Cecil Adams (1986) was sent the gullible letter below:

Dear Cecil:
While discussing a gay acquaintance recently, my friend Mary, a nurse, lauded him by adding, "And he's no damn gerbil stuffer, either."

When I protested that she should not perpetuate cruel stereotypes of our homosexual brethren, she informed me that she personally had witnessed a fellow admitted by her hospital to remove a deceased gerbil lodged in his rectum. That gentleman is now doomed to be tied to a colostomy bag through eternity.

The story is obviously nonsense, but the letter writer took it seriously. Urban legends are like jokes in that they have no authors and circulate anonymously, being polished and improved and gaining accretions. However, jokes, like the one above about the talking bear, are known to be and meant to be obvious fictions, and their sole purpose is to generate laughter. A good teller may choose to give a joke verisimilitude or may exaggerate its fantastic aspects, but will do so as a means to this end. The urban legend, by contrast, must have a certain plausibility, and some, like the letter writer above, may well believe in it, even though it has absurd elements. Many urban legends are, of course, very funny and are told for humorous effect, but this is not a necessary aspect of the legend (Bennett and Smith 1990). Most jokes do not have their origins in urban legends, nor do most urban legends give rise to jokes, but in this particular case the legend and the jokes are very likely connected.

> How can you tell if you're in a gay amusement park? They issue gerbils at the tunnel of love. (Tibballs 2005, 194, joke 988)

> What did the brown hamster say to the white hamster?
> "So, you must be new in town."
> (UCBFA 1990 file V Dirty Jokes H6; collected by Carrie Roller)

The discussion of jokes about bestiality has by chance brought us to the second reason for the strong hostility toward gays, which stems from the classifying of sex between men and sex with animals as among the abominations of Leviticus that break down the fundamental categories of human existence (Davies 1982; Davies 2002, 139–45; Douglas 1966, 53), male and female, human and animal (Leviticus 18:22–24, 20:13–16; Genesis 1:24–31). This view was later reinforced by the theological distinction between the natural and the unnatural, which is not based on detailed empirical observations of the natural world but assumes what that world is like and argues that the natural is that which conforms to its supposed purpose, in the case of sex, procreation; "unnatural vice" then becomes the worst of all possible sexual sins and is deserving of savage punishment.

SOCIAL CLASSES AND THE ENGLISH

As we have already seen, jokes about gay men and about homosexual activity tend to have a social class basis and dimension. Al Reiss Jr. (1963, 272) has noted that lower-class males are obsessed with toughness and masculinity and have a contempt for "softness" and frills, that a negative view of homosexuality is a persistent theme in lower-class culture "manifested in the institutional practice of 'baiting queers' including violence" and that they use the word *queer* as a pejorative term for individuals from a higher social class or for their upwardly mobile peers.

It is here that we can see one reason for the existence of jokes about the sexual preferences of aristocrats, though the appreciation of jokes about aristocrats is common to all the classes. The eighteenth-century French aristocrats mocked by Hogarth discussed earlier were seen as sexually ambiguous because of their effeminate refinement and elaborate concern with dress and hairstyles (Rosario 1997, 73–76). Likewise, the Austrian aristocrats Graf Bobby and Rudi, who are the butt of so many Austrian and German jokes about their stupidity, are also made out to be "queer and degenerate" (Scholten 1971, 23–24). Because aristocrats have an assured status, they are able to indulge in foppishness and to disregard the moral strictures of the populace. Those great gay comic figures, Marcel Proust's prowling Palamède de Guermantes, Baron de Charlus in *Sodome et Gomorrhe,* and Evelyn Waugh's Lord Sebastian Flyte with his teddy bear, Aloysius, and the flamboyant Oxford aesthete Anthony Blanche in *Brideshead Revisted* are all aristocratic.

There are many jokes and comic songs about the homosexual interests and activities of aristocrats,

> When Lord St. Clancy became a nancy.
> It did please the family fancy
> And so in order to protect him
> They did inscribe upon his rectum,
> "All commoners must now drive steerage,
> This arsehole is reserved for peerage."
> (*Rugby Songs* 1967, 172)

Class-based British jokes about aristocrats are popular in anti-aristocratic America and Australia, where the popular image of their own society is that of a rugged frontier or outback, a newly founded society cleansed of the pretensions, refinements, and corruptions of Europe. There is a certain irony in the men without women of the outback or frontier enjoying such jokes.

> Why are there so many queers in the British aristocracy?
> Have you seen their women? (Coote 1996, 169)

> Lady Chichester finds her husband in bed with the butler. "My Lord," she expostulates, "the least you could be is on top." (Legman 1982, 2:151)

These can become ethnic jokes and songs about the English in general.

> Australia is a wonderful place.
> It's full of great sheilas and blokes.
> The air is clear and no one's queer,
> Except in Pommie jokes.
> (In Australian English, sheilas are women and Pommies are Englishmen)
> (http://humour.bluehaze.com.au/2003_08_08.html; accessed September 4, 2009)

The precious "Pommie poofter," "shirt-lifter," and "mattress-muncher," the homosexual Englishman, as opposed to the crude, manly Australian, is a standard figure in Australian humor and has been used by Barry Humphries in his cartoon strip about Barry McKenzie (1988) and in the monologues and memoirs of the Australian diplomat Dr. Sir Leslie Colin Patterson (1985). The other side of this humor is to be seen in a section of the Monty Python *Bruces Sketch*, in which the coarse, raucous, beery members of the Department of Philosophy at the Australian University of Walamaloo, all of whom are named Bruce, greet a new British member of staff, Michael, whom they call New-Bruce:

> **Everybruce:** Australia, Australia, Australia, Australia, we love you, amen!
> **Fourth Bruce:** Crack tube! (*Sound of cans opening*) Any questions?
> **Second Bruce:** New-Bruce, are you a Poofter?
> **Fourth Bruce:** Are you a Poofter?
> **Michael:** No!
> **Fourth Bruce:** No. Right, I just want to remind you of the faculty rules. Rule One!
> **Everybruce:** No Poofters!
> **Fourth Bruce:** Rule Two, no member of the faculty is to maltreat the Abbos in any way at all—if there's anybody watching. Rule Three?
> **Everybruce:** No Poofters!!

Fourth Bruce: Rule Four, now this term, I don't want to catch anybody not drinking. Rule Five!
Everybruce: No Poofters!
Fourth Bruce: Rule Six, there is NO . . . Rule Six. Rule Seven.
Everybruce: No Poofters!!
(http://orangecow.org/pythonet/sketches/bruces.htm)

The exchanges of joking between the English and the Australians often take this form. The Australians are cast as the crude, uncultured ones, the ockers (working-class males) and the larrikins (lacking all propriety), and the English as over refined and lacking in masculinity, which in turn leads to the jokes about Pommie poofters. Masculinity, class, and national identity are all tangled together in the humor (Davies 1990, 259–70). Within conventional status hierarchies, those who are cultured have status in part because to be cultured is a mark of restraint and taste (Kuipers 2006). However, these are also conventionally female attributes, and so the men who have achieved this higher status or belong to a group that possesses it are open to jokes about their being effeminate and by implication homosexual (Kuipers 2006, 65–66). Middle-class men in Australia or in old South Wales, even men of considerable education and cultural achievement, are expected in certain circumstances to affect a degree of plebeian coarseness, to put on the airs and graces of those lower in the social scale and join their mates in a boisterous exchange of blue jokes (Oxley 1978), something that would horrify their Dutch counterparts (Kuipers 2006, 49, 52). There are two systems of power and status, one based on social class and the other on masculinity, and the jokes emerge from the contradictions between them. An awareness of yet further differences between the ways in which these two sets of social pressures are balanced in the otherwise very similar societies of Australia and Britain leads to yet further humor.

Jokes about "queer" Englishmen have also been popular in America. The extremely homophobic (Brottman 2004 and see Legman 1982, 2:55–98) Gershon Legman wrote:

The following is a British story, or one intended to mock the British, "all" of whom are considered practically homosexual at a certain level in American folklore. (This is not altogether folklore.) Two camels slowly approach each other in the desert, their riders identically dressed in excessively long Bermuda shorts and topee helmets. They pause and the riders speak (in

exaggerated British accents): "English?"—"Of cawss."—"Foreign office?"—
"Cinema photawgraphy."—"Oxford?"—"Cambridge."—"Homosesxsh'l?"
—"Certainly nawt!"—"Pit-y!"—and the two camels continue their separate
ways across the desert. (Legman 1982, 2:93; heard in London, 1954, "told
by an American and getting a great laugh from his British audience")

For Legman, American jokes such as this, told in a distinctively
American English but with British accents added, are national or ethnic jokes but exactly the same joke and told in the same way as the one
above is told by the British. However, when they tell it, the emphasis is
on social class, and it is also a joke about men without women. The accent Legman describes as "exaggerated British" will have been perceived
by the British listeners to whom the American told it not as a parody of
their own accents but as that of an English upper-class person, whose
speech patterns they themselves would have found ridiculous. Making
fun of this way of speaking is a part of the repertoire of any skilled British joke teller. An "upper-class voice" might also be pinned on gays in
a joke, since it can sound affected, prissy, and poncy. Yet Legman's joke
is also a joke about tough and masculine men crossing a desert alone
and in a situation that gives rise to many jokes about same-sex behavior
or sex with camels; there are corresponding jokes in French both about
Legionnaires in a distant desert outpost in the Sahara and about Britain's
empire builders.

> In a London club two men sat silently perusing the *Times*. After a long si-
> lence one took his courage into his hands and struck up a conversation.
> You are an officer, I take it?
> But of course.
> In India?
> Yes.
> Was your regiment stationed in Calcutta?
> Yes, indeed.
> Homosexual?
> No.
> Ah, you must be Major Macaulan of the Third Lancers.
> (Nègre 1973, 1:83, joke 179; author's translation from the French)

THE ENGLISH BOARDING SCHOOL

Curiously, many of the class-based jokes and songs come out of the homosexual under life (Goffman 1968) of the "public schools," the all-male,

fee-paying boys' boarding schools where the English elite were educated. There is a pretence that this under life did not and does not exist, but surveys show that the incidence and frequency of past homosexual experience and of genital contact is far greater among those who attended boarding schools than among those who did not (Wellings et al. 1994, 206). Likewise, the memoirs of those who attended these schools, from the historian John Addington Symonds at Harrow in the nineteenth century, to the Christian apologist C. S. Lewis (1955) at Malvern College before the First World War, down to John Peel, the disc jockey who was the victim of homosexual rape at Shrewsbury School in the 1950s (Kami 2005; Peel 2005, 41), and many other autobiographies and biographies speak of it. It often involved relationships between older and much younger boys, and could, as in other single-sex total institutions, involve affection, orgiastic reveling, as in Symonds's time at Harrow, gifts for sexual favors, or as in Peel's case coercion by older or stronger boys. There is a thorough historical account of English public school homosexuality in John R. de S. Honey's (1977, 189–96) comprehensive study, *Tom Brown's Universe*. The phenomenon should not be evaded by the use of evasive terms such as "homosocial" or "intimate male friendship"; it often involved sex.

In 1895, when Oscar Wilde was convicted of gross indecency, the moralist W. T. Stead wrote of the contrast between the "universal execration heaped upon Oscar Wilde and the tacit universal acquiescence of the very same public in the same kind of vice in our public schools. . . . Boys are free to pick up tendencies and habits in public schools for which they may be sentenced to hard labour later on."

Perhaps the best known of the anonymous comic songs that speak of pederasty and bestiality is a parody of and sung to the tune of the Eton Boating Song, a song about boys rowing on the Thames. The original version was written by William Johnson Cory, classics master at Eton and a graduate of King's College Cambridge, a college sometimes ridiculed for the supposed homosexual proclivities of its members. Some of the lines of Cory's original song have been construed as homoerotic. Cory also wrote a collection of poems, *Ionica,* many of which are pederastic in nature, and he was forced to resign under suspicion of taking part in or at least permitting homosexual behavior in the school. Given Cory's background, the parody of his song is not entirely unexpected.

I was taking a ride on a chuff-chuff [child's word for steam train].
It was crowded and I had to stand.
A little boy offered me his seat.
I reached for it with my hand....

***

For we're all queers together
And that's why we go round in pairs.
For we're all queers together
And that's why we're sneaking upstairs.

***

Oh the sexual life of the camel
Is stranger than anyone thinks.
In the height of the mating season
It tries to bugger the sphinx.
But the sphinx's posterior sphincter
Is clogged with the sands of the Nile.
Which accounts for the hump on the camel
And the sphinx's inscrutable smile.

***

For we're all queers together etc....
(*Old Alleynians Tour Song Book;* also *Hymns and Arias*)

In the songs "queer" activities are simply taken for granted as an ordinary aspect of life, as indeed they were in many boarding schools. Some even had their own school-specific slang for the older and younger partners. In Cheltenham College in 1951, the older one was called "homo" and the younger one "bij" from the French *bijou* (jewel). (UCBFA filed under Folk Speech; collected by Karen T. Melgaard in 1965 from an old boy of Cheltenham College, who told her that homosexuality was common in English public schools) Some of the bijoux seem to have been indiscreet (Redfern 2007, 9–10). Other schools had their own terms for these roles.

Even if there had been no such activities, there might well have been jokes simply because they were an all-male institution. That in itself is enough to set off jokes.

What do guys do if they drop their keys in Bowles Hall?
They have to kick them back to their rooms. (UCBFA 1998; collected by Jason Okutake from a female South Asian student at the University of California, Berkeley)

Most of the halls of residence at Berkeley are co-ed, but Bowles Hall was an all-male hall. It was rumored, without any evidence, to house a large gay population, even though the tone of this very traditional hall was aggressively masculine with its members boisterously roaring out drinking songs about girls.

THE MISSING LESBIAN JOKE

There are many jokes about lesbians, but they tend to be either sex jokes or lifestyle jokes that are not attached to any particular place, occupation, institution, or social class, and so are outside the scope of this study. Women are less likely than men to work in isolated locations or to belong to single-sex total institutions. There is a great deal of same-sex contact for the duration between women in women's prisons (Ward and Kassebaum 1966), and lesbians join the armed forces (Shilts 1993), but this has not given rise to many jokes. Jokes about sex in convents tend to be about nuns' involvements with priests or monks or nuns engaging in self-stimulation, even though many lesbian ex-nuns have written about their experiences in the convent (Curb and Manahan 1985). Although there are places and occupations with a relatively high proportion of lesbians, so far these are mentioned only in lesbian humorous writings (Jimenez 2001; Orleans 1992), though with the expansion in the numbers of jokes told by lesbians about lesbians and for lesbians (Bing and Heller 2003), this will probably change.

GAY PLACES AND EFFEMINATE OCCUPATIONS

Most jokes about places where men have sex with men, such as Greece or Qazvin, do not refer to a contemporary reality. Today, though, there are jokes about cities, areas, and resorts such as Fire Island where gay men openly live or visit in large numbers and have visible institutions and celebrations, notably San Francisco.

> Two homosexual men are sitting in a car in San Francisco. The light turns green, and the driver does nothing, so his friend says: "The light was green. Why didn't you go?"
> "Oh," he says, "I was waiting for it to turn pink." (UCBFA Gay and Lesbian jokes, J6; collected by Jason Putter 1994)

How many heterosexuals does it take to change a light bulb in San Francisco?

Both of them.

(UCBFA File Blason Populaire A4 R4; collected by Donna Arndt 1982)

How many straight San Francisco waiters does it take to change a light bulb?

Both of them. (Knott 1985, 73)

California is like a bowl of Granola.

Everything that isn't fruit or flakes is nuts. (Ascribed to Will Rogers)

There are also jokes about members of some occupations dressing too elaborately, too flamboyantly, or too effeminately, possibly in order to impress their particular circle of gay friends.

Officers' batmen often help themselves from their officer's wardrobes if they want to tart themselves up specially for some reason, but this batman might more appropriately have raided a WAAF officer's quarter because, not to put too fine a point on it, he was precious. He was careful to confine his fairy ways to his off-duty hours, but those who had seen him in some bar during these times, giggling with kindred queens, knew him to be "as ginger as a tom cat." He was waiting one evening in the corridor of the Guard Room as an RAF Service Policeman looked over his pass. He was in civvies, dressed in a figure-hugging light check suit, violet shirt, yellow tie, and green suedes. He exuded a delicate odour of sweet violets.

An airman from the flights came in—due for a "forty-eight" and as smartly turned out as only those airmen who usually do a dirty job know how to look. Uniform meticulously pressed and brasses brilliant. He was a beefy bloke and had trouble getting past the batman in the narrow passage and got a good whiff of those sweet violets. He paused and looked the other up and down and then said, quite amiably, "You ought to be wearing f. . . ing ear-rings."

The exquisite appeared shocked—"What!" he bleated. "With tweeds?"

(Dickinson and Hooper 1974, 7–8 plus cartoon, 10)

(A batman was a soldier or airman assigned to an officer as a valet and a kind of soldier servant.)

There are many interesting aspects to the joke about the batman. It is not directly about his sexual preferences, though this is mentioned, but about his departure from conventional masculine appearance, which meets social disapproval in and of itself. Not just gay transvestites but the more numerous heterosexual transvestites can in many jurisdictions get in trouble with the law, and in many social circles a man wearing ordinary male clothing, which by cut or color looks somewhat effeminate, will meet with negative comment, possibly even indignation and abuse. Masculinity and masculine appearance is compulsory; it is a "privilege" that cannot be betrayed without coming up against hostility, particularly from other men. Parents may boast of a tomboy daughter, but a son of sissified appearance or interests, whatever his sexual orientation, is in most societies an embarrassment.

> A titled lady returning home said to her butler, "James, take off my dress. James, take off my bra. James, take off my knickers, and James, don't you ever let me catch you wearing my clothes again." (British 1970s)

In this joke there is a clever switch from a script of wantonness in women to one of transvestism in men. The joke brings us to another important point, which is that men in certain occupations who are seen as effeminate and by implication gay are the subject of jokes. These are either service occupations that deal with what has been seen traditionally as women's work, such as stewards on passenger liners (Baker and Stanley 2003), male "air-hostesses, the trolley-dollies," or else jobs that cater to distinctively or conventionally female interests such as ballet dancers, ladies' hairdressers, fashion designers, florists, window dressers, interior decorators, and caterers (Woog 2001, vii). Ethnic jokes about male Chinese cooks or laundrymen, though only occasionally sexual, have something in common, since these too are seen as women's occupations. There are jokes about valets because they are the servant guardians of upper-class male correctness of dress and neatness, and these are popularly seen as suspect qualities associated with straight-acting gay men.

> Henry Kelly said on his Classic FM show that now that the *Queen Victoria* was in service with the *QEII* and the *Queen Mary* that it was the first time that three "Queens" had sailed together under the Cunard flag. This is not true, as all the steward messes in the fleet will verify. (Cunard Queens 2007)

> Why does it take two gay men to rape a girl?
> One holds her down while the other does her hair. (Knott 1985, 72).

> Two women were walking down the street when they saw two men kissing passionately

"Ugh," one woman said to the other. "That's disgusting. They ought to ship every one of those queers to some island, so we wouldn't have to look at them."

"They can't do that," the other woman said. "Then we'd all have to cut our own hair and decorate our own apartments."

(UCBFA Anglo American file, Gay and Lesbian IJ6; collected in San Francisco 2003. The claim that it was collected in San Francisco is untrue. The same joke with exactly the same wording is in Alvin 1983, 83. The chance of a joke published in 1983 being in oral circulation twenty years later is high. The chance of the wording being identical is zero.)

You know you're absolutely gay when your third-grade teacher asks you for decorating tips. (Cohen 1995, 1)

The crucial aspect is once again masculinity. There quite possibly are a disproportionate number of gay men in these "feminine" occupations and having these interests than in the general, largely heterosexual, population, but the jokes seem to have flourished more since gay men achieved a greater degree of openness and public pride. However, among gay men a regard for both conventional masculinity, as with regular outdoor guy "Bears" (Kampf 2000) and for ultra-tough masculinity as with the Leathermen (Hennen 2008) and the "muscle-beach queers," remains strong and the minority of strongly effeminate gays tend to have less status and to feel badly treated. This comes out in gay humor and particularly gay slang. In addition to the feminizing words used by straight people when joking about gays in general such as pansy, Nancy-Boy, fairy, tinker-bell, queen, faggot (from *faegele*, the Yiddish word for a little bird, related to *Vogel*, bird), fruit (as opposed to masculine meat), puff, powder-puff, mollies (soft, from the Latin *mollus*), Mary-Anns, pillow-biters, mattress munchers (facedown being buggered), there is a rich comic vocabulary about the effeminate, used only or mainly by gay men (Baker 2004; Fosberry 2004). In use among gays, but not commonly used by straight men, are *Bruce, screamer, Minty, swishy, twinkle-toes, helium heels, light on his feet* (like a ballet dancer), *flamer, tissue on fire,* or *"See Tarzan, hear Jane"* when a masculine appearance goes with a nelly voice. There is even a *nellyectomy,* an imagined medical operation that would render a man camper, more effeminate, through the removal of wrist bones, so he can flail his hands in a limp-wristed way (Baker 2004, 167–68). A gay man who usually goes along with the conventions of straight masculine behavior but suddenly starts to camp it up as soon as he enters a gay bar is said to have undergone such surgery.

However, the existence of such a humor indicates the continued salience of ideas of the dominance of masculinity. Departures from it by men, including gay men, such as the limp wrist replacing the firm handshake, ready fist, or steady grasp of the manly man, become intrinsically ludicrous. This is mere humor, but beneath it is the reality that gay personal ads may often specify "straight acting," "no fems" (Hennen 2008, 10), or masculine as in "masculine GM" (Gay Male not General Motors), as a desired characteristic, whereas it doesn't seem to work the other way. Along with this goes the search for "rough trade" such as truck drivers, oil rig mechanics (Woog 2001, 16), marines, or guardsmen (Armstrong 1963, 125, 158–59; Harvey 1971; Richardson 1981, 39), who are prized as casual sexual partners; their very roughness precludes any hint of effeminacy. Those who are effeminate, who may well feel as strongly driven to behave this way as gay men in general are inclined to seek same-sex partners, sometimes feel looked down on by those gays whose equally strong inclinations are to act masculine or who simply choose to conform to wider social conventions. Camp or outrageous effeminate humor or the humor of drag queens breaks through not only the conventions of straight men's masculinity but also that of many gay men.

THE PATTERNS OF TARGETS

The groups who are the butts of jokes about same sex activities come into two main categories. First, there are groups of men, who by reason of their occupation or institution are deprived of the company of women and are portrayed in the jokes as turning to sex with other men, in much the same sense as shepherds in jokes resort to sheep. It is depicted in the jokes not as a preference but as a product of their situation. Under these circumstances the main butt of these jokes, about men without women, is the one who is passive and penetrated and who is seen as being feminized by the activity. Either this role is forced upon him or he has been tricked into it. The penetrated one is often a servant, a member of an ethnic minority, or even a boy (D'Arcangelo 1972).

The second category consists of men seen as having effeminate tastes and dress such as foppish aristocrats or whose occupations are traditionally seen as female ones. This in itself makes them figures of fun, but in addition there may be jokes about their supposed willingness to play the passive role of the penetrated one. There is a curious paradox about the idea of masculine dominance in that it is most strongly upheld by those individuals, both men and women, who belong to the less powerful and influential social classes, which enables their men folk to deride the men of the more educated, cultivated, and powerful strata above them as effeminate and to make jokes about them (Kuipers 2006, 65–66). The qualities of being restrained, civilized, and sensitive that upper-middle-class men see as the basis of their elevated status may well be seen by their lower-middle-class, working- class, and lower-class counterparts as forms of weakness. The civilizing qualities are acceptable in women of all classes. But when men display them, they are perceived in a very ambivalent way, for although they convey social superiority, they also imply a lack of masculine assertiveness. In modern societies, men still tend to have more power than women, but where men and women are of the same class, the power differential by sex is least for those men who enjoy the most social power in general, and those men who occupy a lower rung in the social order know this. Women of high standing may, by reason of their occupying positions of authority or by belonging to a higher social class, exercise considerable power over those very men of the subordinate social classes or ethnic minorities who are so proud of their masculinity. The question of who can exercise power, how, and when is complicated and depends on context. Those who chatter about "power relations" tend to ignore these complexities. The social contradictions between social status and masculinity are important as a factor generating these jokes, and understanding them makes it easier to understand the jokes.

Behind both sets of jokes lies the value that men in these societies place on masculinity. Those who are the butts of the jokes are those who either by choice or by fate have been sexually penetrated by other men and those who have an effeminate appearance, style, or tastes, or whose job implies these. Either way they have lost their masculinity and become the object of jokes.

Note

1. There is a depiction of just such a circle of men in the Turkish/Persian set of pictures *A Shaykh (Shaykh Muhammed Ibn Mustafa Al-Misri) Remembers His Youth*, 1773. A continuous circle of Near Easterners, naked except for their little circular Muslim caps and abbreviated jackets, are buggering one another round and round and round in a circle, their feet shuffling desperately to keep up (Wallace et al. 2007, 121). See also Edwardes (1967, 12) for an account of a supposed Arab rite of nude males dancing in a circle "united *penem in anum*."

For jokes about Buddhist monks, see UCBFA Jokes Chinese File; Levy 1973, 104–106, 129–31; Levy 1974, 218.

FIVE

❧

The Great American
Lawyer Joke Cycle

As we have already seen, many countries have a long tradition of telling jokes about canny, crafty, conniving lawyers, what Galanter (2005, 254) has called "the enduring core" of lawyer jokes. It goes with the law. However, the older jokes were very varied, and jokes about crooked lawyers were mixed in with many other jokes that portrayed them as ordinary human beings with the same foibles as anyone else. In common-law countries with an adversarial system such as England and Wales, Ireland, Australia, and the United States, interactions in court were the source of many humorous anecdotes, often lovingly treasured by the lawyers as the amiable face of their own familiar world and passed on to the public as collections of wit and humor (Jackson 1970). Sometimes these are genuine recollections about named individuals, but often they have been reshaped and polished into joke form and perhaps arbitrarily pinned on a lawyer known to the public. It is often easy to move back and forth between those cousins, or indeed siblings, the joke and the humorous anecdote. Such tales also make for amusing fictional vignettes, as in the celebrated *Forensic Fables* (O 1961). In England and Wales, Australia and Ireland today, lawyers are just one more everyday profession about whose work jokes can be told.

In America and in America alone, there emerged a huge new wave of lawyer jokes in the 1980s, several hundreds of them, which depicted U.S. lawyers as betrayers of trust and as morally deficient objects of scorn.

They included "death wish" jokes, which suggested that America would be better off without any lawyers and suggested ways of killing them off (Galanter 2005, 17). These jokes are unique to America,

> The devil went to see a rising young lawyer in his office and offered him a deal.
>
> "Look what I can do for you," said the devil. "I'll make you the richest and most famous lawyer in America. I guarantee you'll win every case. All I ask in return is that your wife and all your young children must rot in hell forever."
>
> The lawyer thought for a moment and then said, "Okay, but what's the catch?" (Told to me in California; for another version and for the evolution of this joke, see Galanter 2005, 186)

> What's the difference between a catfish and a lawyer? One's an ugly, scum-sucking, cold-blooded, bottom-dredging parasite, and the other one's a fish. (American 2008)

> My parents sent my brother through law school. He graduated and is suing them for wasting seven years of his life. (Fuqua 2000)

> A guy walks into a post office one day to see a middle-aged, balding man standing at the counter methodically placing "Love" stamps on bright pink envelopes with hearts all over them. He then takes out a perfume bottle and starts spraying scent all over them.
>
> His curiosity getting the better of him, he goes up to the balding man and asks him what he is doing. The man says, "I'm sending out 1,000 Valentine cards signed 'Guess who?'"
>
> "But why?" asks the guy.
>
> "I'm a divorce lawyer," the man replies. (http://www.swapmeetdave.com /Humor/Lawyer.htm; accessed March 2010)

Usually when a large new joke cycle or mode of joking gets going in America, it soon spreads to Europe, where the jokes are quickly adapted to local conditions and institutions but remain essentially the same. This is what happened with the huge American joke cycles about Polish stupidity and about dumb and promiscuous blondes, and to this we may add jokes about televised disasters and the death of celebrities. American jokes about lawyers, by contrast, have never taken root outside America. The jokes are known, appreciated, and told in Britain, Europe, Australia, India, and elsewhere, but specifically as jokes about American lawyers; they are not adapted to fit the local legal profession, even though there is often a well established local tradition of telling jokes about lawyers, onto which the new jokes could in principle be grafted. The jokes are told in Europe either as jokes from America or as ethnic jokes about Americans, jokes about a culture the Europeans see as laughably strange and different from their own.

> A truck driver passing through New York stopped to eat at a restaurant. Hardly had he sat down when a man came in dressed in an expensive suit and a bow tie and carrying a briefcase.
>
> The proprietor said to him, "You're a lawyer, aren't you?"
>
> The man replied, "You must be a mind reader. Yes, I am an attorney."
>
> The proprietor immediately produced his hunting gun and shot the lawyer.
>
> The truck driver was amazed and asked the owner to explain what had happened.
>
> The owner replied, "The hunting season on lawyers began yesterday in New York. You don't even need a license. It's great sport."
>
> The driver, delighted, replied, "It sure sounds like it. I just lost my shirt getting divorced." He finished his meal and took the road again.
>
> Only a mile further on, his truck hit a big pothole, a tire burst, and he smashed into a streetlight at the side of the road. As he was getting out of his cab to examine the damage, a huge crowd of men in suits, carrying briefcases, came running toward him waving their business cards and shouting, "Take me, take me. I'll sue the department of roads and bridges for you." The driver promptly pulled out his pistol from the glove compartment and started shooting into the crowd of lawyers. There were dead and wounded everywhere.
>
> A few minutes later, the police came and ordered him to drop his gun. They handcuffed the trucker's hands behind his back, read him his rights, and informed him that he was under arrest.
>
> The bewildered truck driver said, "But I thought it was now open-season for hunting lawyers?"
>
> "Quite right," said the police officer, "but you can't hunt in a baited field." (Author's translation from the French; http://www.uneblague.com /-Avocats-.html; accessed August 23, 2009)

The French have made or kept New York as the setting of the joke. The version in French shows signs of the joke having come from America, and indeed I heard a similar joke in Houston, Texas. Another joke on the *uneblague* (a joke) site refers to a lawyer in a trial in Oklahoma trying to trick a jury into acquitting his client.

The joke below at the expense of their American colleagues circulated among British lawyers by email in 2009.

BEST LAWYER STORY OF THE YEAR, DECADE AND PROBABLY THE
CENTURY!!

Charlotte, North Carolina. USA.

A lawyer purchased a box of very rare and expensive cigars, then insured them against, among other things, fire. Within a month, having
smoked his entire stockpile of these great cigars and without yet having
made even his first premium payment on the policy, the lawyer filed a
claim against the insurance company.

In his claim, the lawyer stated the cigars were lost "in a series of small
fires." The insurance company refused to pay, citing the obvious reason,
that the man had consumed the cigars in the normal fashion. The lawyer
sued . . . and WON!

(Stay with me.)

Delivering the ruling, the judge agreed with the insurance company
that the claim was frivolous. The judge stated, nevertheless, that the lawyer held a policy from the company, which had warranted that the cigars
were insurable and also guaranteed that it would insure them against fire,
without defining what is considered to be "unacceptable fire" and was
obligated to pay the claim!

Rather than endure a lengthy and costly appeal process, the insurance
company accepted the ruling and paid $15,000 to the lawyer for his loss
of the cigars in the "fires."

NOW, FOR THE BEST PART

After the lawyer cashed the check, the insurance company had him
arrested on twenty-four counts of ARSON!!!

With his own insurance claim and testimony from the previous case
being used against him, the lawyer was convicted of intentionally burning
his insured property and was sentenced to twenty-four months in jail and
a $24,000 fine. This is a true story and was the First Place winner in the
recent Criminal Lawyers Award Contest!

ONLY IN AMERICA!

This is, of course, a joke of American origin about lawyers, one re-
sembling an urban legend, and can be found on almost 100 U.S. websites,
including http://www.breakthechain.org/exclusives/cigars.html, where
it is dated 2003. It will have been generally seen as a mere amusing tale,
but those in charge of the breakthechain website feel they have to point
out that the story is false. They comment: "This tale and others like it
give us hope that in this overly litigious society, plagued by frivolous lawsuits and scams, justice does prevail." Quite apart from the source being
American, the sentiments are American, the use of the phrase "in this . . .
society" is peculiarly American, and the joke is presented as reflecting

a contemporary and distressing American problem. However, for the British lawyers emailing it to one another, it is a joke about "them," about those American lawyers who go in for that sort of thing, about someone else's problem. The heading Charlotte, North Carolina, and the ending "Only in America," which were originally put there to give the tale local verisimilitude, have now become the way in which it is known to be a joke about a particular set of outsiders. It would have been easy enough to relocate the joke to Manchester or Munster or Mumbai and tell it about some local shyster, but so strong is the contemporary association of such jokes with a specifically American legal profession that this is relatively unlikely to happen. Curiously, the joke has a distant ancestor that did not have an American setting at all, nor did it include the long tale about the law and the courts. These are not necessary to the joke and are there mainly to underline that it is now a joke about a lawyer.

What is it about American society and the American legal system that sets them apart from those of other stable liberal democratic societies, such that the new wave of lawyer jokes arose only in America? Why did the jokes only boom in America from the 1980s onwards? What had changed? The change was not necessarily sudden, for it may be that only in the 1980s did Americans become aware that many years of slow cumulative change had brought about a very new set of relationships between the lawyers and society. Given that other countries do not have such jokes of their own, how is it that their citizens have come to appreciate these very American jokes?

Since much of what follows is, fairly predictably, critical of the American legal and constitutional order, it needs also to be stated that Europeans are seriously deficient in some of the American constitutional virtues. The best examples lie in the greater willingness and ability of their governments to restrict freedom of speech and in the accumulation of power by centralized and often unelected institutions, which it is very difficult indeed for the individual citizen to challenge. The highly restrictive and archaic British libel laws have a chilling effect on free speech not only in Britain but even in America (American Center for Democracy 2009; Hooper 2003), because wealthy and malignant individuals indulge in "libel tourism"; they are able to obtain damages in a British court against the publisher of a book sold only in America, on the grounds that it might seep into Britain. It is not necessary to prove falsity or to demonstrate malice. Yet there are no British jokes (though much satire, notably in the British fortnightly *Private Eye*) about rich British libel lawyers to match American jokes about tort lawyers. In the Australian state of Victoria, vigorous statements of religious disagreement are prevented by laws prohibiting "religious hatred," and a law to this effect only failed to pass through the British parliament by a single vote. In America such laws would be struck down as unconstitutional. That I am able to write this book at all is a tribute to the First Amendment to the Constitution and American zeal in enforcing and extending it. Were it in their power, many politicians and officials even of the liberal democratic European and Commonwealth countries would be happy to censor out of existence many of my sources both of jokes and factual information, simply because they are annoyed or offended or afraid (Kuipers 2006, 27). The only true believers in and protectors of freedom of speech are American lawyers; they deserve the unqualified gratitude of authors and researchers of all countries.

The peoples of Europe feel as constrained and strangled by arbitrary administrative controls, enforced by intrusive and unchallengeable boards known only by their acronyms, as Americans feel constrained by lawyers and the courts. But there are far fewer jokes in these countries about the insolence of office than there are American jokes about the law's delay. Lawyers are the butt of jokes because they are paid fees and profit openly and directly from litigation. European bureaucrats rob by stealth. A new regulation means more staff. More staff means a larger pyramid. A larger pyramid means higher salaries for those at the apex. Total tort costs may be lower in Europe, but the bureaucrats have to be paid, and taxes are high. The European bureaucracies have done far more to stifle enterprise than the American legal profession.

HOW MANY LAWYERS DOES IT TAKE?

In America there are far more lawyers to tell jokes about, and they are both more visible and more powerful than in other modern democracies with sophisticated economies. As Seymour Martin Lipset (1997, 50) has shown in table 3, America is very much the odd one out. The number of lawyers in America in relation to population was steady throughout the mid-twentieth century, but from the 1960s onwards there was a rapid

Table 3. Litigiousness and Tort Costs in Six Countries.

	Lawyers	Lawyers per 100,000 Population	Tort Costs as % of GNP 1987
United States	780,000	312.0	2.4
Western Germany	115,900	190.1	0.5
England and Wales	68,067	134.0	0.5
Italy	46,401	81.2	0.5
France	27,700	49.1	0.6
Holland	5,124	35.2	—

Source: Lipset 1997, 50. Figures are given for the latest available years.

expansion. There were three times as many lawyers per capita in 2000 as there had been in 1965. Every year another 40,000 are produced. The proportion of the national income spent on legal services doubled between 1960 and 1985. Total civil filings in the federal courts rose from 59,284 to 273,670 between 1960 and 1985, and it can be inferred that a similar rise took place in the state courts (Galanter 2005, 9–10).

> Lawyers and computers have both been proliferating since 1970. Unfortunately, lawyers, unlike computers, have not gotten twice as efficient and half as expensive every 18 months. (http://www.vakilno1.com/lawone-liner.htm)

A rise of this magnitude could not have been merely a product of American economic development. The rise in the number of lawyers in America was quite disproportionate to what was happening in other wealthy countries with modern economies. Also it is very odd that there should have been such an abrupt change from the 1960s. The American economy expanded steadily and grew in complexity and sophistication in the period 1945–60, but without an explosion in litigation and in lawyers to do it. The causes of the marked shift after 1960 lie rather in changes in political expectations and in the exploitation of these by legislation-hungry politicians and in decisions made by the courts. In either case there will have been a big input from lawyers, partly out of crude self-interest but more significantly because, like most other groups, lawyers want the world to conform to their perceptions of what is important and how things should be done. Lawyers want more law, educators more education, doctors more things defined as illnesses, generals bigger armed forces, and civil servants more regulations, not just to get their hands on more power and resources but because their very training and experience lead them to see such expansion as beneficial, indeed natural. Often the benefits do not justify the expenditures; indeed, the net or even direct effects of expanding their activities may be harmful to society, but those asking for more often get more. In late twentieth-century America it happened to be the lawyers who were influential, and their worldview prevailed. Popular American perceptions of the number of lawyers in the United States as excessive and rising do then have a strong basis of truth, though in American mythology the extent of the rise of the lawyers may be exaggerated (Galanter 2005, 223–25). In European countries the fear is sometimes expressed that this "American disease" may spread to them (Galanter 2005, 221; Markovits 2007, 119).

Within America the anti-lawyer commentators' favorite unfavorable comparison is with Japan, another democratic country with a strong modern economy but where lawyers are passing few. Even by European standards lawyers are scarce in Japan; in 2002 it was estimated that there were only 25,000 lawyers in that country for a population of 125 million (Benjamin 2002).

Sometimes the United States versus Japan comparison is stated by Americans just as plain fact and one to the detriment of their own country; sometimes it is used as a source of humor. Lee Iacocca, then of Chrysler, speaking of the lack of litigation among Japanese businessmen, said: "There are more lawyers just in Washington, D.C., than in all of Japan. They've got about as many lawyers as we have sumo-wrestlers" (cited in Benjamin 2002).

Much American humor plays with the idea that the lawyers were to blame for the decline and fall of the once-dominant American automobile industry and the rise of its Japanese rivals based in a country where there are few lawyers to hinder productivity.

> What educational programs should the United States support to ameliorate the burgeoning U.S.–Japan trade imbalance?
> Japanese language lessons for lawyers. (Turkish Law Site/Lawyer jokes)

> Take heart, America. Three monkey wrenches have been thrown into Japan's well-oiled economic machine. It's only a matter of time before that powerful engine of productivity begins to sputter and fail. What could

cause such a sharp turnaround? High interest rates? Increased unemployment? Lower productivity? No, it's something much more economically debilitating—and permanent. Three American lawyers have become the first foreign attorneys permitted to practice law in Japan. What's more, two of them are from New York! The decline has begun. Japan has one attorney for every 10,000 residents, compared to the U.S. ratio of one attorney for every 390 residents. For every 100 attorneys trained in Japan, there are 1,000 engineers. In the United States, that ratio is reversed. But a law that became effective on April 1 permits foreigners to practice in Japan for the first time since 1955. Already, an additional 20 American and 6 British lawyers have applied for permission to open practices in Japan. If anything can slow the Japanese economy, it's the presence of American attorneys. What better way to even our balance of trade than to send Japan our costliest surplus commodity? (http://www.jokes-db .com/Japanese_Jokes/94.html)

It is doubtful whether the eclipse of the traditional manufacturing industry in the United States can be explained in this simple way. However, Japan is a large, effective, modern economy in which "thick trust" between individuals defined by hierarchy, status, and reputation has not been replaced by complete reliance on detailed legal contracts; its very existence disproves the thesis favored by lawyers and indeed by many U.S. sociologists that modernity requires a society of strictly demarcated roles for specific purposes that require legal monitoring. Japan may be exceptional and indeed very un-American, but to claim that Japan is not modern in order to try to save this argument is hopelessly circular.

TORTUOUS TORT

Yet it is not just the numbers of lawyers but the high ratio in America relative to other countries of tort costs to the total value of goods and services produced that is driving controversy. A very large proportion of American lawyer jokes and of other humor about lawyers refers to questions of tort, cases in which redress is sought in the civil courts for some harm that complainants allege they have suffered as a result of the wrong conduct, often, but not limited to, the negligence of others. For the purposes of the jokes, it means suing someone, an activity that can provide considerable rewards for the lawyers who conduct the case. Not only is the aggregate level of tort costs far higher in America in relation to income levels than in other comparable countries, but it has greatly risen over time with the main upward surge taking place in the 1980s, the decade when the great American lawyer joke cycle began. (*U.S. Tort Costs* 2006)

There is a great deal of strong controversy in America about tort reform. The econometric data and arguments involved are way beyond the scope of this book. It is nothing like as important a political issue in other countries, and in no other country are law firms such major contributors to campaign funding. The great American lawyer joke cycle draws on this controversy, and indeed many of the jokes are about lawyers chasing business in the field of tort.

TORT AND AMERICAN LAWYER JOKES

Did you hear about the lawyer hurt in an accident?
An ambulance stopped suddenly.
(UCBFA file Blason Pop, U2 L4; collected by Fiona Nguy 2000.)

How many lawyers does it take to change a light bulb?
Three. One to climb the ladder, one to shake it, and one to sue the ladder company. (UCBFA file Blason Pop U2 L4; collected by Troy Miller 1992)

Everybody in my family follows the medical profession. They're all lawyers. (http://www.vakilno1.com/lawoneliner.htm)

A lawyer was asked if he (would) like to become a Jehovah's Witness. He declined, as he hadn't seen the accident, but would still be interested in taking the case. (Fuqua 2000)

An airliner was having engine trouble, and the pilot instructed the cabin crew to have the passengers take their seats and get prepared for an emergency landing.
A few minutes later, the pilot asked the flight attendants if everyone was buckled in and ready.
"All set back here, Captain," came the reply, "except one lawyer who is still going around passing out business cards." (Fuqua 2000)

These are just jokes, but American humor also embraces both true cases and urban legends about tort cases. Tales of crazy lawsuits abound in most countries, and they may well be collected together and published for the public's amusement. It is the predominance of tort cases in the American humorous collections of the twenty-first century that is remarkable, as is the fame of such cases throughout the English-speaking world, where they are seen as distinctively American and as revealing what law in America is really like.

Perhaps the most famous of these is "The Great American Pants Suit" (W. Olson 2007) of *Pearson v Chung*. In 2005 a U.S. administrative judge sued a small dry cleaning family business run by industrious Korean immigrants in Washington, D.C., for $67 million after they had temporarily mislaid a pair of his suit pants. He demanded an absurdly large sum of money for a trivial mistake on their part. His claim included half a million dollars for emotional distress and ten years worth of payments for car rentals so that he could take his pants to a different dry cleaner. He further argued that their advertisement saying "satisfaction guaranteed" and "same day service" was fraudulent and that he was entitled to payment for all the days during which the advertisement appeared. Even though he represented himself, he asked for another half million dollars to cover his legal expenses. It went to trial in 2007, by which time the Chungs would have been ruined and forced to return to Korea had they not received $100,000 from supporters, much of it channeled through the website about the case set up by the Custom Cleaners Defense Fund. It was widely seen as disgraceful that the claim had been brought and that the U.S. legal system had allowed it to have been brought, particularly after the Chungs had offered the complainant reasonable compensation, which was refused. Walter Olson (2007) drew the general conclusion that lawsuits in America can serve as "a hobby for the spiteful and a weapon for the rapacious," and others related it to the widespread cases of "junk-fax" litigation in which a good deal of money is extorted from small businessmen for some petty breach of consumer protection laws. Many Americans think the American legal system is pants.

For the Chungs, it was harrowing harassment and injustice, but for the world it provided vast amusement, the amusement that things stupid and bizarre so frequently provide. The case was extensively reported in the *Washington Post*, and accounts of it soon appeared in the press, on the internet, and even on the radio in Australia, Canada, Russia, and parts of Asia. America had become a laughing stock. Press agencies and the foreign press love stories of this kind; the Reuters account "Woman Sues U.S. Zoo over Splashing Dolphins" appeared in the *Times of India* in 2009 and also in Australia and the UK. Because America is a major center of attention in the world, these stories spread quickly, whereas the American public's lack of interest in other countries means that foolish legal happenings that take place outside America get no publicity within America. It then seems to everybody that only in America are law and lawyers foolish, which, of course, is quite untrue. But the tort tales from other countries are rarely quite as absurd or bizarre as the American ones, and so one key ingredient of humor about lawyers is missing. European cases can be silly, but by American standards they are rather tame and not very funny, as in the tepid German case below, which somehow became "news":

> Court Rejects Damages Claim in Kebab-Throwing Case
> A German court has rejected an employee's demand that an irate customer pay damages for throwing a half-eaten kebab at her. The claim stems from an altercation in June in which a kebab customer unsuccessfully demanded his money back. He says he then tossed the food behind the counter. The employee claims the customer called her a "stupid cow" and aimed the kebab at her. She says she narrowly avoided the flying kebab and wants at least $390 in damages. (Legal Humor News 2008)

Not surprisingly, Roy L Pearson Jr., who lost his pants and his suit, became the recipient of the 2007 True Stella Award, a class of awards set up by Randy Cassingham to honor "Real Cases of Greedy Opportunists, Frivolous Lawsuits, and the Law Run Amok." Each country has its own comic awards, which reveal much of the culture of that country, such as Australia's annual Ernie Awards (Burgmann and Andrews 2007), presented to Australian men who have made the most outrageously insulting remarks about women in the preceding year. The Ernie Awards are supposed to be a chastening humor to operate within Australia, but outside Australia they have become an affectionate ethnic humor about the entire country. Good on yer, mate! Cassingham is a humorist with a serious purpose. He is seeking to combat what he rightly sees as a social evil, for even when a frivolous case is eventually thrown out, that does not mean the system is working well. Each case of this kind diverts resources and clogs up the courts, such that for genuine claimants, justice is delayed or even denied. Real cases get pushed aside. Yet the well-researched true cases that Cassingham uses to show this are humorous. Let us consider some of his best cases from the 2003 Stella awards.

Shawn Perkins of Laurel, Ind., was hit by lightning in the parking lot of Paramount's Kings Island amusement park in Mason, Ohio. A classic "act of God," right? No, says Perkins's lawyer. "That would be a lot of people's knee-jerk reaction in these types of situations." The lawyer has filed suit against the amusement park asking unspecified damages, arguing the park should have "warned" people not to be outside during a thunderstorm.

Caesar Barber, 56, of New York City who is 5-foot-10 and 270 pounds, says he is obese, diabetic, and suffers from heart disease because fast-food restaurants forced him to eat their fatty food four to five times per week. He filed suit against McDonald's, Burger King, Wendy's, and KFC, who "profited enormously," and asked for unspecified damages because the eateries didn't warn him that junk food isn't good for him. The judge threw the case out twice and barred it from being filed a third time. Is that the end of such McCases? No way: lawyers will just find another plaintiff and start over, legal scholars say.

These cases make a serious point, but they are so absurd as to have provided an incentive for the anonymous "inventors" and circulators of urban legends to try to provide even "better" ones that are somewhat too good to be true. They then try to pass them off as Stella Award cases. The defenders of the existing legal system use the existence of these urban legends to allege that all bizarre cases, including those that have been accurately reported, are fictions of this kind (Cassingham 2005, 11). Yet the fact that the fake cases even seem to be true is itself an indication of how the legal system has come to be perceived.

Terrence Dickson of Bristol, Pennsylvania, was leaving a house he had just finished robbing by way of the garage. He was not able to get the garage door to go up, since the automatic door opener was malfunctioning. He couldn't reenter the house because the door connecting the house and garage locked when he pulled it shut. The family was on vacation, and Mr. Dickson found himself locked in the garage for eight days. He subsisted on a case of Pepsi he found and a large bag of dry dog food. He sued the homeowner's insurance claiming the situation caused him undue mental anguish. The jury agreed to the tune of $500,000.

Mr. Grazinski of Oklahoma City purchased a brand-new thirty-two-foot Winnebago motor home. On his first trip home, having driven onto the freeway, he set the cruise control at 70 mph and calmly left the driver's seat to go into the back and make himself a cup of coffee. Not surprisingly, the RV left the freeway, crashed, and overturned. Mr. Grazinski sued

Winnebago for not advising him in the owner's manual that he couldn't actually do this. The jury awarded him $1,750,000 plus a new motor home. The company actually changed their manuals on the basis of this suit, just in case there were any other complete morons buying their recreation vehicles. (http://www.truthorfiction.com/rumors/o/onlyinamerica.htm)

Both these stories are, as the compilers of "truth or fiction" make clear, complete fabrications, pure urban legends, and as with most urban legends, are believable, shocking, and often funny. Weird tort cases, whether true or made up, are now to be found everywhere in American humor (Jimenez 2001, 8) but rarely in that of other countries. Why does this kind of humor about lawyers remain confined to America? The answer lies in the greater litigiousness of Americans relative to other countries.

CONSTITUTION AND CULTURE

The greater litigiousness of the Americans has its roots in the American social order.

> The emphasis in the American value system, in the American Creed, has been on the individual. Citizens have been expected to demand and protect their rights on a personal basis. The exceptional focus on law here as compared to Europe, derived from the Constitution and the Bill of Rights, has stressed rights against the state and other powers. America began and continues as the most anti-statist, legalistic, and rights oriented nation. The American Constitution intensifies the commitment to individualism and concern for the protection of rights through legal actions. The American Bill of Rights, designed to protect the citizenry against the abuse of power by government, has produced excessive litigiousness. It has fostered the propensity of Americans to go to court not only against the government but against each other. Lipset (1997, 20–21)

If Lipset is right, then the excessive litigation is a product of the very definition and virtues of U.S. society. Lipset (1997, 21) notes that in neighboring Canada there is far greater respect for and reliance on the state and that the Canadian people are much less litigious. The Canadians are also in some respects less free. The egalitarian individualism on which America is founded brings with it an emphasis on self-reliance rather than solidarity, on equal rights and opportunities, not on equality of condition (all of which have been a target for American satirists such as

Sinclair Lewis and Nathanael West); this makes for a disputatious society in which individuals assert their rights and their grievances through the courts to a greater extent than in other countries. These disputes give rise to American jokes about lawyers who are blamed for inciting them, yet in truth the lawyers would not have been able to do so if the culture and national character of America and its fundamental institutions and political origins had been different and less nationally distinctive. The lawyer jokes are jokes about America. More precisely they stem from the clash between the perception of America as essentially harmonious and the reality that the much honored virtues of egalitarian individualism inevitably lead to strife in the courts. The clash is framed as and briefly resolved by jokes about villainous lawyers stirring up conflicts for their own profit.

Rights are a matter of social convention and choice. In America rights are fixed in law, but this too is convention (Riesman 1954, 460). The refusal to accept this view and to see rights as natural may well be a factor in making Americans wish to pursue legal disputes more freely and fiercely and further than appears sensible to outsiders of a more pragmatic and utilitarian disposition. It is an insistence on rights and an obsession with justice that leads to American jokes about all the parties to a legal conflict winning nothing and losing everything and the whole of their substance being taken by the lawyers. The trouble with justice is that there is never enough of it to go round. For most people justice is a decision in their favor.

> "I guess you heard about Ezry losin' his farm?" said the man who was showing him around.
> "No, I hadn't," said the visitor. "How did it happen?"
> "Wal," said the local man, "Ezry got the idea that his neighbor's fence was encroachin' on his land and he got to broodin' on it. Finally he went to see a lawyer who thought so too." (Croy 1948; cited in Galanter 2005, 65)

Or in modern form

> Why are lawyers like nuclear weapons?
> If one side has got one, the other side has got to get one. Once they have been launched, they cannot be recalled. And when they hit, everything gets completely smashed up.

THE IMPORTANCE OF THE AMERICAN CONSTITUTION

In a more paternalistic and deferential society, it would be possible for someone in authority to take possession of such conflicts and prevent those in dispute from ruining one another, but this would require not just restraining the lawyers but restricting the fundamental and inviolable rights of a free-born American. The obvious contrast is with Japan, which is hierarchical and more ethnically homogenous and whose people have a strong sense of collective solidarity and a consensus about how individuals should comport themselves. Because there are in consequence high levels of interpersonal trust and clear shared expectations, this in turn limits uncertainty. There is in Japan less need and less desire to rely on written contracts enforceable in a court of law and less reliance on lawyers. To take legal action against other Japanese to resolve a disagreement is against the very ethos of the society. Japan is not the way it is because it is lawyerless. It is lawyerless because it is Japanese. The Japanese, like the Danes or the Irish, are what they are because of their ancestry and the history and language or religion of their country which set them apart from their neighbors. By contrast, the very definition of America is its founding Constitution, and American national identity is rooted in a legal document. The Americans are a proclamation of "self-evident" truths and rights that are not self-evident to anyone else, and their identity is rooted in a hallowed text to be interpreted and reinterpreted, to be revered and to be haggled over by lawyers. America is based on government not by men but by lawyers. The U.S. Constitution and its amendments have taken on a "sacred" character that in the nation-states of Europe is spread over a series of primordial institutions with which the people identify. After a lecture in Delhi in 1974 (three years after the Indo-Pakistan war), the distinguished Indian anthropologist M. N. Srinivas was asked by an Indian, "What holds India together?" Srinivas replied, "Loyalty to the Indian constitution." The amused and astonished questioner countered, "Are you really saying that our solidarity during the war with Pakistan in 1971 was based on loyalty to the constitution?" Srinivas had no answer to this. India is not America.

Moral controversies that would be resolved in Europe by the legislature, or perhaps by referendum, in America become legal questions.

A key example of this is the liberalization of the abortion laws that happened in many countries in the latter half of the twentieth century. In Britain the law was drastically liberalized in 1967 by an act of Parliament on utilitarian harm-reduction grounds; questions of rights were never part of the Parliamentary debate (Davies 2004, 71–90). In the debates on abortion, the views of the lawyers were unimportant, far less important than the views of the British doctors, for it was seen as a medical welfare measure, with abortions provided free through the National Health Service (Britain's system of socialized medicine). For most Europeans, the American legal controversies about right to life versus right to choose seemed and seem pointless. The arguments only carry weight in America, where the restrictive laws on abortion in place in many individual states were struck down by a legal decision in *Roe v Wade* (1973) based on a tortuously constructed right to privacy derived by taking, interpreting, and adding together various fragments of the Constitution. The point may be made with equal force to the reasoning in the case that may be regarded as a precedent, *Griswold v Connecticut* (1965), which struck down the laws of that state against contraception. The conclusion was sensible, but it was a very odd way to get to it. What this comparison shows is that the dominant moral arguments used in a country are shaped by where the power lies, and in America it lies with the lawyers. Lawyers lie at the very heart of American society. American lawyers are the most American of Americans, and they represent the crucial American preference for due process as opposed to personal discretion. Law and lawyers *are* the very essence of what it means to be an American.

Because of the centrality of law, American perceptions of their legal system are different from those to be found in other democratic countries. Galanter (2002, 2224) refers to an account of American legal consciousness that speaks of three intertwined "perspectives on the legal." These are (i) the law as a transcendent and majestic system; (ii) the law as commonplace, as part of everyday life, a game involving the pursuit of self-interest; (iii) the law as arbitrary and capricious to be coped with by tricks and subterfuge. Americans perceive their legal system in a mixture of these ways depending on circumstances, and no doubt Europeans do, too. However, I would put forward the tentative, but testable, hypothesis that Americans are more likely than citizens of northwestern European countries to see the law as majestic and transcendent and that they are *also* more likely to see it as arbitrary and oppressive. In northwestern Europe, law and lawyers are merely ordinary, everyday phenomena that are joked about from time to time in relation to their observed idiosyncrasies. However, the commonplace is unlikely to become the focus of a massive cycle of lawyer jokes. In America, impossibly high demands are made on a "majestic" legal system which is used to try and resolve all manner of problems that in Europe are the business of politicians, welfare agencies, the ombudsman, or arbitrators. Yet there is also in America more chicanery and more emphasis on winning regardless of whether the outcome is fair or reasonable, which is very visible not only in tort cases but in criminal trials (Brandon and Davies 1973, 239, 243–44; Taylor and Johnson 2007). A very high degree of formal protections of the accused is combined with legal maneuvers, such as fixing the composition of the jury, changing the venue of a trial, or getting vital evidence excluded, so as to load the dice in favor of one side on the other. Verdicts can be overturned on the basis of petty legal technicalities but not by a reconsideration of the evidence. America's is a criminal justice system of the lawyers, by the lawyers, and for the lawyers. The humorists see it as being strictly for the money.

> Lawyer speaks to man being strapped into the electric chair. "It sure would be swell if your last words didn't mention that eyewitness who recanted her testimony, the con that confessed to your crime, the DNA test that proved your innocence, or the fact that I slept through most of your trial." (Shanahan 2005)

> Did you hear about the new O.J. ride at Disneyland?
> It's a dollar to get on but $5 million to get off.

> Johnnie Cochran (defense attorney): O.J., all this blood evidence is very damaging. We've got to get a change of venue to West Virginia.
> O.J.: How come?
> J. C.: Because, in West Virginia, everybody has the same DNA.

> What is the difference between O.J. Simpson and Pee-wee Herman?
> It only took twelve jerks to get O.J. off.

> Q: What's the difference between O.J. Simpson and Christopher Reeve?
> A: Christopher Reeve stood for truth, justice, and the American way.
> O.J. stands for lies and injustice, the American way.

For these, for other versions, and for over 160 more O.J. Simpson jokes, see (http://www.angelfire.com/tn/jokes/oj.html)

The O.J. Simpson jokes grew out of his trial for murdering his ex-wife and a friend of hers in 1994. Simpson was acquitted against the weight of the evidence, but a subsequent civil action found him culpable. Simpson, who was very wealthy, paid his defense lawyers several million dollars. One law for the rich. The key point at issue was where the trial would be held, since this would shape the composition of the jury. In 2008 Simpson was convicted of armed robbery and kidnapping in Las Vegas and sentenced to thirty-three years in jail.

> O.J. Simpson has been found guilty at a court in Las Vegas of armed robbery and kidnapping. In a statement to the court, O.J. said he was sorry—sorry the trial wasn't held in LA.

> The jury has been selected in O.J. Simpson's upcoming kidnapping trial. The judge tried to select a jury of Simpson's peers, but it's hard to find twelve unconvicted murderers. (http://www.dailycomedy.com /hottopic/OJ_Simpson)

A legal system that is held up to be the true embodiment of everything that's excellent but that is strong on tricks and manipulation is likely to be the butt of more jokes than one of not so great expectations but acceptable levels of delivery as in northwestern Europe.

LAWYERS AND MONEY

One striking aspect of American jokes about lawyers is the emphasis on their greed, wealth, and love of displayable possessions.

> A lawyer is settling up with his client.
> "Let's try this," says the lawyer. "You pay me $2,000 down and $250 a month."
> "What!" said the client. "I feel like I'm paying for a new car."
> "You are!" replied the lawyer. "It's a BMW."

> A lawyer was driving his big BMW down the road, singing to himself, "I love my BMW, I love my BMW." Thinking about his car, not his driving, he smashed into a tree. He survived, but his car was completely wrecked. "My lovely BMW! My dear, dear BMW!" he sobbed.
> A passer-by dragged him from the ruins of his car and said, "Thank goodness you weren't killed. But, oh my God, you've lost your left arm!"
> The horrified lawyer screamed in desperation, "My Rolex! My Rolex!"

In October 2009, I heard a version of the American lawyer and Rolex joke told by a Welsh professor of engineering who introduced it specifically as a joke about Americans. It had now become a comic tale not just about the greed of lawyers but also about Americans' alleged materialism and their love of showy, expensive purchases; the joke was essentially the same and funny in the same way it had been when I had heard it in America, but it now drew implicitly on two scripts: an American script about lawyers and a European script about Americans. This is, of course, a very uncertain proposition, for the joke circulates widely in Britain, and there is no evidence available as to how it is generally perceived, other than that its American setting is preserved. The argument depends rather on the existence of many earlier jokes about an excessive American pride in possessions (Davies 1990, 241–47).

There are many JAP jokes on this same theme, and it is worth remembering that the JAP is not only Jewish but American and a Princess. These are not just jokes about Jewish women but jokes about a particular social class, the princess class, within one particular nation. There is nothing particularly Jewish about the content of the JAP jokes or lawyerish about the content of this type of lawyer jokes. Just as the "Polack" jokes were also jokes about unskilled blue-collar workers, these are jokes about a social class, the class of the ostentatious rich.

> What do you say to a JAP baby?
> Gucci, Gucci, goo.

> Jewish Personal Ads
> Jewish Princess, 28, seeks successful businessman of any major Jewish denomination: hundreds, fifties, twenties. POB 27. (Weiss 1996, July 2 issue)

> Rhoda ran into Bobbi on Rodeo Drive, and the two Beverley Hills JAPs were having a genial chat. Suddenly Rhoda looked at her watch. "Darling, I've got to dash," she exclaimed. "Oh, damn!"
> "What's wrong?" Nina asked.
> Rhoda raised her wrist and shook it in Bobbi's face. "My expensive gold watch just stopped. I'll have to take it back to Tiffany's and get it fixed. Can you tell what time it is?"
> "Sure," said Bobbi. She slowly raised her wrist in front of Rhoda's face. "It's exactly eight diamonds past five rubies." (Wilde 1986, 56)

It is important to consider what was happening in the American economy during the decades when the lawyer jokes and the JAP jokes emerged. American has long been a more unequal society than the other English-speaking countries, as we can see by comparing the Gini coefficients (one of the measures of inequality of income; the higher the coefficient, the more unequal) for each of these countries as calculated by the CIA (Central Intelligence Agency 2009). In the United States the Gini coefficient cited by the CIA is 45 while the Gini coefficients for all the other Anglophone democracies are clustered in the mid- to low thirties. Only in America were levels of inequality much higher and rising. The level of inequality of family incomes in America is not even within the same range as the European countries but lies alongside those of Uganda and Iran.

The importance of these figures for thinking about lawyer and JAP jokes is that the widening divergence in incomes and ownership in America that began in the late 1960s was accompanied by a rise in aspirations. Class boundaries became weaker, and those on lower incomes began to compare their lifestyle with that of people much richer than themselves and sought to emulate it by going ever deeper into debt (Schor 1998, 4–7, 11, 39). The common experience became to borrow and to borrow and to borrow, and rising debt crept up from day to day. It became a way of life, as people ceased to save and were trapped in an endless cycle of competitive consumption (Schor 1998, 12, 20, 163–65). The chances of buying a house faded for people on subprime incomes (Schor 1998, 14), and the inept and ill-thought out Carter-Clinton attempt to remedy this by enabling the lawyers to sue banks on behalf of the subprimers to force them to give mortgages even to paupers led to the disastrous crash of 2008–2009.

Lawyers probably did well during these years, years when those in many other occupations were struggling. According to the U.S. Census Bureau (Bishaw and Semega 2008, 32–34), lawyers earn more on average than chief executive officers (CEOs) and nearly twice as much as detectives and criminal investigators. It is fairly easy to see why jokes might be told about lawyers' high earnings, but even more important is the very high spread of earnings within the legal profession (U.S. Bureau of Labor Statistics 2008). At the top end, tort lawyers can make tens of millions of dollars a year, which is rather more than is earned by a defense lawyer in a rural county in Alabama representing an indigent client on legal aid (Freedman 2001).

Rewards *within* many occupations in America become far more unequally distributed as a small group of extremely high earners emerged by the 1990s (Schor 1998, 9–10), and this would have been particularly true of the new winner-takes-all world of the lawyers. This will have intensified yet another social contradiction from which lawyer jokes are likely to emerge. The last decades of the twentieth century saw the destruction of many of the old constraints on competition rooted in custom, convention, or the concept of the lawyer as engaging in a profession as opposed to a business (Gray 1998, 93, 103–15).

> During the 1980s the number of lawyers increased dramatically. The world of staid clubby law firms—a world of assured tenure and little lateral movement, shrouded in confidentiality with retainers from loyal long-term clients—dissolved. It was replaced by a world of rapid growth, increased competition for clients, mergers and breakups, movement from firm to firm, fear of defection and pervasive insecurity. Collegiality was replaced by wariness. Increasingly, lawyers were competitive not with lawyers in other firms but "with their own partners and even the associates coming up the ladder." Established partners might be "pushed off the iceberg." (Galanter 1998, 831)

It sounds like the beginning of a lawyer joke. "Three lawyers were sitting on this shrinking iceberg . . ." "How many lawyers can an iceberg hold?" "I don't need to outrun the polar bear. I only have to outrun you."

The lawyer jokes emerged at a time of tensions within the profession, which helps to explain why so many of these jokes were told by American lawyers themselves (Galanter 1998, 831–32). For those in other occupations in an increasingly insecure labor market characterized by intensified competition and declining fraternity, the lawyer jokes also made sense of the world as they experienced it. Scott Adams's cartoons featuring Dilbert are an expression of this same sense of distrust in a management context. America had become more intensely "American," more competitive, more governed by "contract," more impersonal, more anomic (Gray 1998), and the jokes about lawyers were jokes about this not altogether welcome assertion of American distinctiveness. It is at this time that the word *shark* becomes humorously attached to lawyers rather than extortionate usurers.

> Why won't a shark eat a lawyer?
> Professional courtesy.

A doctor was vacationing at the seashore with his family. Suddenly, he spotted a fin sticking up in the water and fainted. "Darling, it was just a shark," said his wife when he came to. "You've got to stop imagining that there are lawyers everywhere."

(http://www.free-funny-jokes.com/funny-lawyer-jokes.html)

Shark comes from the German *Schurke,* meaning greedy parasite. While no brave soul has gotten close enough to determine where lawyers come from, logic and common sense dictate a similar derivation. Sharks, unlike most fish, have no bones; their skeletons are made entirely of cartilage. Lawyers, too, are spineless—as willing to argue one side of a case as the other. For the right price.

Best known as scavengers of the dead and dying, sharks have well-honed sensors with which they can track the sounds of other injured and struggling beings. They are also equipped with fine senses of smell that allow them to detect minute dilutions of blood (one part blood to one million parts water) up to one quarter mile away. Precisely the distance a hopeful personal injury lawyer will run behind an ambulance to toss a business card. . . . Some sharks even prey on their own kind. The smell and taste of blood in the water can trigger them into an obsessed feeding frenzy, in which they often eat their own bodies while twisting and turning to get more food. This is not unlike the litigation frenzy, where lawyers are pitted against other lawyers, and ultimately themselves, to waste reams of paper while losing sight of a fair resolution for their clients (Fuqua 1996; Sharks and Lawyers 2006).

The shark image might seem a negative one, but all over America "some lawyers have embraced the shark image as a totem, flaunting it on T-shirts, comic signs, and even in advertisements" (Galanter 2002, 2229) as a sign of ferocity and unstoppability. Lawyers' business cards show a vicious shark in suit jacket and tie, with teeth like razors in his mouth for all to see. The lawyer-shark wears gangster dark glasses and carries a briefcase, saying to the world of little clients, "Hi, fish." The lawyers who advertise themselves as sharks want to appear macho and aggressive—"I am going to go in there savagely for you and win." Some lawyers hang dead sharks outside their buildings, and one in Montana keeps a blacktip reef shark in a vast aquarium in his office. In an adversarial legal system, clients want a lawyer who will savage their opponents. As Galanter has shown, the theme of many lawyer jokes is that the "smart guy wins." Writing for Americans, Galanter (1998, 819) adds, "Although the lawyer may violate the canons of fraternity he is a winner who reassures us that we may justifiably pursue our claims even if the rightness of our cause is only relative, for if someone has to lose it might as well be the other guy." The lawyer jokes are about a way of life.

The use of the shark in this way reminds us of the social contradictions that necessarily impinge on American lawyers. To what extent are lawyers members of a profession, and to what extent are they running profit maximizing businesses? To what extent is the lawyer a shark for his client and to what extent a servant of the court? It is an old question, one addressed by John Bannister Gibson, chief justice of Pennsylvania, in *Rush v Cavanaugh* (1845).

> It is a popular but gross mistake to suppose that a lawyer owes no fidelity to anyone except his client and that the latter is the keeper of his professional conscience. He is expressly bound by his official oath to behave himself in his office of attorney with all due fidelity to the court as well as the client and he violates it when he consciously presses for an unjust judgment. . . . The high and honourable office of a counsel would be degraded to that of a mercenary were he compelled to do the biddings of his client against the dictates of his conscience.

Can a lawyer whose self-image is that of a shark say in all honesty that he is exercising the high and honorable office of counsel? Or is he a degraded mercenary? The deliberate use of the shark image by American lawyers in their advertising indicates the inevitable ambiguity of jokes and humor. It is likewise notable not only that many of the best internet sites for lawyer jokes are provided by law firms but also that other joke sites filled with jokes about ambulance chasing lawyers finance themselves through advertisements placed there by lawyers touting for business from the recently injured. Jokes can usually be turned around in this way, given a different gloss, flavored with a touch of irony. "When lawyers are sharks are they nicer to the little fish?" *Tendenz*, intention, purpose resides here in the use of the humor, not in the shark joke itself. The Florida lawyers' referral agency "Whocanisue" even runs "irreverent television spots featuring buxom nurses and a pack of lawyers chasing an ambulance" (Diaz 2009). It must be good for business or they would not use it, though other lawyers were not happy at seeing their profession advertised quite so blatantly. There is another contradiction here, a point of social uncertainty and tension. Are lawyers a profession with restrictive practices conspiring like a cartel against the public, or are lawyers honest businessmen openly competing in the free market?

PROTESTS AGAINST LAWYER JOKES

Sometimes lawyers have protested that the jokes have given them a bad image. A former president of the Pennsylvania Bar Association, John Carpenter (1990), opening for the prosecution of lawyer jokes, said:

> Why am I so sensitive? I must confess to you that I really like lawyers and judges. I admire the way they think and argue and compete. What profession is more disciplined or has a higher standard of ethics? What body of people has done more to craft and sustain civilization and the laws by which we live? This is truly a great and honorable profession. Yet we stand by and watch other people make fun of it and us and, in the spirit of trying to be "good sports," we even join in the self-abuse process—laughing with them and topping their latest lawyer bash with our own. . . .
>
> May I suggest that you and I join together to attack the seemingly impossible job of stamping out "lawyer jokes"? Think about it. Their demise just might begin with me—or you.

Terry Light, J.D., who describes the American lawyer as one who "maintains and drives the most sophisticated civilization in the history of mankind," has added:

> Why is a person treated as a lower life form merely because his professional trademark is a "J.D."? I have been a member of the Bar for 16 years (as of 1991) and have never understood why lawyers sit by idly as others ridicule and humiliate them. . . . My abhorrence of "lawyer jokes" runs deeper than a mere pride in the profession. I am not just a lawyer. I am a husband, a father, a son, a brother, an uncle, a friend, a member of a community, a member of a church, and many other things to other people. I resent those who use me and my profession as whipping boys, because it has a negative impact on how my wife, my sons, my parents, my brother and sister, my nieces and nephews, my friends, and my neighbors perceive me. To be blunt, it just isn't funny and it hurts. (Light 2000)

Their skill in using orotund rhetoric does credit to these two extremely eminent Pennsylvania lawyers. They have assembled every possible cliché from the banal to the high falutin' and flung it at the jury in a truly masterful way. However, they have provided no actual evidence whatsoever that lawyers in general have been harmed by the jokes. The world exists independently of how we feel about it. Their argument contains the commonly held, if fatuous, fallacy that if humor about our group offends us, it must also *ipso facto* have undermined our group's social position. Shoe repairers! Not only have their eminences provided no evidence, but there is no evidence that the jokes have had any effect on society at all. Why should we humor the humorless by outlawing jokes? Lawyer jokes do not even have the trivial effect of influencing short-term attitudes toward lawyers (Olson et al. 1999). The jokes must be funny, or they would not circulate and lawyers would not make so much use of them in their online advertising both directly and by getting the compilers of collections of lawyer jokes to add links to their own websites. Light did, though, make one very good point, namely, that there were many jokes about amoral lawyers on the main television comedy shows in the late 1980s and early 1990s, whereas jokes about other groups were censored out, either because the producers wished to coddle these groups or because the groups had power or powerful protectors who might cause trouble. Television producers and administrators tended to subscribe to the odd thesis that it was acceptable to have jokes about those of high social position but not about those who could represent themselves as underdogs. Very few jokes (other than utterly anodyne ones) are ever told on radio or television in America or Britain about Muslims, both because they can gain support within those media by representing themselves as an underdog minority and also because they are powerful and if annoyed quick to use that power. By contrast, those American attorneys in the late twentieth century who felt offended by lawyer jokes were trapped, because the television writers and their bosses did not care about the possible hurt feelings of individual lawyers, who for them did not matter, and lawyers' organizations (which did have power) were only concerned with using television to manipulate public opinion about far more important questions. They rightly saw jokes as utterly insignificant by comparison. The only exception I know happened not in contemporary America but in Britain in the late 1940s, when a senior person from the Law Society was able to persuade the BBC to stop comedians from telling jokes about solicitors (attorneys) who absconded with their clients' money. The deal was done quietly in that sly, behind-the-scenes British way, paradoxically known as a gentleman's agreement.

The subset of American lawyer jokes that will have tended to upset some lawyers' feelings most were the so-called "death-wish" jokes.

> How do you stop a lawyer from drowning?
> Shoot him just before he hits the water.
>
> What is the ideal weight for a lawyer?
> About three pounds, including the urn.
>
> How many lawyers do you need to roof a house?
> Depends how thin you slice them.
>
> How many lawyers does it take to stop a moving bus?
> Never enough.
>
> If I had but one life to give for my country, it would be a lawyer's.
>
> Why are scientists now using lawyers instead of rats in their experiments?
> 1. There is not an endless supply of rats.
> 2. The researchers don't get attached to lawyers.
> 3. The ethics committee is more likely to approve pain inflicted on lawyers.
> 4. There are some things even a rat won't do.
> One problem remains: you can't extrapolate from the test results to human beings.
>
> Question: What do you call a lawyer up to his neck in cement?
> Answer: Not enough cement.

Terry Light (2000) has cited the last of these jokes and calls it, and by implication the others, "an invitation to genocide," referring to the systematic elimination of lawyers by the Communist Khmer Rouge, Pol Pot's regime in Cambodia. The Khmer Rouge killed nearly 2 million people, more than 20 percent of the Cambodian population, many of them as painfully as possible (Rummel 1994, 159–207). Light added, "If we continue to allow people to drape themselves in the sheep's clothing of "lawyer jokes" and wrongfully portray American lawyers as scabs on society, then we members of the Bar will have only ourselves to blame if the day comes when we are "dealt with" merely because we have certificates on our office walls which read, 'Juris Doctor.'" Light has repeated here in even stronger terms the gross fallacy that, because he is offended by lawyer jokes, they have the power to undermine his profession. Somehow I doubt that lawyer jokes were ever very popular among the Khmer Rouge. The communists in Cambodia who murdered not only lawyers but anyone wearing eyeglasses or showing any signs of education (Rummel 1994, 185) were motivated by an ideology derived partly from the doctrines of Mao Tse-tung and partly from French Marxism, picked up when their leaders went to university in Paris or elsewhere in France. Ideologies kill. Jokes do not. Death-wish jokes are harmless play that no one takes seriously. Ideologies that advocate violence are serious "death wishes" that may well be put into practice, something we shall see in the chapter on the Soviet Union that follows. American lawyers have never had anything like this to fear in the United States. Far more social workers are killed by their clients than are lawyers; there are very few jokes about social workers, but the nature of their work can arouse anger and hostility among clients to a greater extent than is the case with lawyers, fraught though some legal cases may be. People kill when they are stressed, bitter or belligerent, not when they are laughing or after they have been laughing.

Jokes have no effect on the real world out there. It is very unlikely that the cause of tort reform was assisted by the jokes. Tort reformers no doubt enjoy lawyer jokes and deploy them, but they are mere decoration and entertainment; precisely because they are jokes they do not persuade, since everyone knows exactly what jokes are. Likewise, we may dismiss the thesis popular among lawyers that the jokes originated with big corporations, who had them invented to assist in their campaigns against being sued for damages. It is impossible for any institution to create a new joke cycle in this way, impossible to get tens of millions of people to invent and circulate jokes that suit its purposes. You can hire gag writers, you can bribe scriptwriters, you can influence television comedy—but jokes belong to the people. Jokes, including lawyer jokes, emerge spontaneously. They cannot be created by decree, nor can they successfully be repressed. Jokes are democracy.

American jokes about lawyers have had no impact, but they are interesting and important. They are not a thermostat, but they are a thermometer. That the great lawyer joke cycle flourished only in America and that it was accompanied by a great deal of other American humor about lawyers leads us to ask questions about why and how America differs from other comparable liberal democracies. They are a strange tribute to the distinctive American virtues, to the emphasis on rights, legality, due process, limited government, free speech, rugged individualism, and the American dream that anyone can make it.

SIX

☙

The Rise of the Soviet Joke and the Fall of the Soviet Union

The many hundreds, quite possibly thousands, of political jokes told by the citizens of the former Soviet Union and in the satrapies of its empire constitute one of the largest bodies of jokes ever invented. The Soviet jokes were truly a people's humor, an authentic folk humor that could not be published in the countries where the jokes were told. Like all jokes, they were a collective product, for jokes have no authors and no discernible origins, but in the Soviet Union, the jokes had no competition at all from scriptwriters or from gags told by professionals on radio and television. In most countries there is a gap in both style and content between the jokes in oral circulation and those used in the mass media, but they are similar; in the Soviet Union, the humor of the people expressed in the jokes was utterly different from, indeed antithetical to, the official humor authorized and sponsored by the authorities. The jokes traveled to the democratic world and were translated into and published in English, French, German (Beckmann 1969; Isnard 1977; Drozdzynski 1977), and other languages, first by small publishers and later by big commercial ones and were very popular but were very rarely adapted to fit local circumstances; no new *anekdoty* (political jokes) of this type were invented in the democratic countries. The Soviet political jokes covered far more ground and were far more numerous than jokes told in the many merely authoritarian countries with autocratic traditional rulers or dictators such as General Franco (García 1977; Pi-Sunyer 1977). In the case of the latter, political jokes spoke and speak irreverently about those who hold political or military power and their associates, much as they did in the Soviet Union, but that is all they do (Rose 2002), and there are far fewer of them.

THE JOKES OF AUTOCRACY

President Hosni Mubarak asked one of his trusted lieutenants: "Who is great: me or Hitler?"

Lieutenant: "Hitler? He was good for nothing. He brought the world to the edge. He committed suicide. You are, no doubt, great."

Mubarak: "Who do you feel is great: me or Saddam Hussein?"

Lieutenant: "Saddam Hussein? The poor chap could not understand the U.S. machinations. See his end. There is no comparison between you and the former Iraqi president. By all standards you are great."

Mubarak: "Okay. Tell me honestly. Who is great: me or Omar bin Al-Khattab?

Lieutenant: "Omar? He always feared Allah, while you fear none." (Ausaf 2009)

Omar bin Al-Khattab was the second caliph of the Muslim world (634–44) and is revered by Sunni Muslims, the dominant group in Egypt.

Eva Perón was descending in an old-fashioned elevator in a hotel in Buenos Aires with one of the ministers of her husband, President Perón. As they passed the third floor where a party was taking place, some of the revelers saw she was in the elevator and shouted abuse at her.

Shocked, she turned to the minister and said, "Did you hear that? They called me a whore."

"Never mind," he replied. "I've been retired from the army for twenty years, but people still call me 'General.'" (Told to me in Argentina 1991)

A Zimbabwe policeman stops a motorist and asks for a donation: terrorists have kidnapped Robert Mugabe and have vowed to soak him in petrol and set him alight if the ransom is not paid.

"How much are other people giving?" the motorist asks.

"On average about two or three litres." (Macintyre 2008)

THE JOKES OF TOTALITARIAN SOCIETIES

In the Soviet Union, political jokes also routinely made fun of individual leaders, but more important, they were jokes about an entire social and political system. Only the *Flüsterwitze* (the whispered jokes) told in Nazi

Germany (Dannimann 2001; Gamm 1979; Hillenbrand 1995) have come anywhere near rivaling the Soviet ones. In the Soviet Union, jokes about all manner of targets were aggregated into one single genre of political jokes. In consequence, jokes about very varied targets, such as occupations, ethnic groups, regions, men and women, religion, drunks, prison, death and disasters, or the defects of automobiles, often became political in character.

> A drunk fell into a sewer and could not get out. He clutched the bars and tearfully cried out, "But for what, comrades, for what?" (For another version, see Beckmann 1980, 21)

> A new assistant was being taken on at a sobering up station in Russia.
> "What do you do with the drunks?" he asked.
> "If they smell of vodka, we send them back to their factory. If they smell of *samogen* (moonshine), we send them back to their village."
> "But what do I do if I get someone who smells of cognac?"
> "In that case he's a senior party official, so you clean the vomit off his suit and send him home."

> Why has the new Lada (Soviet car) got a heated rear window?
> To keep your hands warm when you are pushing it.

> A Soviet journalist interviews a Chukchi man.
> "Could you tell us briefly how you lived before the October Revolution?"
> "Hungry and cold."
> "How do you live now?"
> "Hungry, cold, and with a feeling of deep gratitude." (Draitser 1998, 76)

The Chukchis live in a remote peninsula in the Arctic northeast of Siberia, Chukhotka, and have a distinctive way of life. Their remoteness led them to become the butt of many Russian ethnic jokes, but this one turns into a joke about Soviet propaganda

> An American tourist goes with a whore in Moscow. Afterwards it is time to pay.
> He puts $20 on the table. "No," she replies.
> He puts down $50. "No."
> He puts $250 on the table. "No."
> "But that's what I pay in Boston," says the American.
> Russian whore: "I don't want your dirty capitalist money. Just take your Pershings out of Europe." (Told to me in 1984 by a colleague who had been a professor at Moscow University)

The intermediate-range American Pershing missile was deployed in Europe by NATO in the early 1980s to counter the SS20 Soviet missiles introduced in 1977. The Soviets devoted much political propaganda to try and get the Pershings removed (Mercer 1986, 114–15) so that they, the Soviets, could have a preponderance of missiles in Europe.

> A Nigerian, a Frenchman, and a Russian were arguing about whose wife had the best ass. The Nigerian proudly declared, "My wife has the biggest ass anyone has ever seen."
>
> "Size isn't everything," said the Frenchman. "My wife has the shapeliest ass of any woman in France."
>
> "Listen," said the Russian, "when I leave for work, I give my wife's ass a good slap, and when I come home again it is still vibrating . . . but that is only because we have the shortest working day in the world." (Told to me in 1984 by colleague who had been at Moscow University; see also Adams 2005, 30, joke 77)

> Who invented barbed wire?
> Michurin. He crossed earthworms with hedgehogs. (Beckmann 1980, 67; Kolasky 1972, 111)

> What is the difference between painters of the naturalist, impressionist, and the socialist realist schools? The naturalists paint as they see, the impressionists as they feel, the socialist realists as they are told. (Lewis 2006)

The very social and political order itself thus became a hyper target for joke tellers, embracing, though by no means eliminating, all other targets. Such a pattern is unique to this particular type of society. In other types of society, jokes about individual politicians often start with a political theme, but are then revealed in the punch line to be ethnic jokes or jokes about sex or drunks. But in the Soviet Union, the opposite often happened, with jokes pretending to be tales about sex or alcohol or ethnic jokes about Jews or Georgians or Armenians, but ending up as jokes about the political system. The jokes begin with a variety of scripts: paintings, genetics, the female posterior, inventions, adultery, children in the countryside, or innocuous census questions that seem to have nothing to do with politics, and yet in the punch line a new opposed script (Raskin 1985, 237) suddenly presents some absurdity of socialism.

In her study of the history of Estonian jokes, Liisi Laineste (2008, 2008a, 109, 128–29) has shown how, during the time of the second illegal

Soviet occupation of Estonia from 1944 onwards (Laar 2007a, 2007b, 2007c), the older traditional jokes with local targets disappeared as they were crowded out by pan-Soviet jokes with political themes. Estonia became part of the "unified 'joke-circulation' of the Soviet Union." Only in the 1990s were the pre-Soviet jokes revived, and new jokes with a local social, cultural, and economic setting started to replace the tide of political jokes, which had been generic to the entire area of Soviet political control. During that time, in Estonia as in the other Soviet imperial possessions and protectorates, ethnic jokes tended to focus on the Russians because they were the dominant nationality. "Russian" was treated as synonymous with "Soviet," much as many contemporary ethnic jokes about Germans refer back to the time of the Nazis.

> How many Germans does it take to change a light bulb?
> Ve are asking ze qvestions here!

Sadly, the Russians, who had been the first victims of communism after the revolution of 1917, became the upholders of that oppression and were identified with it by their subordinate peoples. Today in the now free countries of Eastern Europe, jokes about Russians are just one more kind of ethnic joke, and there are just as many such jokes about ethnic minorities and about both neighboring and distant peoples.

The key question to be asked is why this distinctive pattern of joking existed. What was it about the nature of the socialist societies that led their peoples to invent so many jokes? What do the jokes tell us about the nature of this very distinctive type of society and about the reasons for the very rapid total breakdown of the entire Soviet empire in 1989–91, when all that had seemed solid melted into air? Uprisings and coups that displace a particular ruler or ruling elite are common enough, but it is quite rare for an entire social order suddenly to collapse in peacetime and undergo such a complete transformation.

SOVIET JOKES WERE DIFFERENT

Soviet jokes differed greatly from the jokes that we have discussed in other chapters because of the extremely repressive and intrusive nature of the political and social system and in particular the absence of freedom of speech. The jokes were far more important to the people who told them than are the jokes told in democratic societies, where jokes are merely a laughing matter, sheer entertainment. It is not possible to infer this from the texts of the Soviet jokes alone, either by intuitive guesswork or by the dubious process of asserting what was in the joke tellers' minds by invoking the authority of a cultural or psychoanalytic pseudo-theory or some dubious guru. Rather, we must turn to the quite separate empirical observations of the joke tellers' behavior in social contexts that we know are reasonably representative of the society in general. From these observations we know that in times of terror individuals took considerable, or what they saw as considerable, risks in telling these jokes. It could lead to prison or the labor camp (Draitser 1978, 5). In the later years of the communist regimes, when the terror had abated, jokes played an important role in social life. On meeting an acquaintance an individual might greet him or her with "have you heard the latest *anekdot*?" and an entire social occasion might be dominated by the telling of these political jokes (Yurchak 1997). Under socialism jokes were special. They were also important because the jokes directly conveyed truths about the realities of these societies that were suppressed by the Soviet authorities. The authorities were shamefully supported in their deception by many western scholars and writers. Some of the latter thoroughly sympathized with the Soviet regime and its ideology, but most of them were merely naïve, fearful of bad feeling or even conflict between their own country and the Soviets and thus unwilling to believe that their country's opponent was evil. Others disliked their own society and were so enamored of critical slogans concerning democracy and capitalism that they could not believe that the leaders of the Soviet Union, who mouthed the same slogans, could be tyrants. The jokes of the Soviet era were a better predictor of the future of socialism than were the writings of those myopic or mendacious western observers of and "experts" on the Soviet Union, who utterly failed to predict the sudden and complete crumbling of the entire rotten system. When Humpty Dumpty fell, they were left with egg on their faces.

The jokes about dumb carabinieri, blondes, or orthopedic surgeons, greedy lawyers and sport-despising Jews, the gay Greeks and the fellated French discussed earlier—all constitute social puzzles, puzzles that I have had to try to solve, since they do not correspond directly to reality. They are the product of particular and sometimes not immediately discernible social tensions or of peculiar historical circumstances that have to be elucidated. The problem of explaining the Soviet jokes is different, since they are closely related to real events and experiences. My main task is to explain the nature of the events and processes to which the jokes refer, since these are necessary to a full understanding of the jokes. The most widely circulating western jokes are often very clever and indeed sophisticated in their construction, but they do not usually require much background knowledge. You don't need to know much, or indeed in most cases any, law to understand jokes about lawyers. Likewise, as Władysław Chłopicki and I (Davies and Chłopicki 2004) have shown, American jokes about Polish stupidity make no references at all to the distinctive culture of the Polish people, nor do they require the jokers to possess any knowledge beyond what can be obtained from a high school education and an acquaintance with popular culture and commercial advertising—that is to say, very little and nothing difficult. Understanding the content of such jokes is often easy; it is explaining why particular joke cycles exist at all that is intensely difficult. By contrast, like many jokes about specialized occupations or indeed many Jewish jokes, Soviet jokes often have to be unpacked if they are fully to be understood by outsiders. Indeed they often even have to be explained to the young and free descendants of those who invented and told them during the grim years of socialism.

During the time of Soviet socialism, hundreds, perhaps thousands, of political jokes were invented. They were already common in 1922 (Chamberlin 1957, 27; Lyons 1935; Talmadge 1943, 48). However, the earliest jokes are often inaccessible, so here we will discuss in turn two broad periods of joke telling: the time of high terror and the time of decadence and downfall. The time of high terror lasted from the end of the New Economic Policy (NEP, *Novaya Ekonomicheskaya Politika*), a time when a large element of capitalism was permitted (Levytsky 1971, 48) in 1928 to Khrushchev's denunciation of terror in his secret speech at the Twentieth Party Congress of the Communist Party of the Soviet Union, February 25, 1956. The time of decadence lasted from Khrushchev's speech until the time of Gorbachev's leadership in 1985–91, when his well-intentioned attempts to reform the unreformable led to the final crisis of socialism. First, the terror.

THE TIME OF HIGH TERROR

There never was a time of freedom and security for the individual in the Soviet Union. There were no constitutional checks on state power, no rights to liberty or property, no freedom of speech and assembly, no *habeas corpus,* no guarantees of due process. Only one political party was permitted, and that one was controlled from the center. From the very start, Lenin's Bolsheviks deliberately both incited random terror and employed "disciplined terror" (Andrew and Mitrokhin 2000, 709; Levytsky 1971, 30–31; Sebag Montefiore 2004, 235), and the omnipresent, omniscient, communist secret police, the Cheka (then OGPU, then NKVD, then KGB) suppressed all effective dissent. Nonetheless, the level of terror varied, and it peaked between 1928 and 1956. To call this time Stalinism is misleading in the same sense that it would be misleading to reduce the Nazis to Hitler. The very structure of the Soviet political system and the nature of the ideology that legitimated it made it inherently likely that someone without scruples would come to power, enjoy unlimited power, and prove impossible to dislodge. Ruthless systems call forth ruthless leaders. Absolute power corrupts absolutely. Stalin was simply Lenin's most able pupil (Amis 2003, 138) and extended his ideas (Andrew and Mitrokhin 2000, 709; Pipes 2003, 236; Tolstoy 1981, 4, 10), a point made humorously in Robert Conquest's limerick:

> There was an old Marxist called Lenin,
> Who did one or two million men in.
> That's a lot to have done in,
> But where he did one in,
> That old Marxist Stalin did ten in. (Robert Conquest, cited in Moore 2009)

And they answered one another as they played and said Lenin hath slain his millions and Stalin his tens of millions.

> What is the most boring whodunit in the world? The most boring whodunit is "The History of the Communist Party" because by the third page you know who committed the murders. (Winnick 1964, 6–7)

The era of high terror saw the murder of tens of millions of innocent people and the arbitrary imprisonment and exile of tens of millions of others (Courtois et al. 1999; Reddaway 2008b, 191–95; Rummel 1990; Rummel 1994, 79–89). The jokes of, from, and about the time of high terror (Adams 2005; Chamberlin 1957; Harris and Rabinovich 1988; Krikmann 2004; Talmadge 1943) refer to this and also to the brutal crushing of the peasants and herdsmen with forced collectivization, the deportation of the kulaks (successful entrepreneurial peasants), and the deliberately created famines that verged on genocide in Kazakhstan and in the Ukraine, the famine movingly described by Miron Dolot (1985). The purges and farcical trials of engineers and managers falsely called wreckers and saboteurs, and of intellectuals, army officers, and Party members accused of treason in the 1930s (Conquest 1971; Levytsky 1971), the anti-Semitic persecutions of the Jews, particularly in 1946–53, the "black years of Soviet Jewry" (Kovály 1997, 136, 150, 189; Rosenberg 1997, 260–62; Vaksberg 1994), torture, executions, and labor camps all turn up in the jokes. The jokes are a gallows humor. The harsh employment regulations introduced in 1940–56, when the workers became in effect serfs, forbidden to change their jobs and subject to harsh penalties (including being sent to a labor camp) for petty irregularities, such as being more than twenty minutes late for work (S. Davies 1997, 15, 46–47; Fitzpatrick 1999, 8; Zaslavsky 1982, 4–7), were also a source of jokes.

The spectacular Soviet famines in which millions died were famines deliberately engineered by the government or famines in which aid was deliberately withheld from the starving for propaganda reasons. Those who believed that feeding the people was more important than some imagined glorious future, those who saw that pie on the table was better than pie in the sky were denounced as "philistines" (Vatlin and Malashenko 2006, 143).

> The all-powerful inhabitants of the Kremlin were attacked by body lice, as persistent as one of the Egyptian plagues. Scientists were helpless. Finally Karl Radek—to whom all such witticisms are automatically and quite unfairly attributed—made a suggestion that saved the day:
> "Collectivize them," he is supposed to have said. "Then half of them will die and the other half will run away." (Lyons 1935, 334)

> What is the difference between India and Russia?
> In India one man starves for the people, and in Russia the people starve for one man. (Talmadge 1943, 50)

Mohandas K. Gandhi, the Mahatma, went on hunger strikes in India in 1922, 1930, and 1933 during his nonviolent campaign for Indian independence. He did not die in the jails of the king-emperor but was shot by another Hindu after India had become independent. Stalin starved millions to death in 1932–33.

> Two Russians discussed who was the greater man, Stalin or President Hoover.
> "Hoover taught the Americans not to drink," says one.
> "Yes," replies the other, "but Stalin taught the Russians not to eat."
> (For other slightly differing versions, see Adams 2005, 21; Kolasky 1972, 4. For further famine jokes, see Chamberlin 1957, 28, 31.)

When Herbert Hoover was president (1928–32), he upheld Prohibition. Stalin in 1932–33 was responsible for starving several million people to death. The joke speaks of Russians, but there was an even greater death toll in Ukraine and Kazakhstan, possibly with the intent of destroying those nationalities. A decade earlier, Hoover had headed the American Relief Association, which shipped food to Russia to alleviate the Povolzhye famine of 1921–22, in which several million perished. Many millions more would have died but were able to survive on rations provided by the Americans and the British. After Hoover's relief workers had left, the Soviets persecuted those who had worked with them locally (Levytsky 1971, 42–43). No relief operation was permitted in 1932–33.

> A Russian Jew was walking through the suburbs of Moscow when a car stopped suddenly, a man was thrown out at the side of the road, and the other car sped off. He ran over and saw that it was his old friend Moishe, who had been beaten almost to death by the KGB and was nearly unconscious, his eyes opening and closing.
> "Moishe, Moishe," he cried. "It's me, Abram. Don't you remember me? We were in Auschwitz together."
> "Ah," said Moishe dreamily, "ah yes, Auschwitz." (For another version, see Banc and Dundes 1990, 39–40)

> A Jew fills out one of the official applications.
> "Were you ever a member of any party other than the Communist party?"
> "No."
> "Have you remained on any territory occupied by the enemy?"
> "No."
> "Have you ever been convicted or are you currently under investigation for any criminal activity?"

"No."
"Your nationality?"
"Yes." (Draitser 1998, 125)

After the war, many who had lived in those Soviet territories occupied by the invading German armies were rounded up as collaborators, despite there being no evidence against them. The relatives of those arrested were seen as sharing their guilt. Soviet citizens over the age of sixteen had to carry internal passports. The fifth section was marked nationality, which said which republic the person came from such as Uzbekistan or Armenia. However, if you were Jewish, it said Jew, no matter where you were from. The form-filler in the joke has pleaded not guilty to all the probing questions, but pleads guilty to being Jewish, without it even being mentioned. No other nationality would be perceived in a way that was automatically taken as a sign of blameworthiness. Soviet anti-Semites would refer to the Jews as "natsmen," referring to the give-away fifth section marked nationality (Sebag Montefiore 2004, 311).

Three men were talking in a labor camp about why they had been arrested.
"I was sent here because I was late for work," said the first.
"I was so anxious not to be late that I arrived half an hour early and was accused of being a saboteur," said the second
The third said, "I turned up exactly on time and was accused of owning a foreign watch." (Told to author in 1960s in UK)

Soviet industry could not produce cheap reliable watches for the masses. During their officially permitted, indeed encouraged, time of looting and raping in Eastern Europe in 1944–45 (Aydelott 1993; Iverson 1963, 106), the Soviet soldiers stole as many watches as they could, sometimes wearing three (Fitzpatrick 1999, 8) on each wrist.

A marshal (the highest rank in the Soviet army) is inspecting troops on the parade ground.
"Greetings, comrade infantrymen!"
"We wish you health, comrade marshal!"
"Greetings, comrade tankers!"
"We wish you health, comrade marshal!"
And so on through the artillerymen, pilots, etc."
"Greetings, comrade *chekisty*!"
"Yeah, hi yourself!" (said in a threatening tone) (Adams 2005, 35)

All the soldiers reply respectfully to their most senior officer except the *chekisty,* the members of the secret police, men who could have even a marshal arrested and put to death on a fake charge. During the invasion of Finland and again in World War II, the secret police were stationed behind the front line to shoot any soldiers who did not attack with sufficient vigor.

> Stalin ordered the marshals of the Soviet Union to wrestle in front of him. Marshal Tukhachevsky won every single bout. Stalin was angry. He sent for Marshal Timoshenko, who was huge.
> Timoshenko easily defeated Tukhachevsky. When Tukhachevsky was thrown to the floor, he banged his head. Timoshenko said he was sorry.
> "Don't worry, comrade Timoshenko," Stalin said. "He won't be needing his head much longer." (See Perakh 1998)

Tukhachevsky, one of the Soviet army's most able senior commanders, was executed in 1937. Three of the five other marshals, 13 of 15 generals, 50 of 57 army corps commanders, and 154 out of 186 division commanders disappeared in the great purges of 1936–39. During the purges, absurd, even impossible, confessions of guilt were extracted from the accused by torture and by threatening to torture and execute their wives and children as well. In fairness to the authorities, it should be added that imposing the death penalty on children over the age of 12 was permitted under Soviet law in the 1930s (Tolstoy 1981, 219). The loss of all these officers was one, though not the only, reason for the humiliating defeats an inept Soviet army suffered in 1940 against tiny Finland and again in the early stages of the German invasion in 1941. In 1957, Tukhachevsky and the other officers were rehabilitated.

> Stalin and President Roosevelt had a bet as to which of them had the most loyal and obedient bodyguard. Roosevelt called his bodyguard over and asked him if he would jump out of a high window for him. "No," replied John. "I will not jump. I have a wife and children."
> Stalin's bodyguard, when asked, replied, "Of course, I will jump. For the sake of my wife and children." (Krikmann 2004, 99–100. My translation from the German. Krikmann gives other versions in Estonian, Finnish, and Russian.)

> What is the difference between socialist democracy and capitalist democracy?
> The same as between the electric chair and the armchair. (Witkowska 2008, 129n24)

"I hear that all the Germans in Nazi Germany are going to have a 'people's car' each."

"That's nothing. We all have two vehicles, the NKVD car and the ambulance." (See S. Davies 1997, 95)

On Hitler's instructions, the Volkswagen (people's car) was designed so that every family could afford a small car paid for by installments. The NKVD was the secret police, descendant of the Cheka and ancestor of the KGB.

"They've taken Teruel."

"What? And his wife, too?" (Remembered by Ilya Ehrenburg; cited in Rubinstein 1996)

There are other, slightly differing versions; Raskin (1985, 242) has Guadalquivir.

"Did you hear? They took Saragossa"

"Her husband, too?"

"No, Saragossa is a city."

"What, they're taking whole cities now?!" (Adams 2005, 39)

Both Teruel and Saragossa (Zaragoza) were towns that changed hands in the course of the Spanish Civil War (1936–39), the war in which the Soviet Union ostensibly intervened to support the Republicans against the Nationalists but where it showed more concern about getting the NKVD, a grandchild of the Cheka and an ancestor of the KGB, to eliminate rival Republican and leftist groups (Levytsky 1971, 112–13). Ilya Ehrenburg reported on the war for the press in Moscow, where the citizens were rather more concerned that their friends, colleagues, neighbors, and entire families were being arbitrarily arrested, imprisoned, and murdered than with the squabbles in Spain.

These are just a small sample, but a reasonably representative one, of the kinds of jokes told about the regime at that time. Soviet jokes explored all the weaknesses of the system in a way that often showed great insight and even erudition, which indicates that the intellectuals had had a hand in composing and circulating them. The jokes about famine among the peasants and the hardships of the downtrodden masses generally refer to these peoples' experience of daily life, but what would the humble uneducated toilers have known about Gandhi, Teruel, genetics, or impressionism?

The jokes are humorous, yet they convey truth. Indeed, they are a more accurate portrayal of Soviet history and the nature of socialism than that purveyed by the regime or by sympathetic and influential western intellectuals at the time such as George Bernard Shaw, the racist and homophobic Beatrice Webb, and her tadpole husband, Sidney (Conquest 2008, 126; McElroy 2000) or Walter Duranty (Taylor 1990), who denied that the famines had happened or reduced them to little local difficulties. The show trials of the 1930s, which like the witchcraft trials of the sixteenth and seventeenth centuries had the tortured and tormented accused confessing to the impossible and being led off to execution or deportation to the camps, were described by Professor Harold Laski and the sometime British Member of Parliament D. N. Pritt as entirely just and the accused as utterly guilty. Laski even praised Vyshinsky, a man who in court screamed sarcastic abuse at innocent prisoners, as a model prosecutor (Conquest 2008, 125). The jokes in Bruce Adams's (2005) very thorough *Twentieth-Century Soviet and Russian History in Anecdotes* are a far better guide to what happened and its meaning than are the works of the "revisionist historians" (Pipes 2003, 218–23), who failed to understand the utter centrality of the political in Soviet type societies and could never properly come to terms with the sheer evil to be found there; they were at best equivocal about it.

The jokes were told, as are all jokes, mainly for enjoyment. In and of themselves they are funny because they are cleverly constructed and highly transgressive. The Soviet jokes differ only in that they emerged in a society where the most important prohibited forms of speech were political rather than referring to, say, race or sex or blasphemy. But the context in which they were told and their social and political importance differed markedly from what was the case in free societies. The importance of the jokes to those who told them can be inferred from the risks that so many individuals took in telling and circulating them, when they knew that being reported to the authorities could result in possible imprisonment or deportation and even death (Deriabin and Gibney 1960, appendix; Draitser 1978, 5; Fitzpatrick 1999, 66, 183–86; Zlobin 1996, 223). Individuals took similar risks in Ceausescu's totalitarian Romania (1965–89), where political jokes and cartoons circulated in writing in a country where even typewriters had to be registered and jokes were reproduced using carbons, since photocopiers were guarded to prevent public access (Cochran 1989, 265). In the Soviet Union in the time of terror, even to smile at someone else's joke told at another table could lead to arrest (Conquest 1971, 423), and informers would denounce a joke teller out of fear or from personal malice (Deriabin and Gibney 1960, 173).

There are many jokes that refer directly to the spying on, arrest, trial, and punishment of joke tellers (Cochran 1989, 270; Dolgopolova 1983, 30; Parrott 1977, 32; Fitzpatrick 1999, 185; Kolasky 1972, 3–4, 13; Meyer and Meyer 1978, 110).

> **Prison conversation:**
> "Why are you here?"
> "I told a joke."
> "And what brought you here?"
> "I listened to a joke."
> "And what about you?"
> "I am here because I was lazy! One evening I was at a party. Someone there told a joke. I went home wondering whether I should inform on them right away or wait until the next morning. 'Well,' I thought, 'tomorrow morning will do.' And they came for me during the night!"

> Two judges are eating soup in the restaurant of the "palace." One with a spoon in his hand laughs.
> "Why?"
> "I heard a good joke today."
> "Tell me."
> "I can't tell you. I gave the man who told it five years."
> "You call that a good joke? Good jokes get six years at least." (Told to me in Slovakia 1985)

> A contest for the best political joke was announced.
> First prize—twenty-five years imprisonment.
> Second prize—fifteen years solitary confinement.
> Third prize—ten years and confiscation of all belongings. (Draitser 1978, 29)

> Modern Russian roulette. There are twelve of us telling political jokes. One of us is an informer and we do not know who. (Told to me in Slovakia in 1985)

> Who dug the White Sea Canal?
> The right bank was dug by those who related anecdotes.
> And the left bank?
> By those who listened. (Kolasky 1972, vii)

The canal was built in 1931–33, largely without heavy machinery, dug by the forced labor of hundreds of thousands of prisoners from the Gulag with great loss of life. It was and is of very limited use because it is far too shallow, a white elephant canal.

That people took such risks is both an indication of the importance the jokes had for them and of the strong and interlocking networks of interpersonal trust and solidarity that they had created, that provided them with some degree of independence from an overwhelmingly powerful state (Shlapentokh 1990, 72; Thurston 1991, 541–50). For the authorities and particularly for the secret police, in turn the Cheka, the OGPU, the NKVD and the KGB, henceforth referred to collectively as the KGB, the jokes were also important and even used as a test of public opinion (Andrew and Mitrokhin 2000, 673–74, 726); they regularly collected and sometimes repressed political jokes. Indeed, the KGB files may well turn out to be the best source of ethnographic data on anti-Soviet humorous folklore in general, including graffiti, parody, and *chastushki* (satirical songs or limericks), since other records of these were censored and bowdlerized (S. Davies 1997; Fitzpatrick 1999, 183–86). Jokes are not a way of saying covertly what the teller is unwilling to say directly, for those who told jokes furtively among trusted associates also exchanged political opinions and secrets in private, perhaps in the bathroom with the taps turned on to muffle the conversation (Rubinstein 1996, 171–72), or for the bathroomless majority in the kitchen on occasions known as "filthy togetherness." Mutterings of disbelief, cynicism, fear, and discontent were widespread. Informers passed them on to the authorities, and the items are still there in the Soviet archives (Fitzpatrick 1999, 94–100, 186). The Jewish writer Isaac Emmanuilovich Babel, arrested and tortured in 1939 and murdered by the state in 1940, said it was only possible to talk to one's wife at night and even then under the blanket (Rubinstein 1996); surely he must have told her a muffled joke or two.

Nonetheless, the jokes were so much a part of everyday understanding that people in the Soviet Union and refugees from it would routinely use them better to make a point. As one Uzbek put it, an anecdote could contain "the whole tragedy and drama of an event" (Krikmann 2004, 241). Jokes were told because they had force as well as because they gave pleasure. Jokes were remembered and transmitted better than other aspects of informal culture (Fitzpatrick 1999, 183). Jokes were used as a means of conveying insight, far more than they are or ever have been in or in relation to other kinds of society. However, this is a statement not about the content of the jokes but about the consistently repressive social and political context in which they were told, which gave them a special luster and significance.

THE TIME OF DECADENCE

The jokes of the time of terror were numerous, but far more were called into existence in the years of decadence after 1956, building up to a peak in the early 1980s, the last years of Brezhnev's reign (1964–82), the golden age of Soviet joking (Krikmann 2006, 2–3; Yurchak 1997, 175). It is difficult to be certain about this because many jokes from the time of terror may have been lost or recycled to fit a later era. It is always difficult to try to compare quantities in this way if the number of jokes in circulation is very large. Nonetheless, the work of many scholars does seem strongly to indicate that there were far more jokes in the latter period.

The smaller number of political jokes stemming from the time of terror, relative to its successor, the time of decadence, contradicts the simple version of the thesis that the jokes are a direct product of repression, a view taken by the leading folklorist of jokes, Alan Dundes. Dundes (1971, 51) claimed that "the more repressive the regime, the more numerous the political jokes" and again in Banc and Dundes (1986, 14) that "the more repressive the ideology and system the more ingenious and clever the political wit." Dundes's propositions are wrong. Repression does generate political jokes, but the jokers are also inhibited by fear, so that the Soviet jokes thrived best when the chances of being arrested were perceived as lower and the penalties as less severe. Even during the thaw of the late 1950s, the open and relaxed telling of political jokes became more common (Hellberg 1985, 92–93). It became a social asset to be a good joke teller. By the late 1960s, people would frequently reel out a string of *anekdoty,* the political jokes, when there was an interval in any meeting or classes, and this was even more open and common by the late 1970s (Beam 1982). In 1982 and 1983, my English-speaking Bulgarian colleagues would freely exchange jokes with me in a crowded restaurant in Gabrovo, although Brezhnev, dear Leonid Ilich, was always called "Mr. B," just in case the repeated laughter following the use of his name should alert an informer. The jokes of this milder period were probably more numerous but certainly no less clever and ingenious than those of the time of terror. Political jokes flourished with equal vigor in the 1970s and 1980s in the more relaxed countries, such as Hungary and Poland, as in the most repressive ones, such as Ceausescu's Romania, from which Dundes took his jokes.

The number and possibly even the ingenuity of the jokes are determined rather by the breadth of the state's oppressive reach. Since in a socialist political order the state owns all productive property, including farms, factories, shops, and businesses that purvey services, jokes about economic matters, jokes about shortages and consumption, and jokes about work and employment of necessity become political jokes. Since the key decisions about what to produce were made by the central planners, and the rulers regularly told the people that "life's become better, life's become jollier," even when it had gotten worse, it was both inevitable and just that they should became the butt of so many jokes stemming from the frustrations of everyday life. The jokers faced with sober senses their real conditions of life and laughed at the utterly fictitious official version.

JOKES ABOUT PLANNED SHORTAGES

The single biggest topic of the jokes in both periods (Adams 2005; Banc and Dundes 1986) was the endless shortages, the waiting in line for food and other basic necessities and the deplorable quality of housing and consumer goods. In the time of terror, the standard of living was very low for all, except for a small highly privileged elite who had access to unlimited food through multiple ration books and had privileged access to splendid housing and special TORGSIN shops that sold luxuries. The economic position of the peasantry had been destroyed, and the wages of the workers in the workers' state were forced down to the minimum required to keep the labor force in being; most of a family's income was spent on food, and even then the urban workers were hungry and at times close to starvation (S. Davies 1997, 23–30, 109; Rimmel 1997). With rare exceptions, "the Bolshevik elite showed little sympathy for the plight of ordinary people" (Vatlin and Malashenko 2006, 143). Housing conditions were bad, for heavy industry was given priority in a socialist society addicted to conspicuous production, a society that made a fetish of investment and chased meaningless statistical targets of output. Work was both arduous and dangerous because the unrealistic targets decreed by the planners demanded very long hours of work and the taking of serious physical risks with human life. This was covered up by the periodic persecution of scapegoats, the imagined wreckers and saboteurs (Vatlin and Malashenko 2006, 169), a modern equivalent of burning witches. The jokes reflect those grim times.

> The Commissar of Internal Trade, Mikoyan is ... comparing notes with the Commissar of Health, Dr. Semashko.
> "You haven't accomplished anything," Mikoyan chides his colleague. "When you took office ten years ago, there was malaria in the country, wasn't there? Well, there is still malaria. There was typhus in the country—there is still typhus. There was—"
> "And what has your Commissariat accomplished?" Dr. Semashko interrupts.
> "Mine?" Mikoyan declares proudly.
> "The situation is entirely different. When I took office ten years ago, there was bread in the country, wasn't there? Well, there isn't any now. There was meat then—there isn't any now. There was sugar. . . ." (Lyons 1935, 329–30)

> Co-operative shops, lacking real supplies, would often decorate their shelves with empty tin cans. A simple working woman came into such a shop and asked to buy some canned goods, pointing to the full shelves.
> "My dear woman," the clerk explained, "these are only embellishments."
> "Well, well," the woman sighed. "Let me have two cans of that. We take what we can get these days." (Lyons 1935, 330–31)

Nonetheless, scarcity jokes boomed even more in the time of decadence, when money wages were higher and the standard of living was improving, albeit very unevenly (Burks 1989, 122; Zaslavsky 1982, 52–53, 100, 123). Now that there was some attempt to produce goods for the people, it became even clearer that the planned economy did not work and indeed could not work. Without a market to shape prices, you do not know how to match production to what is demanded by the consumers, either in quantity or quality, or even how to deal with the allocation of capital goods, raw materials, or components. Without a proper legal system, you cannot draw up and enforce contracts. Without competing entrepreneurs, you cannot innovate. It is impossible to run a modern sophisticated economy without these—"in the same sense in which it is impossible for a cat to swim the Atlantic" (Polanyi 1951, 126). All this had been predicted by western economists long before (Hoff 1949), and also by implication the sudden collapse of the entire Soviet system, not just politically but economically.

But first let us look at the jokes:

A brand-new food store has opened—everything looks sparkling and there is a brisk young shop assistant in a crisp white coat.

A customer enters and says, "Wrap me up a pound of meat, please."

The shop assistant takes out a large sheet of paper and says, "Certainly, give me your meat."

General Jaruzelski, the Polish communist leader, is being driven through Warsaw in a limousine.

He sees a long line of people outside a food store.

He tells his chauffeur to stop, and he asks them how long they have been there.

"Six hours," they reply.

"This is dreadful," says Jaruzelski. "I must do something."

An hour later a truck arrives and unloads a hundred chairs. (Told to author by a Polish colleague in the 1980s)

There was a long queue outside a meat shop in Poland. After an hour the manager came out and said, "The delivery of meat will be less than we thought. The Jews had better go home."

An hour later he came out again: "There is even less meat than we expected. Those of you who are not party members will not get any." Most people left.

After a further hour the manager addressed the party members. "I know you are all loyal party activists, so I can tell you the truth. There isn't any meat."

As the activists trudged away, one said to another: "Just as I thought. Yet another Jewish conspiracy." (Told to me by a Polish colleague in the 1980s; for other versions, see Banc and Dundes 1990, 162; Beckmann 1980, 51; Dershowitz 1991, 263)

A Georgian carrying a big basket is flying from Tbilisi to Moscow. A hijacker takes over the flight and demands that the pilot fly to Paris. The pilot agrees, but the Georgian pulls out his knife, cuts the hijacker's throat, and tells the pilot, "Listen here, *genatsvale,* you fly to Moscow and right away." When the plane lands, the Georgian is immediately awarded the highest of medals; he is made a Hero of the Soviet Union. After the award, the KGB take him away and demand, "Why did you really stop the plane being hijacked? You had better tell the truth."

The Georgian replies, "How could I sell my oranges in Paris?"

Question to Radio Armenia: What would happen if socialism were built in Greenland?

Answer: At first snow would be made available only through ration books, and later snow would be distributed only to the KGB officers and their families.

A Russian, a Frenchman, and a Slovak discuss how they live.
Slovak: I live 1 + 2.
Frenchman: What do you mean?
Slovak: 1 kitchen + 2 rooms.
Frenchman: Then I live 1+ 5.
Russian: Ah, but I live 2 + 8.
What do you mean?
Two feet from the road and eight feet below the ground. (Told to me in Bratislava, Slovakia 1985.)

These are jokes with differing illogical mechanisms. The immediate targets are poor Russians and violent, greedy Georgians, and depending on tone and context, either cunning Jews or stupid anti-Semites. However, through every one of the jokes there runs the absurdity of a society without a proper price mechanism to determine what is produced and where to invest. The catastrophic failure of agriculture meant shortages of food, and there was an obsessional investment in wasteful, gigantic prestige projects and in armaments, not in housing for ordinary people. Rents and the price of food were kept artificially low, but this exacerbated the problem, for there were no signals to the planners to provide better housing or even to do repairs, and there were no incentives for the peasants to produce more food. Low prices and high money wages of necessity means queues and incidentally meant drunkenness. The price of oranges was high because too few were grown or imported, and the price of airfares was artificially low because of the planes' military usefulness, so that Georgians who had grown a few oranges or some flowers on their tiny personal plots of land could travel to Moscow, hawk them in the street, and earn enough in a few hours to make the xenophobic Russians resent and envy them. Low prices and rents, together with rationing, superficially seem egalitarian, but only the privileged could get residence permits, apartments, and assorted perquisites, together with better education and health care, through power, *svyasi* (connections, especially dubious ones), and bribery (Brokhin 1975, 95; Hoffman 2002, 7, 17–19); ordinary people could not. Black markets flourished, involving both individuals and entire enterprises. For many individuals the most attractive jobs were those that gave opportunities for moonlighting or the theft of and illicit trading in state property (Andreski 1989, 720–22; Brokhin 1975). Everything in the Soviet empire was in both senses on the left: on the Left ideologically and "on the left" for dishonest personal gain (Hoffman 2002, 18). For state enterprises the black markets and *blat* (exchanges of favors, corruption) were utterly necessary, for otherwise they would have been unable to comply with the fantasies and rigidities of the planners sitting at their desks with input-output matrices. Most enterprises employed *tolkachi* (pushers, fixers) to handle procurements and to expedite deliveries using whatever methods were necessary. Without corruption, the entire economic system would have collapsed much earlier than it did, due to the intrinsic irrationality and contradictions of a centrally planned system. Everyone could see the huge gap between the official pretence of the virtuous "New Soviet man" and the sordid reality of venal "Homo Sovieticus."

FROM SOCIALIST CORRUPTION TO THE NEW RUSSIANS

After the Soviet Union fell, it was this reserve army of the corrupt and the venal, the *nomenklatura* (appointees to senior privileged positions [Theen 1989]), the party bosses, and the foreign trade bureaucrats who gained control over and often ownership of the property that had belonged to the state (Reddaway and Glinski 2001, 29). The KGB members who had learned their trade as gangsters for the party now ran criminal gangs on their own account (Hoffman 2002, 234). State crime had been privatized.

Ordinary Russians had lived for so long under socialism that they lacked the skills needed to operate in the marketplace, for the Soviets had gone to enormous lengths to eliminate the spirit of entrepreneurship and private property. Under socialism it was an "economic crime" to buy and sell goods or set up a small factory, and ordinary people had been taught to hate entrepreneurship and those who made their own money (Hoffman 2002, 18); the only markets they had known were black, and the only business dealings of which managers had experience were corrupt ones. In post-Soviet Russia there was no rule of law, no law enforcement, and no proper legal system to define entitlements, impose restraints, and provide security of contract, and so debts and conflicts were settled outside the law by coercion (Hoffman 2002, 6, 234–35). Many became worse off than they had been under Gorbachev, for all economic security was now destroyed. The Russians had suffered by the establishment of the Soviet Union, suffered while it was held in place by force, and suffered again when it disintegrated.

Terry W. Light, J.D., whose fierce denunciation of American jokes mocking lawyers was quoted in the previous chapter, wrote in 1991 in defense of his most noble and unfairly traduced profession:

> Earlier this year, the *National Law Journal* featured an article on the miserable legal infrastructure of the Soviet Union, a fundamental weakness which will plague that country in its struggle to establish the most basic concepts and institutions necessary for a successful society. That article should be required reading for at least every American lawyer (especially those who would denigrate our profession) and probably for every American. Look it up! And, when you finish reading it, find another lawyer and thank him or her for upholding and perpetuating a legal system which, though far from flawless, maintains and drives the most sophisticated civilization in the history of mankind. (Light 2000)

The author will make a point of personally thanking the next five American lawyers he meets. In fairness there is only one thing worse than having far too many lawyers and that is having far too few. In the absence of enforceable legal contracts in the new Russia, disputes and dept enforcement were settled gangster fashion (Hoffman 2002, 6, 234–35), and in the 1990s there emerged a huge wave of jokes about a newly rich class of shady racketeers, the New Russians (Adams 2005, 160), who flaunted their dubiously gained wealth in front of an impoverished and in many cases more refined and cultured population. In Seth Graham's listing of thirty-four collections of anecdotes brought out up to 1998 by the Minsk publishing house Literatura, there are three separate volumes of jokes about New Russians, whereas other targets, including such internationally popular topics as drunks, blacks, English lords, husbands and their wives' lovers only got one volume each (2003b, 206–207; see also Graham 2003a).

> "Dad, all the lads at my school go there on the bus, but the chauffeur always takes me in the Rolls-Royce. It makes me feel different and left out"
>
> **New Russian:** "Don't worry, my boy. I will buy you a Swedish luxury bus of your own, and you will be able to travel in the same way as all the other boys" (Russian, 1990s)

> A New Russian urgently needs a new bookkeeper.
> "I've got an excellent candidate in mind," says his manager, "but he's still got half a year to serve." (Adams 2005, 164)

Those in power in the Soviet Union, when it still existed, constantly and consistently tried to shift the blame for the system's economic failure onto those below—low-level bureaucrats, collective farmers, or even the workers in particular shops or factories. Aggrieved individuals were even encouraged to complain about minor functionaries, both to the more powerful officials at the center and to the press, and their letters might well be published (S. Davies 1997, 18, 31; Thurston 1991, 551–53); naïve or favorably disposed western observers thought this was democracy in action, when in fact it was one more form of control from the top and a way of diverting discontent onto the little man. What were never printed were the people's complaints about hunger, cold, shortages, and the oppressiveness of official regulations (S. Davies 1997, 31). The system was the very embodiment of socialist morality, and so all its shortcomings had to be defined as the fault of deviant individuals (Deriabin and Gibney 1960, 73, 113, 136). Ridiculing these scapegoats was one of the main purposes of official Soviet humor, which sought to deride rather than to entertain. Journals with biting and stinging names such as Krokodil (Editors of *Krokodil* 1989), Nettles, Porcupine, Hornet, Stag Beetle, and Thistle were a vehicle for satires and cartoons about those who had to face workers, clients, and customers directly, the equivalent of humor about the foreman or supervisor. It was a limited humor about those with a little brief authority. No one holding lasting and serious power was ever ridiculed, nor was the political and economic system itself. It was tame and tactful stuff, and editors could be sacked for straying past the limits of the permissible (Chamberlin 1957, 27; Oring

2004, 216; Sanders 1962, 22–27; Sanders 1982, 21–29; Talmadge 1943, 46). Official humor had a particular defined purpose, and the brief given to writers and cartoonists was to stir up scorn and indignation through derision; being funny was a secondary concern, a way of making this palatable and enjoyable. The official humor was a form of designed order. The patterns that large numbers of jokes exhibit are the opposite; here we have "spontaneous order," the form of order that emerges from the aggregation of a large number of independent individual decisions by economic actors, those carrying out scientific experiments, judges in a common law system, or in this case jokers (Barry 1982; Polanyi 1951). Jokes have no authors and thus cannot have intentions. During a particular telling it is possible to infer the purposes and feelings of that particular teller from the tone and the context but not from the text itself (S. Davies 2002, 221–22, 227–28). That is why it was possible for top party officials such as Karl Radek, senior army officers, KGB men (Deriabin and Gibney 1960; Myagkov 1976, 2), and judges who had convicted others accused of "anti-Soviet conversations" (including humorous conversations) to laugh at the jokes. They laughed because the Soviet jokes were so ingenious and because, even for those who exercised power, jokes were time off from the inhibitions imposed by Soviet political correctness. At a radio producers' conference in Russia, a delegate introduced himself truthfully as the head of Radio Armenia. Everybody laughed because even these senior propagators of the official line, men who had much to lose if the system stumbled, all knew the many jokes based on fictitious broadcasts from "Radio Armenia," also known as "Radio Eriwan" (Hellberg 1985; Schiff 1975, 1978) from the capital of Armenia, which played with the stupidities and the sheer nastiness of the system in absurd ways.

The entire Soviet economic system was summed up in a single joke:

> The Soviet leaders Joseph Stalin, Nikita Khrushchev, and Leonid Brezhnev are traveling on a train. Suddenly, the train stops.
> Stalin tries to solve the problem. The engineer is shot for sabotage and the co-driver is deported to Siberia. The train doesn't budge.
> Now it is Khrushchev's turn. He brings the co-driver back from the labor camp and tells him, "I know you have been in exile for a long time, but please try to remember how to get the train going." He cannot, and the train still doesn't move.

Brezhnev now orders that all the blinds be drawn across the windows and tells the passengers to start rocking in their seats. "Now," he says, "the train is moving."

(There is a sequel in which Gorbachev is also present and says brightly, "Why don't the four of us get out and push.")

The recognition of economic failure and the accompanying hypocrisy was coupled with a rejection of the dominant Marxist-Leninist ideology, something intrusive and omnipresent but in which no one believed. In the jokes its absurdities and contradictions were revealed and the official blathering about peace, justice, and equality was derided.

Question to Radio Armenia: Are there questions you can't answer?
Answer: No. We approach everything in accordance with Marxist dialectics. To any question we can give any answer.

Comrade Mennikh, the most senior of a Latvian group of party lecturers was answering questions after a lecture.
Q: Comrade Mennikh, what will be the outcome of the Communist Party's battle for peace in the world?
A: Comrade, the Communist Party will battle for peace in the entire world so that in the imperialist camp there will be no stone left standing. (Latvians Poke Fun at Communist Past 2003)

What is the difference between socialism and capitalism?
Under capitalism, man exploits man, and under socialism, it is exactly the other way round.

The theory of historical materialism indicates that the intermediate stage between socialism and communism is alcoholism.

What is the Marxist definition of a hole?
A partial negation of a total continuity. (UCBFA File P 65 Political Joke Czechoslovakia; collected by Sylvia Virsik 1986; told originally in Prague 1962)

In his analysis of the social significance of the *anekdot,* Alexei Yurchak speaks of the "cynical realism" of the joke tellers of "late socialism." The jokers were not dissidents, for they felt that their rulers could deploy so much brute force that all change was impossible, but they joked endlessly about the worthlessness of the system and sneered at the few *aktivists* who believed in the ideology (Yurchak 1997, 171). Perhaps the most striking of the jokes of Brezhnev's time were those told about Lenin.

Some were older jokes now recycled, and others were quite new, many of them in response to the jubilee celebrations of the centenary of Lenin's birth in 1970. Jokes about Brezhnev, Andropov, or Chernenko could possibly be seen as mere gibes about old, decrepit, unpopular rulers, but for Russians to devote long joke telling sessions to ridiculing Lenin, the founding father of the Soviet Union, was as if Americans were to devote much time and ingenuity to the endless, relentless mockery of George Washington through jokes.

> Lenin's widow, Krupskaya, visited a school to tell the children what a wonderful man Lenin had been and in particular how kind he had been to children.
> "One day," she said, "Lenin was standing outside his dacha, peeling an apple with his knife. A hungry little boy came and watched him and asked him what he was doing.
> 'Can't you see, little boy,' Lenin said, 'I am peeling an apple.'"
> The children in the school were puzzled. "How does that show how kind Lenin was?" one of them asked.
> "Don't you see?" said Krupskaya in a fury. "Lenin could have cut the hungry little boy's throat, but he didn't." (Told to me by Alexander Shtromas in 1980. For different versions, see Adams 2005, 127–28, jokes 586 and 587; Zand 1982, 67.)

Behind jokes like this lay the cult of Lenin, a secular religion complete with myths and legends, icons, and even pilgrimages to his "imperishable, undecaying" corpse, which was treated almost like a medieval relic (Tamarkhin 1984). An earlier uplifting prayer given to the Soviet Union's colonial subjects, the nomadic Kirghiz, told them:

> In Moscow the great stone-built city
> Where all the people's chiefs are gathered
> In the heart of the city is a tent
> And there reposes Lenin.
> If thou be sad and weary
> And nothing console thee
> Come hither to the tent
> And gaze on Lenin. (Cournos 1943, 161–62)

Lenin was the heart of a heartless hegemony and the soul of soulless socialism, the *samogen* (moonshine) of the people. The cult had begun shortly after his death, and he was turned into gentle "Grandpa

Lenin" (see Raskin 1985, 245, joke 395) who loved children, even though he had been ill at ease with them and was as angry as Elisha (2 Kings 2: 23–25) when the young daughter of another Bolshevik mocked his baldness (Tamarkhin 1984, 128–30, 227–29). The joke also conveys the true but unmentionable fact that Lenin was utterly ruthless and that many children had been done to death or had died of starvation as a result of his decrees. Lenin, like Himmler, may have been too squeamish to cut throats himself, but he was happy to give orders that it be done, as when he decreed that anyone who failed to turn up for work on Christmas Day would be shot (Andrew and Mitrokhin 2000, 709).

The cult was given a new boost after Stalin's death, and an attempt was made under Khrushchev to create a distance between the image of the heroic founder of Soviet communism and Stalin, who was now made to carry the entire blame for the murderous history of the Soviet Union. In 1961 Dora Lazarkina, acting as a kind of Red shaman, told the delegates of the Twenty-second Party Congress of the CPSU of her mystical encounter with the dead Vladimir Ilich Lenin. What follows is a true account of a serious speech and is cited as such by a leading scholar, but how very much like a humorous anecdote it is:

> Yesterday I took counsel with Ilich, and he stood before me as though alive and said, "It is unpleasant for me to be beside Stalin, who brought such misfortune to the party." (Stormy prolonged applause) (Tamarkhin 1984, 259).

Stalin was now ousted from the mausoleum he had shared with Lenin. But they remained comrades in the jokes.

> An old priest died and went to heaven. He was asked if he had one last wish before entering. He replied that he would like to have a conducted tour of Hell. They began in the deepest pit reserved for those whose lives had been utterly evil. There he saw a lake of boiling shit in which stood Hitler and Stalin. Stalin was up to his waist in it and Hitler up to his nose.
> "That's outrageous," said the priest. "Why should Hitler be punished more than Stalin? I suffered under both, and Stalin was just as evil as Hitler."
> "You don't understand," said his guide. "Stalin is standing on Lenin's shoulders." (For variants, see Krikmann 2004, 85)

For a joke to place Lenin under Stalin's feet and completely submerged in Dantean excrement was a shocking heresy, though it might just possibly also be drawing on an earlier and curiously truthful slogan that had been used to elevate Stalin; Stalinism had after all flowed directly from Leninism, and from his devotion to doctrine and disciple (D. Lane 1978, 76), regardless of whether Stalin had been the anointed heir or not. To put both of them in the same moral category and in the same lake as Hitler was to strangle a central Soviet myth, that of the antithesis of socialism and fascism and of the heroic Soviet "anti-fascist" struggle, one curiously suspended during the firm and vicious Soviet-Nazi alliance of 1939–41 (Tolstoy 1981, 94–105).

> Hitler asked Stalin to help him destroy London. Stalin offered him a thousand apartment managers. (Adams 2005, 44)

THE EMPIRE JOKES BACK

A large part of the jokes discussed earlier are Russian, though they would rapidly have spread to the other socialist countries. However, the other nationalities had their own jokes about the Russians, whom they saw as double imperialists who both deprived them of their independence and national identity and imposed on them an alien and oppressive socialist system (Pieckalkiewicz 1972, 326). Empires can be extremely beneficial and bring peace, order, and civilization (Lal 2004) to their subject peoples, but for the East Europeans, that which was called peace was a desert, and the Soviet empire meant rule by a backward nation whose achievements often lagged behind their own.

The Soviet Union itself was a prison house of the nationalities, who resented Russian control and even more the attempted Russification of their countries through cultural and linguistic as well as political domination, the suppressing of distinctive local institutions and traditions, and the moving in of Russian settlers sometimes to the point where the local people felt they were facing the loss of their identity (Kaiser 1976, 125–27). The minority nationalities in this respect had been better off under the Tsars. The Tsarist regimes had imposed Russian military and political dominance, but they had not penetrated or destroyed the local cultures, languages, and religions (Shtromas 1989, 359). The Soviets did undertake such destruction, for they firmly believed that imperialism was the highest stage of socialism.

During collectivization, the Ukrainians and the Kazakhs suffered the most, and attempts were made to suppress their national identity (Levytsky 1971, 68). Between 30 and 40 percent of the nomadic Kazakhs died (Reddaway 2008b, 197), as did 80 percent of their livestock in a real-life enactment of the "moral" of *The Caucasian Chalk Circle* (Brecht 1988, scene 1, 1–8, scene 6, 97, Prologue of 1944, 124–28). After the occupation of their countries under the Soviet-Nazi pact in 1940 and again from 1944, the Estonians declined from being 92 percent of the population of Estonia in 1934 to only 65 percent in 1979, and the Latvians declined from 77 percent to 54 percent in their country due to the murders of 1940 and 1944–53 and to the deliberate bringing in of Russian colonists (Laar 2007c, 57–59; Yardys 1989, 440, 444). It is hardly surprising that there was such intense anti-Russian sentiment in the Baltic States and the Ukraine (Rositzke 1982, 306–307). During World War II, many Ukrainians initially welcomed the German army, and ordinary Lithuanians began shooting at the retreating Russians the day after the Germans invaded (Shtromas 1996, 87–89). The Estonian freedom fighters, the Forest Brothers, resisted the Soviet occupation, ambushed Soviet forces, and attacked quislings from 1944 to 1956 (Laar 2007a). There were high levels of disaffection (Andrew and Mitrokhin 2000, 345–55, 673–74, 683, 705) in most of the puppet states of Eastern Europe. They were all countries where the original communist governments had been imposed by the Soviet army, except in Czechoslovakia, where the takeover followed Soviet-backed electoral fraud and internal subversion. On many occasions, resentment of Russian "double imperialism" led to public protests, riots and even uprisings notably in East Germany in 1953, Hungary in 1956, Czechoslovakia in 1968, and in Poland repeatedly, which were only crushed by Soviet tanks or the threat of tanks. It was Russian nationalism, not socialist internationalism or Marxism-Leninism, that came to motivate the Soviet armed forces and the KGB (Rositzke 1982, 255). It was the sense of being powerful and exercising power over others that sustained the Russians, not ideology, and it was nationalism that led the subjugated peoples to rebel and seek their freedom. During the Hungarian revolution of 1956, the communist order fell apart in a matter of days, for it had been utterly lacking in legitimacy (Shtromas 1981, 100). It is hardly surprising that the citizens of the subordinate nationalities of the Soviet "great brotherhood of nations" told so many jokes about Russia and particularly about the way their own local communists deferred and groveled to the Russians, being unable and unwilling to represent the interests of their own people (Kürti 1988, 328; Rose 2002; Sanders 1982, 22–25).

> Why are there so many Russians in Poland?
> In order to protect our country.
> From what?
> From the Poles taking control of the government. (Brzozowska 2009, 134)

> Polish riddle
> What is the difference between the two sources of energy, the sun and coal?
> The sun disappears into the west, the coal into the east. (Isnard 1977, 30; my translation from the French)

> Under the new Soviet-Hungarian treaty, the Soviets have the right to navigate the Danube upstream and downstream and the Hungarians to navigate it crossways.

> In Slovakia, lavatory paper always comes in two layers. Why?
> One copy has to go to Moscow. (Told to me in Bratislava, Slovakia, 1985)

> What is the most neutral country in the world?
> Czechoslovakia. It does not even interfere in its own internal affairs. (Kolasky 1972, 24)

> What is the largest country in the world?
> Ukraine, because its border is in the Carpathian Mountains, its capital in Moscow, and its population in Siberia (Kolasky 1972, 44; for an Estonian version, see Vesilind 2009, 29)

> Ukrainian on the mutual exchange between Russia and the Ukraine: The Russians take our coal, our oil, our steel, our wheat, our workers, and give us their laws, their language, their labor camps, their prisons, and their police. (Kolasky 1972, 44–45)

> Romania asks Gorbachev for assistance after Chernobyl, and Gorbachev promises it. The Romanians doubt him and ask, "Will the Hungarians be able to deliver?" (Kürti 1988, 333). (This is a cleverly recycled version of a post-1956 joke. Kolasky 1972, 35.)

> One day, while visiting Ulbricht, a party member saw a strange telephone on his desk. He asked, "Comrade Ulbricht, why do you have such

a strange-looking telephone? It has no mouthpiece but only the receiver. What do you use it for?"

"Well, since you ask," replied Ulbricht, "that is our direct line to Moscow."

On a bright sunny day Ulbricht walks out of his office with an open umbrella. "But you don't need an umbrella when the sun is shining," declares a comrade.

"I certainly do," replies Ulbricht. "It's raining in Moscow." (Lo Bello 1968, 242–43; also recorded in French as a Polish joke about Gierek. Isnard 1977, 26.)

> There is a meeting of Communist leaders in Moscow
> Walter Ulbricht takes the first chair. He notices that it has a nail sticking up, but he is a tough German, and he sits on it.
> Next Poland's Gomulka takes a chair. He sees there is also a nail on his chair, but he is not going to be outdone by any German, and he also sits on the nail.
> Then Novotný pulls out his chair.
> "Please, Comrade Khrushchev," he whined, "they forgot to give me a nail."

Antonín Novotný, a hard-line communist, ruled Czechoslovakia with Soviet backing from 1953 to 1968, when the Czechs and Slovaks managed to replace him with the reformer Dubček, who was soon afterwards ousted by an invasion of Soviet tanks. Walter Ulbricht, the East German communist leader, was parachuted into office in 1945 as a Soviet stooge (on Soviet orders he had been pro-Nazi in 1932 and in 1939–41) and was eased out by Brezhnev in 1971. Gierek replaced Gomulka in Poland in 1970.

The jokes reflect the strength of nationalist resentment and the wish to be free of all Soviet control and free of local leaders who obeyed the Soviets and blocked change toward a free society. Unsurprisingly, it was in these outposts of empire that the revolutions of 1989 began. Once Gorbachev had made it clear to the leaders of the East European governments in 1985–86 that he was no longer willing to deploy the Soviet army to keep them in power in the face of local discontent, they were doomed, for they were seen as illegitimate hirelings and oppressors by their own people. In the face of popular unrest, General Jaruzelski dared not impose martial law in Poland in 1989, as he had in 1981, by using the threat of a Soviet-led invasion, so he allowed an election but rigged it so that he thought he was bound to win. Despite the rigging, he lost the elections heavily to Solidarity, and thus began the "Autumn of the Nations." The Berlin Wall came down, and within weeks every single communist government was gone. The people had realized that "the wall is tottering; you only have to push it for it to fall over." The Soviet empire fell, as so many other empires have done, when those in power at the center lost their nerve and would not risk a bloodbath or the possibility of their own forces refusing to shoot; the empire fell when the Russian rulers decided that the rising cost of empire had become greater than the declining benefits. Within two more years the Soviet Union itself had collapsed, and crucial to the collapse was the growth of a strongly nationalist opposition in the outlying republics, particularly in the Baltic republics of Estonia, Latvia, and Lithuania (Laar 2007c, 61–69; Reddaway 2008a, 85). The only nationalism that the Soviet regime could exploit was that of the Russians themselves, for whom an arrogant sense of belonging to a powerful empire, which others feared, may have in some measure compensated for their low standard of living and lack of individual freedom. They were servants at home but masters abroad. There is still a sense of nostalgia among many older Russians for the days when they could watch on television that Roman triumph for the proletarians, the huge military parades in Moscow, nostalgia for all the pomp of yesterday, now one with Nineveh and Tyre, nostalgia for the era of missiles and cosmonauts and the years when their soldiers' boots could walk over lesser peoples for their own good in the name of progress and inevitability. The other countries, by contrast, have museums of the suffering and repression of Soviet times that cast the Russians as the villains.

CONSEQUENCES AND PREDICTIONS

Thus far we have sought to map the content of the political jokes of Soviet times against the history and social, political, and economic realities of the Soviet empire, particularly in the light of the research done since the fall of the system and the opening up of the archives. There is a very good fit between them, but it raises two important questions. First, did the jokes have any effect or any consequences? Second, did the jokes convey truths about the system that could have helped us to predict that it would collapse?

The jokes had no effects on communist society and no consequences. Jokes never do. Jokes did not cause the collapse of the Soviet Union. Jokes are a very, very weak force in a world of much stronger forces. If the probable causes of the collapse were listed in order of importance, the biting political jokes, numerous as they were and however frequently they were told, would not even make the top twenty. The collapse of the Soviet Union was caused by a combination of economic failure, the contradiction between a rigid antiquated system of government and the social and intellectual modernization of society, pressure from the outside by a newly confident and aggressive western leadership that was willing to raise the cost to the Soviet Union of military competition and to undermine peripheral parts of the Soviet empire in Africa and Asia, and the growth of nationalist resentments in Eastern Europe that could no longer be suppressed. There is a detailed summary of these factors in the collection of essays *The Strange Death of Soviet Communism: A Postscript*, edited by Nikolas K. Gvosdev (2008).

It is a foolish sentimental myth that an entire oppressive political order could be brought down by humor, although it is one widely believed and propagated by humorists and humanists who assert it without evidence and then cite one another to prove it, often employing silly military and political metaphors such as "wit as weapon" or "humor as strategy." It would, of course, be quite unfair, if true, to point out that humorists and those who write sententious articles about humor have a strong interest in making their work seem important and that this might shape their opinions. The myth was reinforced by some of the studies made of the role of humor during the Nazi occupation of many countries in Europe during World War II, which produced large numbers of so-called "resistance jokes" about the occupier. After the war the jokes were celebrated and even published (Clément 1945; Jean-Charles 1970) to maintain the pretense that the resistance movement had been effective and as a way of salvaging a few crumbs of national self-respect in those countries that had surrendered completely.

Veni, vidi, Vichy. I came, I saw, I concurred.

For those joke tellers who had lived in the gray area of more or less collaborating, remembering the jokes after the war that everyone had told during it was a way of convincing themselves and others that to have joked was to have resisted. No doubt, after the Berlin Wall fell in 1989, many of those who had been informers for the Stasi (the East German secret police) even frantically read up the collections of German jokes that had been told in the DDR, East Germany, but published in West Germany (Drozdzynski 1977).

The best-known statement of the thesis that jokes are effective resistance is to be found in a wartime article by Obdrlik (1942, 709–16) about the resistance movement in the Czech lands occupied by the Nazis from March 1939 until 1945. It is much and unthinkingly cited by those who wish to believe his conclusions and have not looked carefully, let alone critically, at his rather sparse and subjective data. Obdrlik argued that the numerous Czech jokes circulating in Bohemia and Moravia about the German occupier were proof of the existence of a strong and vigorous resistance movement; its morale was sustained by the jokes, and supposedly the enemy's morale was undermined. However, Chad Bryant (2006, 133–39) was able to show on the basis of detailed empirical work that the Czech resistance movement had been negligible in size and impact and had achieved nothing; its local leaders collected political jokes and put them in its reports back to the Czech government in exile in London as an indicator of resistance, but then they had little else to report. It is likely that the jokes were used as a way of keeping up the morale of small groups, but morale is not a sufficient condition for achieving effectiveness, and most of those who invented and told the jokes were not involved in any political activities at all, any more than the jokers were in the Soviet era.

Those who see jokes as undermining a dictatorship back their case by pointing to the lengths to which the authorities in a totalitarian society have sometimes gone to persecute jokers and infer from this that jokes must be powerful or else they would not be feared. But why should we accept that the authorities' actions were rational? They were after all the same people who purged imaginary enemies in a manner reminiscent of the witchcraft trials.

Some assert that humor is an effective form of resistance, a boost for the oppressed and an underminer of those in power, and others claim that jokes are a safety valve that enable dictatorial regimes to survive and that it is counterproductive to try to suppress them (Cochran 1989, 272; Draitser 1989, 118; Rose 2002, 7–8; Speier 1998, 1395). It is extremely unlikely that jokes have any significant effect one way or the other, and the entire argument is utterly futile and best abandoned.

Political jokes were and are certainly important to individuals trapped in such societies, for they are a way of keeping alive in the imagination an alternative world that is utterly different from that of official total enthusiasm. In a socialist society, jokes are the aspirin of the people taken to suspend political pain; jokes cannot cure the pain, but unlike an opiate, they do not blur a proper perception of its cause. Those who say that political jokes are a safety valve will have to argue that the valve operated more effectively to maintain the regime in being during the time of decadence, when there was a plethora of jokes than it had done in the time of terror when there were fewer. Why then were the peak years of joking in the 1980s followed by rapid collapse? The entire discussion about the effects jokes have, whether as eroders or sustainers or both at once, is pointless because such effects are minute if they exist at all.

Given that the jokes had no discernible effect in or on the Soviet empire, despite being concentrated on a single target and being so important to the jokers that they would in times of terror defy persecution in order to tell them and in times of decadence make them an important part of social life, we can be certain that jokes have no effects in democratic societies with freedom of speech. In the latter societies, jokes are spread over many targets, and those seeking and gaining enjoyment from a relaxed exchange of joke telling rarely concentrate for long on any one target. Jokes are an important part of the lives of individuals, particularly in face-to-face or email communication, but it is wrong to deduce from this that jokes have any impact on society. It is illicit to move between levels in this way. Jokes are a thermometer, not a thermostat; they provide an indication of what is happening in a society, but they do not feed back into and change or reinforce the social processes that generated them in any important way. The argument that jokes "reinforce" the social order is meaningless. Every time we conform to the demands of society or the expectations of our peers, we are of necessity reproducing, re-creating, and reinforcing the social order. Why single out jokes that happen to be congruent with that order for special comment?

Those in a free society who seek to restrain individuals from sharing jokes of which they disapprove are as misguided and intrusive as their Soviet counterparts and about as likely to succeed. They wish to scapegoat the jokers, both because they want to flaunt their power to control one particular area of life and because they are frustrated by their inability to manage the larger social tensions on which the jokes draw. Jokes do not conceal malign intent, but attempts to censor them do. Censorship, whether by states or institutions, under dictatorships or within democracies, is not about consequences; it is merely a way of saying, "We are the bosses around here" and of falsely claiming that a consensus exists when in fact there is a good deal of dissent. Much of the disapproval in the West is directed against popular humor, which often targets not the powerful but those beneath them—the lumpen, the underclass, failed ethnic minorities, and ignorant third-world immigrants. The accusation made by the critical intelligentsia is that such joking reinforces the existing unequal and inegalitarian social order. No one who is seriously trying to understand how systems of stratification work would ever consider them to be upheld to any significant extent by something as trivial as jokes. Material forces, comrades! Being laughed at in jokes is the very least of the losers' problems. But there is a further point, namely, that the broad masses who tell the jokes may indeed support the very social order that the jokes' critics denounce because they want stability and continuity and a settled way of life and do not subscribe to radical egalitarianism. In a plural and democratic society, they have an inalienable right to take such a political stance; rights are not reserved for radicals. But the entitlement to such rights carries with it the masses' right to enjoy jokes congruent with their views. Jokers will, like Sir Toby Belch, ask those radicals who see themselves as the stewards of society and would take the hot jokes out of the jokers' mouths, "Dost thou think, because thou art virtuous, there shall be no more cakes and ale?" (Shakespeare, *Twelfth Night*, act 2, scene 3, lines 97–99).

JOKES AND CARNIVAL

The arguments about the effects of political jokes run parallel to the debates about whether carnivals are functional or disruptive. Joking under communism resembled in certain respects those medieval carnivals in which the rites and rituals of the Church were burlesqued, the social distance between the high and the lowly shrank, the mighty were ridiculed, and the world turned upside down (Bakhtin 1985, 71–96). That is also what jokes under communism did. Slogans, ideological arguments, and political catechisms were parodied and inverted, solemn political rituals and uplifting tales about heroes such as Chapaev or cult figures such as Lenin were reduced to foolishness or even nastiness, and current leaders were shown as complete fools (S. Davies 1997, 174–77). Indeed, it has been suggested that when Bakhtin wrote about carnival, he may have had in mind the popular humorous culture of the Soviet Union, a subject no Russian scholar dared write about (Clark and Holquist 1984, 307–14; Vice 1997, 152–54). Carnivals, though seemingly the antithesis of the social order, might in practice reinforce it and those taking part in carnivals may well be pious and observant when it is not carnival time; Speier (1998, 1395) uses an analogy with carnivals to argue that political jokes are a safety valve. The Soviet regime presumably saw carnivals as a force for undermining, for it allowed and at times encouraged militant atheists and *aktivists* to hold blasphemous carnivals mocking the Orthodox Christian churches (C. Lane 1981, 130). The Roman Catholic Church in Spain must have thought so, too, for under Franco the grotesque carnivals customarily held in Galicia before Lent were banned.

The analogy is deficient in that Bakhtin's carnivals were a social institution, regular, known, and in a sense "licensed" public events, whereas Soviet joke telling in Bakhtin's time was done secretly by individuals who, far from being believers, seem from the KGB files to have felt nothing but alienation and resentment. "Safety valve," like "slippery slope" or "thin end of the wedge," is an unhelpful metaphor that is often employed in persuasive rhetoric, but it does not advance our understanding.

JOKES AS PREDICTORS

Jokes had no effect in the Soviet Union, but we can see them as a predictor of the final collapse. Jokes are not serious, and they are not intended to be. They occupy a world of their own outside the realm of bona fide discourse (Raskin 1985, 100–104). To try to reduce a joke to a serious statement is fatuous, since a joke can be glossed in many ways and enjoyed by those, such as the KGB (Deriabin and Gibney 1960), to whom a parallel serious statement would be anathema. Taken as a whole, the political jokes came closer to telling the truth about the system than the official Soviet version or than those in the free world who accepted that version or failed to contest it with sufficient vigor. Now that the system is gone and there is free access to the archives and to the memories of the people, we can see clearly that the jokes were a better guide to what the system was and to how it might evolve than were the absurdly restrained and at times sympathetic views of a large portion of those who studied the Soviet empire. That is why they were so utterly amazed when it collapsed.

The only scholar who clearly saw, even in the 1970s, that the Soviet empire would disintegrate was Alexander Shtromas, who had been professor of law at Moscow University before being forced to leave for England, where he became a lecturer at two British universities and later at a university in Michigan (Burke 1989; Gvosdev 2008, 6; Shtromas 1981). We would often meet to exchange political jokes and to discuss the fate of the Soviet Union; he saw the jokes as a harbinger of downfall. In his book *Political Change and Social Development: The Case of the Soviet Union*, Shtromas (1981) showed in detail how the collapse of the doomed system would come about. He went on to plan a conference called "The Fall of the Soviet Empire" to be held in Geneva in 1985, and he invited me to give the paper "Humor for the Future and a Future for Humor" (Davies 1989; see also Davies 1998). We were denounced in the Swiss press as dangerous extremists. It was jokes like the following that helped to convince me that Shtromas was right:

> **Russian Social Survey question:** "Where were you born?"
> **Soviet citizen:** "St. Petersburg."
> "Where did you go to school?"
> **Citizen:** "Petrograd."
> "Where do you live?"
> **Citizen:** "Leningrad."
> "Where would you like to live?"
> **Citizen:** "St. Petersburg."
> (Told to me by Alexander Shtromas 1981; see also Adams 2005, 30, joke 77)

St. Petersburg was founded in 1703 by Peter the Great and named after St. Peter. In 1914, when war broke out with Germany, the name was Russianized to Petrograd, even though the original version is Dutch, not German. In 1924, it was renamed after Lenin, who had just died. The socialist system is gone, and so is Leningrad, whose citizens freely chose to expunge the name of Lenin and to return to the old Tsarist and Christian title of their city. Such a transformation was at least thinkable to the joke tellers, but it was utterly beyond the imagination of many "Sovietologists," who thought the Soviet Union was stable and durable and its government legitimate. It is not that the joke tellers thought that such a change of name and regime was at all likely; rather, such jokes revealed a degree of alienation in the population that few other than the perceptive Shtromas were able or willing to recognize.

Jokes can be oddly prescient. In Bratislava in Slovakia in 1985, I was told this joke:

> What is the difference between Gorbachev and Dubček?
> There isn't any, but Gorbachev doesn't know it yet.

In Czechoslovakia they had learned full well what happens to reformers, for their reformist leader Alexander Dubček had been quickly ousted by military intervention in 1968. There was an attempted coup against Gorbachev in August 1991, with strong support from the KGB, but this time there were, as Shtromas had predicted, serious divisions at the top, and not only did the coup fail, but the USSR fragmented. The old guard had lost its nerve. A 19 million-member party imploded without a fight (Pipes 2008, 124); no one believed in what it stood for. A system based on force alone may be in equilibrium, but it will be in unstable equilibrium. So long as it is not disturbed, such a system will remain where it is, as it did under Brezhnev, but once disturbed, it will rapidly fall apart. Gorbachev provided just such a disturbance (Rush 2008, 28; Kontorovich 2008, 67) when he tried to reform the unreformable. Those scholars who had seriously listened to the jokes had been proved right.

Conclusion

Conclusions have been provided at the end of each chapter, and in some cases more general inferences have also been made. The jokes about the French and sex, about American lawyers, about Jewish men and women, and about the Soviet Union have been explained in terms of particular social and political situations and historical events and patterns. The explanations are in many respects self-contained and are specific to those sets of jokes. If the circumstances had been different, the jokes would not have been invented, which is why it is so important to locate and describe those circumstances. To explain the jokes, it was necessary to discuss in detail the evolution of the sex industries of France and their perception by outsiders, the special importance of law in the very construction and definition of the United States, the existence of communities of men living in isolation from women, the unique position of the Ashkenazi Jews in American society, and the breadth of Soviet tyranny that set that society and its dependencies apart not only from democratic societies but from most authoritarian societies as well. It would not be unfair to say that the targets produced the jokes. By contrast, jokes whose theme is stupidity are jokes in search of a target and require a quite different kind of explanation couched in terms of very general cultural patterns that cut across different institutions and societies. One of these patterns, the stupidity jokes told about those held in the grip of traditional sex roles, does, however, also have a relevance to understanding jokes about Jewish men and women, both of whom are portrayed as distancing themselves from this pattern. An understanding of the emphasis on physical dominance that is a key facet of conventional male identities is also essential to understanding jokes about men who have sex with men. But it is the cultural patterns underlying the stupidity jokes that most require further elucidation.

THE EVOLUTION AND TESTING OF THE THESES ABOUT THE TARGETS OF STUPIDITY JOKES

The jokes about stupidity are the most universal of jokes with targets, which is why the book began with them. An understanding of these jokes has also been important to the analysis of Jewish jokes and has relevance to the contrast between a Soviet society based on force and ideology and an American society based on law and commerce.

The new "mind-over-matter" theory seeks to cover all kinds of stupidity jokes about groups and also to cast some light on jokes about the canny. Its strength lies in its comprehensiveness, but how secure the theory is will depend on how far it can successfully accommodate further examples of jokes about "stupid" groups. Here I have in mind not the jokes that might be invented in unknown circumstances at some future time but rather sets of jokes about stupidity not considered here but already in existence that target other quite different occupations, classes, and ethnic groups.

In order to indicate what is meant by *accommodate,* it is necessary first to consider what could have been reasonably predicted on the basis of my earlier theory about stupidity jokes (Davies 1990), one that was designed to apply only to ethnic jokes. In this theory it was claimed that stupidity jokes were always told about those on the edge of a country or a cultural or linguistic area, with the tellers being at the center. The theory states that the order cannot be reversed such that a substantial set of stupidity jokes are told by those at the edge. The rule does not cover and was not designed to cover qualities other than stupidity. The butts of ethnic jokes about the canny, the coarse, the cowardly, the militarist, the drunk, or the teetotal are not distributed in this way. They are quite different. The roots of these other types of jokes lie in highly particular social and historical circumstances, and the same jokes may be told in several countries about a single people, such as the very widespread jokes about the canny Scots and Jews, the cowardly Italian army, the oversexed French, or the drunken Irish. Jokes about canny Scotsmen are invented

Table 4. Stupidity Jokes by Country

Country	Targets
Australia	Tasmanians, Irish
Austria	Burgenlanders, Carinthians
Brazil	Portuguese, Baianos
Britain	Irish
Bulgaria	Šopi, the peasants from the rural area outside Sofia
Canada (east)	Newfoundlanders
Canada (west)	Ukrainians
Colombia	Pastusos from Pasto in Nariño
Czech lands	Slovaks
Denmark	Aarhusians, people of Aarhus
Egypt	Sa'idis of Upper Egypt, Nubians
Finland	Karelians
France	Belgians, French-speaking Swiss (Ouin-Ouin)
Germany	Ostfrieslanders
Greece	Pontians (Black Sea Greeks)
India	Sardarjis (Sikhs)
Ireland	Kerrymen
Israel	Kurdish Jews
Italy	Meridionali (Southerners)
Mexico	Yucatecos from Yucatan
Netherlands	Belgians, Limburgers
New Zealand (North Island)	Irish, Maoris
New Zealand (South Island)	Irish, West Coasters
Nigeria	Hausas
Pakistan	Sardarjis (Sikhs)
Russia	Ukrainians, Chukchees
South Africa	Afrikaners (van der Merwe)
Spain	Leperos from Lepe; Gallegos from Galicia
Sweden	Finns
Switzerland	Citizens of Fribourg/Freiburg
Tadjikistan	Uzbeks
Turkey	Laz
United States	Poles, Portuguese
Yugoslavia	Bosnians, Albanians

Source: Davies 1990, 42.

in Slovakia and told in Slovak, despite Scotsmen being somewhat rare in that country. It is an entirely different pattern in which there is one single target but the jokes and joke tellers are spread over many countries. It is a different pattern and requires an entirely different kind of comparative analysis. By contrast, each country has its own specific local butt of stupidity jokes. I built my original center-edge model in 1990 (see table 4). In the light of the many new examples of ethnic jokes that have turned up since then, how has the old model fared?

From this comparison of thirty-four cases, it was postulated that the butts of the stupidity jokes are similar to those who tell the jokes about them, but they live on the edge of a society or culture in which the joke tellers are at the center. The edge consists of one or more of the following: (a) a geographical or political edge, such as a remote coast, a frontier area, or an offshore island, (b) a cultural and linguistic frontier where a "funny" version of the standard language is spoken, and (c) the economic edge, well away from the important and dynamic economic and administrative centers. The joke tellers at the center are thus able to see the people about whom they tell stupidity jokes as a distorted version of themselves, as themselves seen in a fairground distorting mirror. The butts of the jokes are cousins and country cousins. They are not in any way strange or alien. The asymmetry of position between jokers and joked about is irreversible. Belgium is at the edge of France, Kerry of Ireland, and Newfoundland of Canada; likewise, the Sikhs are unambiguously at the edge of Hindu India, the Pastusos of Colombia, and the Laz of Turkey. It would make no real sense to reverse the pairing and to say that Ireland is at the periphery of Kerry or that Canada lies offshore from a mainland called Newfoundland, except perhaps as a piece of whimsical mathematics. When I say the butts of the jokes are people at the edge, I do not mean that they are, are seen as, or see themselves as socially marginal. The Aarhusians of Aarhus in Jutland, who live at the edge of Denmark, and the Carinthians, who come from a rural border region of Austria, are provincials and thus the butt of stupidity jokes, but they are not in any sense socially marginal; that position is occupied by recent immigrants to those countries who are perceived not as cousins but as culturally alien. In Ireland, the rural Kerryman with a brogue who lives at the far southwestern edge of the country may be laughed at, but he is not socially marginal. That status belongs to the members of the "traveling community," whom most Irish people call "the tinkers." It is the latter who constitute a marginal group that is not fully and properly part of Irish society and whose position has in consequence been the subject of legislation in the Irish parliament. The edge is not the margin. Marginal groups may well be the subject of jokes, but they will inspire a different set of jokes that reflect their social position, which is not that of cousin but of outsider. The center-edge model also provides a clear refutation of the idea that the jokes are a product of hostility or conflict or anxiety or threat. Sometimes there will have been conflict, as there may well be between adjacent neighbors, and sometimes there is no evidence of any; the conflict theory of humor is simply irrelevant. The butts of stupidity jokes may be liked, disliked, or regarded with indifference by the joke tellers. It makes no difference whatsoever to the content of the jokes. Other things being equal, people may well prefer it if their jokes fall on those they dislike rather than on their affiliates, but other things are rarely equal, and the stupidity jokes are told about favored and unfavored cousins alike. The theory predicts that similar jokes should exist in other countries and that the patterns of joking should be the same. In table 5 are listed new examples of countries where ethnic jokes about stupidity are told. The jokes' very existence confirms the first part of the prediction. The pattern of the relationships between the groups who tell the jokes and the groups about whom the jokes are told is also exactly as predicted. They fit the center-edge model.

The ethnic jokes about stupidity that emerge from these new pairs of groups in table 5 are essentially similar in style and content to the jokes that emerged from the original pairs in table 4. They are the same phenomenon.

> Two Alentejos were walking along a dusty road when they decided to take a nap. One suggested they should sleep under a tree at the side of the road, but the other insisted it would be safer to sleep in the middle.
>
> A car driven by another Alentejo came down the road at speed. The driver swerved to avoid them and smashed into the tree.
>
> "You see," said the first Alentejo. "I told you it was safer here than if we had been under that tree." (Told to me in September 2009 in Tartu by a Portuguese paremiologist; see also http://www.tpo.net/humor/Ultra/life/lifed.j.html)

Table 5. Extra Stupidity Jokes by Country

Country	Target
Argentina	Gallegos (in effect, Spaniards)
Estonia	People of islands of Hiiumaa and Saaremaa
Faeroe Islands	Citizens of Klaksvík
Jordan	Sarihis from village of Al Sarih. Tafilians from southern town of Al Tafili.
Malaysia	Orang Asli
Peru	Arequipeños from Arequiba
Portugal	Alentejos (south of the River Tagus/Tejo)
Romania	People of Oltenia
South Korea	People of Choong Chong Do (*do* means province)
Syria	People of Homs and Hama, Kurds
Tangier	Berbers
Venezuela	Gochos

In Choong Chong Do, a father and son were working in a field at the foot of a mountain. A boulder came off the mountain and hurtled down toward the father.

"Father," said the son, "a ... boulder ... has ... come ... loose ... in the mountain... and ... you had better ... watch ..." Splat!

(Told to me by a Korean economist from Choong Chong Do in January 2010)

Two Hiiu men are on the mainland with their fish cart, on their way to the market. It's midnight. One man asks from the other, "How come the moon is here? We left it behind when we left home." The other one answers, "Are you stupid or what? That's not the only moon there is. There are heaps of them up there!"

(Laineste 2008a, 115, and 2008b)

A Kihnu man visited the mainland for the first time to sell his fish on the Pärnu market. He told himself, "The world is wide and large! There are people and villages beyond Pärnu. This means that the edge of the world is somewhere even further away!" (Laineste 2008a, 115, and 2008b)

Why does a man from Homs sleep with one eye open and one eye closed?

He took half a sleeping pill. (Told to me in Damascus, April 1996)

Dos Gallegos:—Sabes, al final encontré trabajo en Santiago.—De que?— De Compostela.

One Gallego says to another: Do you know—I finally found work in Santiago.—As what?—Of Compostela.

Untranslatable pun. *De* can mean "as" or "of." It is an integral part of the name of the great Roman Catholic pilgrimage center Santiago de Compostela, which holds the relics of Spain's patron saint, St. James. There are many other cities called Santiago, such as Santiago del Nuevo Extremo, St. James of the new frontier, the capital of Chile.

(http://usuarios.arnet.com.ar/ngiunta/chistesgalle2.htm; for more Argentinean jokes about Gallegos, see Muleiro 1998, 133–39)

As predicted, these new cases fit the center-edge model well. The theory is confirmed. The people of the Choong Chong province are rustic provincials who speak a different dialect of Korean from that of the capital, Seoul. When a Korean tells a joke about the people of the province having slow and sluggish minds, he or she will imitate the local accent and speak very slowly.

The Orang Asli are the original inhabitants of Malaya (peninsular Malaysia). They live in small rural communities in the northeast of Malaya, often working as loggers, in contrast to the large modern cities of the southwest of Malaya, and they speak an older form of Malay. In addition to joking about them, the Malaysians will use the phrase "that is so Orang Asli," when something stupid or out of place has been done or said.

Klaksvík, a fishing port on the island of Bordoy, is the second largest town in the Faeroe Islands, but it has only 5,000 people and is much smaller than the capital and university town, Tórshavn, on the larger island of Streymoy with 20,000. The Faeroes are a self-governing affiliate of Denmark, so it is not surprising that the jokes follow the same pattern as in Denmark, where the people of Aarhus in Jutland are the butt of stupidity jokes. Aarhus is the second largest town in Denmark but very provincial and far smaller than, and far away from, the capital, Copenhagen. Homs and Hama on the River Orontes in Syria are provincial towns, as are Al Sarih and Al Tafili in Jordan, and Al-Khatib (1999, 268) has suggested that the location of Al Tafili in the southern region is important, much as it is with the jokes about the Sa'idis of Upper Egypt told in Egypt.

The Kurds are a mountain people living in the remote region of Kurdistan, which overlaps Iraq, Iran, Turkey, and Syria, and they are the butt of many stupidity jokes in the Arab countries, including Lebanon, and even in Israel (Khanaka 1990, 60). The Kurds have a distinctive Indo-European language of their own, but they are often bilingual and are the butts of stupidity jokes among the neighboring Arabs because of the distorted way in which they speak Arabic, the dominant language. Communication between Iraqi Kurds and Arabs is on the Arabs' terms. Iraqi Arabs tell jokes about Kurds speaking bad Arabic, but the Kurds have no jokes about Arabs speaking bad Kurdish (Khanaka 1990, 34, 68); it is difficult to know exactly what constitutes good Kurdish because there are competing dialects and no standard language. Kurds speaking one dialect will pass on the stupidity jokes told by the Arabs and tell them about those speaking another form of Kurdish (Khanaka 1990, 27–28, 62). Tangiers is a large cosmopolitan port in Morocco, a center of industry and tourism, while typically the Berbers live in the mountains of the interior.

Few people live in the bleak, dusty, predominantly rural Alentejo region in the south of Portugal with its rolling hills covered in cork-oak trees, and there are many Portuguese jokes about the inhabitants being slow, lazy, and foolish. It is Portugal's answer to Appalachia or the Ozarks. Likewise, Oltenia or Lesser Wallachia is a rural province in the far southwestern corner of Romania. The Gallegos are the people of Galicia, a province of farmers and fishermen in the far northwestern corner of Spain. The local language of the province is in some respects closer to Portuguese than to Castellano, the standard Spanish of Castile. Many jokes are told about them, not just in Spain but also in Argentina and Mexico. Many poor people from Galicia emigrated to Argentina and Mexico, and the word *Gallego* is almost synonymous with *Spaniard* in the latter countries.

(http://bepop.com.ar/humor/Gallegos.html)

The Arequipeños in Peru (Davies 1998, 168–69) and the Gochos in Venezuela live close to the Andes, working as peasants and cattlemen, and like the Pastusos of Colombia, they are socially conservative and speak Spanish with a distinctive accent.

The islands of Hiiumaa and Saaremaa lie off the Estonian coast and at one time would have seemed truly remote. They are very rural, and many of the people are fishermen. They have strong local dialects and accents.

Thus far the original center-edge model has been confirmed, but it has been challenged by the noted Estonian humor scholar Liisi Laineste, on the basis of her longitudinal studies of ethnic jokes in Estonia. The stupidity jokes that existed in Estonia before the Soviet invasion in 1940 conformed to the center-edge model, for they were pinned on the people of the islands of Hiiumaa and Saaremaa or those dwelling on the remote northern coast (Laineste 2008a, 126, and 2008b). During the time of the Soviet occupation of Estonia, all jokes, including stupidity jokes, became political ones (Laineste 2008a, 127, and 2008b), but after Estonia regained its independence in 1991, new patterns of stupidity joking emerged, some based on the old local targets, but others have involved the Finns. The Finns are a neighboring people who speak a language related to Estonian, and both languages are unrelated to any others in the region. During the Soviet occupation, Estonians living close to the Gulf of Finland would watch Finnish television in preference to their own heavily censored programs. So far, so good. The Finns and Estonians are cousins. However, since Finland is bigger and richer than Estonia, Laineste (2005, 12–14) has argued that the existence of the jokes refutes my theory about the center always telling jokes about those on the edge, and not vice versa.

The problem with her claim is that the Estonian jokes about stupid Finns that she cites come from the internet, and there is no indication that they are in general oral circulation. Furthermore, Laineste (2008a, 122, and 2008b) herself notes that there exist in the same internet locations stupidity jokes about Latvians, Estonia's other but linguistically unrelated neighbor, and also many stupidity jokes about the Estonians themselves. The internet in Estonia has become a place for the arbitrary switching around of jokes, and it is not surprising that it is young Estonians who are doing it, for they have the highest rate of internet usage in Europe and a good knowledge of English, the world's international language. It is possible that in the very long run, after many decades or centuries of internet use, all local cultural patterns will collapse, leaving a random global mass of jokes. Viewed from the core of Europe, Estonia and Finland both appear very small peripheral countries, countries on the edge of Russia, on the edge of Scandinavia, and historically on the edge of German culture. Both Finland and Estonia were for a long time under Swedish and then under Tsarist Russian rule. The Swedes were the cultured element in Finland, and the German Baltic barons were the most powerful stratum in Estonia. The Swedes have long told stupidity jokes about the Finns (Davies 1990), and today Russians tell jokes about the Finns, as well as about the Estonians, being slow and speaking bad

Russian (Krikmann 2009). These other countries may well be the sources from which any Estonian jokes on the internet about Finns came. It is difficult to see how Finland could be cast as a country at the center given the overwhelmingly dominant position of the neighbors that it shares with Estonia. Nonetheless, Liisi Laineste's criticism was entirely along the right lines. This is how theories should be tested.

In the case of the new mind-over-matter model constructed to analyze stupidity jokes in general, it is again necessary to look at the most potentially tricky cases, such as the jokes about "stupid" Belgians and about "stupid" aristocrats. The Belgians are clearly geographically and linguistically peripheral to both France and the Netherlands and so fit the center-periphery model of ethnic jokes very well indeed, as do the French-speaking Swiss. But in what sense can the Belgians or the French-speaking Swiss be slotted into the new mind-over-matter model? It is, of course, possible to turn to the very strong emphasis on matters intellectual in French or indeed Dutch culture such that for humorous purposes the phlegmatic Belgians and the slow-spoken Ouin-Ouin may be seen as falling below their own very high threshold of cultivation and as lacking the acute wit of the French or Batavian mind. The French seem to believe that speed and fluency of speech and a ready recourse to abstractions are marks of national intelligence such that the Belgians can be portrayed as stodgy and known only for their comic strips and detective tales. The model holds but in a way that is not entirely satisfactory.

With the stupidity jokes about aristocrats, the problem rather has to do with the nature of the power they exercise, which thus far has been treated as a kind of fossilized force. That is not the whole story, and it is necessary to have recourse to my further model of jokes about the stupid and the canny built in 2007 (Davies 2009) based on the contrast between monopoly and competition; it is a contrast constantly used by economists but one that has also fruitfully been applied to religion (Martin 1979).

MONOPOLY AND COMPETITION

Sometimes powerful groups are the butt of stupidity jokes and sometimes of jokes about being crafty. Which one it is depends on whether they enjoy a monopoly of power or have to compete. Monopoly fits well with comic stupidity, since monopoly power does not have to be achieved through a visible competition, when ability has to be openly displayed in the marketplace or the examination hall. American lawyers have competed and succeeded in both, and that is the basis of their power and the source of the jokes about their being canny. The rulers of the Soviet Union did not have to pass either test, since in that country no one was allowed to compete with them. There was no competition in producing goods and services, no competition for votes, no competing ideologies or policies. The struggles for power within the Communist Party of the Soviet Union will have demanded a certain kind of unscrupulous and rhetorical cunning, but these internal struggles were not visible, and they took place within a framework designed by that self-same powerful elite. Above all, there could be no challenge from outside the party and its approved officeholders, the *nomenklatura*. A single ruling party had a monopoly over politics that extended, at least in principle, to matters economic, cultural, and scientific. In open societies these are areas of strong competition; when they are not, the barriers to such competition can face strong criticism, and pejorative words like *clique, cartel,* or *gatekeeper* are used.

Here we return to the question of why aristocrats are the butt of stupidity jokes. Their connection with ancient and now outdated and unsophisticated means of waging war, such as the horse, is only part of the answer. The other part is that aristocrats often enjoy an automatic social power that has not had to be achieved in competition with others. To enjoy such prestige, it is enough to have the right lineage and inherited titles, and a closed aristocracy can come to take on some of the qualities of a caste (Weber 1948). Aristocrats, peasants, and unskilled workers (including Essex girls), all of whom are the butts of stupidity jokes, are static classes in a modern world where the technical and commercial aspects are constantly changing. These classes are all undifferentiated by skill, and so one set of jokes will do for an entire class, whereas each skilled or qualified group is the butt of highly differing jokes defined by its particular area of work.

In the case of all three models—the center-periphery, the monopoly-competition, and the mind-over-matter model—the unifying ideas have come from the data itself, from looking at a very large number of quite disparate jokes from many countries, from considering a single theme, stupidity, and asking what the targets had in common. It was necessary to shift from the center-edge model to the monopoly versus competition model to the mind-over-matter model to cover extra categories of jokes. All three models continue to have their uses because, taken together, they explain more than any one does on its own. The three contrasts I have deployed are not in any way esoteric but can be and have been used to analyze and understand many other aspects of social life, and they are often underpinned by measureable aspects of the material world. The reason that these three rather than the many other available cultural contrasts have been used to explain the stupidity jokes is because they provide the best fit. They cannot be used to explain kinds of jokes other than those relating to the stupid and the canny, and this is very much a strength; a more general set of categories that purported to encompass all jokes would be so vaguely defined as to be meaningless.

MORE ABOUT MIND OVER MATTER

The relationship in the real world between the jokers and those whom they have comically labeled stupid or canny, by reason of their position on the dimension between mind and matter, may be one of amiable coexistence and cooperation, of indifference, of ambivalence, of conflict and hostility and even hatred, or most likely some mixture of them but in varying proportions. The fluctuating historical relationships between the mandarins, China's scholar-administrators, and the Chinese military, between the Brahmins and the warrior castes, between the leaders of the Church and the feudal warriors, between the samurai and the merchants of Osaka, between aesthetes and hearties—all in their different ways illustrate this variability. Town and country coexist peacefully because they are connected through visits, trade, personal contacts, and longer-term geographical mobility, for individuals move, migrate, and intermarry. Yet their peoples have different outlooks, interests, and agendas, and this can lead to tensions and even political conflicts. In the late nineteenth and early twentieth centuries, American populists led by men with rustic nicknames like "Pitchfork" Ben Tillman and "Sockless Jerry" Simpson (McMath 1993, 136, 182) fought both the selfish protectionism of the tariff-loving manufacturers and their "infant" industries, long since grown to economic adulthood, and the hard money policies of the bankers. William Jennings Bryan, who was to be thrice Democrat candidate for the presidency, warned the bankers in the final words of his speech to the Democratic National Convention in Chicago on July 9, 1896: "You shall not crucify mankind upon a cross of gold." The grasping bankers yet again. For his rural supporters Bryan declared in that same speech:

> Burn down your cities and leave our farms, and your cities will spring up again as if by magic. But destroy our farms, and the grass will grow in the streets of every city in the country. (Cited by Ashby 1987, 53)

The worst conflicts between classes and between town and country have taken place in Marxist countries. In the Soviet Union, the peasants as a class were first split by stirring up envy of the entrepreneurial kulaks, who were sent into exile, and then destroyed by collectivization with millions being murdered by deliberately induced starvation. The remainder were effectively reduced to serfdom to fit in with an ideology designed by and for urban intellectuals holding bureaucratic power. It can work the other way, as with the Marxist Khmer Rouge's mobilization of the peasants against the people of the cities in Cambodia and particularly those who represented the things of the mind (Rummel 1994, 178–89). Lawyers were murdered, and anyone who was literate was in danger; you could be tortured and killed just for wearing spectacles, and your children could be murdered, too. Only 50 doctors survived out of 450, and 5,000 teachers out of 20,000 (Rummel 1994, 192–93). The jokes that poke fun at American lawyers do seem to be a rather different kind of phenomenon.

The Nazis and some fascist parties were mobilized around an attack on those who thought and those who traded. This was linked to their worship of force, to their appeal to instinct as against reflection: *Credere! Obbedire! Combattere!* Believe! Obey! Fight! *Muera la inteligencia! Viva la muerte!* Death to intelligence! Long live death! In Germany, the condemnation of *Händlertum*, merchant commercialism, as opposed to *Heldentum*, idealistic German heroics, was a strong aspect of the Nazis' ideology of anti-Semitism and of their dislike of British and American democracy (Markovits 2007, 62–63). It is force, ideology, and solidarity versus freedom, thought, and trade.

The jokes about the stupid and the canny have no impact on these conflicts, whether mild or intense, democratic or violent, but they emerge from the same sets of social, political, and economic situations. Sometimes these circumstances bring forth wild and contemptible ideologies that lead to tragedy, and sometimes they just produce jokes. Those who laugh at the jokes know that jokes can do nothing to ward off future disasters. Jokes are not a moral enterprise. They don't do any harm, but neither are they a force for good. Canned jokes are a pleasurable escape from the pressures of the world, a brief time when both reality and moral judgment can be suspended. To endow jokes with virtue or worse still with metaphysical or transcendental qualities is sheer foolishness. A particular joke can be used with a suitable gloss and tone to further a moral purpose or even a religious one, but that is not why the jokes came into existence; it is simply an opportunistic use of a joke as a rhetorical device, much like any other verbal trick. It is illicit to work backwards and claim that the beneficence or piety of the teller is an intrinsic property of the jokes they are using.

THE USES AND CONSEQUENCES OF JOKES AND HUMOR

Jokes have no consequences for society as a whole. Those who disagree must accept that the burden of proof lies entirely with those who think such consequences exist. Where is the evidence that would support their case? Jokes have no effect for the same reason that homeopathic medicines do not and indeed cannot cure patients; jokes are so diluted by much stronger aspects of social life as to be utterly trivial in their impact. It is at the aggregate level that the proposition that jokes have effects needs to be tested. *Jokes and Targets* is about social facts and neither concerns itself with particular individual cases nor needs to. The idea that jokes have aggregate effects is the stuff of which moral panics are made.

It is possible that forms of humor other than jokes, such as satire and mockery by a skilled author or cartoonist with a defined purpose, can have a small social or political effect, provided that the humor is aimed at and has an impact on an individual or a small number of individuals in a position to exercise considerable influence. David Low's cartoons about Colonel Blimp may have reinforced the perception of politicians in Britain in the 1930s, such as the dynamic Leslie (later Baron) Hore-

Belisha, that the army leadership was out of date. Some of those personally targeted by humor may wish to avoid personal ridicule or may come to regard a derided colleague as being a liability. Humor can also be used to goad someone into behaving unwisely and intemperately and damaging his or her own cause, thus unmasking an influential person as unstable, irrational, bigoted, or even violent. But is humor a more effective, as distinct from a more entertaining, way of achieving these ends than the alternative solemn means available? The ambiguity built into humor produces a heightened risk of being misunderstood or of producing the opposite effect from what was intended. The audience may fail to grasp irony or come to identify more strongly with the views of those who are being ridiculed. There is a tension between being humorous and being didactic. I have often tried to use humor persuasively in newspapers, magazines, journals, and on the internet in both Britain and America to support the cause of women's ordination, to expose the hypocrisy of the Olympic Games, to defend able bald politicians, to criticize the conduct of jury trials, to deplore the decline in the teaching of the physical sciences, to damn bad art exhibitions, and to oppose the introduction of compulsory ID cards; as an activity it is utterly different from telling jokes. The very nature of canned jokes makes them a poor tool for a persuasive humorist. You might use jokes to attract someone to a place where you have posted a serious persuasive message, but the jokes do not add to its persuasive force. Even in a debate before an audience, a set-piece joke cannot be used as a sword; it is merely decoration on the scabbard. Jokes are entertainment only, a mere laughing matter.

The tellers of canned jokes are rarely trying to achieve any particular outcome. They mainly tell jokes in groups whose sole function is the creation and maintenance of sociability, which also means that the tellers avoid telling "hurtful jokes to people who could feel attacked by them" (Kuipers 2006, 191). The joke tellers are following Thomas Hobbes's injunction:

> Laughter without offence must be at absurdities and infirmities abstracted from persons and where all the company may laugh together. (Hobbes 1840, 46–47)

Hobbes's maxim is very likely a product of what he himself had undergone as a bald philosopher, baited in company by the ringletted rakes of the aristocratic households where he served as tutor or at the court of Charles II (Aubrey 1994). Hobbes had experienced raillery, an exchange in which individuals try to put one another down with humorous remarks such that one emerges humiliated, another triumphant, and the rest having enjoyed a bout of verbal bearbaiting. It is precisely this development that the etiquette of joke telling for sociability is designed to avoid, even in a context of characteristically boisterous, bantering, competitive joke telling (Kuipers 2006, 63, 191).

For working-class and lower-middle-class joke tellers, there are no restraints on what may be joked about, but there are strong conventions about the context and situation in which a particular joke may be told. The joke tellers seek to avoid upsetting or offending or putting down anyone who is present, for that would be against their own etiquette and disrupt the very sociability that is central to their own enjoyment. You do not tell a disaster joke to the newly bereaved, a blasphemous joke to the pious, or a joke that would make one member of the party look small, unless he or she has made it clear that it would not bother them. This is confirmed by the answers individuals give to folklorists collecting jokes when they inquire about when and to whom the informant would be willing to tell that joke. Telling the jokes involves the conscious transgressing of social conventions about what may and may not be said, but it is done within a network of individual understandings.

It is important not to confuse this concern on the part of the joke tellers with the impact a particular joke might have on a particular individual who is present with the very odd view that aggregates of jokes have an effect on society as a whole. The former is based on observation and experience, but the latter is a primitive belief in the magical power of words, the belief that even to utter certain jokes, regardless of situation or context, might cause total social destruction. The patterned aggregates of jokes that have been discussed are social facts that have to be explained in terms of other social facts, but there is no significant feedback from the jokes into the situations that produced them.

Hobbes (1840, 46) says of jokes more generally:

> Also men laugh at the infirmities of others, by comparison wherewith their own abilities are set off and illustrated. Also men laugh at jests, the wit whereof always consisteth in the elegant discovering and conveying to our minds some absurdity of another: and in this case also the pas-

sion of laughter proceedeth from the sudden imagination of our own odds and eminency: for what is else the recommending of ourselves to our own good opinion, by comparison with another man's infirmity or absurdity?

It is possible, though easily contestable, that Hobbes's account is correct and that this is the reason for the universal existence and very widespread popularity of jokes that have targets. However, it does not help us to discern why some are chosen as targets for jokes and others are not. The main purpose of this book has been to answer that much more difficult question.

WHY MIND OVER MATTER?

Behind the way jokes fit the mind-over-matter model may lie the prestige given particularly in the past to those who dealt with the pure world of the spiritual, the elevated, and the abstract over the useful and practical, but today the jokes are best seen as an aspect of a modern world in which change is driven by knowledge and commerce. The "knowledge economy" is not a new phenomenon but one that came with the industrial revolution (Mokyr 2002, 28–77). The value of physical capital is derived not from the brute labor that went into its production but from its embodied knowledge, knowledge not just of science and technology but of the marketplace, of the consumer, competitors, rates of return, and the law. The knowledge economy of today that has produced the computer, the internet, the birth-control pill, and genetically modified crops is just a more sophisticated extension of the knowledge economy that produced the steam engine and the telegraph. Even where the use of force is concerned, as Stanislav Andreski (1968, 222) has noted, "the chief military virtue is nowadays neither physical endurance nor pugnacity but technical inventiveness." Even terrorists whose ideals are primitive have come to realize this and use ever more sophisticated techniques in their attack on the civilized.

MASCULINITY, FORCE, AND STUPIDITY

In jokes, stupidity is often linked to one particular kind of masculinity, that of the gamma double minus males, whose main sense of their own worth comes from being physically able to dominate or obtain women.

The corresponding women are the stupid Essex girls, who are part of that same culture.

> Essex girl's phone rings.
> **Essex man on phone:** "'ello, darling . . . it's me."
> **Essex girl:** "Who?"
> "The bloke that 'ad yer behind the pub last night."
> "Er . . . was it the Red Lion, Rose and Crown, or The Bull?" (Don 1991, 34)

The blonde joke is part of another contradiction, one between the demands of the modern world of work which require self-control and steady intelligent effort and the continued elevation of unreconstructed sex roles in popular entertainment, where, regardless of dumbness, the hyper-attractive woman is relentlessly celebrated. In Australia, women who value intelligence highly give out satirical Elaine Awards, such as the one presented to model Kate Fischer, who is reported as having said, "I'm beautiful. I'm a model. I'm allowed to be dumb" (Burgmann and Andrews 2007, 203).

The entertainment industry provides such women with a male counterpart through film and sport alike. In a postscript to his 1968 study, *Military Organization and Society,* Stanislav Andreski wrote:

> [Nuclear] weapons constituted the last step in the devaluation of martial virtues which began with the invention of gunpowder. When firearms first appeared they were generally condemned on the grounds that they permitted a dastardly weakling to kill a man of strength and valour. Now a sickly woman scientist suffering from an anxiety neurosis may constitute a far greater military asset than thousands of tough and fearless soldiers . . . [yet] cheap literature as well as the mass media propagate the idea of brainless toughness combined with disdain for "egg-heads." There are two possible explanations, which do not exclude each other, of this trend. . . . One is that it is simply engineered by the advertisers who dislike people who think too much and do not buy without asking why, and for this reason foist upon the public the ideal of a brainless tough and a dumb doll. The other explanation of the present cult of male toughness is that it is a spurious compensation for a lost reality when men carried swords and used them habitually . . . the young men of today . . . live in dread of being taken for "chickens" and find in rudeness and "tough speech" the only opportunities for proving their manhood.

Masculinity is treated in jokes as another kind of power, which includes the power to penetrate sexually. It underpins sex jokes of many kinds (Legman 1982). Here it has been put forward as the basis of jokes about sex between men. Those targeted in the jokes and by extension the groups to which they belong have "lost" their masculinity by being the passive, the penetrated, the pogue, the catamite, and thus weak. The widespread condemnation of the behavior of gay men as morally wrong (Laumann et al. 1994, 284) has nothing to do with family life; that only became an issue in the 1980s after older and once forceful arguments had wilted (Davies 2004, 165–79). The real reason for the condemnation is the horror felt at the imagined sexual domination of one man by another. Sodom was not destroyed to preserve the sanctity of family life in Arkansas. The prohibitions of same-sex activities are strongest in the military, where the hierarchical relationships between men must conform to an ordered and disciplined structure that might be disrupted by the presence of a competing sexual relationship of dominance and submission, whether actual or symbolic (Davies 2004, 229–36; *Lustig-Prean and Beckett v United Kingdom* 2000; *Report of the Homosexuality Policy Assessment Team* 1996). The jokes about man dominating man are often associated with all-male groups strongly committed to traditional masculinity, in which individual men and boys compete for masculine status. The use of phrases such as "rugby jokes" or "barrack-room" ballads in the titles of collections of ribald humor mocking the passive partner in male on male sex imply this. The jokes and songs are as much about masculinity and power as they are about sex.

Jewish jokes about Jewish women and about Jewish men are important not only for what they tell us about self-mocking Jewish humor but also because they allow us to stand outside the world of the conventionally masculine and feminine and not only to laugh at it but to understand how much of it is simply arbitrary. It cannot be denied that on average the innate differences between men and women are very large indeed (Baron-Cohen 2003), though many individual men and women may well differ greatly from the averages for their particular sex. This knowledge is based on very strong evidence, evidence from experiments made of the differences between male and female newborns by observers who do not know what sex the babies are, from measuring hormone levels and from direct observations of the functioning of the brain. However, for our present purposes, all this is rather beside the point. What is relevant to the study of jokes is the way in which these innate male-female differences are expressed and in the process magnified or minimized, which differs greatly between societies, in the same society over time, and between social classes or religious groups. Contemporary Sweden is not at all like Kurdistan in this respect, and the French and the Dutch upper middle classes differ greatly from the working classes of those countries (Kuipers 2006, 65). Modern Iceland is not like the Iceland of the sagas. Masculinity is a given, a fact of life, but the important questions are these: what form does it take, how strongly is it upheld, and to which aspects of it is dominance seen as an essential? It is to be hoped that future researchers can draw on a much greater geographical range of jokes than has been possible here and compare them.

THE FORBIDDEN AND THE INCONGRUOUS

A central theme throughout this work has been the way in which humor comes from a perception of the incongruity of social ambiguity and contradictions. Jewish humor is especially rich because it is the humor of those who not only experience these social incongruities in great measure but intelligently reflect on them. In contemporary America, Jewish humor is the humor of those who are both inside and yet self-consciously outside, of those who know how the two social worlds to which they belong differ and are much given to thinking about it. Jewish humor is a relatively modern phenomenon (Oring 1992, 113–17), one that may be seen as a product of conflicting pressures as to whether and in which ways to assimilate or to remain within a distinctive separate tradition. In the late nineteenth century and for much of the twentieth, it was a dilemma heightened by the exceptionally strong hostility directed against the Jews by the very people whose acceptance they sought. Today, at least in the United States, Australia, and Britain, the dilemma is the opposite, for social acceptance brings with it new problems and temptations. Anti-Semitism remains in these English-speaking societies, but it is now the creed of political and religious fragments who are themselves unpopular and despised in these very societies of which the Jews are now a secure part. The creation of the state of Israel, far from undermining the humor of the Jews, has added new dimensions to it. It is not at all surprising that such a high proportion of American comedians and comedy writers are Jewish.

The other great source of contradiction that leads to joking is the gap between how we experience the social world and what we are told it is and ought to be. This is the basis of the American lawyer jokes, where the members of a profession that is one of the central upholders of the ideals of the republic are perceived as behaving in a venal way. The gap between claim and reality was far greater in the Soviet Union than in any democratic country, and this underlies many of the jokes told in that country. Farce followed hard on the heels of tragedy in that most distressful country. The leaders spoke incessantly of peace, equality, and justice, yet most people's everyday experience was of the opposite. It was a system based on force in which there was always a shortage of goods because resources were diverted into armaments or the means for making armaments. The gap in power between the elite and the people was far greater than in other countries, and there was no justice for anyone who dissented. Lenin, who had been a brutal tyrant, was depicted as a benign uncle. Planning led to muddle and corruption. It was a one-party state where the judiciary had no real independence, and yet there was a pretense of elections, of a constitution and rights, of fair trials; all were a false, meaningless, and comic imitation of the "trappings of bourgeois democracy." The Soviet republics and subordinate countries were called independent, and yet they were not. It was no accident that such a social order should have produced more political jokes than any other.

> When was the first Soviet election? When God put Eve in front of Adam and said, "Go ahead, choose your wife."
>
> When we say Lenin, we mean Party. When we say Party, we mean Lenin. And this is how we deal with everything. We say one thing, we mean something else. (Oring 2004, 213)

It was also the society in which there were more things which it was forbidden to say than in any democracy. Jokes involve breaking rules about what may be said openly and directly, which is why there are so many sex jokes and jokes that play with abusive language. Such jokes existed in the Soviet Union as elsewhere, including the grossly obscene *chastushki* (Raskin 1985, 170–77), as did racial jokes about the supposedly simian features of African ambassadors to that country. In a society where there were restrictions on how to speak about economics, science, and art as well as matters that were directly political, there were more "speech rules" to be broken, and so more jokes were invented. It is a great mistake to think that jokes are funny because they circumvent strongly repressed feelings, though in some cases this might be true. Those who are least inhibited tend to be the ones who most enjoy the escape from inhibition that a joke provides. What we directly observe is that the jokers break social rules about how people in their society or group should speak; these may well be rules that people obey out of mere social convention and to avoid conflict with others, particularly with those who have the power to do something nasty to them. Why feel guilty, as distinct from watchful, when telling a joke about Lenin? Are those who cheerfully enjoy smutty talk racked with guilt about their indecencies? Jokes are an escape, but an escape from social constraints on speaking, constraints which the jokers may see as legitimate or which they may feel are a mere nuisance or even an oppressive imposition by others. This is also true of societies with freedom of speech, in which other kinds of imposed patterns of social disapproval are evaded by jokes. This is why disaster jokes, such as those about the death of Princess Diana in a car crash, have long been and remain so popular (Davies 1999 and 2003).

Democratic societies are not rich in political jokes. The Russians joked about nuclear missiles because it was forbidden to oppose the official line concerning their uses and deployment. In Britain the question of nuclear weapons (Mercer 1986) was an issue that utterly divided and nearly destroyed the Labour Party, one of the main political parties. It was the subject of political marches from the Aldermaston Atomic Weapons Establishment and of protests by strange women who camped out in tents next to the RAF base at Greenham Common, where the USAF held its cruise missiles, in either case quite close to my home. The possibility of mutual destruction was the theme of Stanley Kubrick's 1964 comedy *Dr. Strangelove, or How I Learned to Stop Worrying and Love the Bomb*. Why invent jokes about matters that are not only openly discussed but are the subject of prize-winning humor?

There were few political jokes about environmental controversies in either the Soviet Union or the democracies but for opposite reasons. In the democratic world, environmental and health risks and attempts to conceal risk were and are central to politics (Neal and Davies 1998) and also the subject of open satire. There is doubt and cynicism, but very few jokes, since the doubts and cynicism can be openly expressed in both serious and humorous ways. The jokes given below are rare. They have not multiplied in numbers to form a joke cycle. They are highly specific one-off jokes.

> Why are organic fruits and vegetables so expensive?
> It costs more to spray at night. (Told to me by a Californian geneticist in 1988)

> Why is McDonald's 144 times more efficient than the human body?
> It takes the human body twenty-four hours to turn food into shit. McDonald's does it in ten minutes.

These jokes have not given rise to sets of general jokes about fast-food outlets or health food stores or the power of advertising or about popular or official beliefs concerning food. It is always important to consider not only the jokes that exist but those that could exist but do not. The existence of these lone jokes shows that a joke cycle could exist, but their great scarcity shows that such a joke cycle does not exist.

In the Soviet Union, there were many serious environmental disasters, such as the chemical explosion in nuclear waste in Kyshtym in 1957 and the release into the atmosphere of anthrax spores being prepared for use as banned biological weapons in Sverdlovsk in 1979, but there were no jokes about them because the authorities arranged a complete cover-up in a way that is difficult in societies with opposition parties and investigative journalism. Political jokes only began with the Chernobyl nuclear disaster in the Ukraine in 1986, which could not be fully concealed. In the outside world, it was just one more occasion to be celebrated in disaster jokes that broke the enforced total solemnity of speech laid down by western broadcasters in regard to anything from earthquakes to assassinations. In the Soviet Union and Eastern Europe, Chernobyl gave rise to an entire new cycle of political jokes.

> Report in Soviet newspaper: Last night the Chernobyl nuclear power plant fulfilled the entire Five-Year Plan for the generation of energy in five microseconds.

> What were the first two announcements concerning radiation?
> The first: There is no radioactivity. The second: The radioactivity during the second week has subsided considerably, being only one-half of the first week's.

The May Day celebrations were held in Kiev yesterday. In the front row were the party activists.

In the second row were the trade union activists
And in the back row were the radio activists.

The U.S. has declared itself under a unilateral obligation not to attack the USSR first by means of any of its nuclear reactors. (Kürti 1988, 332)

It is not so much the gap between ideal and reality as such that gives rise to jokes but the ban on pointing out that the gap exists. In Britain, it is widely believed that the educational system and the criminal justice system are in serious decline and that the politicians and administrators who tell the public that they are improving are liars and scoundrels. But there are very few jokes about these topics because both the decline and the mendacity are a matter of open debate and public ridicule. In a democracy, mass joking is most likely to occur when the government, the main opposition parties, and the mass media close ranks and exclude from proper political debate an issue that ordinary people feel is important. Jokes reflect hegemony.

What is curious about the American lawyer joke cycle is how much less sophisticated the lawyer jokes were than the political jokes told in the Soviet Union. They require very little knowledge of lawyers and the law. They are merely straightforward jokes about the venal behavior of individuals. It is only the curiously sacred quality of law in the very making and defining of the United States that led to the great cycle of lawyer jokes being told, a set of jokes never taken up outside the United States. The U.S. Constitution is the one aspect of American political life that may not be challenged or ridiculed, even though Jeremy Bentham saw its underlying principles as "nonsense on stilts." The American lawyer jokes can be portrayed as a very indirect evading of the taboo on trashing the Constitution, but their content parallels the straightforward jokes of an earlier time about the celibate priest who sleeps with his pretty young housekeeper, the avowedly teetotal Protestant minister who is a secret tippler, or the rabbi who eats a baked apple but in the mouth of a roast suckling pig. The lawyer ought to be an exemplar, but is not. The American lawyer jokes lack the range and sophistication of the best Soviet jokes, which were not merely about ordinary human failings but played with entire systems of ideas in an intellectual way. Only Jewish jokes have managed to match the political jokes told in Soviet times for sheer depth and ingenuity.

Jokes multiply when there is a tension or contradiction between two sets of behaviors or ways of looking at the world. Often it is between duty and temptation, and sometimes the temptation is represented by some other group. In Jewish jokes, it is the lax gentiles, and American, British, and German jokes about the French can be viewed in the same way. It is one of the reasons why everyone, including lawyers, can laugh at jokes about rascally attorneys. The tension between temptation and duty, like that between the social order as it is held out to be and the reality that is actually experienced, gives rise to jokes because both aspects can be perceived and understood at one and the same time. These are incongruities that obviously relate to important aspects of the jokers' lives.

THE INCONGRUOUS AND THE FORBIDDEN

The joke itself is a tiny analogue of the situation that has given rise to it, for its internal mechanism involves yet another kind of incongruity. A joke begins with a tale or question that could be serious, but if it were, it would be puzzling. Listeners are not given enough information to work out which way it will go, though they well suspect from the overall context of the conversation that there is going to be a funny ending, but they cannot be sure, and the joke teller may well distract and mislead them by the way he or she begins. Even when the listeners suspect a surprise ending, they do not know what kind of surprise to expect. The advantage of having a target in the joke about which there is a known comic script, such as the crooked lawyer or dumb athlete, is that it preserves the initial incongruity but makes it clear that if there is going to be a surprise, roughly what kind of surprise it will be. When a tale begins "two lawyers" or "two athletes," it may turn out to be a joke, but it could equally be a story about a real event involving actual individuals. A "targetless" joke that begins "two utter twisters" or "two complete dumb heads" does not allow for the latter possibility; the beginning is overdetermined. The surprise is undermined. However, if a joke about trickery began "two actuaries" or a joke about stupidity began "two archers," then however good the punch line, the joke might fail because these occupations do not evoke a well-known comic script. The use of a conventional target enables the joke teller to strike the right balance between giving the listeners too much information and giving them too little. Punch lines themselves can be interpreted in more than one way, and even though the listeners may still laugh at the ending, they may not laugh as much as they could have done because they have put a different construction on it, one that is funny but not as funny as the one intended. The mention early on of a specific target that is conventionally associated in humor with a particular quality thus both preserves the initial uncertainty *and* enables the rapid and accurate understanding of the final surprise when it arrives. The target contributes to the very workings of the well-made joke.

> Here is the latest question put to Radio Armenia.
> Would it be possible to create socialism in Switzerland?
> In principle, yes. But what have the Swiss ever done to you?

There is or easily could be a real radio station called Radio Armenia, and the question about Switzerland could have been posed by or put to one of the party's Marxist theoreticians who did have serious if inane discussions of this kind. But the listeners also know that statements that begin with Radio Armenia tend to end up with a punch line that indirectly reveals the absurdity and nastiness of socialism. The ending is additionally funny because it expresses the forbidden. Jokes with targets are constructed in such a way as to be able to play both with incongruity and with forbidden speech and as such provide many of our best jokes.

REFERENCES

ARCHIVAL SOURCE

University of California Berkeley Folklore Archive (UCBFA)

PRINTED AND INTERNET SOURCES

503 World's Worst Dirty Jokes. 1982. New York: Bell. Previously titled *Anecdota Americana*, series 2.

Abrams, Nathan. 2004. Triple Exthnics: Jews in the American Porn Industry. *Jewish Quarterly* 196 (Winter): 27–30.

Abse, Leo. 2000. *Fellatio, Masochism, Politics, and Love*. London: Robson.

Adams, Bruce. 2005. *Tiny Revolutions in Russia: Twentieth-Century Soviet and Russian History in Anecdotes*. New York: Routledge Curzon.

Adams, Cecil. 1986. Is It True What They Say about Gerbils? A Straight Dope Classic from Cecil's Storehouse of Human Knowledge, March 28. http://www.straight dope.com/columns/read/478/is-it-true-what-they-say-about-gerbils.

Adams, Scott. 2002. *Dilbert and the Way of the Weasel*. New York: HarperCollins.

Al-Khatib, Mahmoud A. 1999 Joke Telling in Jordanian Society: A Sociolinguistic Perspective. *Humor: International Journal of Humor Research* 12 (3): 261–88.

Alexandrian, Sarane. 2006. Education in Love in the Age of the Enlightenment. In *The Triumph of Eros*, ed. Dimitry Ozerkov, Satish Padiyar, and Sarane Alexandrian, 35–44. London: Fontanka.

Alvin, Julius. 1983. *Gross Jokes*. New York: Zebra.

Amelunxen, Clemens. 1992. *Of Fools at Court*. Berlin: Walter de Gruyter.

Amis, Martin. 2003. *Koba the Dread: Laughter and the Twenty Million*. London: Vintage.

Andreski, Stanislav. 1968. *Military Organization and Society*. 2d ed. With a foreword by A. R. Radcliffe-Brown. London: Routledge and Kegan Paul.

———. 1989. The Prospects for Poland in the Event of a Cessation of Soviet Control. In *The Soviet Union and the Challenge of the Future*, ed. Alexander Shtromas and Morton A. Kaplan, 3:717–24. New York: Paragon.

Andrew, Christopher, and Vasili Mitrokhin. 2000. *The Mitrokhin Archive*. London: Penguin.

Anecdota Americana: Five Hundred Stories for the Amusement of the Five Hundred Nations That Comprise America. 1933. New York: Faro.

Aquisti, Danilo. 1988. *Carabinieri la Superbarzelletta*. Rome: Napoleone.

Aristotle. 1975. *Ethics of Aristotle: The Nicomachean Ethics*. Trans. J. A. K. Thomson and H. Tredennick. Harmondsworth: Penguin.

Armstrong, Arnold [pseud.]. 1963. *The Mortarboard Spartans*. London: Frederick Muller.

Ashby, LeRoy. 1987. *William Jennings Bryan, Champion of Democracy*. Boston: Twayne.

Ashton, John. 1888. *English Caricature and Satire on Napoleon I*. London: Chatto and Windus.

Attardo, Salvatore. 2001. *Humorous Texts: A Semantic and Pragmatic Analysis*. Berlin: Mouton de Gruyter.

Aubrey, John. 1994. The Brief Life: An Abstract of Aubrey's Notes on Thomas Hobbes. In appendix to Hobbes, *The Elements of Law, Natural and Politic with Three Lives*, ed. J. C. A. Gaskin. Oxford: Oxford University Press. Orig. pub. 1680.

Ausaf. 2009. Saudi and Egyptian Humour. *Radiance* 47 (19) (August 9). www .radianceweekly.com (accessed September 2009).

Austin, James C. 1978. *American Humor in France: Two Centuries of French Criticism of the Comic Spirit in American Literature*. Ames: Iowa State University Press.

Avnery, Uri. 2006. *Mon dieu, mondial! (Balls instead of Bullets)*. June 25. http:// www.redress.btinternet.co.uk/uavnery161.htm (accessed December 21, 2009).

Aydelott, Danise. 1993. Mass Rape during War. *Emory International Law Review* 7: 585–631.

Ayling, Stanley. 1972. *George III*. London: Collins.

Aymé, Marcel. 1933. *La jument verte*. Paris: Gallimard.

Baker, Paul. 2004. *Fantabulosa: A Dictionary of Polari and Gay Slang*. London: Continuum.

Baker, Paul, and Jo Stanley. 2003. *Hello Sailor! The Hidden History of Gay Life at Sea*. Harlow: Pearson Education.

Bakhtin, Mikhail M. 1985. *Rabelais and His World*. Bloomington: Indiana University Press.

Banc, C. [pseud. Banc means joke in Romanian], and Alan Dundes. 1986. *First Prize, Fifteen Years! An Annotated Collection of Romanian Political Jokes*. Cranbury: Associated University Presses/Fairleigh Dickinson University Press.

———. 1990. *You Call This Living? A Collection of East European Political Jokes*. Athens: University of Georgia Press.

Baron-Cohen, Simon. 2003. *The Essential Differences: The Truth about the Male and Female Brain*. New York: Basic.

Barry, Norman. 1982. The Tradition of Spontaneous Order. *Literature of Liberty* 5: 7–58.

Bauer, Thomas G., and Bob McKercher, eds. 2003. *Sex and Tourism: Journeys of Romance, Love, and Lust*. New York: Haworth Hospitality.

Bayor, Ronald H. 1978. *Neighbors in Conflict: The Irish, Germans, Jews, and Italians of New York City, 1929–41*. Baltimore: Johns Hopkins University Press.

Beam, Alex. 1982. Introduction to Arie Zand, *Political Jokes of Leningrad*. Austin: Silvergirl.

Beckmann, Petr. 1969. *Whispered Anecdotes: Humor from behind the Iron Curtain*. Boulder, Colo.: Golem.

———. 1980. *Hammer and Tickle: Clandestine Laughter in the Soviet Union*. Boulder, Colo.: Golem.

Bell, John Joy. 1929. *Hoots*. Dundee: Valentine.

Bellus, Jean. 1957. *Clémentine Chérie*. London: Arthur Barker.

Benjamin, Chris. 2002. Japan's Writ Rarely Runs to Lawyers. *Guardian* (London), July 8. http://www.guardian.co.uk/business/2002/jul/08/japan.internationalnews.

Bennett, Gillian, and Paul Smith, eds. 1990. *A Nest of Vipers*. Sheffield: Sheffield Academic Press.

Bergson, Henri. 1924. *Le rire: Essai sur la signification du comique*. Paris: Editions Alcan. Orig. pub. 1900.

Bermant, Chaim. 1986. *What's the Joke? A Study of Jewish Humour throughout the Ages*. London: Weidenfeld and Nicolson.

The Best of 606 Aggie Jokes. 1976. Dallas: Gigem.

Die besten Graf Bobby Witze. 1982. Rastatt: Moewig.

Bing, Janet, and Dana Heller. 2003. How Many Lesbians Does It Take to Screw in a Light Bulb? *Humor: International Journal of Humor Research* 16 (2): 157–82.

Bird, Kai, and Martin J. Sherwin. 2006. *American Prometheus: The Triumph and Tragedy of J. Robert Oppenheimer*. London: Vintage.

Bishaw, Alemayehu, and Jessica Semega. 2008. *U.S. Census Bureau, American Community Survey Reports ACS-09: Income, Earnings, and Poverty Data from the 2007 American Community Survey*. Washington, D.C.: Government Printing Office.

Blonde Discrimination Is No Joke in Hungary. 2004. *Cape Times*, November 24. http://www.iol.co.za/index.php?set_id=1&click_id=24&art_id=vn2004112403 5214167C871988 (accessed August 28, 2009).

Blyth, Henry. 1972. *Skittles: The Last Victorian Courtesan*. Newton Abbott: Readers Union.

Bode, Carl. 1969. *Mencken*. Carbondale: Southern Illinois University Press.

Bonfanti, Joe. 1976. *Italian Jokes*. New York: Leisure.

Boronson, Warren. 2008. The Truth about Jews and Sport. *New Jersey Jewish Standard*, August 8.

Boyarin, Daniel. 1997. *Unheroic Conduct*. Berkeley: University of California Press.

Bracewall, Michael, Marco Livingstone, and Jan Debbault. 2007. *Gilbert and George*. London: Tate.

Brandon, Ruth. 1992. *Being Divine: A Biography of Sarah Bernhardt*. London: Mandarin.

Brandon, Ruth, and Christie Davies. 1973. *Wrongful Imprisonment*. London: Allen and Unwin.

Brecht, Bertolt. 1988. *The Caucasian Chalk Circle*. Trans. James and Tania Stern. London: Methuen.

Brewer, E. Cobham. 1894. *The Dictionary of Phrase and Fable*. Leicester: Galley.

Brokhin, Yuri. 1975. *Hustling on Gorky Street*. London: W. H. Allen.

Brottman, Mikita. 2004. *Gershon Legman and the Psychopathology of Humor*. Hillsdale: Analytic Press.

Brunvand, Jan Harold. 1973. "Don't Shoot, Comrades": A Survey of the Submerged Folklore of Eastern Europe. *North Carolina Folklore Journal* 21: 181–88.

———.1981. *The Vanishing Hitchhiker: Urban Legends and Their Meanings.* London: Picador.

Bry, Clémentine, Alice Follenfant, and Thierry Meyer. 2008. Blonde Like Me: When Self-Construals Moderate Stereotype Priming Effects on Intellectual Performance. *Journal of Experimental Social Psychology* 44: 751–57.

Bryant, Chad. 2006 The Language of Resistance: Czech Jokes and Joke-Telling under Nazi Occupation, 1943–45. *Journal of Contemporary History* 41 (1): 133–51.

Brzozowska, Dorota. 2009. Polish Jokelore in the Period of Transition. In *Permitted Laughter,* ed. Arvo Krikmann and Liisi Laineste, 127–69. Tartu: ELM Scholarly Press.

Buitenen, Paul van. 2000. *Blowing the Whistle: One Man's Fight against Fraud in the European Commission.* London: Politico's.

Bullock, J. M. 1935. Peers Who Have Married Players. *Notes and Queries* 169 (10): 92–94.

Bureau of Labor Statistics. U.S. Department of Labor. 2008. *Occupational Outlook Handbook, 2008–2009* ed. http://www.bls.gov/OCO/.

Burgmann, Meredith, and Yvette Andrews. 2007. *The Ernies Book: 1000 Terrible Things Australian Men Have Said about Women.* Crow's Nest: Allen and Unwin.

Burke, Thomas. 2008. Father Tongue. In *Queer and Catholic,* ed. Amie M. Evans and Trebor Healey, 117–28. New York: Routledge.

Burks, Richard V. 1989. The Coming Crisis in the Soviet Union. In *The Soviet Union and the Challenge of the Future,* ed. Alexander Shtromas and Morton A. Kaplan, 1:115–65. New York: Paragon.

Burns, Robert. 1868. *Poems and Songs.* Edinburgh: William P. Nimmo.

Burns, Stan, and Mel Weinstein. 1978. *The Jewish Book of World Records.* Los Angeles: Pinnacle.

Cain, Julien. 1970. Introduction to Honoré Daumier, *Lawyers and Justice.* New York: Leon Amiel.

Caniff, Milton. 1945. *Male Call.* New York: Simon and Schuster.

Carpenter, John. 1990. President's Sidebar. *Pennsylvania Lawyer,* November. Cited in http://www.brann-light.com/Pub-TWL/lawyer_jokes.htm.

Carroll, Lewis. 1968. *Sylvie and Bruno Concluded.* In *The Works of Lewis Carroll.* Feltham: Spring. Orig. pub. 1893.

Cassingham, Randy. 2005. *The True Stella Awards, Honoring Real Cases of Greedy Opportunists, Frivolous Lawsuits, and the Law Run Amok.* New York: Dutton.

Central Intelligence Agency. 2009. *The World Factbook.* https://www.cia.gov /library/publications/the-world-factbook/fields/2172.html (accessed July 20, 2009).

Cerf, Bennett A. 1943. *The Pocket Book of War Humor.* New York: Pocket.

Chabin, Michelle. 2005. Arab Players Key to Israel's Success. *USA Today,* June 3. http://www.usatoday.com/sports/soccer/world/2005-06-03-arab-israel-team_x .htm (accessed January 22, 2010).

Chamberlin, W. H. 1957. The Anecdote: Unrationed Soviet Humor. *Russian Review* 16 (3): 27–34.

Chambers, Pearl. 1958. *Below the Neckline.* London: Neville Spearman.

Chanfrault, Bernard. 1992. Stereotypes of "Deep France" in the Almanach Vermot. *Humor: International Journal of Humor Research* 5 (1): 7–31.

Chang, Jung-fu. 1997. *A Simulation Matching Approach of Mate Selection: An Integration Study*. PhD diss., University of Reading.

Chaucer, Geoffrey. 1926. *The Canterbury Tales*. In *The Works of Geoffrey Chaucer*, ed. Alfred W. Pollard et al. London: Macmillan. Orig. pub. 1387.

Chesney, Kellow. 1970. *The Victorian Underworld*. London: Maurice Temple Smith.

Clark, Katerina, and Michael Holquist. 1984. *Mikhail Bakhtin*. Cambridge: Harvard University Press.

Clément, André. 1945. *Les 100 meilleures histoires de l'occupation*. Paris: Le Sourd.

Cochran, R. 1989. "What Courage!" Romanian "Our Leader" Jokes. *Journal of American Folklore* 142 (4–5): 259–79.

Cohen, Joseph. 1995. *You Know You're Gay When . . . : Those Unforgettable Moments That Make Us Who We Are*. Chicago: Contemporary.

Cohen, Rich. 1998. *Tough Jews*. London: Jonathan Cape.

Cole, William, and Douglas McKee. 1960. *French Cartoons*. London: Panther.

———.1962. *You Damn Men Are All Alike*. Greenwich: Fawcett/Gold Medal.

Collins, Dick. 1998. *Historia Urinalis*: Re-reading *Les trois meschines*. *French Studies* 52 (4): 397–408.

Conquest, Robert. 1971. *The Great Terror: Stalin's Purge of the Thirties*. Harmondsworth: Penguin.

———. 2008. Academe and the Soviet Myth. In *The Strange Death of Soviet Communism*, ed. Nikolas Gvosdev, 125–35. New Brunswick: Transaction.

Cooper, Alan. 1996. *Philip Roth and the Jews*. Albany: State University of New York Press.

Coote, George. 1998. *The Politically Incorrect Joke Book*. Norman Park QLD, Australia: Gap.

Cournos, John, ed. 1943. *A Treasury of Russian Life and Humor*. New York: Coward-McCann.

Courtois, Stéphane, ed. 1997. *Le livre noir de communisme: Crimes, terreures, et Repression*. Paris: R. Laffont.

Crime: Easy Money. 1955. *Time*, April 18.

Croy, Homer. 1948. *What Grandpa Laughed At*. New York: Duell, Sloan and Pearce.

Cunard Queens. 2007. *Rum Ration: The Navy Network*. http://www.navy-net.co.uk /Jokes/jid=989/sortby=rate/ad=asc.html.

Curb, Rosemary, and Nancy Manahan, eds. 1985. *Breaking Silence: Lesbian Nuns on Convent Sexuality*. London: Columbus.

Curzon, Daniel. 2006. *The Big Book of In-Your-Face Gay Etiquette*. San Francisco: Igna.

Daninos, Pierre. 1954. *Les carnets du Major Thompson*. Paris.

Dannimann, Franz. 2001. *Flüsterwitze und Spottgedichte unterm Hakenkreuz*. Wien: Ephelant.

D'Arcangelo, Angelo. 1972. *Angelo D'Arcangelo's Gay Humor Book*. New York: Lancer.

Daumier, Honoré. 1970. *Lawyers and Justice*. Introduction by Julien Cain. New York: Leon Amiel. Orig. pub. c. 1851.

Davies, Christie. 1978. *Welsh Jokes*. Cardiff: John Jones.

———. 1982. Sexual Taboos and Social Boundaries. *American Journal of Sociology* 87 (5): 1032–63.

———. 1986. Jewish Jokes, Anti-Semitic Jokes, and Hebredonian Jokes. In *Jewish Humor*, ed. Avner Ziv, 75–96. Tel-Aviv: Papyrus.

———. 1989. Humor for the Future and a Future for Humor. In *The Soviet Union and the Challenge of the Future*, ed. Alexander Shtromas and Morton A. Kaplan, 3:299–319. New York: Paragon.

———. 1990. *Ethnic Humor around the World: A Comparative Analysis.* Bloomington: Indiana University Press.

———. 1992. Review of Gloria Kaufman, ed., *In Stitches: A Patchwork of Feminist Humor and Satire. Humor: International Journal of Humor Research* 5 (4): 431–36.

———. 1996. Puritanical and Politically Correct: A Critical Historical Account of Changes in the Censorship of Comedy by the BBC. In *The Social Faces of Humour: Practices and Issues*, ed. George Paton, Chris Powell, and Steve Wagg, 29–61. Aldershot: Arena.

———. 1998. *Jokes and Their Relation to Society.* Berlin: Mouton de Gruyter.

———. 1999. Jokes on the Death of Diana. In *The Mourning for Diana*, ed. Tony Walter, 253–68. Oxford: Berg.

———. 2000. Goffman's Concept of the Total Institution: Criticisms and Revisions. In *Erving Goffman*, ed. Gary Alan Fine and Gregory W. H. Smith, 239–54. London: Sage.

———. 2002. *The Mirth of Nations.* New Brunswick, N.J.: Transaction.

———. 2003. Electronic Humor about Disasters. In *Of Corpse: Death and Humor in Folklore and Popular Culture*, ed. Peter Narváez, 15–34. Logan: Utah State University Press.

———. 2004. *The Strange Death of Moral Britain.* New Brunswick, N.J.: Transaction.

———. 2009. A General Theory of Jokes Whose Butts Are the Stupid and the Canny. *Acta Ethnographica Hungarica* 54 (1): 7–19.

Davies, Christie, and Władysław Chłopicki. 2004. Dowcipy o Polakach w Ameryce-znamienny wytwór współczesnego społeczeństwa masowego. In *Aspekty współczesnych dyskursów, Język a komunikacja*, ed. Piotr P. Chruszczewski, 59–61. Series 5. Tome 1. Kraków: Tertium.

Davies, Sarah. 1997. *Popular Opinion in Stalin's Russia: Terror, Propaganda, and Dissent, 1934–1941.* Cambridge: Cambridge University Press.

De Witt, Hugh. 1970. *Bawdy Barrack-Room Ballads.* London: Tandem.

Deriabin, Peter, and Frank Gibney. 1960. *The Secret World.* London: Barker.

Dershowitz, Alan M. 1991. *Chutzpah.* New York: Simon and Schuster.

Diaz, Missy. 2009. Whocanisue Website Skirts the Rules for Lawyer Ads. *South Florida Sun Sentinel*, October 4. http://www.sun-sentinel.com/news/palm-beach/boca-raton/sfl-who-can-i-sue-p100409,0,4368025.story.

Dickinson, Dicky, and Bill Hooper. 1974. *Clangers in Uniform.* Tunbridge Wells: Midas.

Dolgopolova, Z. 1983. *Russia Dies Laughing: Jokes from Soviet Russia.* London: Unwin.

Dolot, Miron. 1985. *Execution by Hunger: The Hidden Holocaust.* New York: Norton.

Don, Basil (pseudonym based on Basildon in Essex). 1991. *The Very Best of Essex Girl Jokes.* London: Attica.

Donald, Diana. 1996. *The Age of Caricature: Satirical Prints in the Reign of George III*. New Haven: Yale University Press.

Douglas, James W. B., J. M. Ross, and Howard Russell Simpson. 1971. *All Our Future*. London: Random House.

Douglas, Mary. 1966. *Purity and Danger*. London: Routledge and Kegan Paul.

Dover, Kenneth J. 1978. *Greek Homosexuality*. London: Duckworth.

Dowling, Linda. 1994. *Hellenism and Homosexuality in Victorian Oxford*. Ithaca, N.Y.: Cornell University Press.

Draitser, Emil. 1978. *Forbidden Laughter*. Los Angeles: Almanac.

———. 1989. Soviet Underground Jokes as a Means of Entertainment. *Journal of Popular Culture* 23 (1): 117–25.

———. 1994. Sociological Aspects of the Russian Jewish Stories of the Exodus. *Humor: International Journal of Humor Research* 7 (3): 245–67.

———. 1998. *Taking Penguins to the Movies*. Detroit: Wayne State University Press.

Drozdzynski, A. 1977. *Der politische Witz im Ostblok*. Munich: DTV.

Dundes, Alan. 1971. Laughter behind the Iron Curtain. *Ukrainian Quarterly* 27: 50–59.

———. 1980. Misunderstanding Humour: An American Stereotype of the Englishman. In *Folklore Studies in the Twentieth Century*, ed. Venetia J. Newall, 10–15. Totowa: D. S. Brewer, Rowman and Littlefield.

———. 1987. *Cracking Jokes*. Berkeley, Calif.: Ten Speed.

Durkheim, Émile. 1982. *The Rules of Sociological Method*. Ed. Steven Lukes. Trans. W. D. Halls. New York: Free Press. Orig. pub. 1895.

Editors of *Krokodil* magazine. 1989. *Soviet Humour*. London: Sidgwick and Jackson.

Edwardes, Allen. 1967. *Erotica Judaica: A Sexual History of the Jews*. New York: Julian.

Ehrenfeld, Rachel. 2009. UK Libel Laws Chill Another American Book. *Legal Project:* Forbes.com.

Elgart, J. M. 1973. *Still More over Sexteen*. Vol. 3. Secaucus: Castle.

Elias, Norbert. 1982. *State Formation and Civilization*, vol. 2 of *The Civilizing Process*. Oxford: Basil Blackwell. Orig. pub. 1939.

Enodreven. 2005. Posh and Becks. *Crypt Magazine* 43, Crypt jokes. http://cryptmag3 .site11.com/Online/43/PoshandBecks%20.html (accessed January 20, 2010).

Fairbanks, Charles, Jr. 2008. The Nature of the Beast. In *The Strange Death of Soviet Communism*, ed. Nikolas Gvosdev, 61–75. New Brunswick: Transaction.

Fairfax, René [pseudo. John Haselden]. 1991. *'Allo 'Allo! The Complete War Diaries of René Artois Based on the BBC Television Series by Jeremy Lloyd and David Croft*. London: BBC.

Fantoni, Barry, ed. 1982–2008. *Private Eye's Colemanballs*. 14 vols. London: Private Eye and Andre Deutsch.

Feynman, Richard P. 1986. *Surely You're Joking, Mr. Feynman*. London: Unwin.

Field, Tim. 2003. *Jokes about Those Friendly Lawyers*. www.suyccessunlimited.co .uk/humour/lawyer.htm.

Finer, Samuel E. 1978. *The Man on Horseback: The Role of the Military in Politics*. Harmondsworth: Penguin.

Fitzpatrick, Sheila. 1999. *Everyday Stalinism: Ordinary Life in Extraordinary Times: Soviet Russia in the 1930s*. New York: Oxford University Press.

Fletcher, Lynne Yamaguchi. 1992. *The First Gay Pope and Other Records*. Boston: Alyson.

Forney, Ellen. 2008. *Lust: Kinky Online Personal Ads from Seattle's* The Stranger. Seattle: Fantagraphics.

Forth, Christopher E. 2004. *The Dreyfus Case and the Crisis of French Manhood*. Baltimore: Johns Hopkins University Press.

Fosberry, Charles T. 2004. *Gay Slang*. London: Abson.

Freedman, Michael. 2001. *Plaintiff Lawyers*. http://www.forbes.com/forbes/2001/0514/132.html (accessed March 8, 2010).

Freud, Sigmund. 1991. *Jokes and Their Relation to the Unconscious*. London: Penguin. Orig. pub. 1905.

Frevert, Ute. 1995. *Men of Honour*. Cambridge: Polity.

Frommer, Myrna Katz, and Harvey Frommer. 1995. *Growing Up Jewish in America: An Oral History*. New York: Harcourt Brace.

Frosh, Anthony. 2009. Tough Frummes—Religious Jews Making a Career in the Ring. *Galus Australis Jewish Life in the Antipodies,* November 26. http://galusaustralis.com/2009/11/tough-frummes-religious-jews-making-a-career-in-the-ring/.

Frumkin, Vladimir. 1989. Liberating the Tone of Russian Speech: Reflections on Soviet Magnazidat. In *The Soviet Union and the Challenge of the Future,* ed. Alexander Shtromas and Morton A. Kaplan, 3:277–98. New York: Paragon.

Fuller, Thomas. 1811. *The History of the Worthies of England*. 2 vols. London: Rivington. Orig. pub. 1662.

Fuqua, James. 1996. *Sharks and Lawyers—A Comparative Study. James Fuqua's Law Jokes,* September 13. http://www.jamesfuqua.com/lawyers/jokes/sharks.shtml (accessed November 5, 2009).

———. 2000. *James Fuqua's Law Jokes, Shorter Lawyer Jokes*. http://www.jamesfuqua.com/lawyers/jokes/short.shtml (accessed August 23, 2009).

Galanter, Marc. 1998. The Faces of Mistrust: The Images of Lawyers in Public Opinion, Jokes, and Political Discourse. *University of Cincinnati Law Review* 66 (3): 805–45.

———. 2002. Changing Legal Consciousness in America in the View from the Joke Corpus. *Cardozo Law Review* 23 (6): 2223–40.

———. 2005. *Lowering the Bar: Legal Jokes and Legal Culture*. Madison: University of Wisconsin Press.

Gamm, Hans-Jochen. 1979. *Der Flüsterwitz im Dritten Reich*. Munich: Deutscher.

García, P. [pseud. José García Martínez]. 1977. *Los Chistes de Franco*. Madrid: Ediciones 99.

Gardner, Gerald. 1994. *Campaign Humor*. Detroit: Wayne State University Press.

Gatrell, Vic. 2006. *City of Laughter: Sex and Satire in Eighteenth-Century London*. London: Atlantic.

Gaulet, Laurent. 2005. *L'official de l'Humeur 2006*. Paris: First.

Gilbert, William S., and Arthur Sullivan. 1996. *Iolanthe, or The Peer and the Peri*. In *The Complete Annotated Gilbert and Sullivan*. Oxford: Oxford University Press. Orig. pub. 1882.

Ginger, Ray. 1974. *Ray Ginger's Jokebook about American History*. New York: New Viewpoints.

The Girls from La Vie Parisienne. 1962. London: Panther.

Goffman, Erving. 1968. *Asylums.* Harmondsworth: Penguin.

———. 1990. *Stigma.* London: Penguin. Orig. pub. 1963.

Goldman, Stuart. 1999. Women on the Warpath. *WorldNetDaily Commentary,* October 8. http://www.wnd.com/index.php/index.php?pageId=4855 (accessed December 21, 2009).

Goody, Jack. 1982. *Cooking, Cuisine, and Class: A Study in Comparative Sociology.* Cambridge: Cambridge University Press.

Gorer, Geoffrey. 1955. *Exploring English Character.* London: Criterion.

———. 1971. *Sex and Marriage in England Today.* London: Nelson.

Graham, Seth B. 2003a. The Wages of Syncretism: Folkloric New Russians and Post-Soviet Popular Culture. *Russian Review* 62 (1): 37–53.

———. 2003b. *A Cultural Analysis of the Russo-Soviet Anekdot.* PhD diss., University of Pittsburgh. http://etd.library.pitt.edu/ETD/available/etd-11032003-192424/unrestricted/grahasethb_etd2003.pdf.

Gramont, Sacha. 1969. *The French: Portrait of a People.* New York: G. P. Putnam.

Gray, John. 1998. *False Dawn.* London: Granta.

Grayzel, Susan R. 2002. *Women and the First World War.* London: Longman.

Grish, Kristina. 2005. *Boy Vey! The Shiksa's Guide to Dating Jewish Men.* New York: Simon Spotlight Entertainment.

Grosskurth, Phyllis. 1964. *The Woeful Victorian: A Biography of John Addington Symonds.* New York: Holt, Rinehart and Winston.

Grossmith, George, and Weedon Grossmith. 1994. *The Diary of a Nobody.* Ware: Wordsworth. Orig. pub. 1889.

Guillois, Mina, and André Guillois. 1980. *Encyclopédie de l'amour en 2000 histoires Drôles.* Paris: Fayard.

Gurock, Jeffrey S. 2005. *Judaism's Encounter with American Sports.* Bloomington: Indiana University Press.

Gvosdev, Nikolas K., ed. 2008. *The Strange Death of Soviet Communism: A Postscript.* New Brunswick: Transaction.

Halkin, Hillel. 2008. Man into Machine. *Jerusalem Post,* August 28. http://www.jpost.com/Home/Article.aspx?id=112592.

Hall, J. Mortimer. 1934. *Anecdota Americana.* 2d series. Boston: Humphrey Adams.

Hallett, Mark. 2000. *Hogarth.* London: Phaidon.

Halperin, David M. 2002. *How to Do the History of Homosexuality.* Chicago: University of Chicago Press.

Handwerker, Haim. 2008. Jewish, Yes. American, Yes. But Am I a Princess? *Haaretz.com,* March 11, 2008.

Harris, Ben. 2009. First Date 2.0: ShidduchVision Aims to Ease Shidduch Crisis. *JTA,* June 30. http://jta.org/news/article/2009/06/30/1006250/new-program-aims-to-alleviate-shidduch-crisis.

Harris, David A., and Izrail Rabinovich. 1988. *The Jokes of Repression: The Humor of Soviet Jews.* Northvale, N.J.: Jason Aronson.

Harris, Harold A. 1976. *Greek Athletics and the Jews.* Cardiff: University of Wales Press.

Hart, Harold H. 1971. *The Bawdy Bedside Reader.* New York: Bell.

Harvey, Ian. 1971. *To Fall Like Lucifer.* London: Sidgwick and Jackson.

Hay, Peter. 1989. *Harrap's Book of Legal Anecdotes.* London: Harrap.

Hearne, John. 2009. Hunting the Celtic Tiger. *Spiked on Line,* September 22. http://www.spiked-online.com/index.php/site/printable/7427/.

Hebrew Jokes and Dialect Humor. 1902. Philadelphia: Royal.

Heddendorf, Russell. 2009. *From Faith to Fun: The Secularisation of Humour.* Cambridge: Lutterworth.

Hellberg, Elena F. 1985. The Other Way Round: The Jokelore of Radio Yerevan. *ARV: Scandinavian Yearbook of Folklore* 41: 89–101.

Hennen, Peter. 2008. *Faeries, Bears, and Leathermen: Men in Community Queering the Masculine.* Chicago: University of Chicago Press.

Herbert, Susannah. 1998. French List Historic Brothel. *Electronic Telegraph,* February 12, issue 993. www.telegraph.co.uk.

Hibbert, Christopher. 1998. *George III: A Personal History.* London: Viking.

Hillenbrand, F. K. M. 1995. *Underground Humor in Nazi Germany 1933–1945.* London: Routledge.

Hobbes, Thomas. 1840. Human Nature or the Fundamental Elements of Policy. In *The English Works of Thomas Hobbes,* 4:1–76. London: Bohn. Orig. pub. 1650.

Hoff, Trygve J. B. 1949. *Economic Calculation in the Socialist Society.* London: W. Hodge.

Hoffman, David E. 2002. *The Oligarchs: Wealth and Power in the New Russia.* New York: Public Affairs.

Hofstadter, Richard. 1964. *Anti-intellectualism in American Life.* London: Jonathan Cape.

Honey, John R. de S. 1977. *Tom Brown's Universe.* London: Millington.

Hooper, David. 2003. The Carter-Ruck Chill. *Guardian* (London), December 23.

Houlbrook, Matt. 2005. *Queer London.* Chicago: University of Chicago Press.

House, Brant, and Edna Bennett. 1956. *Love from France.* London: Arthur Barker.

Humphreys, Laud. 1970. *Tearoom Trade: Impersonal Sex in Public Places.* Chicago: Aldine.

Humphries, Barry, and Nicholas Garland. 1988. *The Complete Barry McKenzie.* London: Methuen.

Hungary to Ban Blonde Jokes? 2004. *Ummah.com Muslim Forum.* http://www.ummah.com/forum/showthread.php?t=46291.

Hymns and Arias. http://www.odps.org/glossword/index.php?a=term&d=5&t=68 (accessed February 15, 2010).

Isnard, Armand. 1977. *Raconte . . . Popov! Les histories drôles de derrière le rideau de fer.* Paris: Mengès.

———.1991. *L'encyclopédie des meilleures histoires drôles.* Alleur Belgium: Marabout.

Iverson, William. 1963. *The Pious Pornographers.* New York: William Morrow.

Izzy [pseudo.] 2009. Ask Izzy #3 Sailing Solo. September 9. http://galusaustralis.com/2009/09/ask-izzy-3-sailing-solo/.

Jackson, Stanley. 1970. *Laughter at Law.* London: Mayflower.

Jarrett, Dere. 1976. *The Ingenious Mr. Hogarth.* London: Michael Joseph.

Jean-Charles. 1970. *La Bataille du Rire, 1939–1945.* Paris: Presses de la Cité.

Jewish Personal Ads. 1996. *Fun People Archive,* June 7. tp://www.langston.com/Fun_People/1996/1996BDX.html (accessed February 16, 2010).

Jimenez, Laura. 2001. *Hear Me Out: A Dose of Lesbian Humor for the Whole Human Race.* San Jose: Writers Club Press.

Jokes from the Late Nineteenth Century. 2008. http://www.innocentenglish.com /classic-old-funny-jokes/jokes-from-the-late-nineteenth-century.html (accessed October 10, 2009).

Jones, Baird. 1987. *Sexual Humor.* New York: Philosophical Library.

Kaiser, Robert G. 1976. *Russia, the People and the Power.* New York: Pocket.

Kami, Alex. 2005. Peel's Childhood Rape Revelation Praised by Campaigners. *Guardian* (London), October 10.

Kampf, Ray. 2000. *The Bear Handbook: A Comprehensive Guide for Those Who Are Husky, Hairy, and Homosexual, and Those Who Love 'em.* Binghamton, N.Y.: Harrington Park.

Karbusický, Vladimir. 1998. *Jewish Anecdotes from Prague.* Prague: V Ráji.

Kelly, Peter. 1989. The Other Russia—Past and Present. In *The Soviet Union and the Challenge of the Future,* ed. Alexander Shtromas and Morton A. Kaplan, 3:22–39. New York: Paragon.

Khaldûn ibn, Abd-ar-Rahmân, Abû Zaid, ibn Muhammad ibn Muhammad. 1950. *An Arab Philosophy of History.* Trans. Charles Issawi. London: John Murray. Orig. pub. 1377.

Khanaka, Shayee Hussain Ahmad. 1990. *Kurdish Humor: An Analysis of Ethnic, Political, and Sexual Jokes in Iraq.* MA thesis, University of California, Berkeley.

Kipling, Rudyard. 1940. *The Definitive Edition of Rudyard Kipling's Verse.* London: Hodder and Stoughton.

Knott, Blanche [pseud.]. 1985. *Outrageously Tasteless Jokes.* London: Arrow.

Kolasky, John, ed. 1972. *Look Comrade—The People Are Laughing: Underground Wit, Satire, and Humour from behind the Iron Curtain.* Toronto: Peter Martin.

Kontorovich, Vladimir. 2008. The Economic Fallacy. In *The Strange Death of Soviet Communism,* ed. Nikolas Gvosdev, 45–46. New Brunswick: Transaction.

Ková1y, Heda. 1997. *Under a Cruel Star: A Life in Prague, 1941–68.* Teaneck, N.J.: Holmes and Meier.

Kovner B. [pseud. Jacob Adler]. 1936. *Laugh, Jew, Laugh: Short Humorous Stories.* Trans. Abraham London. New York: Bloch.

Kramer, Stanley. 1980. *The Joke's on Them.* New York: Leisure.

Krausz, Ernest, and Gitta Tulea. 1998. *Jewish Survival: The Identity Problem at the Close of the Twentieth Century.* New Brunswick, N.J.: Transaction.

Kravitz, Seth. 1977. London Jokes and Ethnic Stereotypes. *Western Folklore* 36 (4): 275–301.

Kreeft, Peter J. 2004. *Angels and Demons: What Do We Really Know about Them?* San Francisco: Ignatius Press.

Krikmann, Arvo. 2004. *Netinalju Stalinist.* Tartu: Estonian Literary Museum,

———. 2006. Jokes in Soviet Estonia. Paper presented at the 18th ISHS conference at the Danish University of Education, Copenhagen. http://haldjas.folklore.ee /~kriku/HUUMOR/Nlj_sovpol.pdf.

———. 2009. Finnic and Baltic Nationalities as Ethnic Targets in Contemporary Russian Jokes. In *Permitted Laughter,* ed. Arvo Krikmann and Liisi Laineste, 73–95. Tartu: ELM Scholarly Press.

Kuipers, Giselinde. 2006. *Good Humor, Bad Taste: A Sociology of the Joke.* Berlin: Mouton de Gruyter.

Kumove, Shirley. 1986. *Words Like Arrows: A Treasury of Yiddish Folk Sayings.* New York: Warner.

Kürti, László. 1988. The Politics of Joking: Popular Responses to Chernobyl. *Journal of American Folklore* 101: 324–34.

Kutchinsky, Berl. 1978. Pornography in Denmark: A General Overview. In *Censorship and Obscenity,* ed. Rajeev Dhavan and Christie Davies, 111–26. London: Martin Robertson.

Laar, Mart. 2007a. *The Forgotten War: Armed Resistance Movement in Estonia in 1944–56.* Tallinn: Grenader.

———. 2007b. *Estonia in World War II.* Tallinn: Grenader.

———. 2007c. *Bird's-Eye View of Estonian History.* Tallinn: Grenader.

Laineste, Liisi. 2005. Targets in Estonian Ethnic Jokes within the Theory of Ethnic Humour (Ch. Davies). *Folklore* 29: 7–24. http://www.folklore.ee/Folklore/vol29/davies.pdf.

———. 2008a. Politics of Joking: Ethnic Jokes and Their Targets in Estonia (1890s–2007). *Folklore* 40: 109–88.

———. 2008b. *Post-Socialist Jokes in Estonia: Continuity and Change.* Tartu: Tartu University Press.

———. 2009. Political Jokes in Post-Socialist Estonia (2000–2007). In *Permitted Laughter,* ed. Arvo Krikmann and Liisi Laineste, 41–72. Tartu: ELM Scholarly Press.

Lal, Deepak. 2004. *In Praise of Empires: Globalization and Order.* London: Palgrave Macmillan.

Lane, Christel. 1981. *The Rites of Rulers: Ritual in Industrial Society in the Soviet Case.* Cambridge: Cambridge University Press.

Lane, David. 1978. *Politics and Society in the USSR.* Oxford: Martin Robertson.

Lanoux, Armand. 1983. *Madame Steinheil ou la connaissance du Président.* Paris: Bernard Grasset.

Latvians Poke Fun at Communist Past. 2003. *BBC News,* April 11. http://news.bbc.co.uk/1/hi/world/europe/2940235.stm (accessed February 27, 2010).

Laumann, Edward O., John H. Gagnon, Robert T. Michael, and Stuart Michaels. 1994. *The Social Organization of Sexuality.* Chicago: University of Chicago Press.

Laumann, Edward O., Christopher M. Masi, and Ezra W. Zuckerman. 1997. Circumcision in the United States: Prevalence, Prophylactic Effects, and Sexual Practice. *Journal of the American Medical Association* 277 (13): 1052–57.

Leake, Jonathan. 2003. The Future Looks Bad for Redheads. *Times on Line,* November 16. http://www.timesonline.co.uk/tol/news/uk/health/article1019030.ece (accessed August 22, 2009).

Lederer, Richard. 2003. *The Cunning Linguist.* New York: St. Martin's Press.

Legal Humor News. 2008. *Legal Humor,* April 14. http://www.legalhumour.com/Blog/Legal_Humour_News/LHN_080414.html.

Legman, Gershon. 1982. *No Laughing Matter: An Analysis of Sexual Humour.* 2 vols. Bloomington: Indiana University Press.

Lemonier, Marc, and Alexandre Dupouy. 2003. *Histoire(s) du Paris Libertin.* Paris: La Musardine.

Levitt, Steven D., and Stephen J. Dubner. 2006. *Freakonomics.* New York: Harper.

Levy, Howard Seymour. 1973. *Japanese Sex Jokes in Traditional Times.* Washington, D.C.: Warm-Soft Village Press.

———.1974. *Chinese Sex Jokes in Traditional Times.* Taipei Taiwan: Chinese Association for Folklore.

Levytsky, Boris. 1971. *The Uses of Terror.* London: Sidgwick and Jackson.

Lewis, Ben. 2006. Hammer and Tickle. *Prospect* 122: 28–33.

Lewis, C. B. 1884. *Sawn-Off Sketches.* New York: G. W. Carleton.

Lewis, C. S. 1955. *Surprised by Joy: The Shape of My Early Life.* London: Geoffrey Bles.

Lewis, Paul. 2006. *Cracking Up: American Humor in a Time of Conflict.* Chicago: University of Chicago Press.

Lewis, Sinclair. 1950. *Babbitt.* New York: New American Library. Orig. pub. 1922.

Light, Terry W. 2000. I Hate Lawyer Jokes. http://www.brann-light.com/Pub-TWL /lawyer_jokes.htm.

Lipset, Seymour M. 1997. *American Exceptionalism: A Double-Edged Sword.* New York: Norton.

Lo Bello, Nino. 1968. I Heard Jokes behind the Iron Curtain. In *The New Catholic Treasury of Wit and Humor,* ed. Paul Bussard. New York: Meredith.

Loos, Anita. 1925. *Gentlemen Prefer Blondes: The Illuminating Diary of a Professional Lady.* New York: Boni and Liveright.

———.1928. *But Gentlemen Marry Brunettes.* New York: Brentano's.

———.1977. *Cast of Thousands.* New York: Grosset and Dunlap.

Lopez, Billie Ann. 2003. Old Viennese Humor: Graf Bobby and Baron Rudy. *Virtual Vienna Net,* October 21. http://www.virtualvienna.net/main/modules .php?name=News&file=print&sid=120. (accessed February 2009).

Low, David. 1956. *Low's Autobiography.* London: Michael Joseph.

Lyons, Eugene. 1935. *Moscow Carousel.* New York: Alfred A Knopf.

Macintyre, Ben. 2008. A Zimbabwe Joke Is No Laughing Matter; Tyrants May Try to Ban It, but Humour Has a Way of Seeping through the Cracks of Any Dictatorship. *Times on Line,* June 27. http://www.timesonline.co.uk/tol/comment /columnists/ben_macintyre/article4221062.ece.

McCabe, John. 1961. *Mr. Laurel and Mr. Hardy: An Affectionate Biography.* New York: New American Library.

McElroy, Wendy. 2000. A Webb of Lies. *Free Market* 18 (2).

McKercher, Bob, and Thomas G. Bauer. 2003. Conceptual Framework of the Nexus between Tourism, Romance, and Sex. In *Sex and Tourism,* ed. Thomas G. Bauer and Bob McKercher, 3–17. New York: Haworth Hospitality.

McMath, Robert C., Jr. 1993. *American Populism: A Social History.* New York: Hill and Wang.

Markfield, Wallace. 1974. *You Could Live If They'd Let You.* New York: Knopf.

Markovits, Andrei S. 2007. *Uncouth Nation: Why Europe Dislikes America.* Princeton, N.J.: Princeton University Press.

Martin, David. 1979. *A General Theory of Secularization.* Oxford: Basil Blackwell.

Mason, Jackie. 1989. *Jackie Oy.* London: Robson.

Masters, R. E. L. 1962. *Forbidden Sexual Behaviour and Morality.* New York: Julian Press.

Matthews, Arthur, and Graham Linehan. 1998. *Father Ted: The Craggy Island Parish Magazines*. London: Boxtree.

Maupassant, Guy de. 1880. *Boule de suif et autre contes de la guerre*. Paris: Magnier.

Maurois, André [pseud. Emile Salomon Herzog]. 1940. *Les Silences du Colonel Bramble*. Paris: Nelson. Orig. pub. 1918.

Mayhew, Henry. 1950. *London's Underworld*. London: Spring. Orig. pub. 1862.

Melly, George. 1978. *Rum, Bum, and Concertina*. London: Futura.

Mercer, Paul. 1986. *Peace of the Dead*. London: Policy Research.

Meyer, A., and P. Meyer. 1978. *Le Communisme est-il soluble dans l'alcool?* Paris: Du Seuil.

Mika, Niclas, Michael Shields, and Paul Boulding. 2008. Jokes Making the Rounds on Financial Crisis. *Reuters Factbox*, October 20. http://uk.reuters.com/article /idUKTRE49J30120081020 (accessed January 2009).

Mokyr, Joel. 2002. *The Gifts of Athena*. Princeton, N.J.: Princeton University Press.

Moore, Charles. 2009. *Penultimata*: Tranquil Reflections on a Passionate Past. Review of Robert Conquest's *Penultimata*. *Daily Telegraph*, August 3.

Morrison, Blake. 2009. David Beckham, Icons of the Decade. *Guardian* (London), December 22. http://patrickhenrypress.info/?q=node/110699.

Mr. J. 1984. *Giant Book of Dirty Jokes*. Secaucus: Castle.

Muleiro, Pepe. 1998. *Los Mejores Chistes de Siglio*. Buenos Aires: Grijalbo.

Munn, Bill. 1965. *We Wish You a Kosher Christmas*. Newark: Samuels.

Myagkov, Aleksei. 1976. *Inside the KGB*. Richmond, Surrey: Foreign Affairs.

Myers, James. 1984. *Grandpa's Rib-Ticklers and Knee-Slappers*. Springfield, Ill.: Lincoln-Herndon.

Neal, Mark, and Christie Davies. 1998. *The Corporation under Siege*. London: Social Affairs Unit.

Necchi, Paolo. 2006. Heard the Latest about the Carabinieri? *Florentine* 35 (June 15). http://www.theflorentine.net/articles/article-view.asp?issuetocId=509.

Nègre, Hervé. 1973. *Dictionnaire des Histoires Drôles*. 2 vols. Paris: Fayard.

Norden, Edward. 1991. Counting the Jews. *Commentary* 92 (4): 36–43.

Norden, Helen Brown. 1937. *The Hussy's Handbook*. New York: Farrar and Rinehart.

Northcutt, Wendy. 2000. *The Darwin Awards*. London: Orion.

Norton, Rictor. 2006. *Mother Clap's Molly House*. Stroud: Chalford.

Novak, William, and Moshe Waldoks. 1990. *The Big Book of Jewish Humor*. New York: HarperPerennial.

O [pseud. Theo. Mathew]. 1961. *Forensic Fables*. London: Butterworths. Orig. pub. 1926–32.

Obdrlik, Antonin J. 1942. "Gallows Humor"—A Sociological Phenomenon. *American Journal of Sociology* 45 (5): 709–16.

Old Alleynians Tour Song Book. http://www.alleynian.org/rugby/OA_Tour_Song _Book.pdf (accessed February 15, 2010).

Olson, James, M., Gregory R. Maio, and Karen L. Hobden. 1999. The (Null) Effects of Exposure to Disparagement Humor on Stereotypes and Attitudes. *Humor: International Journal of Humor Research* 12 (2): 195–220.

Olson, Kirby. 1996. Bertie and Jeeves at the End of History: P. G. Wodehouse as Political Scientist. *Humor: International Journal of Humor Research* 9 (1): 73–88.

Olson, Walter. 2007. The Great American Pants Suit. *Wall Street Journal,* June 18. http://www.opinionjournal.com/editorial/feature.html?id=110010225.

Olsvanger, Immanuel. 1947. *Röyte pomerantsen.* New York: Schocken. Trans. Beatrice Santorini. http://www.ling.upenn.edu/~beatrice/humor/royte.html.

Oring, Elliott. 1981. *Israeli Humor: The Content and Structure of the Chizbat of the Palmah.* Albany: State University of New York Press.

———. 1984. *The Jokes of Sigmund Freud: A Study in Humor and Jewish Identity.* Philadelphia: University of Pennsylvania Press.

———. 1992. *Jokes and Their Relations.* Lexington: University Press of Kentucky.

———. 2001 Review of Jefferson S. Chase, *Inciting Laughter. Humor: The International Journal of Humor Research* 14 (2): 207–10.

———. 2003. *Engaging Humor.* Urbana: University of Illinois Press.

———. 2004. Risky Business: Political Jokes under Repressive Regimes. *Western Folklore* 63 (3): 209–36.

Orleans, Ellen. 1992. *Still Can't Keep a Straight Face: A Lesbian Looks and Laughs at Life.* Bala Cynwyd, Pa.: Laugh Lines Press.

Orso, Ethelyn. 1979. *Modern Greek Humor: A Collection of Jokes and Ribald Tales.* Bloomington: Indiana University Press.

Orwell, George. 1982. *The Lion and the Unicorn.* London: Penguin. Orig. pub. 1941.

———. 2008. *Animal Farm: A Fairy Story.* London: Penguin. Orig. pub. 1945.

Ovid [Publius Ovidius Naso]. 16 BC. *Amores,* book 1.

Oxley, Harry G. 1978. *Mateship in Local Organization.* St. Lucia: University of Queensland Press.

Ozerkov, Dimitry. 2006a. The Triumph of Eros. In *The Triumph of Eros,* ed. Dimitry Ozerkov, Satish Padiyar, and Sarane Alexandrian, 11–34. London: Fontanka.

———. 2006b. French Prints of the Gallant Age in Paris and St Petersburg. In *The Triumph of Eros,* ed. Dimitry Ozerkov, Satish Padiyar, and Sarane Alexandrian, 45–54. London: Fontanka.

Ozerkov, Dimitry, Satish Padiyar, and Sarane Alexandrian, eds. 2006. *The Triumph of Eros: Art and Seduction in Eighteenth-Century France.* London: Fontanka.

Pareto, Vilfredo. 1968. *Traité de sociologie général.* 2 vols. Geneva: Librairie Droz. Orig. pub. 1917–19.

Parrott, Cecil. 1977. *The Serpent and the Nightingale.* London: Faber and Faber.

Pastis, Stephen. 2009. *Pearls before Swine. San Francisco Chronicle,* April 19.

Patai, Raphael. 1977. *The Jewish Mind.* New York: Charles Scribner's Sons.

Patel, M. S. 1946. *Witty Tales of Badshah and Birbal.* Bombay: Thakkar.

Patterson, Sir Les [pseud. Barry Humphries]. 1985. *The Traveller's Tool.* London: Michael O'Mara.

Pearl, Cora. 1983. *Grand Horizontal: The Erotic Memoirs of a Passionate Lady.* New York: Stein and Day.

Pearsall, Ronald. 1969. *The Worm in the Bud: The World of Victorian Sexuality.* London: Weidenfeld and Nicolson.

Pearson, John. 1975. *Edward the Rake.* London: Weidenfeld and Nicolson.

Pease, Allan. 1998. *The Ultimate Book of Rude and Politically Incorrect Jokes.* London: Robson.

Peel, John. 2005. *Margrave of the Marshes.* London: Bantam.

Perakh, Mark. 1998. Laughing under the Covers. http://members.cox.net/marperak
/jokes (accessed February 27, 2010).

Pieckalkiewicz, Jaroslaw. 1972. *Public Opinion Polling in Czechoslovakia, 1968–69: Results and Analysis of Surveys Conducted during the Dubcek Era.* New York: Praeger.

Pipes, Richard. 2003. *Vixi.* New Haven, Conn.: Yale University Press.

———. 2008. 1917 and the Revisionists. In *The Strange Death of Soviet Communism,* ed. Nikolas Gvosdev, 91–108. New Brunswick: Transaction.

Pi-Sunyer, O. 1977. Political Humor in a Dictatorial State: The Case of Spain. *Ethnohistory* 24 (2): 179–90.

Pitman, Joanne. 2003. *On Blondes.* New York: Bloomsbury.

Polanyi, Michael. 1951. *The Logic of Liberty.* London: Routledge and Kegan Paul.

Prell, Riv-Ellen. 1999. *Fighting to Become American.* Boston: Beacon.

Proust, Marcel. 1954. *Sodome et Gomorrhe,* Vol. 4 of *A la recherche du temps perdu.* Paris: Gallimard. Orig. pub. 1922.

Quennell, Peter. 1950. Introduction to *London's Underworld,* ed. Henry Mayhew. London: Spring. Orig. pub. 1862.

Quercy, Jean-Marie, and Mariola Korsak. 1993. *Histoires Drôles du Monde Entier.* Paris: Zelie.

Raphael, Marc Lee. 2001. *Jewishness and the World of "Difference" in the United States.* Williamsburg: College of William and Mary.

Raskin, Victor. 1985. *Semantic Mechanisms of Humor.* Dordrecht: D. Reidel.

Reddaway, Peter. 2008a. The Rise of Popular Dissent. In *The Strange Death of Soviet Communism,* ed. Nikolas Gvosdev, 77–87. New Brunswick: Transaction.

———. 2008b. The Arithmetic of Atrocity. In *The Strange Death of Soviet Communism,* ed. Nikolas Gvosdev, 191–98. New Brunswick: Transaction.

Reddaway, Peter, and Dmitri Glinski. 2001. *The Tragedy of Russia's Reforms: Market Bolshevism against Democracy.* Washington, D.C.: U.S. Institute of Peace Press.

Redfern, Walter. 2007. *French Laughter.* Oxford: Oxford University Press.

Redgrove, H. Stanley, and Gilbert A. Foan. 1939. *Hair-Dyes and Hair-Dyeing Chemistry and Technique.* New York: Chemical.

Reiss, Albert J., Jr. 1963. The Social Integration of Queers and Peers. In *The Problem of Homosexuality in Modern Society,* ed. Hendrik M. Ruitenbeek, 249–78. New York: Dutton.

Report of the Homosexuality Policy Assessment Team. 1996. London: Ministry of Defence.

Richardson, Frank. 1981. *Mars without Venus: A Study of Some Homosexual Generals.* Edinburgh: W. Blackwood.

Richardson, Joanna. 1971. *La Vie Parisienne, 1852–70.* New York: Viking.

Richman, Marsha, and Katie O'Donnell. 1978. *The Shikse's Guide to Jewish Men.* New York: Bantam.

Riesman, David. 1954. *Individualism Reconsidered and Other Essays.* Glencoe, Ill.: Free Press of Glencoe.

Rimmel, Leslie A. 1997. Another Kind of Fear: The Kirov Murder and the End of Bread Rationing in Leningrad. *Slavic Review* 56 (3): 481–99.

Roberts, Mary Louise. 2010. The Silver Foxhole: The GIs and Prostitution in Paris, 1944–45. *French Historical Studies* 33 (1): 99–128.

Rockaway, Robert A. 1993. *But He Was Good to His Mother: The Lives and Crimes of Jewish Gangsters*. Jerusalem: Gefen.

Rogers, Ken. 2010. *The Lost Tribe of Everton and Scottie Road,* Liverpool: Trinity Mirror Media.

Roppatte, Vincent, and Sherry Suib Cohen. 1985. *The Looks Men Love.* New York: St. Martin's Press.

Rosario, Vernon A. 1997. *The Erotic Imagination: French Histories of Perversity.* New York: Oxford University Press.

Rose, Alexander. 2002. When Politics Is a Laughing Matter. *Policy Review* 11: 7–8, 50–71.

Rosenberg, Elliott. 1997. *But Were They Good for the Jews?* Secaucus: Card.

Rositzke, Harry. 1982. *The KGB: The Eyes of Russia.* London: Sidgwick and Jackson.

Rosner, Joseph. 1965. *The Haters' Handbook.* New York: Delacorte.

Rosten, Leo. 1970. *The Joys of Yiddish.* London: W. H. Allen.

Roth, Philip. 1969. *Portnoy's Complaint.* London: Jonathan Cape.

Rounding, Virginia. 2003. *Les Grandes Horizontales.* New York: Bloomsbury.

Royot, Daniel. 1978. Postscript to *American Humor in France,* ed. James Austin, 120–36. Ames: Iowa State University Press.

Rubinstein, Joshua. 1996. *Tangled Loyalties: The Life and Times of Ilya Ehrenburg.* New York: Basic Books.

Rudnick, Paul. 2009. Holly or Challah? *New Yorker,* December 21.

Rugby Songs. 1967. London: Sphere.

Rugoff, Milton. 1971. *Prudery and Passion.* New York: Putnam.

Rummel, R. J. 1990. *Lethal Politics: Soviet Genocide and Mass Murder since 1917.* New Brunswick, N.J.: Transaction.

———.1994. *Death by Government.* New Brunswick, N.J.: Transaction.

Rush, Myron. 2008. Fortune and Fate. In *The Strange Death of Soviet Communism,* ed. Nikolas Gvosdev, 21–30. New Brunswick: Transaction.

Rutland, Peter. 2008. Sovietology: Notes for a Post-Mortem. In *The Strange Death of Soviet Communism,* ed. Nikolas Gvosdev, 151–70. New Brunswick: Transaction.

Sanders, Jacquin. 1962. The Tactful Satirists. *East Europe* 11 (2): 22–27.

———.1982. The Seriousness of Humor: Political Satire in the Soviet Block. *East Europe—Euromonitor* 11 (1): 21–29.

Saper, Bernard. 1991. A Cognitive and Behavioral Formulation of the Relation between Jewish Jokes and Anti-Semitism. *Humor: International Journal of Humor Research* 4 (1): 41–59.

Schiff, Michael. 1975. *Radio Eriwans, Auslands-Program.* Frankfurt-am-Main: Fischer.

———.1978. *Radio Eriwans antwortet.* Frankfurt-am-Main: Fischer.

Scholten, Carol Grace. 1971. Modern German Humor: Jokes of German University Students about Fellow Germans, Americans, Frenchmen, and Russians. MA thesis, University of California, Berkeley.

Schor, Juliet. 1998. *The Overspent American: Upscaling, Downshifting, and the New Consumer.* New York: Basic.

Schweinickle, O. U. 1920. *The Book of a Thousand Laughs.* http://www.csufresno.edu/folklore/drinkingsongs/html/books-and-manuscripts/1920s/1928-the-book-of-a-thousand-laughs/index.htm.

Sebag Montefiore, Simon. 2004. *Stalin: The Court of the Red Tsar*. London: Phoenix.

Seifikar, Palmis. 2003. Asses and Cuckolds: Regional Ethnic Jokes from Iran. MA thesis, University of California, Berkeley.

Selitz, Bruce, et al. 1987. *The Jewish Adventurers' Club*. New York: Dell.

Seventeen Jewish Singles Ads. 2005. *Jewish Sightseeing*, February 10. http://www .jewishsightseeing.com/jewish_humor/jewish_singles_ads/2005-02-10-seventeen _singles_ads.htm.

Shafer, Harry T., and Angie Papadakis. 1988. *The Howls of Justice: Comedy's Day in Court*. San Diego: Harcourt Brace Jovanovich.

Shanahan, Danny. 2005. *Innocent Your Honor: A Book of Lawyer Cartoons*. New York: Abrams.

Sharks and Lawyers. 2006. From the 'lectric Law Library's Stacks. http://www.lectlaw .com/files/fun06.htm.

Sharot, Stephen. 1998. Judaism and Jewish Ethnicity: Changing Relationships and Differentiations in the Diaspora and Israel. In *Jewish Survival*, ed. Ernest Krausz and Gitta Tulea, 87–119. New Brunswick, N.J.: Transaction.

Shilts, Randy. 1993. *Conduct Unbecoming: Gays and Lesbians in the U.S. Military*. New York: St Martin's Press.

Shlapentokh, Vladimir. 1990. *Soviet Intellectuals and Political Power: The Post-Stalin Era*. London: Taurus.

Shtromas, Alexander. 1981. *Political Change and Social Development: The Case of the Soviet Union*. Frankfurt-am-Main: Peter Lang.

———. 1989. Multinationalism and the Soviet Future. In *The Soviet Union and the Challenge of the Future*, ed. Alexander Shtromas and Morton A. Kaplan, 3:353–95. New York: Paragon.

———. 1996. The Baltic States as Soviet Republics: Tensions and Contradictions. In *The Baltic States: The National Self-Determination of Estonia, Latvia, and Lithuania*, ed. Graham Smith, 86–117. Basingstoke: Macmillan.

Shtromas, Alexander, and Morton A. Kaplan. 1989. *The Soviet Union and the Challenge of the Future*. 3 vols. New York: Paragon.

Silly Money. 2009. http://www.comedy.org.uk/guide/tv/silly_money.

Smith, Paul. 1983. *The Book of Nasty Legends*. London: Routledge and Kegan Paul.

———. 1986. *The Book of Nastier Legends*. London: Routledge and Kegan Paul.

Smythe, Reg. 1963. *Happy Days with Andy Capp*. London: Daily Mirror/Fleetway.

Sol the Answer Man [pseud. James David Besser]. 1990. *Do They Keep Kosher on Mars?* New York: Collier.

Southworth, John. 1998. *Fools and Jesters at the English Court*. Thrupp: Sutton.

Spalding, Henry D. 1973. *Encyclopedia of Jewish Humor*. New York: Jonathan David.

Speier, Hans. 1998. Wit and Politics: An Essay on Laughter and Power. *American Journal of Sociology* 103 (5): 1352–1401.

Spencer, Herbert. 1969. *Principles of Sociology*. Abridged ed. Ed. Stanislav Andreski. Basingstoke: Macmillan. Orig. pub. 1876–96.

Stalzer, Anton. 1982. *Graf Bobby: Der Witz in Person*. Vienna: Wiener.

Stead, W. T. 1895. The Conviction of Oscar Wilde. *Review of Reviews* 11: 491–92.

Stivers, Richard. 1976. *A Hair of the Dog: Irish Drinking and American Stereotype*. University Park: Pennsylvania State University Press.

Suetonius, [C. Suetonius Tranquillus]. 121 AD. *De vita Caesarum,* book 1: *Caius Julius Caesar.*

Swineford, Edwin J. 1989. *The Wits of War: Unofficial GI Humor—History of World War II.* Fresno: Kilroy Was There Press.

Symonds, John Addington. 1975. *Studies in Sexual Inversion: Embodying "A Study in Greek Ethics" and "A Study in Modern Ethics."* New York: AMS Press. Orig. pub. 1928.

Szasz, Thomas. 1990. *The Untamed Tongue.* La Salle, Ill.: Open Court.

Talmadge, I. D. W. 1943. The Enjoyment of Laughter in Russia. *Russian Review* 2 (2): 45–51.

Tamarkhin, N. 1984. *Lenin Lives! The Lenin Cult in Soviet Russia.* Cambridge: Harvard University Press.

Tateishi, John. 1999. *And Justice for All: An Oral History of the Japanese American Detention Camps.* Seattle: University of Washington Press.

Taylor, Sally J. 1990. *Stalin's Apologist, Walter Duranty: The* New York Times's *Man in Moscow.* New York: Oxford University Press.

Taylor, Stuart, Jr., and K. C. Johnson. 2007. *Until Proven Innocent.* New York: Thomas Dunne.

Telushkin, Rabbi Joseph. 1992. *Jewish Humor: What the Best Jewish Jokes Say about the Jews.* New York: William Morrow.

Theen, Rolf H. W. 1989. The Nomenclatura in the USSR: Instrument of Policy and/ or Obstacle to Reform. In *The Soviet Union and the Challenge of the Future,* ed. Alexander Shtromas and Morton A. Kaplan, 2:435–75. New York: Paragon.

Thurston, Robert W. 1991. Social Dimensions of Stalinist Rule: Humor and Terror in the USSR, 1935–1941. *Journal of Social History* 40: 541–62.

Tibballs, Geoff. 2005. *The Mammoth Book of Dirty, Sick, X-rated, and Politically Incorrect Jokes.* New York: Carroll and Graf.

Tolstoy, Nikolai. 1981. *Stalin's Secret War.* London: Cape.

Took, Barry. 1975. *The Max Miller Blue Book.* London: Robson.

Torberg, Friedrich. 2008. *Tante Jolesch, or the Decline of the West in Anecdotes.* Riverside, Calif.: Ariadne.

Turkish Law Site/Lawyer Jokes. http://www.turkhukuksitesi.com/turkishlaw/lawjokes.shtml (accessed 8 March 2009).

Twain, Mark. 1894. *Pudd'nhead Wilson's Calendar for 1894.* http://etext.lib.virginia.edu/railton/wilson/calendar.html (accessed March 2, 2010).

———. 1897. *Pudd'nhead Wilson's New Calendar* in *Following the Equator* http://etext.virginia.edu/railton/wilson/pwequat.html (accessed March 2, 2010).

Uberoi, J. P. Singh. 1967. On being unshorn. *Transactions of the Indian Institute of Advanced Study* 4: 89–100.

Umeasiegbu, Rems Nna. 1986. *Ask the Humorist: Nigerian Jokes.* Enugu, Nigeria: Koruna.

Urquhart, Conal. 2005. A Guide to Dating Jews Earns Author "Nazi" Tag. *Observer,* August 28.

U.S. Tort Costs Reach a Record $260 Billion, According to Tillinghast Study. 2006. http://www.insurance-canada.ca/business/other/Tillinghast-US-Tort-Costs-603.php (accessed March 8, 2010).

Vaksberg, Anatoly. 1994. *Stalin against the Jews.* New York: Knopf.

Van de Walle, E., and H. V. Muhsam. 1995. Fatal Secrets and the French Fertility Transition. *Population and Development Review* 21 (2): 261–79.

Vatlin, Alexander, and Larisa Malashenko. 2006. *Piggy-Foxy and the Sword of Revolution.* New Haven: Yale University Press.

Vesilind, P. Aarne. 2009. *Estonian Jokes.* Tallinn: Punkt and Koma.

Vice, Sue. 1997. *Introducing Bakhtin.* Manchester: Manchester University Press.

Vinen, Richard. 2006. *The Unfree French: Life under the Occupation.* New Haven: Yale University Press.

Vreck, Françoise. 1999. Fidélité en humour. In *Humour, Culture, Traduction(s),* ed. Antoine Fabrice and Mary Wood, 29–38. Lille: Cahiers de la Maison de la Recherche, Université Charles-de-Gaulle.

Wallace, Marina, Martin Kemp, and Joanne Bernstein. 2007. *Seduced: Art and Sex from Antiquity to Now.* London: Merrell.

Wallis, Keene. 1945. *French Cartoons of the Twentieth Century.* New York: International Publications.

Ward, David A., and Gene G. Kassebaum. 1966. *Women's Prison: Sex and Social Structure.* London: Weidenfeld and Nicolson.

Waugh, Evelyn. 1945. *Brideshead Revisited.* London: Chapman and Hall.

Weber, Max. 1948. *From Max Weber: Essays in Sociology.* Ed. and trans. H. H. Gerth and C. Wright Mills. London: Routledge and Kegan Paul.

Weininger, Otto. 1906. *Sex and Character.* London: W. Heinemann.

Weiss, Marty. 1996. *Virtual Jerusalem, Jewish Humor.* http://franshaul.tripod.com/humor/humorl.htm.

Weiss, Philip. 2008. Shiksa Countries Are for Practice. *Mondoweiss,* September 10. http://mondoweiss.net/2008/09/ shiksa-countries-are-for-practice.html (accessed March 8, 2010).

Wellings, Kate, Julia Field, Anne M. Johnson, Jane Wadsworth, and Sally Bradshaw. 1994. *Sexual Behaviour in Britain: The National Survey of Sexual Attitudes and Lifestyles.* Harmondsworth: Penguin.

West, Nathanael [pseud. of Nathan Wallenstein Weinstein]. 1961. *A Cool Million, or The Dismantling of Lemuel Pitkin.* In *The Collected Works of Nathanael West.* Harmondsworth: Penguin. Orig. pub. 1934.

What Rugby Jokes Did Next. 1970. London: Sphere.

Whitaker, Brian. 2006. *Unspeakable Love: Gay and Lesbian Life in the Middle East.* Berkeley: University of California Press.

Wiener, Martin J. 2004. *English Culture and the Decline of the Industrial Spirit, 1850–1980.* 2d ed. Cambridge: Cambridge University Press.

Wilde, Larry. 1978. *The Complete Book of Ethnic Humor.* Los Angeles: Corwin.

———. 1986. *The Ultimate Jewish Joke Book.* New York: Bantam.

Wilde, Oscar. 1981. *The Picture of Dorian Gray.* Oxford: Oxford University Press. Orig. pub. 1891.

Winnick, Charles. 1964. *USSR Humor.* Mt. Vernon, N.Y.: Peter Pauper.

Winokur, Jon. 2005. *Ennui to Go: The Art of Boredom.* Seattle: Sasquatch.

Wit and Humor of Business. 1908. Philadelphia: George W. Jacobs.

Witkowska, Joanna. 2008. Creating False Enemies: John Bull and Uncle Sam as Food for Anti-Western Propaganda in Poland. *Journal of Transatlantic Studies* 6 (2): 123–30.

Wodehouse, P. G. 1986. *Thank You, Jeeves.* New York: Harper and Row. Orig. pub. 1934.

Wolff, H. A., C. E. Smith, and H. A. Murray. 1934. The Psychology of Humor: A Study of Responses to Race Disparagement Jokes. *Journal of Abnormal and Social Psychology* 28 (4): 341–66.

Wood, Ghislaine. 2007. The Illusory Interior. In *Surreal Things: Surrealism and Design,* ed. Ghislaine Wood, 39–57. London: V and A.

Woog, Dan. 2001. *Gay Men, Straight Jobs.* Los Angeles: Alyson.

Yardys, Stanley V. 1989. The Baltic States in the Soviet Union: Their Present State and Prospects for the Future. In *The Soviet Union and the Challenge of the Future,* ed. Alexander Shtromas and Morton A. Kaplan, 3:439–78. New York: Paragon.

Youngman, Henny. 1974. *Take My Wife . . . Please! Henny Youngman's Giant Book of Jokes.* New York: Citadel.

Yurchak, A. 1997. The Cynical Realism of Late Socialism: Power, Pretence, and Anekdot. *Public Culture* 9: 161–88.

Zand, Arie. 1982. *Political Jokes of Leningrad.* Austin: Silvergirl.

Zaslavsky, Victor. 1982. *The Neo-Stalinist State: Class, Ethnicity, and Consensus in Soviet Society.* Armonk, N.Y.: M. E. Sharpe.

Zinoman, Jason. 2008. He's Telling You This for the Last Time. *New York Times,* March 22.

Zlobin, Nikolai. 1996. Humor as a Political Protest. *Demokratizatsiya* 4 (2): 223–32.

LAW CASES CITED

Griswold v Connecticut (1965) 381 U.S. 479; 85 S Ct 1678; 14 L.Ed 2d 510

Lawrence v Texas (2003) 539 U.S. 558 41 S.W. 3d 349

Lustig-Prean and Beckett v United Kingdom (2000) 29 EHRR 548

Modinos v Cyprus (1991) 13 EHRR 485

Roe v Wade (1973) 410 U.S. 113; 93 S Ct 705; 35 L.Ed. 2d 147

Rush v Cavanaugh (1845) 2Pa187 1845 WL 5210 (Pa) Barr 187

INDEX

Page numbers in *italics* refer to tables.

Aarhusians Jutland, Denmark, 66, 256, 259

abortion laws, 200

Abrams, Nathan, 129

Abse, Leo, 95–96

actresses, 6, 101, 102, 127

Adams, Bruce: jokes about New Russians, 235–36; and Soviet Jokes, 14, 16, 80, 216, 226, 239, 251; and Soviet jokes about shortages, 230, 241; and Soviet jokes in the time of terror, 221, 222, 223, 225

Adams, Cecil, 169–70

Adams, Scott, 205

adultery, 78–80, 86, 99

Aggie jokes, 23, 27, 29–30, 40

aggression, playing with, 3, 273

Alentejos, 257, 260

Al-Khatib, Mahmoud A., 259

Al-Khattab, Omar bin, 214

Allen, Woody, 46–47, 132

all-male institutions, 160–63, 164, 166, 174–77, 271

'Allo!'Allo! (television series), 109–110

ambiguity built into humor, 3, 5, 267, 272

Americanism, 114. *See also* United States

anal sex, 154, 155–56

Andreski, Stanislav, 234, 269, 270

Andropov, Yuri, 239

anecdotes, 4, 9, 11, 12

Animal Farm (Orwell), 168

anonymity of jokes, 4

anti-Semitism, 101, 113, 223, 233, 265, 272

aphorisms, 11

Après la Guerre (song), 105

Arabs and Arab countries, 72, 164, 214, 260

Arequipeños, 260

Argentina, 260

aristocrats, 32–35, 90–92, 171–72, 262, 263

Arisztid and Tasziló jokes, 34

Armenia, 233, 237

art and artists, 18, 49, 78, 85, 89, 92, 94, 101–103, 216

athletes. *See* sports and stupidity jokes

Attardo, Salvatore, 74

Australia: Elaine Awards, 270; Ernie Awards, 195; ethnic jokes, 66, 133, 195, *255;* freedom of speech in Victoria, 189; and homosexuality, 171–73; and lawyer jokes, 1, 184, 185, 194; and sex-with-sheep jokes, 167, 168; social classes, 171–73; and sport, 151; and wartime jokes, 104–105, 107

men jokes, 155–58, 161, 162, 172, 181;
and sex-with-animals jokes, 168–69;
and social classes, 174; and stupidity
jokes, 254, *255, 257–62, 258*; targets
of, 66, 249. *See also specific ethnicities*
*Ethnic Humor around the World: A
Comparative Analysis* (Davies), 13, 19
etiquette of joke telling, 267–68
Eton Boating Song (parody), 175–76
Europe: bureaucracies of, 189; and economic crash of 2008–2009, 61; law
and lawyers of, 185–86, 200–201; and
migration of jokes, 185–86; and sexy
blonde jokes, 73; and sodomy laws,
156. *See also* Eastern Europe
European Court of Human Rights, 156
European Union, 60, 62, 156, 189
evidence collection, 17–18
exclusion/inclusion, 153
eyeglasses, 46–47, 265

Faeroe Islands, 259
Falstaff, Sir John (Shakespearian char-
acter), 30
families as joke topic, 13
Fannie Mae, 59
Fantoni, Barry, 40
farmers and farmhands, 62
Fascist ideology, 265
Faure, Felix, 99–101
feudal era, 32
Feynman, Richard, 141
"filthy togetherness," 228
financiers, 55–59
Finer, Samuel, 35
Finland, 224, 261–62
Finnish immigrants, 43
First Amendment rights in the United
States, 188–89, 212
fishermen, 62, 64–65, 66
Flegenheimer, Arthur "Dutch Schultz,"
142
Flüsterwitze (whispered jokes) in Nazi
Germany, 214–15
"foaf" (friend of a friend) tales, 12
folklore archives, 13, 15
Fontaine, Jean de la, 89

food and drink as joke topics, 13
forbidden jokes, 3, 4, 278
force, use of, 26, 27–29, 31, 37
Ford, Gerald, 75
Foreman, Yuri, 151
Forensic Fables (O), 184
Fortune, John, 58
Fragonard, Jean Honoré, 89
France and French sex jokes, 76–112;
and adultery, 78–80, 86, 99; and artists, 102; blonde jokes compared to,
111–12; brothel culture of, 86–87, 97–
98, 99, 107–108, 109; cartoons, 84–85;
cuckolds, 78, 79, 89; dumb-blonde
jokes, 41; and England, 90–91; erotica
and pornography of, 88–93; and Felix Faure, 99–101; and genders, 69,
272; and "go-fuck-like-the-Greeks"
phrase, 156; high culture of France,
101–104; and homosexuality, 158; language borrowings from French, 85;
and lawyers, 186, *190*; and *ménage á
trois*, 78, 79–80; and military defeats,
104–105, 107–110; and motives of joke
tellers, irrelevance of, 87–88, 103; and
oral sex, 80–84, 95–96, 99–101, 106;
origins of jokes, 86–87; and politics,
110–111; portrayal of French population, 77; sex equated with France, 85;
and sex tourism, 93–99, 103, 109; sexual connotations of French language,
74; sexual image of France, 103; sexy-
blondes jokes, 70; social context of, 16,
17; wartime in France, 87, 104–109, 110
Franco, Francisco, General, 213, 250
Franco-Prussian War, 105
freedom of speech, 188–89, 212, 274
*French Cartoons of the Twentieth Cen-
tury* (Wallis), 85
Freud, Sigmund, 93
frivolous lawsuits, 192–97
Frommer, Myrna and Harvey, 126,
140–41
Fujian province in China, 155

Galanter, Marc: American perceptions
of legal system, 14; death wish jokes,

Christie Davies is Emeritus Professor of Sociology at the University of Reading, UK. He was president of the International Society for Humor Studies in 2008–2009. His previous books include *Ethnic Humor around the World: A Comparative Analysis* (IUP, 1990), *Jokes and Their Relation to Society,* and *The Mirth of Nations.*